Vietnam's Forgotten Army

From the Bibliography of
VN: Peace or Freedom
Local Author

Aug 2022

This book is dedicated to those who fought to defend South Vietnam.

Contents

Thank you for your support:

HÀ H.TƯỜNG, Ed. D.
Vietnam: Peace or Freedom

Acknowledgments		ix
Foreword by James Webb		xiii
Preface: Welcome to America		xvii
Introduction: Welcome to Vietnam		1
1	Coming of Age in a Time of War	11
2	A War Transformed: Battle, Politics, and the Americanization of the War, 1963–1966	31
3	Fighting Two Wars: Years of Attrition and Pacification, 1966–1967	65
4	A Time for Heroes: The Tet Offensive	95
5	After Tet: The Year of Hope	124
6	Hamburger Hill: The Untold Story of the Battle for Dong Ap Bia	157
7	A War Transformed: Vietnamization, 1969–1970	177
8	Shattered Lives and Broken Dreams: Operation Lam Son 719	197
9	The Making of a Traitor	229
10	Journeys Home: Life in the Wake of a Lost War	273
	Conclusion	298
	Notes	305
	Bibliography	329
	Index	339
	About the Author	350

Acknowledgments

It was through and because of the course I teach on Vietnam War history at the University of Southern Mississippi that that I not only came to a real study of the Vietnam War but also came to have occasion to travel to Vietnam, where I met Pham Van Dinh. Many veterans participate in the course, and it was because of them that Vietnam became my passion. I owe each of these brave men my gratitude and my undying respect. Many veterans have participated in my class over the years, but, at the risk of slighting some, I would like to thank the late Roy Ainsworth, Charles Brown, and especially John Young. Also, I would like to thank Dr. Leslie Root and Dr. Raymond Scurfield, himself a Vietnam veteran, for their undying devotion to the Vietnam veteran population and for their help in making our trip to Vietnam a reality.

Several key administrators and colleagues at the University of Southern Mississippi helped to make both the journey to Vietnam and this book possible. Dr. Tim Hudson, then Dean of the College of International and Continuing Education, gambled that a trip to Vietnam would not be a disaster. In the History Department, I owe special thanks to our past chair, Dr. Charles Bolton. Finally, I would like to thank the dedicated and overworked staff of what is now the Office of International Education in the College of Arts and Letters: Susan Steen, who now is the Director of the Office of International Education, Frances Sudduth, Sylvia McNabb, and Melissa Ravencraft. As always, I would like to thank the Administrative Assistant of the History Department, Shelia Smith, for both her friendship and her constant help.

In my research for this project I relied in the expert help of a fine group of archivists and field experts. I would like to thank several persons and the institutions that they represent: Mitchell Yockelson and Cliff Snyder of the National Archives Records Administration; Dr. Jim Ginther, Personal Papers Archivist at the Marine Corps University Research Archives of the Gray Research Center in Quantico, VA; Craig

Tibbets of the Australian War Memorial; Dr. James Reckner, Steve Maxner, and their staff at the Vietnam Center at Texas Tech, a true leadership team in the field of Vietnam studies; Mike Sloniker of the Vietnam Helicopter Pilots Association; and the staff at the Air University Library at the U.S. Air Force Air War College.

Much of my research relied on oral histories conducted with numerous Vietnam veterans. I would like to thank Dr. Curtis Austin, Dr. Stephen Sloan, and the late Suzy Rodriquez, at the Center for Oral History and Cultural Heritage at the University of Southern Mississippi, for their advice and help in the process. I would like to thank Joe West, of Counterparts, An Association of the Second Indochina War & Their Foreign Counterparts, for helping me locate several U.S. advisers to ARVN units. Rick Ryan and the Australian Army Training Team Vietnam Association were indispensable in locating AATTV advisers to ARVN units. When all else failed, I turned to Major General (Ret.) Benjamin Harrison for help in identifying, locating, and making crucial first contact with several of my veteran subjects. Without his gracious help in many ways, this book would not have been possible.

A number of other people provided me with very specific aid at different points in the project. Courtney and Trang My Frobenius, of Vietnam-Indochina Tours, were both instrumental in helping me organize a successful trip to Vietnam and first introduced me to Pham Van Dinh. They were also pivotal in my interview process with Dinh. I would also like to thank Jim Williams for allowing me access to several interviews with U.S. helicopter pilots. I owe Ned Devereaux a special debt of gratitude for providing me with information on the life of Tran Ngoc Hue.

One of the best things about being a historian is working with others who are so knowledgeable in the field. During the years that it took to plan and execute this project, I was lucky to have a group of history-minded friends who allowed me to bounce ideas off them in conversations in places that ranged from London pubs to the Internet. For their help in this regard, I would like to thank Chris McCarthy, Dale Andrade, Lewis Sorley, Robert Brigham, Bruce Davies, Sean McKnight, Gary Sheffield, Stephen Badsey, Dennis Showalter, Mary Kathryn Barbier, Paul Harris, Stephen Maxner, Lam Quang Thi, Terry Whittington, Martin Loicano, and Scott Catino.

Being lucky enough to work in a very collegial department and to live in a town known for its southern hospitality, I also owe special thanks to a sterling group of colleagues and friends who have supported my work in so many ways. At the risk of slighting some others, I would like to single out the following for special thanks: Kim Herzinger, William Scarborough, Glenn Harper, Sean Farrell, Mary Beth Farrell, David Clapp, Jim Hogan, Paul Lyon, Richard McCarthy, David Pumford, David Tisdale, Ryan Schilling, Kyle Zelner, Phyllis Jestice, Andrew Haley, and Danielle Haley. While I was at the Air War College, Toshi Yoshihara, Adam Cobb, and Colonel Jeff Hood all helped out as I labored to finish the manuscript. Most instrumental in my work at the Air War College, though, were the students of seminar "Sweet 16." They were my friends and my military conscience, and they kept me on my intellectual toes. I owe all my thanks to these people especially: Ismail Al Awadhi, Chris Bargery, Enrique Biosca-Vasquez, Sean Boyle, Stephen Fisher, Kathleen Hightain, Robert Howell, Shawn Jansen, Patrick Kelly, Dejudom Kongrsri, Paul (Murph) Murphy, Kenneth (Easy) Rizer, Lawrence (Migs) Roberts, James Sohan, and Janice Wallace.

I would like to offer my special thanks to my colleagues in the History Department, Kevin Dougherty and Michael Neiberg, along with James Willbanks, at the U.S. Army Command and General Staff College, for reading and offering comments on this project while it was in manuscript form. Along the same lines, I owe a deep debt of gratitude to Deborah Gershenowitz, at New York University Press. I very much appreciate the faith that she placed in me and the hard work she put in helping me convert an idea first into a manuscript and then into a book. I would also like to thank my agent, Tom Wallace, and Despina Gimbel and her staff at New York University Press for their considerable efforts in bringing this project to fruition.

There is no way that this project would have ever been undertaken or brought to fruition without the aid of my family, and I would like to thank them all for their help: Wanda Stegall; Terry Smith; La Mae, Dan, Brian, Aaron, and Nicholas Ortman; Steve, Carmen, Amber, Matthew, and David Wiest; Robert and Susan Wiest; Jeanne, Jackson, and Juliana Keene; Grace Trosclair; Everett and Nellie Guillory; Don and Denise Guillory; and Ben, Ruby, and Victoria Buckle. My greatest thanks, though, go to my wife, Jill (CEO of the Wiest household and my best friend), and to my beloved children, Abigail and Luke.

I owe the greatest debt of gratitude to all of those veterans who shared the story of their lives with me and made this book possible, especially Pham Van Dinh and Tran Ngoc Hue. Sadly several of the persons interviewed for this project have passed away since the time of our interviews, including Max Kelly, Cecil Fair, Ngo Quang Truong and Pham Van Dinh. All of these men were eager to share their wartime experiences and to help the present generation learn from the past, but for Dinh the project was special. He realized that the interviews for this book were going to be his only chance to tell the truth of his actions. The interviews in many ways served as his confessional. I am honored that all of the men who took part in this project chose to entrust their memories to me. All of the above-mentioned persons deserve credit for this finished work. I only claim the mistakes as my own.

Foreword

James Webb

I have worked for many years to help bring reconciliation both inside Vietnam and between Vietnam and the United States. In this process I have come to know and respect many people inside the Vietnamese government. I have become friends with people who served in the Army against which I fought. I have strengthened and nurtured my respect for those Vietnamese who fought alongside the Americans. And I have, on more than a few occasions, met Vietnamese who switched their loyalties as the war began to go badly for the South Vietnamese. In human terms, few of us have the standing to condemn anyone who decided to choose a different side in a brutal, seemingly never-ending war. But loyalty to one's comrades is the glue that binds all military service. It is a far stronger cohesive factor than the political reasons that compel a nation to fight. It transcends even the time a nation is at war, because wars have consequences for those who fight them that carry over, not only into the rest of their lives but to the generations that follow.

One cannot begin to comprehend the tales of Harry Hue Tran, a great soldier who paid dearly for his loyalty but who must answer in his honor to no one, and of Pham Van Dinh, whose journey was less painful but in the end more complicated, without understanding this distinction.

And to understand that distinction, it is important to look not at the Vietnam that is emerging year by year into the world community but at the Vietnam that initially grew out of the dark days of the war itself.

I first returned to Vietnam in March 1991, visiting Hanoi and Saigon, which had been renamed Ho Chi Minh City following the communist victory in April 1975. Hanoi was dirt-poor, its streets dark at night from lack of electric power and with hardly a motor vehicle on the roads other than the aging Russian staff cars used by government officials. Saigon was a step upward but was still shaking like a cowed dog from the impact of the communist takeover. Everywhere in Saigon, private conversations inevitably began with a glance outward and the comparative phrase "before 1975," as if life could be divided just as completely by that demarcation as Christians seek to divide it with the phrases "B.C." and "A.D."

In truth, the country was just beginning to climb out of its status as a hard-core Stalinist state. A "bamboo curtain" had been lowered following the communist victory in 1975, preventing the outside world from scrutinizing the brutal retaliatory processes through which the country had been unified. Rebuffing most of the outside world, the Hanoi government had closely aligned itself with the Soviet Union, which until its own downfall had heavily subsidized the Vietnamese economy and trained its government officials in outmoded socialist economic practices. Media visits were rare, and those that were allowed were tightly monitored by the government. Tourist visas were also few. The secret police, controlled by the powerful Ministry of the Interior, were everywhere. It was not uncommon for naïve and unknowing Western visitors to be followed by government agents on the streets and for their conversations to be monitored while they were in their hotel rooms.

Unlike many Americans who were allowed into Vietnam at that time, I had strong cultural referents through which I could evaluate the human dramas that unveiled themselves before my eyes as I made my way along the streets of Saigon. I had spent my entire adult life immersed in the study of East Asian cultures and had spent time in the region as a journalist. During the war, I had fought as an infantry Marine on some of Vietnam's bloodiest battlefields. And, most important, after the war's tragic end, I had spent countless hours assisting Vietnamese refugees who had made their way, often at great cost, to the United States. Through that process I had gained invaluable insights into the intricacies of Vietnam's culture, the perspectives of the Vietnamese regarding the stakes involved in the war, and the internecine battles among Vietnamese on both sides that had rarely made it into American debates about the reasons we were there or why we did not prevail.

This first return to a country that I have always deeply loved literally overwhelmed me. As one of only a small handful of Americans roaming the city, usually by way of a xichlo pedicab, I was both celebrated as a returning hero and inundated with intense, emotional barrages. Again and again, Vietnamese men and women came up to me, clasping my hands, at times with tears in their eyes. "It has been so hard, sir," was a common refrain. "We always knew you would come back."

Some had stories so compelling that at times it seemed that simply listening to them without being able to help was an act of disloyalty. One morning, as I walked, an Amerasian youth caught up to me, jumping down from his bicycle and confronting me as a small crowd gathered around us. He was shivering with intensity as he pointed to his own mixed African and Asian features. "LOOK AT ME," he screamed. "I AM NOT VIETNAMESE! MY FATHER WAS A SOLDIER, KILLED AT CU CHI! THEY GIVE ME NOTHING! YOU ARE AMERICAN, YOU MUST HELP ME!"

But one particular place roused my passions and infused me with a determination to seek a much-needed justice.

In the spring of 1991, perhaps a thousand Vietnamese men spent their days and nights huddled in an open park, just across from Saigon's old railroad station. Asia is a land of extremes, and few visitors seemed to take notice of who these beggar-like men were or to ask how they had come to spend their days in utter desperation, some of them openly shooting heroin and most of them living lives devoid of hope. But in that park was the graphic evidence of a classic societal inversion. These were soldiers from the former South Vietnamese Army. Many of them had held high rank and had great responsibilities. After the fall of South Vietnam, a million people had been marched off to reeducation camps. Some 240,000 had stayed in the camps longer than four years, and some had remained for more than thirteen years. More than fifty thousand had died in the camps. Upon their release, these veterans and their families were branded as traitors and were cut off from jobs, homes, and schooling. Many had been sent far from their homes to live in so-called New Economic Zones, and many who were living in the park had secretly made their way back to Saigon. Those who had been allowed to return to their homes were typically not permitted to work, even at menial tasks such as pedaling the ubiquitous xichlo pedicabs.

Over the years, many of these South Vietnamese veterans would be allowed to emigrate to the United States under special programs.

Like Harry Hue Tran, given a new life in our country, they and their families have had the opportunity to thrive and to succeed. And yet, there is more to be done. The bamboo curtain that fell over Vietnam for so many years after 1975 caused their stories to be lost, even as our country fell into accepting a shorthand version of the war itself as simply a misguided effort by an incompetent army and a corrupt government against a nationalist political system.

There is more to this story, and it deserves to be told. Not only did these people lose everything—their homes, their professions, and, ultimately, their country—but they and their comrades have been misrepresented by historians and political commentators who overwhelmingly misunderstood the reasons that they fought and the excellence that so many of them brought to the battlefield. This misunderstanding still haunts us, and we will never put the Vietnam War into proper focus until it is corrected.

The stories of Harry Hue Tran and Pham Van Dinh inform us, on the level of Greek tragedy, of the costs of war and the price of loyalty. They also bring into the American literary marketplace a much-needed comprehension of the price the Vietnamese on both sides paid on a battlefield that is too often gauged exclusively by American casualties. Through the stories of these two soldiers, perhaps the Vietnamese themselves, no matter their personal histories, can begin to repair the fractures that still divide them.

Preface

Welcome to America

It seemed an auspicious day to begin life anew. On 11 November 1991 —Veterans' Day—the airliner carrying Tran Ngoc Hue[1] (who goes by the nickname Harry), along with his wife and his three daughters, prepared to touch down at National Airport in Washington, DC. After years of suffering and effort and four tiring days of travel, the Vietnamese émigrés felt a palpable sense of relief wash over them as they neared their new home and freedom. The other passengers on the airliner paid little heed to Hue and his family, who seemed to be only a small but typical portion of a vast Vietnamese migration. After all the flotsam and jetsam of America's failed war and Vietnam's failed peace, a massive throng, dubbed the "boat people," had been entering the United States in a steady stream for years. This soft-spoken Vietnamese family was just another set of refugees—lucky enough to flee a nation stricken with famine and discord, but unlucky enough to have to begin a new life as penniless outcasts far from their beloved homeland.

Had they but looked more closely, Hue's fellow passengers would have noticed that three fingers on Hue's left hand were missing, part of the terrible physical scars suffered in eight years of combat—scars earned in the service of South Vietnam, a nation that no longer exists. Hidden were the mental scars of thirteen brutal years behind bars in North Vietnamese prisons. Walking slowly into an uncertain future, Tran Ngoc Hue and his family were among the last off of the airliner. Anxiously awaiting the Trans' arrival were their American sponsors. U.S. Marine Lieutenant Colonel David L. Wiseman had been Hue's close friend and military adviser in Vietnam and had listened helplessly on a radio as Hue's unit was surrounded and destroyed in Laos.

While Hue suffered through the destruction of South Vietnam and seemingly unending years of imprisonment, Wiseman had pursued a lonely and nearly hopeless crusade to find his lost comrade in arms.

As Hue emerged into the crowded terminal Wiseman knew that his twenty-year-long search for his friend had finally come to an end. At the age of forty-nine, for Tran Ngoc Hue the Vietnam War was finally over, but the struggle to reclaim his life had just begun.

A decade later, an airplane carrying Pham Van Dinh made its final approach into Louis Armstrong International Airport, in New Orleans. Dinh traveled alone and almost unnoticed on the long journey from Saigon. A successful businessman in a modernizing Vietnam, Dinh was once the compatriot and military brother of Tran Ngoc Hue and also bears scars from years of defending South Vietnam. However, the mental burden carried by Dinh was of a much different nature, as was the cause of his arrival in the United States. Where Hue had come to America to make his way into the future, Dinh was flying into his own tortured past.

Dinh's arrival in New Orleans was low key and unheralded, with no joyous airport reunion. Greeted cordially at the airport by an academic, Dinh drove away, wanting only to tell the story of his role in the war. Aware that his story of the honor and bravery of South Vietnam would find little acceptance in today's Vietnam, Dinh hoped that a land far removed from his own would welcome both him and his tale and that he could reclaim a part of his lost youth.

Dinh also hoped to reach out to his old comrades, and toward that end he planned to speak at a public gathering of students and Vietnam War veterans. He hoped to build bridges between two countries that had shared a common, tragic war. When news spread, though, that Dinh would deliver a public address, a firestorm of protest erupted, especially within the veteran community, for Dinh was not just a nearly forgotten South Vietnamese hero. He had also surrendered his entire unit in battle and had defected to North Vietnam. Dinh was a traitor. Some thirty years after his defection, Dinh dared to hope that the Vietnam War and his actions in the conflict had lapsed into the realm of history. He was quite mistaken. Dinh left a nation still so pained by war that it would not allow him to tell his story. He entered a nation that remains so pained by his actions that it did not want to hear his story.

While Tran Ngoc Hue's welcome to America served as a cathartic conclusion to a war that had persisted far too long, Pham Van Dinh was thoroughly enmeshed in a past that neither he nor his old friends could forgive. History had come full circle.

Introduction

Welcome to Vietnam

IN MAY 2001, on a day that seemed oppressively hot even to a Mississippi native, while relishing an ice-cold bottle of water in the lounge of the Huong Giang (Perfume River) Hotel in Hue City, Vietnam, I discovered that sometimes a book can quite literally walk up and introduce itself to you. I was in Vietnam on the third and final week of a study-abroad program for my home university, the University of Southern Mississippi. The program, in its second year, was very much a labor of love and was designed to take a group of U.S. students and veterans to Vietnam to learn of "our war" through the eyes of its participants in the land where it was fought. The trip, though, had a deeper personal meaning. While too young to fight in the war, in many ways I grew up with Vietnam. As a child, I watched the war on the evening news, a war so complex that even my father could not explain it fully. Vietnam had always been a part of my life and represented a mystery that needed solving.

After working diligently for years in an effort to learn the facts of the Vietnam War, I felt that something was still missing, so I decided to go to Vietnam. Sitting there that afternoon in Hue City, after having slopped through rice paddies, slithered through the tunnels of Cu Chi, and listened while three U.S. veterans related tales of war and survival that were at once both horrible and touching, I felt more able to grasp the reality of the conflict. I even had the chance to meet and learn from our ex-adversaries, both from the North Vietnamese Army (NVA) and from the Viet Cong (VC). On that steamy afternoon, I awaited the arrival of the last piece of the historical puzzle, a veteran of the South Vietnamese military.

At the age of sixty-four, Colonel Pham Van Dinh, tall, ramrod-straight, and still a commanding presence nearly thirty years after his war, walked into the hotel and introduced himself to me in nearly

perfect English. The ex-Army of the Republic of Vietnam (ARVN) officer was scheduled to take us on a battlefield tour during which he
would describe the ARVN's epic struggle to recapture Hue City during the Tet Offensive, in 1968. I knew little about Colonel Dinh other
than that he had fought heroically in the battle and that he was brave
enough to risk the ire of his own government by talking to my group.
After some polite conversation and a sweltering battlefield tour of the
city, we all boarded a bus for the drive to visit the old U.S. Marine
base at Khe Sanh, site of the historic siege in 1968.

After a winding journey down Route 9, we reached the abandoned U.S. Marine base at Camp Carroll. Dinh asked the driver to
stop and instructed the group to exit the bus, and we were soon
tramping after him up the steep slope. What had been a center of
bloody fighting for so long during the war was now a nondescript
hilltop covered by new-growth tropical forest. After a short climb, we
came upon a particularly battered-looking memorial that seemed to
occupy the geographic center of the middle of nowhere. Much of the
writing had faded and some of the sculpture work had fallen to the
ground, but Dinh needed no help in telling the group of the mon-
ument's meaning. The crumbling concrete edifice marked the spot
where Dinh had surrendered his entire regiment to the North Vietnamese during the Easter Offensive of 1972, after which he had changed
sides and joined the enemy.

After our return to Hue, Dinh took me aside and asked if I would
like to write a book about his life and career. It took me a moment to
process the information. The man was a walking mystery, the only
man of such high rank to fight on both sides in the Vietnam War.
My next book was standing right there in front of me. Colonel Dinh
warned me that there was much more to his story and that it would
not be safe for him to conduct interviews in Vietnam. I would have
to get him to America, where he could speak in freedom. It was a moment of classic and blinding irony. The communist government to
which Dinh had defected during the war would not allow him to
speak of his pre-1972 past; more than half his life was an unacceptable
and dangerous embarrassment in the brave, new Vietnam. I had gone
to Vietnam hoping to gain a fuller understanding of the American war
in that country. Instead, I had discovered another war entirely, a Vietnamese war.

Upon my return to the United States, I read what little I could find on South Vietnam and the ARVN, while Dinh, after calling in favors and convincing his government that he would not defect, eventually obtained an exit visa. After nearly a year, Dinh joined me for a month of interviews, during which it became clear that the convoluted course of his military career was central to understanding a Vietnam War that was much more complex than I had ever realized. However, I had a major problem. The critical evidence in the unfolding story came from a man who was a traitor, so corroboration of Dinh's account of the war was paramount. As a result, I contacted as many U.S. and Australian advisers who had served with Dinh as possible. I also searched out members of the American Vietnamese community who had known Dinh. The details gleaned from these sources were invaluable in painting a fuller and more reliable portrait of the hero turned traitor. During my continued research, though, a single name kept recurring: Lieutenant Colonel Tran Ngoc Hue. Several people, ranging from U.S. advisers to South Vietnamese generals, told me that I needed to interview Hue as a balance to the story of Dinh. As luck had it, I discovered that Hue lived in Falls Church, Virginia.

After meeting Hue's family over a wonderful, traditional dinner and convincing them that I meant their father no historical harm, he and I sat down to work at the kitchen table in his comfortable suburban home. I had stepped into the world of the Vietnamese expatriates, at once both exotically foreign and as American as apple pie.[1] Full of an ardent patriotism for two countries, one of which is now a distant memory, the Vietnamese expatriate community is a living, vibrant entity all its own. Tran Ngoc Hue's home served as an introduction to the community and presented an interesting juxtaposition of things American and things Vietnamese, things new and things old. As I leafed through a proffered collection of family photos, I could not help noticing that the same album contained pictures of Hue's daughter's graduation from the University of Maryland and pictures of Hue's graduation from the Vietnamese National Military Academy, the West Point of South Vietnam. I looked up from the tangible metaphor of Vietnamese expatriate life and was happy to note that Hue was in good spirits, even though he was aware that I had interviewed and was writing a book about the despised traitor Dinh. Only as I listened to the tales of my soft-spoken host did I come to realize that Dinh and Hue had once been friends, brothers-in-arms in the crucible of war. Their lives had once been mirror images but had come to dramatically different ends. I realized that the story of Tran Ngoc Hue was indispensable; he was the untarnished hero to Dinh's tortured traitor. Only with the inclusion of an account of Hue's life would the story become whole.

Mirrored Lives

At its heart, *Vietnam's Forgotten Army* is a story of two men at war. From their beginnings in the villages surrounding prosperous Hue City in central Vietnam, the lives of Pham Van Dinh and Tran Ngoc Hue seemed to be intertwined. Though they did not know each other as children, in part because of ties of family and faith, both gravitated toward careers in the military. The elder of the two by nearly five years, Dinh blazed a path that Hue soon followed into the ranks of the officer class of the ARVN. Once in the military, the two men came to know each other well, for they shared a common drive, ability, and devotion to their fledgling nation. The two returned to the Hue City area to assume their commands. Noticed for their military and intellectual prowess, both men enjoyed meteoric rises, sometimes shared the same U.S. advisers, and even commanded the same elite unit, the Hac Bao (Black Panther) Company of the 1st ARVN Division, at different times. After both of the young men had been chosen to become the military protégés of the legendary commander of the 1st ARVN Division, General Ngo Quang Truong, Dinh and Hue next rose to iconic fame as the two brightest young stars in the ARVN for their exploits in the battle for Hue City during the Tet Offensive of 1968. As the two comrades-in-arms reached their military maturity, they watched in dismay as the war unraveled around them, a soul-wrenching process that led Dinh and Hue, so similar in so many ways, to shockingly different conclusions. While Hue fought on to the end against bitter odds, Dinh chose to become a traitor. In the wreckage of their war, Dinh became a hero in the new, communist Vietnam in which Hue was an imprisoned outcast. Even though their lives had seemingly diverged completely, Dinh and Hue remained inexorably linked even during a Vietnamese Diaspora that spanned both decades and continents.

Making sense of the reasons why the lives of Dinh and Hue were so intertwined and yet came to such different military conclusions and understanding the fundamental reality of their decision-making processes as the war came to its end requires use of historical tools outside the realm of simple biography. To understand Pham Van Dinh and Tran Ngoc Hue, it is necessary first to understand the complex reality represented by the institution to which both men dedicated their lives—the Army of the Republic of Vietnam. *Vietnam's Forgotten Army*, then, is not only a dual biography of Dinh and Hue but also a study of the institutional strengths and weaknesses of the ARVN and its place in the wider Vietnam War. While an understanding of the ARVN is a necessary prerequisite to the story of Dinh and Hue, a vivid picture of the lives of the two men is essential for a fuller understanding of the ARVN. Together, the careers of Pham Van Dinh and Tran Ngoc Hue included very nearly the entirety of the Vietnam War and its military aftermath. Hue served in the ARVN from 1963 until his capture in Laos in 1970, then spent thirteen years in the prisons of North Vietnam, and finally lived under house arrest in Saigon before emigrating to the United States in 1991. Dinh served in the ARVN from 1961 until his surrender during the Easter Offensive in 1972 and then served in the NVA until his retirement in 2003. Seeing the conflict through the eyes of Dinh and Hue, then, offers a unique historical opportunity to view both the depth and the complexity that was Vietnam at war.

ARVN: The Forgotten Army of Vietnam

The ability of South Vietnam to persevere in its struggle for survival hinged on the efforts of the Republic of Vietnam Armed Forces, but especially on the Army of the Republic of Vietnam. Caught amid a historiography that is focused squarely on the cathartic American experience in Vietnam, the ARVN and its struggles have until recently been historically invisible. When not ignored in traditional Western accounts of the conflict, the ARVN often receives only passing, damning reference as a collection of bumbling cowards who were reflective of a political and national system that was broken beyond repair. Even when the ARVN receives more balanced treatment, the proclivities of Western historiography are obvious. Two major studies exist regarding the Easter Offensive of 1972, which took place after the vast majority of U.S. troops had exited Vietnam and which was arguably the ARVN's most important battle of the entire conflict. While the works are well researched and of great importance, their very titles indicate an American focus on what was quintessentially an ARVN battle: Colonel G. H. Turley's *The Easter Offensive: The Last American Advisors, Vietnam 1972,* and Dale Andrade's *America's Last Vietnam Battle: Halting Hanoi's 1972 Easter Offensive.*[2]

That South Vietnamese nationalism was porous, leaving reservoirs of popular indifference or outright support for the enemy, and that the ARVN was certainly a flawed instrument does not mean that South Vietnamese nationalism did not exist or that the ARVN was predisposed to failure. Certainly the South Vietnamese state and the ARVN were imperfect. Even so, South Vietnam fought for twenty-five years, and the ARVN lost more than 200,000 dead. After the war, millions chose to flee South Vietnam rather than live under the suzerainty of their brothers from the North.[3] It is apparent that the ARVN, having fought for so long and suffered so much, was not a historical parody, peopled by cardboard cutout officers and men. Only by putting a more human face on the ARVN and by understanding its complexities can historians truly begin to understand the nature of that troubled institution—and thus the nature of the Vietnam War.[4]

The breadth and depth of Dinh's and Hue's military experiences allows for a tantalizing and revealing glimpse into the inner workings of the South Vietnamese military. Dinh began his military career as an aspirant officer and at the time of his surrender was in command of a regiment, while Hue commanded units that ranged in size from platoons to battalions. Both were sensitive observers and fully recognized the ARVN's potentially fatal weaknesses, including debilitating internal political infighting and corruption, that both adversely impacted the ARVN war effort and nearly cost them their lives. Dinh and Hue, though, also witnessed something far too often forgotten—South Vietnamese military bravery and devotion, amid a continuous cycle of war against a stalwart foe. Though the costs were high and the odds long, the ARVN fought on, even after U.S. withdrawal from the conflict had arguably dashed any hopes for ultimate victory, a victory that both Dinh and Hue believed had come agonizingly close before their military lives and the life of their fledgling nation tragically were destroyed.

A close examination of the lives of only two young officers cannot propose to represent all of the ARVN. However, examining the extraordinary lives of Dinh and Hue serves to place the Vietnam War into the critical and understudied rubric of the South Vietnamese military experience. If Dinh, Hue, and the ARVN were of the same martial stock as their communist foes, NVA and VC forces that were so lauded by the bested Americans, it poses an entirely new question. Instead of asking in wonder why the South Vietnamese fought at all, why not ask why, with such sterling raw material, South Vietnam did not win its war? With the aid of the American colossus on the side of South Vietnam, why is it not reserved for the descendants of the North Vietnamese to wonder at the nature of their eventual defeat? If the ARVN was not fatally flawed, if it had even a chance to seize a nationalist mantle, if even some of its leaders were wise and brave, if its men were more than pitiful excuses for modern soldiers—then the questions become much more vexing. Perhaps the ARVN has served as the excuse for America's lost war for too long, and it is time to consider more fully America's role in the defeat of a nation that actually did have a chance to survive.[5] The questions concerning the nature of the flawed relationship between the ARVN and the United States, though, come full circle in the troubled end to Dinh's career, for Pham Van Dinh not only represents what was good and right about the ARVN; he also perhaps represents the worst of the ARVN. In the end, he chose to abandon his country and became a traitor. It will be the central focus of this work to attempt both to explain why Dinh changed so much while Hue did not and to discern how the most critical decisions of their lives were reflective of the Vietnam War as a whole.

A Flawed and Tragic Alliance

Above all else, Pham Van Dinh and Tran Ngoc Hue were combat commanders and leaders of men in battle. In the crucible of combat, the two comrades witnessed an ever-changing war, from the pre-1965 chaos of guerrilla war, to the pitched battles of the "big-unit" war after the arrival of American combat units, to the urban maelstrom of the Tet Offensive, to the press toward presumed battlefield victory in the wake of Tet, to the grim realities of the American withdrawal from the conflict. As battlefield commanders of such long standing, Dinh and Hue occupied a critical, yet poorly understood, position at the nexus of the American and the South Vietnamese war efforts. Victory in Vietnam would come not through the might of American arms alone but rather through a complete symbiosis of U.S. and ARVN effort. Instead, though, the military relationship between the United States and South Vietnam remained fatally flawed, as the Americans and the ARVN fought two different wars in the same country. In the formative years of the combined war effort, the American military essentially pushed the ARVN to one side in an attempt singlehandedly to destroy the communist threat. Made secondary in their own war for independence, ARVN units struggled first to find and then effectively to play their role in the ever-changing conflict.

At the confluence of the two wars in Vietnam stood the U.S. and Australian advisory efforts. Tasked with aiding ARVN units in becoming effective combat adjuncts to the American war, the advisers were both critical to the war effort as a whole and important observers of the reality that was the ARVN. In a role all too often regarded as only secondary to the dominance of American combat units, the advisers toiled in near anonymity in the jungles and rice paddies alongside their ARVN allies. Dinh and Hue worked with and often became close friends of their advisers, who came and went with monotonous regularity in their one-year tours of duty. At the sharp end of the Vietnam War for so long, the careers of Dinh and Hue provide a vantage point from which to view the successes and failures of the combined U.S.-ARVN war. Testimony from their advisers, so uniquely placed as observers of the critical overlap of the war efforts, also reveals the combat and social realities of an allied war effort that was fatally bifurcated.

At its heart, this is a story of two men at war. From initial skirmishes with a Viet Cong force that was only just finding its military balance, to first clashes with the vaunted NVA, to massive battles of attrition alongside their American allies, to the invasion of Laos and the Easter Offensive, Dinh and Hue fought gallantly in an intensely difficult war that seemingly had no end. Like characters from a Greek tragedy, the comrades soldiered on, only to have their lives and the lives of their families fall victim to forces beyond their control.

Both men were living testaments to the great strengths of the ARVN and of the American war in Vietnam. However, their lives also bore witness to how the weaknesses of the ARVN combined with the flawed symbiosis of the American war to doom South Vietnam to eventual defeat. While the mirror image lives of Dinh and Hue reveal much about the nature of both the ARVN and the American war effort, it is as their war neared its end, as their lives were shattered, that the central question of their wartime experiences becomes clear. As their war came crumbling down around them, both Dinh and Hue made difficult choices in deadly circumstances, choices that exacted their own retribution. Both men, the traitor and the hero, believe that they acted honorably in the most difficult decisions of their lives. That such can be the case in a war gone wrong is truly remarkable and does much to illustrate the immense complexity that was South Vietnam at war. However, the vexing question remains: how could two men who were so similar and so driven choose to follow such vastly different paths of honor as their country and war imploded around them?

A Note on Sources

While the present study makes extensive and careful use of the myriad archival and secondary sources available to researchers concerning the military effort in the Vietnam War, extensive written and taped interviews with Vietnamese, American, and Australian participants in the events described in the book form the core of what is in many ways a personal story of young men who were involved in the most dramatic and difficult events of their lives. The evidence provided by these archival sources and personal remembrances serves both to corroborate and to add depth to the focus of the book—the military careers and lives of Pham Van Dinh and Tran Ngoc Hue. *Vietnam's Forgotten Army* utilizes more than fifty-five hours of oral interviews with Pham Van Dinh and Tran Ngoc Hue as its bedrock source. In many ways, the interviews with all of the veterans involved were almost conversational in nature and as such do not lend themselves to long direct quotations. Additionally, for several of the interviewees, English is their third language. Out of respect for the source material, the author chose not to edit the grammatical structure of the interviews to cobble together material for quotations. However, all material within the study that is expressive of an opinion of one of the veterans is taken directly from an interview with that veteran. Any opinions expressed by sources external to the story or by the author are clearly indicated. In an effort to keep endnotes to a minimum, the beginning of each chapter makes clear which tapes from the Dinh and Hue collections the author utilized in writing that chapter. Similarly, footnotes within the chapters make clear which other taped and written sources the author utilized. All taped interviews utilized by the author are available for use by researchers and are housed in the Center for Oral History and Cultural Heritage at the University of Southern Mississippi. Similarly, all written interviews are available and are housed in the McCain Library and Archive at the University of Southern Mississippi.

1

Coming of Age in a Time of War

SENSING THAT THE looming spread of World War II to the Pacific was the historic moment for which he had long waited, in early 1941, disguised as a Chinese journalist, Ho Chi Minh slipped from exile in China across the border to Vietnam, his first return to the land of his birth in thirty years. In the jungles of the rugged limestone hills near Pac Bo, Ho gathered his closest confidants and told them that the time had come to form a broad front of "patriots of all ages and all types, peasants, workers and soldiers," to fight both the Japanese and the French, who then occupied the nation. The conspiratorial moment heralded the founding of the Viet Nam Doc Lap Dong Minh, or, more simply, the Viet Minh, and presaged more than three decades of tumult and violence; a conflagration that was at once part of a world war, a colonial war, a cold war, and a civil war.[1]

Born in 1937 and 1942, respectively, Pham Van Dinh and Tran Ngoc Hue were children of the storm that Ho created and came of age in an era defined by war and uncertainty. Reared in the heartland of the nation, near Vietnam's ancient capital of Hue City, Dinh and Hue were very much alike. Children of families that boasted proud military traditions that dated back to the era of Vietnam's imperial glory, both young men were drawn to military life and into the conflict that defined their generation. Events led both Dinh and Hue down a historical channel different from that taken by Ho and to the support of a noncommunist nationalism and a war in defense of South Vietnam. In a nation where Confucian values of family and honor are of the utmost importance, Dinh and Hue were drawn to the support of South Vietnam for the most Vietnamese of reasons, following paths blazed by their fathers.

Family Matters

Pham Van Dinh was born in Phu Cam Village, in Thua Thien Province, near Hue City, in central Vietnam, on 2 February 1937.[2] Dinh's father, Pham Van Vinh, and his mother, Cong Ton Nu Thi Nhan, were Catholics, a religion whose adherents were normally bitterly opposed to the communists. In a nation where reverence for one's ancestors and ties to the land are paramount, when the nation was split by the Geneva Accords, in 1954, tens of thousands of Catholics, in an extraordinary move, fled their homeland in the north to be free of communist rule. These Catholics and their southern brethren formed the core of support for South Vietnam and for an alternative to a communist form of nationalism.

In Vietnam, the traditional customs of *on* (a high moral debt) and *hieu* (filial piety) undergird social reality and enshrine the family as the central unit of life. The historian Robert Brigham explains:

> The idea of *on* was instilled in Vietnamese at a young age. Children were taught that they owed their parents a moral debt of immense proportions. The debt could never be fully repaid, but children were expected to try to please their parents constantly and to obey them faithfully. A child's greatest comfort would come from the knowledge that he had reduced the burden of work on his parents. The debt did not diminish with age. As parents grew older, responsibility for their care rested more heavily on the children's shoulders. A person who chose to dismiss the moral debt and live according to his or her own aspirations and desires was ostracized in a society where social standing within the family determined everything, even what a person called him- or herself and others. Repaying the debt also extended to the ancestors and the generations to come. To show gratitude for the accumulated merit and social standing that his or her ancestors had provided, each person owed the next generation his or her best effort not to diminish the family's position within the xa (village).[3]

Vinh's family had close kinship links that predisposed them to the support of the South Vietnamese state and noncommunist Vietnamese nationalism. Vinh was a cousin of Ngo Dinh Diem, the first president of South Vietnam. Nhan was a distant relative of Vietnam's last emperor under the French and the first South Vietnamese head of state, Bao Dai, and as such was a member of the royal family. The complex web of relationships virtually ensured that Pham Van Dinh would be a loyal supporter of South Vietnam. Though the ties of kinship existed, they did not gain the family much in the way of preferential treatment. Vinh was a musician and eventually became a warrant officer in the French-supported Vietnamese National Army (VNA) of Bao Dai; he even spent a year living in France. Later, he rose to command the band of the 1st Division of the Army of the Republic of Vietnam (ARVN). Vinh was a warrant officer at the outset of the presidency of Ngo Dinh Diem and remained a warrant officer at the time of Diem's assassination.

Vinh's family was staunchly middle class and urban in a nation of peasants, further inclining it to support the Diem regime. Class ties also marked the Vinh family, and those like it, for importance and influence under Diem's rule; the officer class of the ARVN, like the merchant class, was overwhelmingly middle class and urban. The education level and loyalty of the class as a whole made for good officer material. However, the class was demographically narrow and arguably separated from the wants, needs, and desires of the vast majority of the Vietnamese citizenry.

Pham Van Dinh thus came by his support for South Vietnam quite naturally as a member of a southern, Catholic, middle-class, urban family. He was, indeed, exactly what outsiders would expect to find when researching the background of a South Vietnamese officer. Even in the case of his family, though, things were not simple in the chaos that was post–World War II Vietnam. In 1945, Vinh's elder brother had opted to join and fight with the Viet Minh against French colonialism, and he remained a supporter of the Viet Minh until his death shortly after the communist victory at Dien Bien Phu in 1954. The conflict in Vietnam was much more complex than most American histories of the war allow. It was, in many ways, a true civil war, pitting brother against brother and splitting families—even families in which all ties seemingly led to support of South Vietnam, as in the family of Pham Van Dinh.

Tran Ngoc Hue was born in Hue City on 4 January 1942. The Tran family had long followed the Nguyen emperors of Vietnam and had moved south with the tide of Vietnamese expansion hundreds of years prior to Hue's birth. The family had a storied military tradition in service of the Vietnamese state. Raised on stories of his family's martial bravery, Hue longed to emulate his heroic ancestors, including his great-great-grandfather General Nguyen Tri Phuong, a fabled Vietnamese hero who fought valiantly against encroaching colonialism and who committed suicide in 1873 when Hanoi finally fell to French rule. With regard to family military prowess of a more recent vintage, Tran Ngoc Hue's uncle, Tran Huu Dieu, was a prominent military officer in the Bao Dai regime before 1945, while several of Hue's cousins served in the VNA and later the ARVN. Most importantly, though, Hue's father, Tran Huu Chuong, remained true to the family tradition and served as a junior officer in the VNA. As momentous events ripped Vietnam apart, Chuong stood against colonialism and against communism. Rejecting both the Viet Minh and the French, Chuong sought another path toward true independence for his homeland, a noncommunist form of Vietnamese nationalism, and eventually swore loyalty to the new nation of South Vietnam. Chuong hoped for the reunification of his country, but under noncommunist rule—a hope that soon became the motivating force in the life of young Tran Ngoc Hue.

Hue's mother, Nguyen Thi Nghia, was Catholic, whereas his father, Chuong, was a Buddhist. Though Nghia held true to her own religion, the Tran children were raised Buddhist, the religion of the vast majority of the Vietnamese people. While many Buddhists feared dominance by an avowedly atheist communist regime, the Buddhist community in general did not feel the same level of persecution and resulting anticommunist unity that characterized the Catholic minority in Vietnam. In the case of the Trans, adherence to Buddhism meshed well with support for noncommunist nationalism. However, the situation, especially within the upper echelon of the Buddhist power structure, was exceedingly complex.

Buddhism in Vietnam lacked coherent organization, with most Vietnamese Buddhists practicing an eclectic mix of Asian religions under the loose organization of the Buddhist faith. Even at the very highest levels, Buddhism in Vietnam was fragmented, pulled in different directions by different sects and different charismatic leaders. In general, much of the Buddhist leadership not only stood against communist rule but also sometimes railed against the dictatorial tendencies of Ngo Dinh Diem, with often bloody results. Some of the more politically able Buddhist leaders even saw their movement as a logical middle ground between the extremes represented by Ho Chi Minh and Ngo Dinh Diem. To some, then, Buddhism represented a neutralist hope to end the war while still attaining the goals of Vietnamese nationalism, while, to others, those who passed as neutralist Buddhist leaders were little more than communist stooges.[4]

Though his family was not rich (his home did not even have electricity until 1952), Pham Van Dinh's parents toiled and sacrificed to put their nine children through private Catholic schools. The young Dinh appreciated and honored the hard work put in by his father, but his mother was the primary influence on his life. Throughout his life, Dinh was quite conscious of the fact that his mother reveled in his success, a fact that urged him ever onward to provide her with further honor and prestige.

At the age of eight, Dinh enrolled in the prestigious Pellerin School in Hue City. The staff of the Catholic school was made up, in the main, of priests and other religiously affiliated teachers who often taught classes in French and followed a French classical educational pattern. Dinh remained in the school for some thirteen years, a rarity in a country where few could afford even a short period of expensive private education. Though Dinh was much less well off than many of his classmates, he realized even then that his access to such a good education placed him in the upper stratum of Vietnamese society.[5]

It was a heady time to be a young schoolboy, as great events shook the very foundations of modern Vietnam. While he was in school, the Viet Minh came to power, the French returned and were eventually defeated, the Geneva Accords split Vietnam, and South Vietnam rose in opposition to the communist state of North Vietnam. All the while, Dinh watched the events from the safety of his school, as his elders made the critical decisions of their lives. Dinh's teachers were Vietnamese Catholics and as such mainly stood against both French colonialism and communism. However, a few of his teachers were old-style proponents of French rule, while others were avowed supporters of the Viet Minh.

Though he was aware of the cases in favor of both French and communist rule over Vietnam, Dinh was more influenced by his family background and natural predilections, which led him to adopt the majority viewpoint of the teachers and students at Pellerin School. Accordingly, Dinh developed a personal level of support for noncommunist nationalism in Vietnam and eventually supported the Ngo Dinh

Diem regime. In his case, it was a natural occurrence that had to happen and required little thought.

In the elite school, the teachers pushed their pupils to excel; reaching heights of excellence was their duty to their family. It was also their duty to the state. The faculty, whether Viet Minh, Francophile, or southern nationalist, also taught the students that they were the natural leaders of Vietnamese society. They would be the military commanders, political leaders, and business magnates of the future, charged with lifting Vietnam from its present period of chaos and discord.

As his time in school neared its end, Dinh, who had always excelled in his studies, knew his place in society. Though there were many avenues of advancement open to him, Dinh chose to seek a career in the military. He could have just done his required national service and spent much of the coming war behind a desk. However, Dinh was driven—for himself, his family, and his nation. Thus, he chose to enter the Thu Duc Reserve Officers School outside Saigon and to pursue a career as a combat officer in the infantry. Again, it just seemed the natural and proper thing to do. As he set out on his military journey, it was with high expectations. He did not hope or dream; he *knew* that he would become a general.

The family of Tran Ngoc Hue remained in Hue City until the chaotic period at the close of World War II. The occupation of the city by Japanese troops, and the subsequent turmoil in the nation, forced the Trans to flee to their ancestral village of Ke Mon, twenty kilometers to the northeast. Most of Hue's family remained in Ke Mon, a Viet Minh–dominated area, for the next decade. Chuong, however, rejoined his unit in the VNA and took part in the fighting against the Viet Minh. The situation was difficult for young Hue, living in "enemy" territory and under constant scrutiny while his father was away fighting in the unending conflict.

During this stage of the war, two events provided Tran Ngoc Hue with very powerful motivation for his future career in the South Vietnamese military. Ke Mon was something of a battleground area and suffered at the hands of both sides in the conflict. In 1950, while only eight years old, Hue witnessed a Viet Minh ambush of a Vietnamese government patrol—soldiers like his father. After a brief firefight, the government soldiers realized that they were outnumbered and outgunned and chose to surrender. The Viet Minh fighters stripped the prisoners in an act of ritual humiliation and tied their hands behind their backs. Hue then watched in horror as the Viet Minh buried the government soldiers alive, not wanting even to waste bullets to kill them. It was an act of barbarity that Hue never forgot.

Such an act could not go unpunished, and French forces soon arrived in Ke Mon to administer justice. As was often the case, the Viet Minh had fled, but it made no difference. An example had to be made. Much of the local population was rounded up and herded into a few buildings, while French soldiers put several homes in the village to the torch. Hue's house was not burned, but the soldiers burst into the building and gathered the family into a single room. Then two French soldiers forced one of Hue's young cousins away and took turns raping her. Thus, Hue came to hate the French occupiers as well as the Viet Minh. Neither the communists nor the French had brought anything but death and destruction to Ke Mon. Both were evil and had to be fought. Only support for the Vietnamese government forces, represented by his father, seemed to be justified. Both Dinh and Hue came to their support of South Vietnam naturally, but Tran Ngoc Hue was also driven by the strong and less mutable force of revenge when he dedicated his life to noncommunist Vietnamese nationalism and fought for the nation that became South Vietnam.

Soon Hue went off to a unique boarding school far to the south in Vung Tau. Based on a French model, the Truong Thieu Sinh Quan was a school dedicated to the education of the sons of ARVN officers and men, a school meant to mold the military leaders of the future. Hue received not only a general education based on the French classical model but also a military tutelage served with heavy doses of South Vietnamese patriotism. Hue learned that he was a natural leader of his people and that the ARVN was the vehicle through which Vietnam would achieve peace and reunification. Most importantly, though, Hue learned much regarding his sacred duty. He and his future cadre of South Vietnamese leaders were "responsible for the peace and prosperity of his people." Very much like Dinh, Hue learned his place in society in school, while also learning of his duty to lead his people in war. Adding his new lessons to his hatred of the communists, he found that his next move was natural. Hue enrolled in the prestigious Vietnamese National Military Academy at Da Lat. Hue's mother was initially disturbed by his decision and feared for her son's life. However, she too had been affected by what she knew of the Viet Minh and

Tran Ngoc Hue (second from the left) as a thirteen-year-old student at Truong Thieu Sinh Quan school for the children of ARVN officers and men. Photograph courtesy of Tran Ngoc Hue.

put patriotism before family and urged her son forward with his decision. With his drive and his grim determination, coupled with his prodigious academic skills, Tran Ngoc Hue did not hope or dream—he, too, *knew* that he would become a general.

The popular Western perception is that Ho Chi Minh and his followers were the only inheritors of the mantle of Vietnamese nationalism. As a result, it is common belief that very few, for quite special and narrow reasons, chose to follow the corrupt and dictatorial regime of South Vietnam, which was, after all, only an American creation. It follows, in this version, that the leaders of the South Vietnamese regime, and its military, were in the main Catholics who had a religious score to settle with the communists or were grasping urbanites who sought only to gain economically from their association with the regime. These few men were not leaders in the true sense of the term. They were self-serving and greedy, not heroic. They led the ARVN badly and gave the soldiers themselves little more than a meaningless death.

Pham Van Dinh and Tran Ngoc Hue were and are clearly exceptional. They were the best of the best—and became the bright young stars of the ARVN. However, just a cursory glance at their background and upbringing reveals that the situation in Vietnam and in the ARVN was much more complicated than most Westerners care to believe and defies the common mythology that characterizes America's lost war as one in defense of a bumbling and hopeless ally. The roots of noncommunist nationalism in Vietnam ran much deeper than the roots of the Viet Minh. Though the communists were by far the best-organized nationalist organization after World War II, they did not corner the market on Vietnamese patriotism. There existed a reservoir of support for a noncommunist solution to Vietnamese independence.

That Dinh and Hue were urban, comparatively wealthy, and well connected certainly set them apart in Vietnam and predisposed them both to support of the South Vietnamese regime. However, their motivations were varied and complex and were directly tied to Vietnamese history and culture, especially to the very important concepts of family and duty. These men were certainly not ragtag peasants; they were well educated and urbane. However, their background did not create an unbridgeable distance between them and the men they were destined to lead into battle. As throughout Vietnamese history, the leaders in the coming war were from the elite of society, and the soldiers were from the peasantry. Dinh and Hue stood as the inheritors of thousands of years of Vietnamese military tradition. They were raised to be proud, if paternalistic, leaders of men. They were raised to be the leaders of a great nation.

Birth of an Army

As both Dinh and Hue began their training, they prepared to enter a military force of only recent and questionable vintage. The ARVN was shaped by its colonial past and recently reshaped in the image of its new American sponsors. As such, it attempted to strike an uncomfortable balance between things at once both Vietnamese and Western and displayed the strengths and weaknesses inherent in both systems. Before considering the military careers of Dinh and Hue, it is necessary to outline the complex organization that they proposed to join—the Army of the Republic of Vietnam.

Typical of European efforts at colonization, in the nineteenth century the French had created Vietnamese indigenous units, such as the

Annamese Rifles and the Tonkin Fusiliers, both to aid in efforts to col-
onize Vietnam and to give the colonized a sense of participation and
control within the French system.[6] After World War II and the onset of
the struggle with the Viet Minh, the French chose to alter their relationship with Vietnam and its military forces. Tiring of war after years
of fighting, the French had seen the need to grant Vietnam a greater
level of independence, in part to subvert support for the Viet Minh.
As a result after long bouts of haggling, the French came to terms with
Emperor Bao Dai that granted Vietnam a surprising amount of control
over its own destiny. As part of the agreement, the French-trained Vietnamese National Army (VNA) was born, in 1950.

While a draft for the new army, the precursor of the ARVN, eventually was instituted, forces for the VNA originally were drawn from
the indigenous colonial units. The move once again raises the important question of motivation. Little has been written about the ARVN
and even less about the short-lived VNA, but the scholarship that
does exist suggests that they were both doomed from the outset. The
traditional view holds that the colonial legacy of the VNA and the fact
that it served an emperor whom many judged to be a French stooge
meant that the VNA and later, by extension, the ARVN always lacked
public support. The Vietnamese, with a long tradition of resisting in-
trusions on their sovereignty, saw the VNA and the ARVN as serving
to perpetuate foreign control or influence in Vietnam. Thus, the VNA
inherited the unpopularity of the Vietnamese indigenous forces, and
the ARVN inherited the unpopularity of the VNA.[7]

Yet, even with the French only edging toward acceptance of the
idea of Vietnamese independence, millions of Vietnamese chose to
support the fledgling Bao Dai regime over the specter of the permanent triumph of communist forces in Vietnam. Whether motivated by
religion, anticommunism, self-preservation, or greed, many chose Bao
Dai as a middle ground between support of the French and support of
the Viet Minh. These supporters believed that it was more patriotic,
even more Vietnamese, to follow their own emperor and his more traditionalist form of nationalism than to support Ho Chi Minh and the
foreign and uncomfortably European concept of Marxism.[8]

Though certainly at a disadvantage for being considered something of a foreign force, the VNA and later the ARVN were not fatally
flawed by the connection. Indeed, the VNA and the ARVN could po-

tentially draw upon a wellspring of potential popular support that had existed in Vietnam for generations. It would fall to the government of South Vietnam and its American sponsors to form a political and military system worthy of that support, which would draw from the same martial spirit that made the Viet Minh such hardy adversaries and tap into the nationalism that had allowed Vietnam to fight for an entire millennium against the Chinese.

Systemic and practical problems plagued the VNA from its inception. Under the indigenous system, the French, in part as a method of continued military control, never promoted Vietnamese personnel beyond the rank of junior officer. Thus, there was a chronic shortage in the VNA of Vietnamese officers for command or staff positions above company level.[9] After the VNA transformed into the ARVN with the creation of South Vietnam, the force grew exponentially, and the officer shortage became even more acute. Making matters worse, the French system of officer training was rather chaotic and left the overextended VNA officer corps to undergo hit-or-miss on-the-job training in combat. Additionally, since the VNA officers had come from "native" colonial units, they were closely wedded to their French colonial sponsors, a cadre of Francophile officers who formed a close-knit group, which quickly realized its importance to and power within the new Vietnamese state. The political power wielded by the Francophile officer class, and the subsequent politicization of the military as a whole, continued to grow after the foundation of South Vietnam and became one of the chief problems facing a nation already plagued with myriad difficulties.

During their final, troubled years of colonial rule, the French were sidetracked by practical military matters posed by their battle against the Viet Minh and spent little time and effort on the construction of the VNA.[10] By the time of the French defeat at Dien Bien Phu, in 1954, the VNA had only a rudimentary general staff, no artillery, no heavy armor, no logistic capability, and few Vietnamese officers above the rank of lieutenant. On paper the VNA numbered about 150,000 men at the time of the end of French rule, but many of its battalions were considerably under strength due to desertion and defection to the victorious Viet Minh. That the VNA suffered a nearly complete breakdown of combat capabilities after the withdrawal of the French following the Geneva Accords is hardly surprising.[11]

Enter the United States

In the wake of the French failure in Vietnam, the United States entered the fray in defense of containment against communist expansion. U.S. sponsorship meant the founding of a new military—the Army of the Republic of Vietnam. The job of creating a viable military force out of the wreckage of the VNA was no easy task, but to American policymakers it was far better than the alternative of sending American ground forces into the area. The task fell to the 342-man-strong Military Assistance and Advisory Group, Vietnam (MAAG).[12]

Beginning in 1955, the leadership of MAAG, initially Lieutenant General John O'Daniel and then Lieutenant General Samuel Williams, had to build the ARVN effectively from scratch using what little they had, including the flawed but necessary cadre of VNA officers. MAAG's task was monumental and included everything from training officers to bringing in mountains of supplies. In their haste to ready for a war that many judged to be close at hand, MAAG based the construction of the ARVN on the recent experience of the Korean War and advocated a conventional force ready to face an invasion from North Vietnam.

The leadership of the new Vietnamese Joint General Staff disagreed with MAAG's design for the ARVN, countering that South Vietnam was more likely to face an insurgency than an invasion, and contended that the ARVN should be constructed as a more lithe force based on maneuverability and sustainability within the Vietnamese cultural system.[13] In his memoir of the period, a frustrated General Tran Van Don lamented that such arguments "fell on deaf ears."[14] Williams did not relent and eventually settled on creating an ARVN of seven standardized infantry divisions whose task it was to stand against a North Vietnamese invasion long enough for American forces to arrive on the scene to save the day as they had in Korea.

Diem agonized over the decision to create an American-style army in South Vietnam and recognized that his own generals held a different vision for the army, but by 1956 domestic needs and the promise of American funding overrode his own generals' arguments. The United States chose, with Diem's approval, to create a mirror image of the American military in South Vietnam and labored to construct an ARVN built on the primacy of conventional firepower and lavish logistical support. However, the American plan ran considerable risk, for South Vietnam, a developing nation, could not hope to support the considerable logistic, armament, and training needs of such a military on its own.

The social pressures that accompanied raising and equipping a large, conventional military in a small, developing country were legion and showed a lack of empathy with the needs of the peasant population. Reliant on labor-intensive wet-rice agriculture for their survival, whether they supported the government of South Vietnam or not, many young men refused to abandon their work in the fields and the welfare of their family to join the military. Unable to rely on volunteerism to supply the military with manpower, South Vietnam turned to a draft system that was riddled with abuses, including serial draft dodging and payment of draft substitutes, to provide 65 percent of the army's total troop levels, making it one of the most heavily conscripted armies in history. Men were pulled away from their important familial duties for years, which led to a chronic problem with desertion. Still, the ARVN fought long and hard, and one study indicated that if the United States had mobilized the same proportion of its adult male population as did South Vietnam, it would have sent eight million men per year to Vietnam.[15]

MAAG's reliance on conventional operations also created a westernized ARVN that stood apart from its people and from the nation's own martial past. Promising counterinsurgency techniques based on small units of territorial forces raised on the local level and tied intrinsically to the people were ignored in favor of standard Western tactics of attrition for the next twelve years. To MAAG, a possible insurgency was only a diversion that threatened to take attention away from a potential communist invasion. In 1955, Diem had railed against the Americans' traditionalist approach to the conflict, telling Williams, "We should start Guerrilla Warfare of our own. . . . The Army does not understand, as it sees only the classic military solution."[16] While Diem remained fascinated by elements of counterinsurgency, developing the secondary but infamous Agroville and Strategic Hamlet Programs, MAAG continued to ready the ARVN for a replay of Korea. Thus, MAAG restructured the ARVN quickly, in an American mold, and readied it for a conventional war that never came.[17] In the words of Lieutenant General Ngo Quang Truong:

When fighting finally broke out, it did not take the form of a conventional, Korean-style invasion. It rather began as a brush-fire war fought with subversive activities and guerrilla tactics away from urban centers. Waged day and night, this small war gradually gained in tempo, nipping away at the secure fabric of rural areas. In the face of the growing insurgency, ARVN units found themselves ill-fitted to fight this type of war for which they had not been trained.[18]

As the numbers of American advisers increased, it became obvious that the problems plaguing the ARVN were by no means of a single causation. Again Truong comments:

> During the first few years the effort of U.S. advisers met with considerable obstacles, particularly in the area of training. Several years of hard fighting on all battlefields from north to south and living close to French forces—and undoubtedly under their influence—had instilled a certain psychology of intractability, unruliness and complacency among the Vietnamese military cadre. Their adjustment to the American way of doing things was painful and slow. They found American training and warfare methods too inflexible, too mechanical, and not realistically adapted to the Vietnam battlefield. The language barrier and cultural difference also formed a wide and seemingly unbridgeable gap. To a certain extent, the Vietnamese were not interested in training and did not think it was necessary. After all, they felt they were experienced enough and knew how to fight this kind of war. American tactical advice was something they thought they could do without.[19]

Old Leaders and a New Generation

Ngo Dinh Diem realized that the support of the ARVN—no matter its military might—was the single most important factor that kept his government in power. His generals quickly learned their importance to the new government and did not delay in benefiting from their considerable power and influence. With only limited loyalty to the new state of South Vietnam, many military leaders turned to political games of power brokering and graft rather than to the business of readying for war with North Vietnam. For his part, Diem came to value political loyalty from his military commanders over bravery and combat effectiveness. For the remainder of the conflict, the leadership of the ARVN became intertwined with the state, and the line between politics and the military became so blurred that no regime in Saigon could survive without military support, which made the ARVN synonymous with the government.[20] The ARVN was and remained both the main power base of the South Vietnamese government and its governing apparatus, a system rife with potential political liabilities.[21] To advance within the ARVN ranks, officers had to be well connected and politically loyal even if they were not necessarily among the nation's best military leaders. Once one reached the higher ranks, it became of paramount importance to stay there, so one of the major jobs of the ARVN became defense of the government and the status quo against political enemies, rather than battling the growing insurgency.[22]

That the South Vietnamese officer corps suffered from grave deficiencies and was overly politicized is beyond doubt. However, the only serious studies of the officer corps have focused on the elite within the system—the generals who had connections to the French regime and came to dominate the ARVN and the South Vietnamese political system. These were men from a different time and a different war, men whom the historian Ronald Spector referred to as a "group whose behavior was shaped by the firm conviction that no duty or obligation of citizenship was so compelling that it could not be avoided through judicious use of money and family connections."[23] These men were not the hope for the future; they were the relics of the past. Anthony James Joes brings up a very important point in his study, *The War for South Vietnam*:

> This morale-breaking favoritism and its accompanying back-biting, sycophancy, and corruption were endemic throughout Diem's officer corps, hobbling the efforts of thousands of officers who were doing their best to save their country.[24]

There were indeed thousands of officers who fought hard and well, as any quick survey of American advisers regarding their opinions of their ARVN counterparts confirms.[25] These dedicated ARVN officers were hamstrung by their overly politicized and ineffective top level leadership—in Joes's words, "Diem's officer corps." This initial leadership of the ARVN proved in the main to be fatally flawed. The task of transforming the ARVN officer corps and indeed the ARVN itself fell to a new cadre of leaders with only dim memories of a colonial past, leaders who had American advisers and who were loyal to South Vietnam, the only nation that they could remember. Fired both by new loyalties and by Vietnamese tradition, Pham Van Dinh and Tran Ngoc Hue embodied this new type of leader. A great deal can be learned about the Vietnam War by looking at the nature and fate of the more junior-level leadership of the ARVN during the conflict. Here one finds an ongoing struggle for the soul of the ARVN and the South Vietnamese state. Would the junior leadership have time to transform the ARVN, or would it succumb to the pressure and the dysfunction that were its inheritance?

Battle

The ARVN of 1960 was an army that stood on the brink of failure. It was preparing, and poorly, for the wrong war. Its leaders were largely unresponsive to American demands for change. It had not had enough time to train. Its important territorial element had been ignored. It had no logistic capability. Perhaps worst of all, though, was the fact that the ARVN was hopelessly tied to the corrupt, brutal, and inefficient Diem regime, which had done little to appeal to the various groupings of sects, ethnicities, economic groups, and nationalist groups that constituted South Vietnam. The government and the military had been much more concerned with gaining power than with deserving power. While Diem made significant efforts to create a new nation where none had existed before, he had not done enough. His regime and his military did too little to call upon the power of their own people; did too little to take the mantle of nationalism away from the communists. South Vietnam lacked politically and militarily in the critical area of leadership. Francophile generals and despotic, personalistic rulers were able to take the new nation only so far. Nearly every American report from the time is filled with warnings that South Vietnam lacked leadership; its leaders were too political, too corrupt, too lazy, too selfish, too tied to the flawed system. To build something new and better, though, would take time and patience, something that the United States in the end did not have.

Initially the ARVN performed rather well against weaker, outmatched opponents, mainly the private armies of the various independent religious sects within South Vietnam. However, the situation worsened in 1960 as the communists recovered both from their own exertions and from the promulgation of societal revolution in the North and chose to seek an armed overthrow of the Diem regime in the South through the foundation of the National Liberation Front, dubbed the Viet Cong. At the outset, the Viet Cong found good recruiting in the South, for the Diem government had only in part spread its rule into the South Vietnamese hinterlands and had failed to undertake meaningful land reform, which left many peasants landless, penniless, and only tangentially connected to the distracted and distant central government. The developing ARVN, sidetracked as it was by political issues, failed to provide security throughout the countryside, leaving many rural areas vulnerable to Viet Cong penetration. While it was more than double the size of the Viet Cong, the ARVN failed to achieve meaningful victory.

As the Viet Cong campaign of terror spread, American and South Vietnamese officials found themselves at a loss to explain why the ARVN failed to stamp out the insurgency. Attributing the survival of the rebels to the use of guerrilla warfare tactics, the United States responded in 1960 by sending military advisers to the field with the ARVN and by 1965 had reached the point where each ARVN battalion was accompanied by a five-man American advisory team. Though the move was a step forward, the South Vietnamese and their American sponsors had erred in the belief that a military defeat of the guerrillas would end the insurgency. Guerrilla tactics were but one part of the problem, though the carefully planned hit-and-run attacks did worry the ARVN greatly. The real strength of the insurgency lay in its burgeoning political organization. Until Saigon responded with a political answer, involving governmental and economic reform—creating a state and a national organization that earned the devotion of its people—a military solution to the guerrilla problem remained impossible.[26]

In spite of the challenges, the ARVN performed better by 1962 and had grown to a strength of 219,000 men. Across much of the country, South Vietnamese forces reasserted control over many areas that had fallen under Viet Cong control, prompting U.S. Deputy Ambassador William Truehart to exclaim that he was "tremendously encouraged" by ARVN success that was "little short of sensational." [27] Even the notoriously optimistic North Vietnamese official history of the war admits that in 1962 the ARVN was on the offensive everywhere to such an extent that "rightest and negativist tendencies" appeared among the soldiery and "liberated areas and areas where the masses had seized control shrank. Guerrillas from a number of villages and hamlets were forced to move to other areas or flee to our base areas." [28]

As the ARVN continued its resurgence, the U.S. commitment to the conflict had also deepened, as demonstrated by the arrival of Lieutenant General Paul Harkins, in February 1962, to head the new Military Assistance Command, Vietnam (MACV). The United States's trust in the ARVN seemed well placed, for as one North Vietnamese account lamented during the first months of 1963, ARVN successes continued apace as South Vietnamese government forces mounted between 1,500 and 2,000 operations per month. The study grudgingly noted that "Protracted and large-scale [ARVN] operations launched unremittingly against any given region were more numerous and fiercer than the previous year." [29]

That the ARVN still suffered from obvious deficiencies, though, was evidenced by the botched Battle of Ap Bac, in 1963. An ARVN force, advised by American Lieutenant Colonel John Paul Vann, had located a VC force of some three hundred men and closed in for the kill. Outnumbering their foes by more than five to one and possessing a critical firepower advantage, the ARVN planned to surround and annihilate the VC unit. Manning strong defensive emplacements, the VC fought well, but the ARVN did not. Hampered by ineffective command, the ARVN assault was poorly coordinated and allowed the VC to slip away into the night. What should have been an easy victory was at best a costly draw. Though the battle at Ap Bac was arguably presented in a biased manner by the American media,[30] it and other battles indicated that problems remained in the ARVN. Even so, the successes of 1962 and 1963 demonstrated that the ARVN was resurgent and that there was little danger that the Viet Cong would shatter the ARVN or overthrow the Diem government.[31] The period of optimism and relative calm, though, was short lived as the structural weaknesses of the South Vietnamese state gave way, leading to governmental and military implosion.

Pham Van Dinh and Tran Ngoc Hue made their decisions to enter the Army of the Republic of Vietnam at a tumultuous time. Though in ways their backgrounds were rather standard for the ARVN officer class, their motivations served to set them—and many of their generation—apart from the group of officers that dominated the military and political system of South Vietnam. In time, both young men would become fully aware of the shortcomings that so plagued their military. Both men would also realize that without meaningful reform, the ARVN and South Vietnam might not survive the difficult struggle. Born to and trained for positions of leadership within South Vietnam, both Dinh and Hue were certain, as are so many idealistic young people, of their importance and ability. They would set the proper example. They would change things. When they became generals, as they knew they would, they and their generation would overcome the problems bequeathed to them by their military forbearers. They were both certain that they needed only a chance—and for that chance they both needed time.

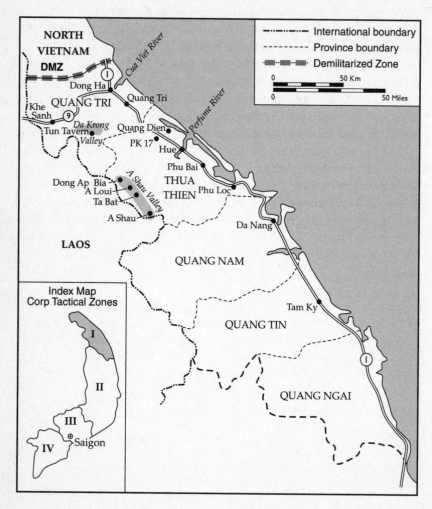

I Corps Tactical Zone

2

A War Transformed

Battle, Politics, and the Americanization
of the War, 1963–1966

IT WAS A heady time to be a leader of men in South Vietnam, and, even as they faced their first tests in battle, Dinh and Hue also became swept up in some of the most important political events of their time. In the coming years, the onset of governmental chaos and discord at the highest levels shook the ARVN to its very core and left the survival of the nation in doubt. In the wake of the cacophony of political intrigue and change, the United States chose to make the war in Vietnam an American war and devoted U.S. combat forces to the fray, which fundamentally altered the nature of the entire conflict. The next four years were formative to the wartime experiences of Dinh and Hue and taught them the reality of South Vietnam at war while the conflict itself became nearly unrecognizable as small-unit guerrilla war gave way to an ever-increasing number of American and North Vietnamese troops engaged in pitched battle. As their world changed around them, both Dinh and Hue retained their optimism and believed that, with the continued help of its American allies, South Vietnam would emerge victorious from a war transformed.

Training

At the age of twenty-four, Dinh began his military training and became part of "Class 9" of the Thu Duc Reserve Officers School in 1961.[1] The school, based on the U.S. Army's Officer Candidate School at Fort Benning, Georgia, produced more than 65 percent of the officers who served in the ARVN. Dinh and the other officer candidates went through nine months of training and received a reserve commission in the ARVN at the rank of aspirant, one level below second lieutenant.[2] Trained by both Vietnamese officers and U.S. advisers, Dinh quickly mastered the art of small-unit command, graduated in the top ten of his class, and learned that being a good officer meant more than understanding tactics. It meant earning the respect of those under his command and leading by example—a lesson often only poorly learned in the ARVN.

After graduation from Thu Duc, Dinh spent a short stint as a mortar platoon leader in the 3rd Regiment of the 1st ARVN Division. The war as Dinh first experienced it was an insurgency in its early stages, and much of Dinh's sector south of the Demilitarized Zone (DMZ), later famed as the single most dangerous place in South Vietnam, remained in a state of relative calm. As a result, Dinh's first command did not involve combat, and in January 1962 he attended the South Vietnamese Ranger School. The demanding physical regimen of the program lasted for three months and focused on jungle warfare and counterinsurgency techniques. After graduating fifth in his class, Dinh underwent additional training in the Jungle Warfare School in Malaya, where he learned British techniques of counterinsurgency.[3]

After completing his advanced training, Dinh received an assignment to the Phu Bai Training Center, where he worked to transform ARVN draftees into effective soldiers. However, faced with a growing insurgency and an expanding war, the ARVN as a whole had little time to devote to unit training. Indeed, U.S. military advisers often cited "poor training, or its complete absence,"[4] as one of the critical weak points of the ARVN. Of special concern was a worrisome lack of unit training. For example, in 1964, fifteen ARVN battalions had received no formal unit training whatsoever, and had to learn their military craft through the crucible of "on-the-job training" in battle.[5] Dinh's stint at Phu Bai, though, was something of an exception in that it occurred during a period of relative calm in his area of operations. During most of 1962 and 1963, Dinh remained at Phu Bai, working with training companies of some sixty men, each for a three-month period. Dinh immersed himself in the lives of his trainees, overseeing everything from their weapons training to their physical fitness— whatever it took to prepare raw recruits for the rigors of battle. In Dinh's mind, his charges left Phu Bai as trained and competent soldiers, but he was aware of a grave training deficiency—one that the Americans did not readily notice.

Even at this early stage of his career, Dinh realized that the ARVN was at a disadvantage, not in tactical prowess but in the critical psychological war for the "hearts and minds" of the people. The ARVN's communist adversaries could claim victory over the French and could portray themselves as the purveyors of a national war for independence. The ARVN, though, could be seen as a relic of the colonial past, which gave the Viet Cong a critical edge.[6] As a result, Dinh believed that the ARVN had to do a better job of convincing the people of the evils of communism and of the righteousness of its own cause. That task had to begin with the soldiers who made up the rank and file of the ARVN, the men who would defend the state of South Vietnam as well as function as the most compelling image of that state. However, since the Saigon government lived in constant fear of a military coup, nationalism and patriotism played an insignificant role in ARVN training. In the words of one ARVN enlisted man, Nguyen Van Chau, "Most soldiers that I knew understood little about why we were fighting. Anticommunism was more abstract to us than scientific political theories. Not once did any of my instructors mention a proactive political agenda."[7] In Dinh's view, the concentration on the mechanics of training never wavered, which left ARVN soldiers technically sound but at a critical disadvantage against their more politically astute foes in the areas of morale and leadership. Other nations had been born in war, but the ARVN arguably never coalesced into a military force possessed of a unifying political ideology.

As Dinh was completing his training at Thu Duc in 1961, Tran Ngoc Hue entered the prestigious Vietnamese National Military Academy (VNMA) at Da Lat. Founded by the French in 1950, the VNMA maintained exacting entrance qualifications and was one of the premier national service institutions in the whole of Asia. Cadets before 1965 went through a rigorous, two-year course of study and received a regular commission at the rank of second lieutenant.[8] Though prestigious, the VNMA could produce fewer than two hundred graduates annually, not nearly enough to meet the constant demand of the ARVN for new officers. Thus, Thu Duc Reserve Officers School, attended by Dinh, which produced several thousand officers per year, remained of critical importance. An understandable rivalry developed between the graduates of the two institutions,[9] with VNMA graduates often feeling superior to their Thu Duc brethren.

Hue excelled at his studies, which included lessons on leadership and patriotism. Driven by his personal hatred for the communists,

Tran Ngoc Hue at the time of his graduation from the
Vietnamese National Military Academy. Photograph
Courtesy of Tran Ngoc Hue.

Hue, like Dinh, learned to respect and love his men and learned his
duty of sacrifice for his fledgling nation. The lessons of the VNMA
stressed ideals of service that linked closely with Vietnam's martial
heritage, which tied service to South Vietnam to the nation's glorious
past.

The ARVN that Hue joined in November 1963 as a second lieutenant had undergone massive expansion as the war in Vietnam changed.
In 1960, the ARVN had contained 150,000 men in seven infantry divisions, one airborne brigade, a Ranger force of 9,000 men, and three
Marine battalions. By 1962, the strength of the ARVN had risen to

219,000 men, organized into four corps, nine divisions, one airborne brigade, one Special Forces group, three separate regiments, one territorial regiment, eighty-six Ranger companies, and nineteen separate battalions and associated support units. Militia-style forces (the Civil Guard and the Self-Defense Corps, later to be reorganized into the Regional and Popular Forces) added another 176,500 men to South Vietnam's total force under arms.[10] The situation at this early juncture of the conflict warranted optimism on the part of Dinh and Hue. Though the lack of individual and unit training remained a problem, morale and leadership were sometimes questionable, and the government had only nominal control in much of the Vietnamese hinterlands, the ARVN in 1963 still held its own in a brushfire war against the emerging force of the Viet Cong. Even though American advisers remained quite concerned that the ARVN sometimes suffered major reverses like that at the Battle of Ap Bac, there appeared to be no immediate threat to the nation of South Vietnam. The future was not bleak but would turn dark very soon.

Chaos

As Hue completed his training at the VNMA and Dinh served at Phu Bai, political turmoil swept across the nation, altering the nature of the war and very nearly shattering the ARVN. President Ngo Dinh Diem had always been a controversial figure, but he had, with American support, beaten all odds and created a functioning government and military in South Vietnam. However, Diem had a dictatorial bent that greatly worried his American sponsors. Additionally, members of the ARVN's command elite on the one hand coveted Diem's power and prestige and on the other fretted about his individual consolidation of authority. Though many within the U.S. government, including President John F. Kennedy and Secretary of Defense Robert McNamara, remained Diem supporters, an influential grouping, led by Ambassador Henry Cabot Lodge, became more and more worried that Diem's style of rule and the preference shown to the Catholic religious minority in South Vietnam had alienated the various powerful Buddhist groupings in the country.

In 1963, fear became reality as cities across South Vietnam erupted into open conflict between the Buddhist movement and the Diem regime. Though the exact nature of the events remains shrouded by a cloak of duplicity and lies, a cadre of ARVN leaders saw the crisis as an opportunity to overthrow the increasingly unpopular Diem while retaining the backing of his all-important American sponsors. As a result, on 1 November, a military coup led to the downfall and assassination of Ngo Dinh Diem.[11]

Though the United States hoped that the new military leadership of Vietnam would both provide a greater level of stability and prosecute the war with more vigor, it was wrong. For the next two years, the rampant politicization of the military became increasingly obvious as leading generals launched a succession of coups and countercoups aimed at gaining or retaining power. The ongoing political instability in Saigon caused such consternation in Washington that after a short visit to Vietnam in December 1964, McNamara reported:

> The situation is very disturbing. Current trends, unless reversed in the next two to three months, will lead to neutralization at best and more likely to a Communist controlled state. The new government is the greatest source of concern. It is indecisive and drifting.[12]

Washington's fears resulted in efforts by the new U.S. Ambassador, Maxwell Taylor, to rectify the situation. Taylor's intervention, though, was ineffective and demonstrated both a political naiveté and a considerable level of hubris. In mid-December 1964, Taylor invited several leading ARVN generals to a steak dinner at General William Westmoreland's residence, where he warned the South Vietnamese military luminaries against further coups and military interference in politics. Certain that he had gotten his point across, Taylor was furious when, only a few days later, the ARVN leadership carried out yet another governmental change. Taylor called the leading ARVN generals to his office and scolded them for their actions, saying, "We cannot continue to carry you forever if you do things like this. . . . Do all of you understand English? I told you clearly at General Westmoreland's dinner that we Americans were tired of coups."[13]

Taylor's admonitions failed, and South Vietnam endured a period of political instability that was of paramount importance to its continuing weakness and eventual downfall. In the twenty months following Diem's death, the nation had nine different governments as members of the military leadership struggled among themselves for ultimate political power in South Vietnam. The political and military chaos struck the ARVN like a typhoon and served to destroy much of the fitful gains made by the South Vietnamese military in recent years.

Each new government made sweeping changes in the command structure of the ARVN, with presumed loyalty to the new regime as the litmus test for high military office. ARVN officials on the province or corps level often had ultimate political authority over their area of operations, and some even ruled as feudal barons. As generals on the national level grasped for power, they formed complex, competing alliance systems with some powerful local military leaders and worked to oust others, who were supporters of rival generals, from power. As the struggle for military and political control became more chaotic, the leadership of the ARVN fragmented into smaller and smaller groups of loyalty.[14] The gamesmanship between members of the upper-level command intensely frustrated loyal young combat officers like Dinh and Hue, who became more committed than ever to doing their jobs well, swimming against the tide of politicization and eventually supplanting the now obviously out-of-touch and dangerous military relics of the French colonial past.

In the wake of political instability, ARVN morale plummeted, and a military that had been holding its own against the Viet Cong both stagnated and lost the initiative as offensive operations and pacification efforts in several areas simply ground to a halt. Communist forces used the chaos to their advantage and built their forces in South Vietnam from a total of 30,000 in November 1963 to 212,000 by July 1965. As the ARVN dawdled, the Viet Cong seized control of large swathes of countryside, and sizable communist units roamed much of the nation at will.

A communist document prepared in March 1965 assessed the situation in South Vietnam:

> The balance of forces between the South Vietnamese revolution and the enemy has changed very rapidly in our favor. . . . The bulk of the enemy's armed forces and paramilitary forces at the village and hamlet level have disintegrated, and what is left continues to disintegrate.[15]

Emboldened by their newfound strength and hoping for the ultimate defeat of the Saigon regime before American power could be brought to bear, the Viet Cong launched a series of assaults on villages and district towns, which heralded a sea change in the conflict.[16]

With the bumbling Saigon regime seemingly perpetually on the razor's edge of collapse, the situation to many American observers now warranted direct U.S. involvement in combat operations lest containment fail. As a result, the administration of President Lyndon Johnson began a tumultuous debate over the issue of committing American troops to battle—a move that would save South Vietnam for the time being but would bring dire consequences.

Dinh and Hue watched with great concern as events played out after the downfall of Diem much to the detriment of the ARVN. The newly minted officer Hue realized that the upper levels of ARVN command were full of plotting, selfish time servers who had no true loyalty to the new state of South Vietnam. For Dinh, the results of the coup were somewhat more personal. Because of his kinship ties to the toppled regime, Dinh languished under house arrest in his quarters at the Phu Bai Training Center with no contact with his family while the new ARVN leadership scrutinized his actions and attempted to divine his loyalties. In the end, the new regime allowed Dinh to remain in the military, though his family did not emerge unscathed as his father had to, in Dinh's words, "retire due to his age." Shortly thereafter, Dinh moved from his training position to the command of the 2nd Company, 3rd Battalion, 3rd Regiment of the 1st ARVN Division.

The endemic national chaos manifested itself on a local level through a parade of ARVN commanders who came and went with monotonous regularity during the ensuing months. In a single year, command of the 1st ARVN Division changed hands four times, while Dinh also had to deal with three different regimental and four different battalion commanders in the same time period. Though junior officers like Dinh and Hue tended to remain in place, the constant flux of senior officers played havoc with the morale of soldiers and the effectiveness of operations in the hitherto relatively peaceful area of I Corps.

Realities of Command

As political intrigue wracked the nation, Dinh went about his business as a second lieutenant and a company commander and learned much about the mutable nature of the conflict that came to dominate his entire life. During the first months of 1964, Dinh's 2nd Company, 3rd Battalion, 3rd Regiment worked out of the regimental base area of PK 17, located off Highway 1, seventeen kilometers north of Hue City. Dinh's company engaged in search-and-destroy missions, designed to deny the Viet Cong access to local villages as sources of supplies and recruits. The area was relatively peaceful at the time, and Dinh's sweeps resulted in little contact. Even so, Dinh learned that the physical reality of command in the ARVN involved difficult moral choices.

Dinh worked hard to earn the respect of his men, remaining with them in the field while other ARVN officers began a trend of skulking away from their units as often as possible to enjoy the comforts of the cities. Dinh also avoided the corruption that plagued the ARVN. Though officers' pay in 1964 (in Dinh's case 5,000 piasters per month, or the rough equivalent of $150), augmented by a family allowance, proved adequate for most, still the overly politicized officer class found ample opportunity to augment their earnings. At lower levels of command, two types of graft appeared most often. Each ARVN soldier received a monthly allotment of twenty-one kilos of rice, but many officers kept some of that allotment for their own use and profited from its sale. Additionally, officers kept "ghost soldiers" on their roles—soldiers who had deserted or had been killed—and pocketed their pay. Soldiers in some units did not have enough to eat, while other units remained chronically under strength due to the ghost soldier phenomenon. The abuses associated with corruption in the ARVN were detrimental to morale and caused ARVN soldiers to question the loyalty of their own officers.

As the war lingered on, pay for both enlisted men and officers failed to keep pace with the rising tide of inflation,[17] and during the late stages of American involvement in the conflict, ARVN officers and men could feed neither themselves nor their families on their dwindling pay. According to Lieutenant General Dong Van Khuyen:

> Low pay compounded by inflation put the average serviceman in a pathetic predicament, forcing him to struggle with himself between moral uprightness (which meant poverty and a life of penury for his wife and children) and corruption (which jeopardized combat effectiveness and perhaps the survival of the nation). Because of their chosen probity, a number of officers had to live off their parents'

incomes, moonlight during off-duty hours in such jobs as carrying passengers on Honda mopeds, reduce their material needs to a minimum, and be content with a life of frugality and destitution.[18]

The situation became so bad that in 1968 the South Vietnamese Joint General Staff authorized an investigation into the inadequacy of ARVN pay, the alarming results of which indicated that "no soldier could exist on his current salary." Two years later, a CIA study of ARVN pay indicated that pay was so low that it covered "only one third to one half of a soldier's expenses." Making matters worse, civilian laborers were much better off than ARVN soldiers, and their American counterparts made princely sums by comparison, further damaging the ARVN's already fragile morale. As a result, more and more officers turned to graft, and the morale of the rank and file sank to critically low levels.

The poverty experienced by ARVN soldiers had an important and troubling connection to the concepts of *on* and *hieu*. Entire families, with one-third of ARVN soldiers having to care for an extended family of ten or more,[19] had to subsist on the meager wages of ARVN officers and carry on even though the men were absent during the most important agricultural times of the year, the times when a family normally produced its livelihood. The emasculating inability to care for one's family left many soldiers torn between their all-too-often poorly understood duty to their nation and their traditional obligation to their loved ones. An ARVN enlisted man, Nguyen Tang, explained the problem simply: "My primary role in life is to provide for my family and to venerate my ancestors. It was very difficult to leave the village . . . even if it was under threat . . . to fight. I would rather have died with my family at home than leave them and not be able to care for them."[20]

The desire to return home both for reasons of *on* and *hieu* and to aid in planting or the harvest were powerful motives behind much of the endemic desertion that plagued the ARVN. In many cases, though, family members simply followed soldiers to their base areas, which resulted in the ad hoc establishment of shantytowns of camp followers near military complexes. In a long war, the proximity of family sometimes served to bolster ARVN morale. However, a chronic lack of adequate housing, sanitation difficulties, and marginal educational opportunities in the "family camps" were sources of constant worry for many ARVN soldiers. The nearness of family, though, proved most distracting in times of major military actions, when ARVN soldiers had to choose between fighting with their unit for the good of the nation and deserting to defend their family as part of their *on* and *hieu*.

Realities of Combat

In June 1964, Dinh's battalion moved south into the operational area of the 2nd ARVN Division near Tam Ky in Quang Nam Province, which put an end to the deceptive period of peace that the battalion had enjoyed. The Viet Cong were much more active in the area, and the 2nd Division, which had responsibility for the region, had called for aid, and was reinforced by the 3rd Battalion. The three rifle companies of the 3rd Battalion quickly settled into a routine of constant motion, which normally consisted of ten days spent on security operations sweeping the villages in the area between the coast and the foothills followed by ten days operating at the battalion command post. The missions were deadly serious and often resulted in running battles with elements of a resident Viet Cong force of company strength and additional communist forces that infiltrated the area from the nearby highlands.

Though fighting in the area was chronic, two battles from this period stood out in Dinh's mind. In early July, Dinh received his "baptism by fire" when his unit came under attack in an open rice paddy while approaching a village. The ARVN soldiers rushed forward, and the enemy, true to form, quickly retreated. Dinh and his men questioned the local villagers and received frustratingly few answers. After searching the village, Dinh made a show of leaving the area but secretly left a squad behind in an ambush position. As expected, later that night the Viet Cong returned, and Dinh's men attacked and drove the enemy force away, killing two. Dinh's quick thinking and ingenuity had won the day in his first battle, yet he found the dubious loyalty of the villagers to be quite troubling.

For six months, Dinh's unit swept its area of operations, sometimes making no contact, often discovering booby traps or receiving sniper fire, and engaging in battle on more than ten occasions, usually against enemy forces no larger than a platoon. Armed with weapons of older U.S. vintage, including M-1 carbines and Browning automatic rifles, the 3rd Company and its parent units consistently bested the Viet Cong. As a result, against prevailing historical wisdom, Dinh believed that the ARVN, regardless of its weaknesses, was holding its own in the conflict. Even so, on a wider level, more and more enemy units seemed to be slipping into the area, and little tangible progress was evident despite the ARVN's considerable exertions.

On 18 December 1964, the escalation of the war that so concerned McNamara and Taylor became more apparent to Dinh as a reinforced battalion of Viet Cong regulars attacked the positions of the 3rd Battalion, 3rd Regiment in an area some eight kilometers west of Tam Ky. The attack came in the predawn hours, while Dinh's company was out on operations. He was so near to the battalion command post, though, that he could hear and see the fighting as Viet Cong sappers penetrated the ARVN defensive perimeter and threw satchel charges into the various command bunkers that dotted the base. During the fighting, the battalion commander fled, leaving the unit commanded by its assistant. Even so, the ARVN soldiers fought bravely and eventually repelled the Viet Cong invaders, losing thirteen dead and killing fifteen. Hours later, forewarned by the attack on the battalion command post, Dinh and the roughly eighty-five men under his command were ready when a Viet Cong company charged into their defensive position. Well trained and confident, Dinh's men repulsed the attack, losing four dead and three wounded. The next day, Dinh's men discovered seventeen enemy bodies and numerous blood trails where the Viet Cong had removed additional dead and wounded. Dinh had fought hard and well and had achieved the first major victory of his career, which resulted in his promotion to lieutenant—a sign that he had been marked for greater things.

The months of action, though, left Dinh with the impression that the war was being fought incorrectly on the tactical level. His men were winning the battles, but Dinh wondered if they were not losing the war, for soon after the fighting ended ARVN forces habitually left the area, which allowed the Viet Cong to return both to exact their retribution against any civilians who had collaborated and to reimpose their control. Dinh, along with many other young ARVN combat officers, wished that his forces could stay in place longer to educate the people regarding why they should support the government of South Vietnam. He also realized that many of the villages that were supposedly under government control actually were not and that the Viet

Cong ruling infrastructure simply melted away when ARVN forces were present, only to return once the armed threat had passed. The Viet Cong were busy proselytizing the people, especially the vast number of landless peasants who, without money and without security, were most vulnerable to their call. While the government offered little in the way of true security or economic benefit to this lowest class of the peasantry, the Viet Cong promised to give them land and hope.[21]

Dinh had struck upon one of the central weaknesses of South Vietnam's war; it was the Viet Cong who held the upper hand in the war for the hearts and minds of the people. While involved in constant attritional sweeps, the ARVN could not alter the fact that, in the words of the former intelligence analyst Cao Van Thu, "The Communists did an excellent job in ideological training, even if the party's message was pure propaganda. In South Vietnam we did nothing to prepare the countryside for the needed sacrifice."[22]

The Art of Leadership

During this tumultuous time, after his own stint learning techniques of counterinsurgency in Ranger school, Tran Ngoc Hue received his first command as part of the 3rd Company, 1st Battalion, 1st Regiment of the 1st ARVN Division. He reported to the company commander, Lieutenant Chiem Uc, at the Ta Bat Fire Base in the infamous A Shau Valley, some five kilometers east of the Laotian border. The rough terrain around Ta Bat was fast becoming a Viet Cong staging area as the communist forces expanded their war efforts. To this point in the conflict, the Viet Cong and North Vietnamese forces in the I Corps area had largely remained in their safe havens across the Laotian border or hiding in the difficult terrain of the mountain jungles. However, having seized the initiative across the country as the ARVN as a whole faltered, the Viet Cong increased their efforts to move into the fertile and heavily populated lowland areas to gain resupply and reinforcements, as evidenced by the struggles that Dinh's unit faced further to the south. The ARVN, and later U.S. forces as well, hoped to stand in their way.

Hue took over as a platoon commander and assistant company commander and quickly set the leadership standard that he would follow for the remainder of his career. Hue demanded strict discipline from his soldiers, realizing that they were the representatives of South Vietnam and that indiscipline or brutality on their part would only turn the local population into supporters of the enemy. Leading by example, Hue depended on long-serving noncommissioned officers for advice and took care to learn much about and to form close relationships with his men. Scrupulously honest and fair, Hue earned the love and respect of his men, concepts of vast importance in the Vietnamese military tradition, and morale in the unit soared.

That Hue and Dinh received special praise for being competent and honest officers who knew and practiced the art of leadership is both important and troubling. As a whole, the ARVN officer class was below the standard expected by their American sponsors. There were thousands of motivated and wonderful leaders of the caliber of Dinh and Hue. However, there were also thousands of officers who led poorly, were overly politicized, and were blatantly corrupt. Thus, the standard of the ARVN officer class was by no means uniform and ranged from the very good to the tragically bad. There were many systemic reasons for the spotty nature of ARVN command, including the reality of a war that seemingly had no end, matters of social standing, and specific problems in training and operations.

Dinh and Hue are not representative of the ARVN officer class as a whole but are representative of the potential found within that class. That both Dinh and Hue were good leaders carried great importance at the tactical level, for the effectiveness of an ARVN unit was tied directly to the personality and capabilities of its commanding officer.[23] According to the historian Thomas Cantwell:

> ARVN's combat performance was directly linked with sound leadership. If an officer was motivated, and experienced, his men were loyal and performed well on the battlefield under trying circumstances. Unlike American units, where experienced troops and NCOs could compensate for a weak commander, ARVN relied on one man —the officer in charge. Vietnamese soldiers did not lack the ability to fight or the desire to win. When led well, they performed commendably, according to the testimonies of MACV advisers. Conversely, weak officers could not expect results. Relying on one man created new problems—if a well-respected battalion officer were killed, his men panicked and the unit could disintegrate.[24]

Dinh and Hue represented the possibility of a bright future for the ARVN, while their less capable brethren represented an important systemic problem and a possible fatal weakness of the ARVN. Rectifying this weakness had to become a central priority of both South Vietnam and the United States during the conflict, but such a program would be long and arduous, since the weakness was rooted in and tied to the entire structure of the South Vietnamese state. Instead, both South Vietnam and the United States turned to more simple military solutions to the complicated war in Vietnam.

Hue's initial combat operations closely resembled those of Pham Van Dinh, search-and-destroy missions designed to inflict casualties and keep the enemy off balance. Because of the hotly contested nature of the area, on his very first patrol Hue took the initiative and altered the previously predictable path that his platoon had taken out of the base camp on its sweeps. Having deceived the enemy, Hue then proceeded to a location that intelligence had indicated was a Viet Cong base area. The intelligence proved correct, and Hue's assault came as a total surprise, netting several prisoners and interrupting a Viet Cong plan to attack Ta Bat. The victory garnered Hue praise from both his men and from his superiors and marked him as a rising young combat commander.

The 3rd Company operated in the A Shau Valley for most of 1964, running constant search-and-destroy missions amid the rugged terrain. Although his unit often discovered mines and booby traps and made sporadic, fleeting contact with enemy units, even in this remote area, fighting near and among a resident civilian population formed a central part of the war's growing dynamic. On one occasion, having taken sniper fire from a hilltop village, Hue's unit counterattacked. In the fighting, several of the buildings in the village burned to the ground, and two enemy guerrilla fighters perished. Amid the rubble, Hue located the now orphaned children of the fighters. Hue and his company adopted the children, naming the boy Anh-Dung Tran and the girl Anh-Thu Tran. The men cared for the children, gathering money for their clothing and sending them to school. When Hue left the 3rd Company, the children remained behind in the care of his men. Although he continued to check on their welfare for years, amid the tumult of war and captivity Hue eventually lost contact with his adopted children.

As victories piled up for his command and his reputation grew, Hue, like Dinh, began to suspect that the ARVN's conduct of the war was flawed. While his unit swept through villages for short periods of violent activity, the Viet Cong were with and among the people for the remainder of the time, eating with them, marrying them, earning or forcing their support, and quite possibly governing them. While search-and-destroy tactics seemed militarily effective, since the enemy suffered higher body counts and usually fled from battle, Hue realized that ARVN tactics achieved little meaningful success in the war for the hearts and minds of the people. In Hue's view, the wrong medicine was being used to cure the disease, and the ARVN was "fighting the wrong war." Instead of clumsy search-and-destroy missions against guerrilla forces that wished to avoid battle, Hue represented many young ARVN officers in his belief that the ARVN should make better use of its territorial forces, locally raised units made up of the people and therefore intimately familiar with the area, to provide true and meaningful rural security. Instead of sweeping through an area, only to leave it vulnerable to Viet Cong retaliation, such units would be resident, a permanent fixture for the protection of the populace. With security in the hands of territorial forces, the ARVN could then strike the Viet Cong using the VC's own stealthy guerrilla tactics.

Though they were in different situations at different levels of command, both Dinh and Hue had reached the same conclusion and realized very early on that the war of rural security and for the hearts and minds of the people was critical to achieving ultimate victory. Through search-and-destroy tactics, the ARVN forces in I Corps usually bested the Viet Cong in battle, but the situation regarding government control of the countryside changed little. As is often the case in war, the commanders at the very lowest level in Vietnam were able to discern problems with the nature of the ongoing fighting before those at a much higher rank. As a result of their experiences, many of Dinh and Hue's ARVN compatriots and their American advisers questioned the military emphasis placed on searching for and destroying enemy units over the provision of rural security. Lieutenant Colonel Arthur P. Gregory, who served as an American adviser in the Mekong Delta, published his assessment of the war in the respected magazine *ARMY* and stated, "Most of us are sure that this problem is only fifteen per cent military and eighty-five percent political. It's not just a matter of killing Viet Cong, but of coupling security with welfare."[25]

The conventional vision that the main objective of warfare is the destruction of enemy forces, though, dominated both the ARVN and the U.S. military. The concept was, indeed, so deeply ingrained that the leaders of both forces refused to listen to innovators from below who were convinced that the military concept was not only ineffective but also counterproductive in the new type of counterinsurgency war faced by the ARVN and the U.S. military in Vietnam.[26] Despite their growing concerns, as 1964 drew to a close, neither Dinh nor Hue believed that defeat was imminent or even possible. However, both men also knew the reality of the situation and realized that victory was not near and that the war would be long and arduous.

An American War

After the comings and goings of numerous failed military-based governments in Saigon, the February 1965 fall of the government of General Nguyen Khanh heralded a return to stability and the political arrival of a group of military mavericks known as the "Young Turks." The clique of military officers, led by General Nguyen Van Thieu and Air Vice Marshal Nguyen Cao Ky, by mid-June had muscled its way into political domination of South Vietnam and, internal power struggles notwithstanding, remained in power until the fall of Saigon in 1975. Both Dinh and Hue looked to the return of stability as an opportunity to achieve needed systemic reform in the ARVN. However, their faith was sadly misplaced, for, though the worst problems of the era of political turmoil came to an end, the Thieu/Ky regime did little to address the systemic problems plaguing South Vietnam and the ARVN. According to the historian Thomas Cantwell:

> The Thieu-Ky administration inherited the same problems of previous governments and was unable to correct them. If their government were to succeed, it would have to build a power base outside of ARVN. However, the Thieu regime never won popular support . . . and relied on ARVN to keep it in power. After 1965, military staff played a greater role in national politics than ever before. President

Thieu managed to survive as he appointed trusted staff to senior positions in the Army and the government regardless of ability. Diem began this policy and succeeding Presidents continued it to protect their political base.[27]

Of more immediate importance to the transforming nature of the war in Vietnam, though, was the beginning of direct American involvement in the conflict on 8 March 1965, heralded by U.S. Marines splashing ashore near Da Nang. The optimism shared by Dinh and Hue sprang in part from a narrow view of the war based on their experiences in I Corps, where the military situation was fairly stable compared to that in other areas of the country where the Viet Cong had been more active and successful since the collapse of the Diem regime. Through Viet Cong successes, the perceived impending defeat of South Vietnam, and increasing attacks on U.S. interests initially led the Americans to launch a sustained bombing offensive dubbed Operation Rolling Thunder, the situation did not change dramatically for the better. The resultant initial troop requests of General William Westmoreland, the commander of Military Assistance Command, Vietnam (MACV), quickly escalated in the wake of ARVN battlefield reverses at Song Be and Dong Xoai, near Saigon, during the late spring.[28]

Opinion within the U.S. government regarding the introduction of ground forces was by no means unanimous. Ambassador Taylor was particularly concerned and argued that an infusion of American forces into the war "would simply encourage the South Vietnamese armed forces to let the United States carry the full burden of the war effort . . . would raise the specter of French colonialism and encourage a majority of the population to turn against the United States." Regardless of Taylor's prescient warnings, distracted by its own political battles and by the domestic Great Society Program, the Johnson White House made the fateful decision to begin the American ground war in Vietnam in earnest.[29]

The poor performance of much of the ARVN in 1963 and 1964 had proven to Westmoreland and others that the ARVN was not combat ready and that direct U.S. involvement in the war on a massive scale was required. Initially, most within the ARVN welcomed direct U.S. intervention in the conflict and were rather overawed by the skill and firepower displayed by their allies. The relationship, though, was not one of equals and portended a fundamental, and subtly dangerous, change in the ongoing conflict. As American forces took over many of the combat responsibilities, the ARVN became spectators instead of participants in what should have been its war.[30]

In essence, the U.S. policy of creating an effective ARVN was now utterly secondary to the advancing American effort to win the war through purely military means. Instead of striving for unity of effort and command, which Westmoreland contended would smack of colonialism, the United States simply decided to win their war for them. As Maxwell Taylor later reflected, "We never really paid attention to the ARVN Army. We didn't give a damn about them."[31]

Some 60 percent of the ARVN was shunted aside into providing local security, a task for which it was poorly trained. Though many within South Vietnam, including both Pham Van Dinh and Tran Ngoc Hue, realized that rural security was critical to achieving victory in the conflict, the provision of rural security, often termed pacification, remained secondary in the American system of warfighting and was hamstrung by a singular lack of support from the South Vietnamese government. Realizing that they were being relegated to what the Americans considered to be a backwater war, ARVN units accepted the new division of labor in the war with reluctance, since most would have welcomed the opportunity to conduct mobile operations alongside their American allies. Additionally, with the ARVN now shouldering the load of rural security, the important territorial elements of the South Vietnamese military, the Regional and Popular Forces, which were much better suited to the task of local security and pacification, were even further marginalized.[32] The shift threw the ARVN into systemic and command chaos, leaving the force to retool and retrain yet again to face a new challenge.

Nearly 40 percent of the ARVN, though, remained engaged in combat operations. The morale and combat effectiveness of these units initially skyrocketed, but the improvement was something of an illusion. Massive U.S. firepower and logistic support virtually ensured tactical victory in battle, but the ARVN quickly became dependent upon that support instead of developing its own capabilities. South Vietnam became wedded to a conventional style of war that alone it could not economically or socially ever hope to support, and when American presence and assistance were no longer available, the morale and combat effectiveness of ARVN units became uncertain.[33]

General Ngo Quang Truong, considered by many to be the finest

combat officer in the ARVN and who later served as divisional commander to both Dinh and Hue, commented on the effects of the American assumption of control of the Vietnam War:

> Resorting to the use of combat force meant that the U.S. advisory ef-
> fort and level of military assistance up to that time had either fallen
> short of their goal or were not enough. . . . Entering the war with
> the posture and disposition of a fire brigade, the Americans rushed
> about to save the Vietnamese house from destruction but took little
> interest in caring for the victims. Only after they realized that the vic-
> tims, too, should be made firefighters to save their own houses, did
> Americans set about to really care for them. Valuable time was lost,
> and by the time the victims could get onto their feet and began to
> move forward a few steps after recovery, the fire-brigade was called
> back to the home station.[34]

After a training period at the Jungle Warfare School in Malaya,
in the autumn of 1965 Hue returned to I Corps and became the aide-
de-camp to General Nguyen Van Chuan, the commander of the 1st
ARVN Division. It was a challenging experience for the young combat
officer, for in his new position Tran Ngoc Hue tracked the operational
situation of the entire division. Additionally, Hue became a trusted
confidant of Chuan and worked with both U.S. and ARVN unit commanders to make the tactical plans of 1st ARVN Division a reality.

As Hue made the transition to war at a new level, the command
life of Pham Van Dinh also underwent a fundamental change. In late
1964, General Chuan had decided that the 1st ARVN Division required a rapid-reaction force, an elite unit that constantly stood ready
to aid other units of the division in battle. As a result, a call for volunteers went out to participate in the formation of the Hac Bao (Black
Panther) Company. Once trained and operational, the reinforced company, numbering more than two hundred men in five rifle platoons,
packed a firepower punch equivalent to that of most ARVN battalions and was the first truly airmobile unit in the ARVN.[35] Its tasks included intervening in battle whenever a unit of 1st ARVN Division
was threatened, rescuing downed pilots, providing security for sensitive convoys, and verifying important intelligence finds. In short, the
Hac Bao served as the 1st ARVN Division's fire brigade, reacting to
any threat across the length and breadth of the 1st ARVN Division's

area of operations (AO). The job was varied and dangerous, as the 1st ARVN Division stood watch over what now had become the most heavily infiltrated and deadly area of operations in South Vietnam.[36] The unit, based near the airfield in the Citadel of Hue City, had to be ready for action on a moment's notice and had the highest priority for air and artillery support.[37]

In February 1965, Pham Van Dinh received the signal honor of being appointed as the second commander of the Hac Bao, proof of his rising reputation as a combat officer. In his new position, Dinh took orders directly from the 1st ARVN Division commander and was accompanied into battle initially by a mixed team of American and Australian advisers, another testament to the importance of the unit, since the advisory effort only rarely extended below the battalion level. Though the ARVN in general was notoriously inept at airmobile operations at this point in the war, in part due to communications and language difficulties between ARVN officers and their American pilots,[38] a rigorous training regimen instituted by Dinh and his own English-language skills made the Hac Bao the effective exception to the rule. The Hac Bao normally had access to five troop carriers and two attack helicopters for major operations and thus utilized true airmobile tactics even before the first American units came on the scene, setting the stage for much of the future tactical reality of the Vietnam War.

After becoming conversant with the reality of airmobility, including training in entering and exiting the aircraft under fire (because the Vietnamese usually were of slighter build than the Americans, a troop carrier could hold twelve ARVN soldiers as opposed to six Americans), rappelling out of hovering aircraft, being extracted via a harness, and coordinating firepower, the Hac Bao prepared for its first mission. Wearing what would become the trademark Hac Bao black beret, which trumpeted the unit's elite status, Dinh realized the importance of the new command: it could make his career. However, the job was high risk and could result in his death or failure as a commander, as well. In March 1965, on nearly the same day that the first American Marines splashed ashore at Da Nang, General Chuan ordered the Hac Bao to reinforce two squads of territorial forces that had been ambushed by a platoon of Viet Cong.

Dinh and his advisers flew on the lead aircraft and picked an appropriate Landing Zone (LZ), while attack helicopters softened the enemy positions located in a village forty kilometers to the southeast of

Members of the Hac Bao Company training for airmobile operations, 1971.
Photograph VA001053, Douglas Pike Photograph Collection, The Vietnam
Archive, Texas Tech University.

Hue City. The Hac Bao hit the LZ in a rice paddy some one hundred
meters away from the enemy positions under cover of fire from the attack helicopters. The Viet Cong seemed stunned by the aerial ambush
and fled the contact, many running out into the open only to be
gunned down by the Hac Bao and its supporting helicopters. It was a
quick and easy victory for Dinh, which netted seven enemy dead and
five weapons captured, while the Hac Bao suffered no casualties. General Chuan paid a visit to his victorious unit and praised Dinh's ac-
complishment.

For the next several months, the Hac Bao operated throughout the
1st ARVN Division's area of operations (AO), from the infamous
"Street Without Joy" to the A Shau Valley to the area just south of the
Demilitarized Zone (DMZ). The Hac Bao ran nearly continuous operations in all manner of terrain, from beaches to rice paddies to the
triple-canopy rainforest of the mountainous border with Laos. Most of
the engagements, up to fifteen per month, were small in nature, with

the Hac Bao arriving to aid a unit that had suffered an ambush. Usually, the Hac Bao moved by helicopter, eventually provided by the U.S. Marines from their base at Phu Bai, but on some operations the unit moved by vehicle or on foot, whatever the 1st ARVN Division commander required.[39] In July, the Hac Bao pinned an enemy company inside a village along the coast; Dinh's men drove the enemy from the battlefield; they killed sixteen of the enemy and captured two mortars, a machine gun, and ten individual weapons at the cost of one Hac Bao dead and three wounded. For the victory, Dinh received promotion to captain.

As Chuan's liaison, Hue often came into contact with the Hac Bao and its dashing young commander. The 1st ARVN Division was a tightknit community, and Dinh and Hue had each long been aware of the other's military fortunes. It was in 1965, though, while stationed in the Hue Citadel, that the two rising young stars of the division came to know each other well and work together on a regular basis. As each recognized the other's ability and dedication to the cause of South Vietnam, Dinh and Hue developed a strong mutual respect. Their time in the Hue Citadel also impacted their lives greatly in that General Chuan recognized their abilities and took both Dinh and Hue under his wing as his protégés, an event that placed the lives of the two comrades into lockstep, with Dinh, the elder, leading the way, while Hue followed closely behind through the command ranks of the 1st ARVN Division.

Even as success in their new assignments set their own personal futures in motion, both Dinh and Hue became aware of a disturbing change in the balance of their war. At the beginning of 1965, there were an estimated five thousand enemy fighters operating in the 1st ARVN Division's AO, giving the ARVN and the incoming American forces a vast numerical superiority. Additionally, large enemy units did not often maneuver in the open lowland areas, where they would be exposed to potential destruction by U.S. air power and firepower. However, as the year wore on, it became obvious to all concerned that the nature of the war in I Corps had changed. In August 1964, partly in response to increased American involvement in the conflict, the North Vietnamese had decided to send their first regular combat forces to the south.[40] The result of that decision meant that by mid-1965, more and more North Vietnamese and Viet Cong forces, estimated at fifty thousand men, had infiltrated into or near the 1st ARVN

Division AO. These forces remained in the highlands or across the border, but their mere presence indicated that the war had changed irrevocably. It was no longer a brushfire war against scattered elements of the Viet Cong but was instead a war in which the well-supplied and heavily armed regular units of the NVA played an ever greater role.

From his newfound, broad vantage point alongside General Chuan at 1st ARVN Division headquarters, Hue witnessed the disturbing new direction that the war had taken. Where in his estimation the ARVN had controlled the tempo of fighting in I Corps against the Viet Cong, the massive infusion of North Vietnamese soldiers had tipped the balance in the enemy's favor. In his view, the ARVN and the incoming Americans now played a more passive role, reacting to enemy incursions and operations. In his words, "before we had looked for them, now they looked for us."

On 21 October 1965, the changing nature of the war became deadly clear to Dinh and the Hac Bao. Shattering the illusion that large enemy units would not operate in the open lowlands, a North Vietnamese battalion of the 83rd Regiment launched a surprise night assault on the positions of the 1st Battalion, 1st Regiment of the 1st ARVN Division near the village of Thon Hoi Yen, in the coastal areas of Quang Tri Province. After a brief struggle in which North Vietnamese forces penetrated the ARVN perimeter, killing ten, the North Vietnamese disengaged from battle and retreated into Thon Hoi Yen. The 1st ARVN Division reacted quickly, sending an additional battalion of troops and the Hac Bao to launch a counterstrike against the North Vietnamese. It was to be Dinh's first operation against the "new" enemy, the NVA, and it was a confrontation that Dinh entered with great confidence.

By midmorning on the 22nd, aerial reconnaissance had reported enemy forces in Thon Hoi Yen, and a Hac Bao platoon went to reconnoiter the position. The North Vietnamese waited until the Hac Bao members were within twenty meters and then opened fire, making early use of the soon-to-be familiar tactic of "hanging onto the belts" of their opponents.[41] Under covering fire, the platoon withdrew, and it was now obvious that the war had changed dramatically. The Viet Cong had prosecuted a guerrilla war; it normally struck only from ambush and then fled to fight another day when the ARVN brought its power to bear. Unlike the Viet Cong, though, the better disciplined and motivated North Vietnamese had dug in and were spoiling for a fight.

Shortly after noon, the ARVN attack, involving two battalions and the Hac Bao, rolled forward, beginning with a tank assault on the enemy positions. Suddenly, though, fire rang out from Thon Hoi Yen. Such an assault would have crushed the resistance of a guerrilla force, but the North Vietnamese were better armed than the Viet Cong and responded to the assault with both antitank and antiaircraft weapons. Two tanks were destroyed, and the commander on the scene, Lieutenant Colonel Nguyen Van Duong, ordered the armor to retreat out of the range of enemy fire. In the fighting, Dinh was surprised and somewhat disheartened to learn that the North Vietnamese possessed such advanced weaponry. Most disturbing was the fact that the North Vietnamese infantry carried the infamous AK-47, which far surpassed the M-1 still in use in the ARVN. Although the organic firepower of the ARVN had always outclassed that of the Viet Cong, the low priority given to the ARVN weaponry left it consistently outgunned by the NVA. The disparity in weaponry led both to unfavorable battlefield performance and low morale.[42]

Still, Dinh and the Hac Bao were anxious to attack the enemy positions. Later in the afternoon of the 22nd, the ARVN struck again, launching an infantry assault on the dug-in NVA defenders under the cover of artillery fire, but still Thon Hoi Yen did not fall. Duong then decided to hold the infantry back while he called upon his trump card, constant application of firepower delivered by air strikes and heavy artillery. After the punishing barrage, ARVN forces swept into Thon Hoi Yen, only to find that the North Vietnamese had fled. The ARVN operation accounted for twenty-five enemy killed, two captured antiaircraft guns and four captured antitank guns.

The ARVN victory, though, came at a price. During the fighting, ARVN forces also lost twenty-five dead, including five from the Hac Bao. During the entire period prior to October, the Hac Bao had lost only four dead, even though the unit was almost constantly involved in minor battles. In those struggles, the Hac Bao had faced smaller Viet Cong units that had fled once they had lost the initiative in battle. The North Vietnamese now seemed ready to fight harder and both pay and exact a higher price, which forecast a much more difficult struggle for the ARVN and its American supporters. The losses hurt Dinh, who was extremely close to his men. The units under his command were, in Dinh's words, "even more important than my family," a turn of phrase that is laden with Vietnamese cultural significance and indicates a mutual debt of honor. Dinh made certain to collect his dead from the battlefield and returned their bodies to their families for proper funerals, which was of the utmost importance in the predominantly Buddhist nation.

While the quality of leadership in the ARVN remained an open question for many outside observers, Dinh's performance with the Hac Bao not only earned him the respect of his superiors within the ARVN but also that of the American and Australian advisers who served with the 1st ARVN Division. Australian Army Training Team Warrant Officer Terry Gill, who served with the Hac Bao for six months before moving on to advisory positions with other ARVN units, recalled:

> I found him [Dinh] to be a very energetic character, open to ideas & new tactics, even though he had seen more combat than most advisers who were attached. He was a good leader & usually led from the front. The Hac Bao were a very successful unit. Their success, in my opinion, stemmed in part from the fact that Dinh was a favorite with I Corps HQ. Also the unit was well equipped & well trained & led, had very high morale & was detested & feared by the VC & NVA alike. The unit was so feared that in short order its advisers had about $25,000 bounty placed on them by the NVA—and probably more for Dinh & his officers.[43]

Both Dinh and Hue, though they watched from two very different vantage points—one as a combat officer and the other from the more strategic level of a general's aide—came to understand that the nature of their war had changed irrevocably. The arrival of sizable NVA units on the battlefield indicated that the conflict was mushrooming in scale beyond that of the guerrilla war with which the ARVN was so familiar. Across South Vietnam, clashes erupted between arriving NVA and American units, fighting that presaged a war that was beyond the ARVN's capabilities to fight alone. However, as evidenced by the struggle at Thon Hoi Yen, the new situation also had great advantages. Because of the arrival of the talented Americans and through the use of their overwhelming firepower, it seemed that even the stalwart North Vietnamese would fall to inevitable defeat.

It was a time of great optimism for both Dinh and Hue, who, like their ARVN brethren, believed that, together, American and South

Vietnamese forces would smash any opponent, no matter how well armed and disciplined. Additionally, both Dinh and Hue believed that the presence of American forces would provide the military protection necessary for the South Vietnamese state and the ARVN to come of age. With American help, they both believed that the politicized rancor that beset the South Vietnamese military would be brought under control. The two comrades were representative of the great hopes of their generation of young ARVN leaders in their belief that there were two ways forward to victory in their war: massive U.S. firepower to provide victory against both new and old foes on the battlefield and South Vietnamese military and governmental reform to make the battlefield victories sustainable in the long term. Suddenly, though, the hopes of Dinh and Hue were nearly dashed as South Vietnam descended again into a period of chaos that threatened the survival of the country.

The Buddhist Crisis

As the new year of 1966 began, a devastating wave of tumult and discord swept across South Vietnam. Though it had been but one part of Diem's overthrow, the Buddhist movement had remained active and powerful in the years after his fall. The Buddhists represented a somewhat splintered opposition group and enjoyed intermittent relations with the various Saigon regimes that came and went with great rapidity. Buddhist protesters often took to the streets, especially during the brief rule of General Nguyen Khanh. When Thieu and Ky took power, in 1965, the Buddhist movement attempted some form of unity through the apparatus of the newly founded Unified Buddhist Church, the important leaders of which included Thich Tam Chau and Thich Tri Quang.[44] Although the Buddhists enjoyed support throughout the nation, their leading strongholds were Hue and Da Nang, both in the ARVN I Corps AO.

In 1966, the Buddhist leadership, especially the more militant Thich Tri Quang, based in Hue City, led a renewed movement against the Thieu/Ky regime. Although many Buddhists within South Vietnam remained loyal to the government, turmoil once again wracked the nation. Many South Vietnamese, including Pham Van Dinh and

Tran Ngoc Hue, believed that at least some of the more militant leaders such as Thich Tri Quang were nothing more than pawns of communism. Many within the Buddhist camp, though, saw themselves more as representing a true political middle ground between the extremes represented by Ho Chi Minh and the Thieu/Ky regime and as the best hope for neutralism and peace.[45] Meanwhile, Thieu and Ky perceived the Buddhist movement, especially in the I Corps area, as a serious political challenge. Making matters worse, the commander of I Corps, General Nguyen Chanh Thi, was a quite powerful figure who ruled over the area like a feudal fiefdom, and Thieu and Ky believed that he would work with the Buddhists to overthrow them. In March, Ky decided to confront Thi, which led to the latter's ouster, explained in a later government report that contended that Thi had been "granted permanent medical leave to correct a serious sinus ailment." Ky chose General Nguyen Van Chuan, commander of the 1st ARVN Division as Thi's replacement and placed General Pham Xuan Nhuan in command of 1st ARVN.[46]

As General Chuan and his aide-de-camp Tran Ngoc Hue settled into their new positions, the Hue and Da Nang areas erupted into an inferno of political dissent.[47] The controversial dismissal of Thi sparked calls from Buddhist leaders for the ouster of the Ky government.[48] Protests broke out across the I Corps AO, and a general strike shut down business in Da Nang. It was a difficult time for General Chuan, who chose not to confront the protesters as long as they remained peaceful. As both Chuan and Hue looked on, though, the protests spread over much of Vietnam, including Saigon, but remained at their most virulent in Da Nang and Hue City. Making matters worse, the protests became more multifaceted in nature and included not only Buddhist activists but also students and workers. Grouped together into an uneasy alliance dubbed the "Struggle Movement," the protesters spoke out against government corruption, had a growing anti-American sentiment, and demanded peace. Thus, the Buddhists served as the center for a storm of growing proportions that the Thieu/Ky government could not ignore.[49]

Initially, Ky attempted political maneuvering and even outright bribery to calm the trouble in I Corps. Inexplicably, these measures included sending General Thi back to the area he once controlled. Thi made a few speeches, often full of sarcasm aimed at the government, and remained in the area working on the fringes of the Struggle Movement. On 1 April, Ky sent General Pham Xuan Chieu to I Corps in an effort to win Thi over to full support of the Saigon government. When Chieu arrived in Hue City to speak with Thi, he was ambushed by a student mob, which took him captive, placed him in a pedicab, and drove him around the city before releasing him.[50] If matters were not bad enough, ARVN forces in the area began to side with the Struggle Movement, defecting from the government in entire units. Some of the defecting ARVN soldiers were driven by a desire to support the goals of the leadership of the Struggle Movement; others, however, simply followed scheming senior officers such as Thi, who saw the turmoil as a chance to seize political power in a scenario that had been all too common in the tumultuous years between the fall of Diem and the rise of Thieu and Ky. As a result of the deteriorating situation, the Saigon government became increasingly concerned about the loyalty of its command team in the area—General Chuan at I Corps and General Nhuan at 1st ARVN Division Headquarters.

Crisis was at hand, and as the ARVN fractured once again, officers and men across the length and breadth of I Corps had to choose sides: would they would remain loyal to their government or join the adherents of the Struggle Movement? The decision would be most difficult for Pham Van Dinh, who would face the unenviable prospect of either betraying his government or betraying his divisional commander.

Confrontation

Pressured both by members of his own regime and by his American supporters, Ky decided that the time had come to strike hard against the dissidents in I Corps. On 4 April, Ky unwisely announced his intentions, terming Da Nang an "enemy-held city," giving the Struggle Movement time to prepare a defense. On 5 April, Ky arrived at Da Nang airbase at the head of a force that included two South Vietnamese Marine battalions, and an additional Marine battalion and two ranger battalions soon followed. Ky's brash actions had an immediate effect; both Thi and Nhuan proclaimed their open support of the Struggle Movement, while riots and protests broke out in many areas of the country. Nhuan sent units of the 1st ARVN Division south from their base areas around Hue to block any government drive on that city and to stand ready to reinforce ARVN units in Da Nang that supported the Struggle Movement. In a tense standoff, with government troops facing off against troops that supported the Struggle Movement, it seemed that South Vietnam stood on the brink of another civil war.[51]

Surprised by the level of resistance, Ky, humiliated, backed down from his confrontational stance, declaring that Da Nang was not occupied by communists after all, and he attempted to conciliate the leaders of the Struggle Movement by promising a shift to democracy. Ky flew back to Saigon the very next day and on 10 April began withdrawing government forces from the Da Nang airbase. The Struggle Movement had won the first phase of the confrontation but had sealed its own doom. The Thieu/Ky regime neared collapse and, though it appeared to be conciliatory for the next month, it had to strike back against the Buddhists and their ARVN allies to retain power and the all-important support of the United States.

During talks with the Buddhist leadership concerning the possibility of elections and the end of military rule, Ky secretly moved ever closer to a second armed attempt to end what he viewed as a rebellion. One of Ky's first moves was to replace General Chuan, who he felt had done too little against the Struggle Movement, with General Ton That Dinh as commander of I Corps. Chuan and his aide Hue traveled to Saigon for reassignment. Having lulled the Struggle Movement with promises of change, Ky struck again on 15 May. With no warning, two South Vietnamese Marine battalions, reinforced by two airborne battalions, which received support from tanks and aircraft of the South Vietnamese Air Force, swept into Da Nang and seized important sites, including the mayor's office and I Corps headquarters. General Dinh, the new I Corps commander, objected to the move and was in turn replaced by General Huynh Van Cao. Dinh promptly fled to Hue City, where he joined Thi and Nhuan as part of the Struggle Movement.[52] Da Nang had fallen quickly to government control, with the remaining Buddhist supporters retreating to the relative safety of local pagodas, which left Hue City as the main holdout of the Struggle Movement and as the next target on Ky's list.

General Nhuan and the leadership of the Struggle Movement struck back by sending units of the 1st ARVN Division to block the route that government forces would have to take between Da Nang and Hue City. To Pham Van Dinh and the Hac Bao fell the task of guarding a bridge near Lang Co Village just north of the Hai Van Pass.

The bridge formed a natural bottleneck on Highway 1, the main route to the north, and Dinh was ordered to defend the bridge against attacks by ARVN troops loyal to the government. Dinh was very troubled by the nature of his new assignment, for he viewed the Viet Cong and the North Vietnamese as his enemies and did not relish the idea of fighting ARVN units instead. Also Dinh had watched as the 1st ARVN Division had slipped into lethargy during the crisis, running hardly any combat operations. As a result, many of the painstaking gains of previous years had been lost. Though the Viet Cong and the ARVN followed something of a "live and let live" policy in I Corps during the crisis, the communists had used the opportunity further to build their strength and seize control over several villages in the area. Dinh estimated that some 30 percent of the villages that had once been controlled by the government were now under the control of the Viet Cong; villages that his men would have to fight and die to recapture.

On 17 May, General Cao, the new I Corps commander, flew by helicopter to Hue City for a meeting with the officers, including Dinh, of the 1st ARVN Division. Cao informed the assembled officers that the insurrection had to end and that the 1st ARVN Division once again had to follow the orders of the Saigon government. The tense meeting failed to reach a resolution, and Cao returned to his helicopter to depart. Before he could leave, though, an ARVN lieutenant, Nguyen Tai Thuc, fired two rounds at Cao from his pistol. The American gunner on the helicopter returned fire, killing Thuc and wounding several others.[53] Though Dinh wisely held his counsel amid a group of officers who supported the Struggle Movement, he agreed with Cao's statements. To Dinh, the violent incident reinforced the notion that the ARVN was headed for a struggle against its own instead of focusing attention on the war with the Viet Cong and the North Vietnamese.

Just days later, on 19 May, the situation became even more chaotic when General Cao refused to attack the Buddhist holdouts in the pagodas of Da Nang and was replaced as commander of I Corps by General Hoang Xuan Lam, the sixth I Corps commander in three months.[54] To Dinh, the growing chaos and waste became too much to bear, and, after nearly two weeks guarding the bridge at Lang Co, he decided to take desperate action. Dinh realized that most of the forces of the 1st ARVN Division had departed Hue City to guard its approaches, which left the city itself and the 1st ARVN Division Headquarters defenseless. If the Hac Bao could only utilize some ruse to reach Hue City, the company would be able to seize General Nhuan, put an end to the uprising, and return the Saigon government to control over the ARVN forces in I Corps.

Dinh ordered the Hac Bao aboard trucks, telling his men that they were going back to Hue City to get fresh supplies. He also hoped to use that subterfuge with any ARVN troops loyal to the Struggle Movement that barred their path; after all, Hue City was the logistic base of the Hac Bao. Supporters of the Struggle Movement, though, spotted the Hac Bao convoy, and Dinh soon found his advance blocked by ARVN tanks and infantry. The commander on the scene ordered Dinh into his compound, but Dinh refused. Amid the tense standoff, General Nhuan achieved a direct telephone link to Dinh and demanded to know his intentions. Dinh informed his divisional commander that he was seeking resupply, and Nhuan responded by ordering the Hac Bao back to the bridge at Lang Co. Nhuan then relieved Dinh of command and informed him that he would be put before a military tribunal to answer for his actions.[55]

Fearing for his life, Dinh accompanied his U.S. adviser to the MACV compound at Phu Bai while awaiting paperwork regarding his fate. However, during the night, a small plane arrived to carry Dinh to Da Nang, where he later flew on to Saigon. The Thieu/Ky regime was grateful for Dinh's actions and marked him for even higher levels of command after the conclusion of the crisis. General Nguyen Ngoc Loan, head of the Vietnamese police and central to the defeat of the Struggle Movement in Da Nang, even offered Dinh a command under his purview. Dinh demurred; he wanted to return to the command of the Hac Bao and wanted an end to the uprising that had so debilitated the ARVN.

While Pham Van Dinh and Tran Ngoc Hue were both in Saigon, government forces massed and tightened their grip on Hue City, while serious anti-American rioting broke out in the city. Though General Nhuan refused to use 1st ARVN Division troops against the civilian population of Hue City, he finally realized that the forces arrayed against the Struggle Movement were too strong. In the end, he professed his loyalty to the Saigon regime and removed the 1st ARVN Division from the defense of the city, leaving the way open to a government takeover of the area.[56] On 18 June, three airborne battalions, under the command of Colonel Ngo Quang Truong, entered Hue City and within forty-eight hours had reestablished control. Though it would take some time to root out the final pockets of resistance, the Buddhist uprising of 1966 was at an end.

A New Beginning

The upheavals had taken a heavy toll on the fighting ability of the ARVN forces in I Corps, especially the 1st ARVN Division. For two months, South Vietnam's military efforts in the area had ground to a halt, leaving the Viet Cong and the North Vietnamese free to conduct antigovernment activities. In August, MACV reported that the ARVN units in the area were still suffering from the aftereffects of the Buddhist crisis and that offensive operations had yet to be planned.[57] The task of rebuilding the shattered 1st ARVN Division fell to its new commander, Brigadier General Ngo Quang Truong. A Buddhist from the Mekong Delta and a graduate of Thu Duc, General Truong was the right man for the job. He possessed strong character and organizational abilities and was even later lauded by General Norman Schwarzkopf as the "most brilliant tactical commander" that he had ever known.[58]

Truong toiled diligently to raise the performance of a division that after the uprising had been rated as marginal. A true combat leader who cared little for politics, Truong took great care to handpick his senior officers and insisted that his battalion commanders be majors with extensive combat experience. The innovative commander also took great care to provide for better training for and utilization of his territorial forces, which greatly augmented the combat strength and ability of the 1st ARVN Division. Due to Truong's care and his ability to develop a divisional esprit de corps, the 1st ARVN Division rose to a new level of efficiency and served as a model of what the South Vietnamese military could become. In 1968, U.S. Secretary of Defense Clark Clifford stated that the 1st ARVN Division was "comparable in quality to any U.S. Army division."[59]

General Ngo Quang Truong's command was an exciting time for both Pham Van Dinh and Tran Ngoc Hue. The 1st ARVN Division finally had a true leader who planned to take the war to the enemy rather than engage in politics. With Truong in command, Dinh, who still languished in Saigon, was ecstatic when he received the call to return to the command of the Hac Bao. For Tran Ngoc Hue, his time as aide-de-camp to General Chuan, who had moved on to direct military training for the Vietnamese Joint General Staff in Saigon, was nearing its end. As the reputation of the 1st ARVN Division once again rose, Tran Ngoc Hue yearned for a return to combat and decided to work hard to achieve a transfer to the unit that he had come to respect so much while he and Dinh had worked closely together in Hue City —the Hac Bao. After the travails of the previous year, both Dinh and Hue represented the predominant view of the officers of their generation and looked to the future with great optimism and hope of victory. Now that the Americans were taking over much of the military burden and the South Vietnamese regime had suffered through its great crisis and reform had begun, certainly the worst of the war was behind them. Neither man gave any thought to the possible worst-case scenario, for it was too outlandish to even suggest that American forces would withdraw from the conflict, leaving it unfinished, and that the South Vietnamese regime and military would not fundamentally change, leaving the ARVN unready and alone to fight a war transformed.

3

Fighting Two Wars

Years of Attrition and Pacification, 1966–1967

WHILE SOUTH VIETNAM labored to recover from a disaster of its own making, on a strategic level it was the time for which General William Westmoreland, Commander of the Military Assistance Command, Vietnam (COMUSMACV), had been waiting, time to take the battle to the enemy and win the Vietnam War. Westmoreland, perhaps the most controversial military figure in modern American history, had famously forecast that the war would take place in three short stages. First, the United States had to build up its forces in Vietnam and ready the all-important logistical infrastructure to support those forces. In the second stage, utilizing a massive firepower advantage and the tactical mobility provided by the helicopter, Westmoreland proposed to lock enemy forces in battle and destroy them. The American warfighting edge would place an unacceptable level of attrition on communist forces, allowing for stage three, which involved a drawdown of U.S. military involvement in the wake of successful negotiations.[1] Though the first stage of his strategy frustratingly had taken longer than he had hoped, by October 1966, Westmoreland finally felt that he had sufficient troops and resources to begin his war of attrition in earnest.[2] American forces could finally, in Westmoreland's words, "just go on bleeding them until Hanoi wakes up to the fact that they have bled their country to the point of national disaster for generations."[3]

Initially, Westmoreland concentrated American offensive actions in the area around Saigon and in the Central Highlands and waited for the monsoon rains to clear before launching his attritional program in the areas bordering on the Demilitarized Zone (DMZ). The large search-and-destroy operations were designed to bring the enemy to battle so that his forces could be attrited by American firepower. For example, Operation Attleboro (September–November 1966) saw twenty-two thousand U.S. and ARVN troops, supported by air power and artillery fire, conduct operations into the Viet Cong stronghold of War Zone C, northwest of Saigon. The seventy-two-day operation was declared a success, since enemy forces suffered some 1,100 dead. However, shortly after the U.S./ARVN withdrawal, the VC reoccupied the area and were operating as before.[4]

While some of the quintessential American attritional operations of the war progressed in the south, the III Marine Amphibious Force (MAF), under the command of Lieutenant General Lewis Walt, remained mainly on the defensive in its I Corps area of operations. The Marines' task was extremely difficult, for the Viet Cong now infested much of the lowlands of I Corps, while strong NVA regular units threatened the area from positions across the DMZ and from three major base areas in Laos. The Marines undertook their defensive mandate with great skill and became involved in a wide variety of missions, which included constructing a string of bases along the DMZ as a barrier to infiltration, facing down ever more aggressive probing attacks by the NVA, and developing an innovative pacification scheme through use of Combined Action Platoons (CAPs), which integrated Marines into South Vietnamese territorial units.[5] The tasks were all difficult in their own way and often involved considerable debate between the Marines and Westmoreland regarding the tactical focus of the war. Arguably, though, it was the slow construction of the series of bases along the DMZ that posed the greatest difficulty in the face of spirited NVA opposition. The ongoing ordeal caused one Marine officer to remark, "With those bastards you would have to build the [demilitarized] zone all the way to India, and it would take the whole Marine Corps and half the Army to guard it. . . . Even then they'd probably burrow under it."[6]

In the autumn of 1966, the situation in I Corps worsened. NVA and VC infiltration and attacks increased dramatically, sparking bloody and protracted fighting south of the DMZ around places that would soon become part of Marine lore, from Khe Sanh, to the Rockpile, to Con Thien. With the Marines embattled and fearful that the initiative in I Corps was shifting to the NVA, Westmoreland rushed reinforcements to the area. The Americal Division took over operations in the southern sector of I Corps, which allowed the Marines both to shift the strength of their 1st Division northward and to concentrate the entire 3rd Marine Division along the DMZ. For the remainder of the year, the

Marines fought a series of engagements with the NVA from the coast to the mountainous border with Laos, famed and bitter battles that formed both part of Westmoreland's plan for attrition and part of the NVA plan to lure American forces away from the cities in preparation for its Tet Offensive.

The fighting in northern I Corps was anything but typical at this stage in the Vietnam War. Proximity to the DMZ and the enemy's Laotian base areas meant that the Marines usually faced NVA regular forces, who enjoyed a constant stream of resupply and ample artillery support, making the fighting unlike the guerrilla war that predominated further south. The war in northern I Corps was also more static as NVA and Marine units traded hammer blows, the bloody nature of which gave the area its nickname of the Dead Marine Zone.

As the Marines faced the VC and the NVA in pitched battles of increasing size and ferocity, the ARVN struggled to find its place in the new American war and found its efforts to be considered only secondary to Westmoreland's war of attrition. Understanding the role of the ARVN within Westmoreland's scheme is central to understanding why the flawed symbiosis of U.S. and South Vietnamese blood and sacrifice failed to achieve ultimate victory.

The 1st ARVN Division, based in Hue City, toiled alongside the III MAF in the defense of Quang Tri and Thua Thien provinces in the north, while the 2nd ARVN Division, based in Da Nang, performed similar duties in Quang Nam and Quang Ngai, the southernmost provinces of I Corps. The 1st ARVN Division of Brigadier General Ngo Quang Truong operated within the complex military reality of a war divided into three separate, yet related levels. At the highest level, ARVN forces sometimes worked in concert with the Marines in battle against NVA infiltration and incursions, even sharing responsibility for some of the outposts that made up the defensive shield along the DMZ. Much of the ARVN combat power, though, was dedicated to a secondary role of fighting the Viet Cong units operating in the lowlands, hoping to drive enemy forces away while the defensive shield prevented their return.

At the local level, protected by this double layer of defense, it was the task mainly of the Regional and Popular Forces to drive the Viet Cong from de facto political control over many of the hamlets and villages of I Corps. This process of gaining local security, known as pacification, also fell under the purview of the ARVN in the new American system of warfighting, and it was left to Truong and his compatriots to find a way for the ARVN to eradicate communist control over the peasantry. Once driven out, the Viet Cong could be held at bay by the combined power of the ARVN and the Marines, leaving behind a situation in which the control of the South Vietnamese government could spread and mature, leading—it was hoped—to victory.

Rising Battlefield Stars

After the tumult of the Buddhist Crisis of 1966, Pham Van Dinh returned to the command of the Hac Bao, which then continued to take part in what Dinh refers to as the "Rice War," in which the ARVN attempted to deny the Viet Cong access to the lowlands, which served as their source of supplies, especially rice. ARVN units endeavored to keep the Viet Cong bottled up in its highland strongholds and to attack any unit that ventured out in search of food or recruits. During the remainder of Dinh's tenure as the unit's commander, the Hac Bao fought as many as fifty engagements with enemy forces as part of the "Rice War." Typically, the Hac Bao came to the support of ARVN units in need, arriving in American helicopters. The engagements were small-unit affairs, usually involving no more than a company of enemy soldiers and often only platoons or squads. The Hac Bao fought well, always driving the enemy from battle and inflicting heavy casualties while suffering few of its own. Dinh's continued battlefield success caused General Truong to inform General Cao Van Vien, Chief of the Vietnamese Joint General Staff, that "One day Dinh will take my place," as 1st ARVN Division commander.[7] By January 1967, Truong had decided that Dinh, who was becoming well known even among the Americans in the area, deserved the command of a battalion.[8]

As Dinh's star rose further, Tran Ngoc Hue yearned for a return to combat. Having made the proper connections as a member of General Chuan's staff, Hue could have avoided the return to the dangerous life of a front-line officer. Instead of, in his words, "taking the door" to a safe and easy life, though, Hue believed that he had "something special," to offer to his nation and that his place was on the battlefield. Hue had every reason to avoid combat, for in March 1967 he married Cam, the chief nurse in the emergency room of Quang Tri Hospital. Though they soon had a child and she greatly feared losing her beloved husband, Cam assented to Tran Ngoc Hue's desire to honor his duty to his country and to return to war. Hue knew that death or capture was a very real possibility, but he also believed that Cam would look after their family if need be.

In February 1967, General Truong offered Dinh the command of the 2nd Battalion, 3rd Regiment of the 1st Division.[9] The command, though, came with a catch. General Truong also wanted Dinh to take over as Chief of Quang Dien District in Thua Thien Province. It was a puzzling offer, for the post of district chief was in the main a political position that involved providing local security. While concerned with rural governance, most district chiefs commanded only the Regional and Popular Force units (RF/PF) in their area. Dinh, though, would be not only a district chief but also a battalion commander as part of an innovative program in which ARVN forces and the RF/PF worked in tandem to achieve local security. It was Dinh's assigned task within this new system to take his battalion to Quang Dien District, drive off resident Viet Cong units, and uproot the local Viet Cong infrastructure. Dinh was elated. Under the new structure, his forces would no longer sweep through areas and then leave; they would be in Quang Dien to stay.

Shortly after Dinh's departure from the Hac Bao, Tran Ngoc Hue achieved his desired transfer to the unit and resumed his career as the company's assistant commander. As the Hac Bao continued its regimen of battle, Hue's intelligence and leadership ability immediately became apparent to his new comrades and to his superior officers. As he had with the 3rd Company in the A Shau, Tran Ngoc Hue led the Hac Bao into battle from the front, exhibiting tremendous personal bravery. Honest and forthright, yet a stickler for discipline, Hue became a popular leader among the men of the Hac Bao. As a result of Hue's efficient combat leadership, only two months after his arrival with the Hac Bao, General Truong marked the rising young star to take command of the elite unit.

In a short time, both Dinh and Hue, so similar in their level of dedication to the ARVN and South Vietnam, had proven themselves to the demanding, no-nonsense General Truong. As had General Chuan before him, General Truong took the two young officers under his tutelage; Dinh and Hue were and would remain Truong's protégés. Within the ARVN and the U.S./Australian advisory community, Truong was well known for choosing his line officers with great care.

Unlike some other ARVN divisions, there were no political hacks or cronies among the combat leaders of 1st ARVN Division. Within his exacting standards of excellence, it is revealing that Truong chose Dinh and Hue for the two most important commands he had to offer to such young officers—in Dinh's case, the command of a battalion tasked with the success or failure of an important experimental project and, in Hue's case, the command of the most elite formation within the 1st ARVN Division.

The lives and careers of the two comrades had crossed once again as they made ready to experience Westmoreland's war from two very different perspectives. Tran Ngoc Hue and the Hac Bao were to occupy the sharp edge of the ARVN's ongoing war of attrition, while Pham Van Dinh entered the shadowy, politicized world of the war of pacification at the very heart of the Vietnam War, which represented either the best hope for a South Vietnamese victory or the surest path to eventual defeat.

Pacification

The South Vietnamese had been involved in some form of pacification, often with U.S. aid and support, since 1954 in an attempt somehow to separate the VC insurgents from the people, their presumed source of support and succor. Even more important, pacification promised to provide the rural population with security and justice, necessary precursors to winning widespread popular support for the fledgling South Vietnamese government. Colonel Nguyen Van Dai, a South Vietnamese police commandant, put the case for security bluntly, stating that "Most of the South Vietnamese have a very simple dream. They wanted to have peaceful lives and not worry about having food. They didn't want to be afraid of someone capturing them or torturing them or killing them. They supported anyone who could bring peace."[10] However, the various South Vietnamese pacification efforts, including the Agroville and Strategic Hamlet programs, had been halting, had suffered from lack of governmental support, and had eventually failed to meet the people's security needs. To be fair, the efforts had faced truly daunting odds in trying to uproot the Viet Cong Infrastructure (VCI) from villages where it had long been in power and where the forces of the government had no writ and little support.

In the critical war for the countryside, though, the South Vietnamese government too often countered the VC only by foisting ineffective local despots upon the population while providing neither true security nor any sustained reason to adhere to a southern nationalism. Frequent coups and political misadventures served only to make the situation worse, and as a result the pacification effort reached its nadir in 1965, with the Saigon government exerting meaningful authority over as little as 25 percent of its own population.[11] Much of the peasantry lived in constant fear, while the Viet Cong achieved nearly free control of vast swaths of the countryside.

With support for an independent South Vietnam, and indeed the war effort itself, at a critical point, it fell to the Americans to rejuvenate the failing pacification scheme and to provide for rural security. Nevertheless, both the American style of war and the temperament of COMUSMACV proved ill suited to the task. Westmoreland's senior intelligence officer, Lieutenant General Phillip B. Davidson, put the situation succinctly by stating that "Westmoreland's interest always lay in the big-unit war. Pacification bored him."[12] Westmoreland believed that his attrition method would win the conflict quickly and make the difficult tasks of rooting out support for the VC and providing for the security of the people moot points. He thus left the issue of pacification in the hands of the South Vietnamese. In essence, then, the United States fought a bifurcated war effort, with the lion's share of resources and attention given to continuing battles of attrition.[13] Pacification—the struggle for the allegiance of the people of South Vietnam—languished, a nearly forgotten part of the American war, until formation, in May 1967, of Civil Operations and Revolutionary Development Support (CORDS) under Robert Komer, the former special assistant to President Johnson for national security affairs.[14] Only after the Tet Offensive and the advent of General Creighton Abrams as COMUSMACV did pacification efforts become integrated into the wider war and achieve marked success.[15]

Left to their own devices, the South Vietnamese made efforts toward pacification that achieved few meaningful results. The social, political, and military reforms required to succeed in pacification would have involved a difficult and protracted effort, something arguably beyond the ability or desire of the self-interested and politicized military class that controlled the South Vietnamese state. It is easy to see why, insecure in its own power and truly believing that the Americans would prove victorious as Westmoreland promised, the South Vietnamese regime placed little real emphasis on efforts that could have in the end undermined its own authority. The South Vietnamese government thus aped the American view of the conflict, setting aside trends toward true counterinsurgency and leaving the ARVN to fight as an adjunct to the "big-unit" war, a war that it could not support without significant U.S. aid—another disturbing effect of the Americanization of the conflict in Vietnam.

The South Vietnamese government continually planned and launched successive pacification programs with noble titles such as the Rural Development Program and the New Model Pacification Program. However, the schemes had little substance, were overly complex, and involved a bewildering array of tasks ranging from efforts to achieve a higher rice yield per acre to tactical problems of providing security for embattled villagers. The muddled organization of the various pacification programs fell to an uneasy, three-tiered alliance of civilian and military organizations. In general, civilian cadre undertook the social and economic parts of the campaigns, while security was the purview of the admittedly substandard RF/PF.[16]

Within the muddled and chaotic world of pacification, Pham Van Dinh occupied a position of special importance. As a district chief, he would be the local representative of the pacification effort and would have both the indispensable local knowledge of and control over individual hamlets and villages in his AO. As such, district chiefs, usually young officers of the rank of either major or lieutenant colonel, faced myriad tasks ranging from combat operations to hamlet security to economic development projects of all types.[17] Usually aided by a team of eight U.S. advisers, district chiefs could call upon a variety of military forces in their pacification efforts, including three to six Regional Forces companies, capable of maneuver, and often up to forty Popular Forces platoons, usually wedded to defensive tasks in individual hamlets or villages. These forces formed the local defensive shield tasked with defending hamlets and villages from Viet Cong incursions and protecting the village and hamlet officials, Revolutionary Development cadre, policemen, and members of other civilian organizations intended to aid the local populace.[18]

Many district chiefs were simply political appointees who ran their commands like small fiefdoms and engaged in all manner of graft and corruption while providing the people with little in the way of true security. Village chiefs in many districts were absentee and visited their village only to collect taxes and thus abdicated their considerable role in local security. In such situations, Popular Forces platoons often did not exist or were left on their own, unsupported and unaided, to man small, static defensive posts in a countryside awash with Viet Cong sympathizers. These posts gave the illusion of government control in an area, when in reality the PF contingent never dared venture out of the confines of its defensive positions. In other cases, district chiefs were honest but inexperienced ARVN combat officers who resented assignment to pacification duties and longed for a return to the quick career advancement of a combat slot[19] and neglected both the training and the tactical utilization of the military forces at their command.

Regional and Popular Forces

Placed by General Truong at the fulcrum point of the war of pacification, the battle for the hearts and minds of the people, Pham Van Dinh quickly discovered that the troops normally tasked with pacification, the Regional Forces and the Popular Forces, were fundamentally flawed. The RF/PF had grown out of the Civil Guard and the Self Defense Corps militia, groupings of paramilitary forces founded in 1955 and initially tasked with internal security duties. Such "hometown" forces, in the opinion of General Truong, implied "the ability to recognize and identify the enemy among the masses, a familiarity with all accesses, hiding places in the hamlets, a working relationship and close touch with the population, and above all, the people's cooperation and support."[20]

Realizing their importance, the South Vietnamese initially supported the creation of territorial forces capable of playing a significant counterinsurgency role. However, the United States disagreed, preferring instead to aid in the construction of a more traditional military force in South Vietnam, leaving the territorial forces out of the Military Assistance Program. As a result, the territorial forces remained poorly trained and underutilized and in some cases actually became part of the problem in sensitive rural areas.[21] Instead of defending the population, territorial forces were often employed to harvest coffee, plant rice, or catch fish with party boats for their corrupt province chief.[22] In the words of General James Lawton Collins, who served as senior U.S. adviser to Vietnamese Regional Forces and Popular Forces, "Many units were little more than armed bands of young men; others were private armies and gangs 'federalized' into the service of the government of Vietnam."[23]

Beginning in 1960, though, as the insurgency became a more serious threat in South Vietnam, the American attitudes toward the territorial forces began to change. By 1964, the territorial forces were integrated into the ARVN command structure and became known as the Regional Forces and the Popular Forces. In their new incarnation, the RF/PF enjoyed a somewhat less chaotic command structure and assumed their roles as defenders of the provinces, districts, villages, and hamlets of South Vietnam. However, the attention and improvement had come ten years too late and could not quickly overcome years of neglect and stagnation.

At the beginning of the American war, then, instead of an effective armed local force standing against insurgency, the RF/PF were a testament to the shortsightedness of the overall American and South Vietnamese war effort. At the heart of the problem, the RF/PF suffered from a nearly complete lack of training.[24] After 1964, with the belated American recognition of the important security function of the territorial forces, there began something of a crash course of training for RF/PF units, but that training still fell 60 percent short of desired goals.[25] Only with the high value placed on pacification after the founding of Civil Operations and Revolutionary Development Support, in 1967, did the training of RF/PF units begin to meet anything like uniform military standards.

Throughout the Vietnam War, the RF/PF suffered from constant problems of leadership. The best officer candidates went to the ARVN, which saw the territorial forces as a poor cousin that afforded fewer chances for advancement. The village and district chiefs who commanded territorial forces were often corrupt bureaucrats who never visited their troops, stole their meager funds, knew little of military command, and fled at the first sight of danger. The RF/PF also suffered from very low rates of pay, well below the wages earned by their ARVN brethren. Finally, since the RF/PF served locally, family matters were a constant problem. When the Viet Cong attacked, the RF/PF soldier faced the choice of defending his outpost or defending his family.[26]

Making matters worse, the RF/PF carried outdated weaponry, receiving only U.S. armament of World War II vintage, including the M-1 carbine after 1960. At the same time, Viet Cong units began to receive AK-47s and RPG-7s, seriously outclassing the organic firepower of the RF/PF, which also received the lowest priority for fire support of all kinds and thus could not even normally call upon the massive U.S./ARVN preponderance in artillery and air power to tip the balance of battle in their favor. A study of III Corps in 1967 revealed the disturbing reality that, out of 234 RF/PF friendly-initiated actions in which calls went out for fire support, nearly 200 actions received no such support.[27]

Although their tasks of local security were seemingly mundane, the RF/PF suffered the highest number of casualties of any allied force in the conflict. Spread thinly across the countryside and lacking in logistical and firepower support, the RF/PF outposts quickly became a favorite target for massed Viet Cong or NVA attacks. The situation was at its worst in 1968 as some 477 RF/PF outposts were overrun during the first month of the Tet Offensive.[28] Additionally, while ARVN and U.S. divisions, brigades, and battalions could rest and recuperate or even just find times of lull in their combat duties, the same could not be said of the small-unit war of the territorial forces. In a war with no frontline, the RF/PF were always on the frontline, with no safe haven and no R&R. Instead, the RF/PF faced a war of constant engagement, always on patrol and always on alert for an enemy that could be anywhere—even in their own villages and hamlets. For the RF/PF, war was the state of daily life, a slow and never-ending battle of attrition that lasted, for some soldiers, for twenty years.

It is no wonder that the morale and effectiveness of the RF/PF, only partly trained, poorly led, undergunned, and unsupported, remained low. That RF/PF forces continued to fight at all is a testament to the tenacity of the South Vietnamese population and serves as further indication that there existed a true reservoir of support for Southern nationalism—a reservoir that both the United States and South Vietnam failed to cultivate sufficiently.[29] It was this backwater of the war, the shadowy world of pacification—the purview of political incompetents and the war zone of the flawed RF/PF—that Dinh now prepared to enter.

The War for the Countryside and the War of Attrition

In 1967, Quang Dien District, located in the fertile lowlands just a few kilometers north of Hue City, contained a population of some forty-six thousand people scattered in eight main villages and a collection of scattered subsidiary hamlets. The area was noted for its rice production and as such was a constant target of Viet Cong infiltration in efforts to secure supplies. In the ongoing "Rice War," it was the task of U.S. and ARVN forces to meet and defeat main units of the VC and the NVA that sought access to the lowlands, but the barrier they provided was porous. As a result, a sizable VC presence existed in the area that proved very difficult for the RF/PF to remove. Thus, although there were two RF companies in the district and each village fielded a PF platoon, in 1967 the situation in Quang Dien District remained very much in doubt, leaving the Viet Cong dominant over half of the villages and hamlets of the district and in control of much of the area's resources. In the words of one American adviser familiar with the area, the Viet Cong "infested the countryside."[30]

The series of events that had led to Dinh's appointment as district chief of Quang Dien began in 1965, when Army Chief of Staff General Harold K. Johnson commissioned a group of American military and civilian experts to study the problem of rural security in South Vietnam in the "Program for the Pacification and Long-Term Development of South Vietnam" (PROVN). The conclusions of the study were striking and suggested a move away from the current emphasis on search and destroy and urged a reliance on pacification and the effort to win the civilian population over to the cause of the South Vietnamese government. The final version of the PROVN study concluded:

> The situation in South Vietnam has seriously deteriorated. 1966 may well be the last chance to ensure eventual success. "Victory" can only be achieved through bringing the individual Vietnamese, typically a rural peasant, to support willingly the GVN. The critical actions are those that occur at the village, district, and provincial levels. This is where the war must be fought; this is where that war and the object beyond it must be won.[31]

In short, PROVN repudiated the entire American military policy since the development of MAAG, including the creation of ARVN in the image of the U.S. Army. As a solution, PROVN advocated what so many of the younger commanders of field units, including Dinh and Hue, and their advisers had long supported. Instead of ARVN and U.S. forces sweeping through areas only to leave them vulnerable to reinfiltration by the Viet Cong, PROVN called for the creation of security forces "associated and intermingled with the people on a long term basis."[32] One specific proposal involved the assignment of regular ARVN battalions to province and district pacification duties, with the RF/PF converted into a police force. Under the proposal, it would fall to the better-armed, better-trained, and better-led ARVN to root out the VC infrastructure while the RF/PF concentrated on keeping the peace where pacification had already succeeded.

The proposals were so unsettling that even PROVN's sponsor, General Johnson, forbade discussion of the study or even acknowledgment of its existence outside the Pentagon. Eventually the Joint Chiefs of Staff and McNamara were briefed on the study and forwarded a copy on to Westmoreland for his comments.[33] Still retaining his faith in his war of attrition, Westmoreland rejected the promising scheme. With the full support of neither its original sponsor nor the commander in the field, PROVN proved to be a missed opportunity and failed to alter the balance of the war in Vietnam. Even though he did not support the idea of intermingling the ARVN with the people, Westmoreland chose to allow individual ARVN commanders to assign infantry battalions to province or district pacification duties on an ad hoc basis.[34]

In 1967, MACV took the idea one step further with the U.S.-South Vietnamese Combined Campaign Plan, which envisioned attaching regular ARVN infantry battalions to provinces to achieve "unity of effort." Under the plan, corps commanders decided on a case-by-case basis when to assign regular units to provincial authorities to act as security forces. However, the innovative plan to use ARVN troops in true pacification efforts faced opposition, both tacit and overt, at nearly all levels of the allied command structure. For his part, Westmoreland regarded the idea as something of a stopgap measure that took forces away from the "big-unit war." While some elements of the Saigon administration saw the policy as the best way to integrate regular forces into the security effort, most South Vietnamese commanders viewed the practice with varying levels of distaste. Divisional commanders often saw the detachment of battalions to province duties as a threat to both their combat strength and their all-important political power. The implications of the plan to detach battalions to province control reverberated even at the very highest levels of power. President Nguyen Van Thieu counted many of the divisional commanders among his strongest backers, while provincial leaders were often supporters of his political arch-rival, Nguyen Cao Ky.[35] Thus, a wholesale shift of battalions to provincial control threatened a sea change in the continuing bitter political and military struggles that so plagued South Vietnam, and as a result the policy of shifting ARVN battalions to provinces and districts languished. The failure of the policy, one that could have better linked the ARVN to the people, is in many ways a testament to the myriad failings of the Vietnam War itself—sacrificed to the American desire to fight a big-unit war of attrition and to the political failings of the South Vietnamese regime.

Young, innovative, and less concerned with politics than many of his brethren, General Ngo Quang Truong was one of the few ARVN divisional commanders who saw the opportunities in and chose to take advantage of the new policy, opting to station Dinh and the 2/3 ARVN in the Quang Dien District for a single year. While many ARVN officers resisted assignment to what they considered the less important role of pacification support,[36] Dinh saw the assignment as irresistible. He had long realized that true control over the countryside represented the best chance for victory for South Vietnam. From his earliest combat experiences near Tam Ky, in Quang Nam Province, Dinh had come to believe that sweeping through villages only to leave them to the mercies of the Viet Cong was a fundamental mistake. He now had the chance to fight the war in the right way.

By 1967, fifty-three maneuver battalions of the ARVN were dedicated to some sort of pacification support role.[37] However, these units still acted as a mobile, inner shield of defense against the Viet Cong, occupying a sort of middle ground between the war of attrition and the war of pacification. These units patrolled from base camps to drive off enemy units and interdict their lines of supply. The role of 2/3 ARVN, though, was fundamentally different. Dinh was one of but a very few ARVN officers who was both district chief and commander of a battalion. Because of his dual role, 2/3 ARVN became an organic part of the defense of Quang Dien District, not only augmenting the efforts of the RF/PF but also living alongside the villagers and peasants.

Quang Dien District in February 1967 had become a focal point of enemy activity as the VC and the NVA sought to exert control over the productive lowlands, not only to seize more supplies but also to divert ARVN and U.S. attention from Hue City in preparation for the upcoming Tet Offensive.[38] In the face of the onslaught, the district's poorly trained and led RF/PF forces had in some cases simply melted away, leaving a VC force of battalion strength to roam the countryside in relative safety. Dinh's arrival, though, turned the tables on the Viet Cong. Not wanting to risk prolonged combat with an ARVN battalion, the resident main-force enemy units quickly withdrew into the highlands and set their sights on softer targets in other districts. However, Quang Dien remained thoroughly infiltrated by the Viet Cong infrastructure, and Dinh felt that the local RF/PF forces were too poorly armed, trained, and commanded to pose a real threat to VC domination of the area, much less to stand in defense against renewed attacks by main force units. The arrival of 2/3 had evened the odds in Quang Dien, and Dinh came to believe that stationing ARVN battalions as organic forces within districts—the ARVN and the people as one—was quite possibly the answer to the pacification war.

The pacification system, though, was not Dinh's to change, leaving him to labor under the chaotic double-command structure that was a staple of the bifurcated war. As a battalion commander, he, along with his ARVN forces, reported to his regiment. However, as a district chief, he, along with his RF/PF component, reported to the province chief. Sometimes the dual command structure worked at cross purposes, and elements of his ARVN battalion were often called away to engage in combat duties elsewhere. In addition, his RF company often departed to undertake province duties with no prior warning. Thus, even with Dinh's near-unity of control, the command situation remained rather unpredictable, and, for ARVN units across the country that were merely attached to provinces or districts, the situation was immeasurably worse.

Training also was an area of critical concern for Dinh. The RF/PF soldiers, in his view, were competent and dedicated, but none of the forces under his command had undertaken any unit training whatsoever, leaving them at a potentially fatal disadvantage against the

VC and the NVA. Dinh worked to train the units himself and pressed the importance of formal unit training and the acquisition of better armament on the province chief. To his immense frustration, though, Dinh was told that Quang Dien was at war and that the RF/PF had to fight now and simply could not afford the luxury of unit training—an oft-repeated refrain throughout South Vietnam.

Though he could not change the maddening command structure or the training inadequacies of the RF/PF, Dinh could alter the organizational flaws that plagued Quang Dien. In South Vietnam, many district chiefs bought their offices in order to become the local representatives at the heart of a national system of corruption that reached breathtaking proportions. The district chiefs would in turn appoint their cronies to serve in critically important pacification positions as village chiefs. The district chief, who paid a cut of his profits to the province chief, collected money from his cronies, who in turn collected money from the people. The most popular form of corruption at the local level remained the "ghost soldier" phenomenon. Village chiefs, who often only rarely visited the village under their control, would claim to head a PF platoon, when in reality none existed. The village chief would pocket the soldiers' pay, while paying a cut to the district chief. As a result, villagers paid taxes to a distant and noncaring government while receiving no security, so it is little wonder that such villages proved easy prey for Viet Cong domination.

Disgusted to discover such a corrupt and dysfunctional system in Quan Dien, Dinh decided to appoint trusted noncommissioned officers who were native to the area to serve as temporary village chiefs. Aided by a local chief chosen from the village population, Dinh's men reorganized and trained village and hamlet defense forces and saw that the local chief learned his job well and received all of the support he needed. Dinh also sent an ARVN company to the four villages under enemy domination to live with the people and provide security, raising and training PF platoons where none had previously existed. In addition, the ARVN soldiers became increasingly familiar with the people and their needs, working with them rather than being distant and uninterested overlords. Theirs was no longer a war of search and destroy and seeking combat; theirs was now a war of administration and security.

Under the new system, pacification flourished in Quang Dien. Protected by the might of an ARVN battalion, Quang Dien was no longer an easy target, and VC main-force incursions dropped accordingly. With ARVN companies living in the villages, the VC infrastructure fled or went deep underground, denying the insurgents access to the people. Rice production went up, and ARVN soldiers made certain that the crop did not wind up in the hands of the VC. The changes in Quang Dien took time and were punctuated by instances in which 2/3 had to leave the area for short periods of combat. However, Dinh was able to report to General Truong that Quang Dien District had been pacified—and the task took only six months, not the allotted year. The situation was indeed so changed that Dinh's American adviser, Captain James Coolican, reported that in an area once "infested" with VC, there were no major incidents of violence even at night and that he felt comfortable walking alone in the local villages.[39] It was a significant victory, vindicating Dinh's view regarding the flawed overall nature of the Vietnam War, a victory that won him further recognition and a promotion to the rank of major.

In his dual role of district chief and battalion commander, Dinh worked with two American advisory staffs, a district staff for pacification support and a battalion staff for combat support. Coolican served as Dinh's battalion adviser, and his opinions are of special importance. Initially, Coolican was excited to learn that he had been assigned to 2/3 ARVN, because of Dinh's hard-earned military reputation as "a real warrior." However, the situation soon changed. The relationship between the two men was rather distant and formal, but Dinh often spoke to Coolican of the successes gained through utilizing an ARVN battalion as organic district support. Even so, for Coolican, both Dinh and the situation were "uninspiring." Coolican was a combat adviser, and it was the task of both him and his team to aid Dinh and his battalion in battle. However, in Quang Dien, there was little fighting, and Coolican felt that Dinh did not seem interested in looking for and engaging the enemy. In Coolican's words, Dinh "became more interested in being the district commander rather than the battalion commander." Coolican recognized that, as district chief, Dinh was honest and had achieved considerable success. However, Dinh spent the majority of his time on matters of pacification throughout the district and often went back to Hue to meet with Truong and the divisional staff.

With little combat in the offing, Coolican felt that his talents and those of his staff were underutilized, and he put in for a transfer.

The relationship between Dinh and Coolican is illustrative of the continued bifurcation of the war. Coolican was in Vietnam for only a year. He was a combat adviser and wanted to serve a real purpose in that role. For Dinh, though, it was already the sixth year of war; the pace of his war and his role in pacification at the time were simply different and foreign to the American interpretation of the nature of conflict. By and large, Americans fought the Vietnam War as eight separate, but related, one-year wars as they came and went on their single-year tours of duty. However, for the South Vietnamese, the war was very much a long-term prospect that was often to be fought at a pace that seemed maddeningly slow to their American counterparts. Coolican, incidentally, would get his chance to make a difference in combat; in November 1967, he became the adviser to Captain Tran Ngoc Hue and the Hac Bao.

After assuming command of the Hac Bao in the summer of 1967, Tran Ngoc Hue put his men through their paces at their barracks in Hue City to improve the company, especially in the areas of small-unit tactics and individual martial arts. Most important, though, Hue concentrated on teaching his men why they were fighting—to save the civilians of South Vietnam from the atrocities of the Viet Cong that Hue remembered all too well. In the brutal civil war, examples of atrocities were never hard to find—villagers tied together and shot by the Viet Cong, children with their hands cut off, civilians made to dig their own graves before being buried alive.[40] Considering that the men of the Hac Bao were natives of the Hue City and its surrounding villages, witnessing the barbaric treatment of their neighbors served as a powerful motivator, and the unit maintained a grim resolve and unity of purpose unmatched in the ARVN.

The Hac Bao still acted as the rapid-reaction force of the 1st ARVN Division, which posed a unique challenge to a man who had by and large led only small units and then spent years as a general's aide. Hue, though, would not face the challenge alone, but would instead fight alongside and with the aid of the first in a long succession of American advisers. Captain Bob Jones had served as senior adviser to the 1st Battalion, 3rd Regiment of the ARVN before his transfer to the Hac Bao and had come to both respect his South Vietnamese counter-

Captain Bob Jones and Tran Ngoc Hue await the arrival of helicopters before an operation with the Hac Bao. Photograph Courtesy of Bob Jones.

parts and understand the critical role individual leadership in ARVN fighting units. Upon their first meeting, Jones came to the conclusion that Hue embodied the best of the ARVN—a strong leader and an even better person. The two forged a close relationship, and Hue worked hard to familiarize his new comrade in arms with Vietnamese culture, ranging from how to shoot and eat water buffalo while on extended missions in the field to tutoring Jones on the details of Vietnam's glorious past through visits to the collection of imperial tombs around Hue City.

The Hac Bao were engaged at the very heart of the ARVN efforts in the ongoing war of attrition. On average the unit remained in its base area in Hue City for only three days before spending a week to ten days in the field on operations that invariably resulted in contact with the enemy. Thus, the Hac Bao fighters were nearly constantly engaged in combat, ranging from a battle at Lang Vei near the Laotian border, where the Hac Bao lost two helicopters upon insertion to the extraction of an ARVN unit from a trap near Phu Bai to calling in fire support on Viet Cong forces negotiating the coastline at night while Hac Bao troopers calmly waded in the water collecting tiger shrimp for dinner. The fighting mainly involved bitter clashes of small units— a constant hum of battle that imposed a slow but steady level of attrition on both sides. Jones was dismayed at the cost of battle to the ARVN, especially to the wounded, who could expect only minimal care and had to rely only on the support of their families after their sacrifice in service of South Vietnam. Together Hue and Jones formed a lethal combat team, exemplifying what was good about the U.S. advisory effort in Vietnam.

Advisers

The U.S. advisory effort in South Vietnam was one of long standing, originally falling to the 342 men of MAAG in the wake of the Geneva Accords. Though their resources were few, the task facing the advisers was far reaching—the creation of a South Vietnamese military capable of standing on its own. The challenging task attracted many of the best young officers in the U.S. military, eager for advancement, desirous of combat, and believing in the need to protect South Vietnam from communist aggression. The situation, though, changed with the advent of overt American involvement in Vietnam in 1965, as U.S. officers increasingly saw posting to an advisory position as less than desirable and instead preferred to lead Americans in combat rather than either advising South Vietnamese or becoming involved in pacification support.

As the Vietnam War transformed itself, the advisory effort grew in every way imaginable, defying easy explanation and generalization. Advisers served at every level, from Westmoreland as the chief U.S. adviser to the South Vietnamese military to Bob Jones, who labored in constant combat alongside Tran Ngoc Hue at the company level. There were military advisers like James Coolican, whose task it was to aid South Vietnamese units in battle. There were training advisers associated with ARVN schools and training centers. However, there was also a wide variety of pacification advisers, including a high number of civilians, who helped the South Vietnamese with matters of local security and economic development. Thus, the advisory effort changed from year to year, from region to region, and indeed from person to person.

Most important, the active participation of U.S. combat units in the ground war both overshadowed and fundamentally altered the role of the advisory effort.[41] U.S. advisers no longer concentrated on training the South Vietnamese military to fight its own war, a shift in emphasis that would have untold consequences. Instead, American advisers served a multiplicity of roles designed to enable ARVN units to fight as an adjunct force within the rubric of the American war. In the words of General Westmoreland, the duties of the adviser

> [i]ncluded coordinating both artillery and helicopter and fixed wing air support; acting as a conduit for intelligence; developing supply and service programs; improving communications between combat units and area commands (provinces and districts); and providing special assistance in such areas as psychological warfare, civic action, and medical aid.[42]

Although a tactical adviser had to be something of a jack of all trades, his most important role was that of combat air support and artillery support coordinator.[43] In this capacity, the U.S. adviser held something of a trump card over his ARVN counterpart. Firepower, especially in the form of devastating air strikes, was *the* critical force multiplier of the war and often enabled U.S. and ARVN units to persevere against heavy odds. That force multiplier was the purview of the American adviser, meaning that he held life and death itself in his hands. Some ARVN commanders felt emasculated and railed at the paramount power wielded by U.S. advisers. However, in most cases, U.S. control over air power was simply a fact of life and formed an important part of the adviser/counterpart relationship.

U.S. advisers served at all levels, including senior advisers and advisory staffs at both corps and division headquarters, but arguably the most important role in what was for the ARVN a small-unit war fell to the battalion advisory staff. Generally speaking, a battalion advisory team consisted of three U.S. personnel, and sometimes Australian personnel, including a captain, a first lieutenant, and a sergeant. Although an advisory chain of command existed and advisers served as part of a corps-level advisory team, in many ways the role of tactical advisers was ad hoc and personal in nature. Westmoreland himself had accepted that the advisory effort was more a "one-on-one," interpersonal relationship than something mandated and systematic. In essence, it was up to the adviser to form a fruitful relationship with his Vietnamese counterpart.[44]

The success of the U.S. advisory effort, then, relied to a great extent on the ability of the individual advisers themselves, who had perhaps the most daunting jobs of any American soldier in the war—fitting into a foreign culture and military, forging a relationship with a counterpart in what was his war, accompanying his unit into often-constant combat, all with very little mandate but a wide latitude for individual action. For such an effort, individual adviser training had to be paramount.

Preparation for advisory duty, however, was minimal. At first, many advisers went to the U.S. Army Special Warfare School at Fort Bragg for a six-week course that stressed counterinsurgency techniques and included some general background on Vietnam as well as a cursory study of the Vietnamese language. Some graduates went on to a further course of intensive language instruction at the Defense Language Institute, in Monterey, California.[45] The training left most potential advisers with little knowledge about the culture they were about to inhabit, unable to speak the difficult tonal Vietnamese language, and with only a limited understanding of the tactical and personal challenges they were soon to face.

Both Pham Van Dinh and Tran Ngoc Hue were able to speak fluent English and could thus communicate effectively with their advisers. For the vast majority of U.S. advisers, however, the inability to communicate often left them shut out and unable to understand or fit into the intricate Vietnamese web of religious and local relationships. Many advisers in the end were unable to form a true bond of comradeship with their host unit, held at arm's length by the reality that they were able to speak only through an interpreter or directly to the unit commander using his own broken English. The historian Andrew Krepinevich has referred to the lack of language training as "cultural hubris" on the part of the United States that violated the basic rule of counterinsurgency—becoming "as familiar as possible with the people and the area that you are trying to win over and control."[46] For his part, General Vien wondered at the problem, stating:

I know of no single instance in which a U.S. adviser effectively discussed professional matters with his counterpart in Vietnamese. The learning and development of a new language seemed to have no appeal for U.S. advisers who must have found it not really worth the effort because of the short tour of duty in Vietnam.[47]

In many cases, advisers served the standard one-year tour of duty; however, in "hardship posts," especially in service with ARVN combat battalions, advisers served for only six months in the field before rotating to a safer position.[48] The short tours not only further limited the ability of the adviser to come to terms with his situation but also ruled out any true institutional memory. Thus, often, every six months a new adviser brought with him a new regimen and style, leaving his counterpart to adapt accordingly over and over again. Again, General Vien put the resulting situation well:

One year was indeed short as a tour of duty since it included the unproductive time spent in familiarization with environment and job, usually about three months. . . . As a result, it was impossible for some ARVN commanders to work with any particular adviser long enough to develop a fruitful relationship. . . . As a result, both sides often abstained from committing themselves to any long-range undertaking.[49]

The most difficult problem facing American advisers, though, was that they and their South Vietnamese counterparts were engaged in fighting two maddeningly different wars. The U.S. adviser, usually young and fresh, had but one year to make his mark on the war in Vietnam. For the South Vietnamese commander, though, the war was quite different and must have seemed endlessly long. In some cases, the South Vietnamese had fought the war for decades. They had seen many brave and brash U.S. advisers come and go, and they realized that their next U.S. adviser would in all likelihood want to prosecute the war differently from his predecessor.

U.S. advisers, often with great frustration, took note of the differently paced wars and argued that sometimes even the best ARVN units lacked a true offensive spirit.[50] However, after spending time in the field with their ARVN counterparts, many advisers found that they had learned much regarding the Vietnamese soldiers' view of their war. James Coolican, for example, entered his advisory tour ready for combat and ready to make an immediate difference, so much so that he had requested transfer to the Hac Bao. On the last day of his tour, Coolican sat on a rice paddy dike after briefing the incoming adviser who was going to take his place. As he waited for the helicopter to come and take him away, Coolican realized that he was both emotionally and physically exhausted after six months in nearly constant combat. As he waited to return home, he could not help but wonder how the situation looked to Tran Ngoc Hue, who had fought the war for years and would fight it for years to come. Hue could not look forward to a trip back to "the world." Standing next to Hue was a new adviser, anxious and excited to make his difference in the war. Coolican knew that the situation would be repeated over and over again and wondered how the South Vietnamese were able to do it. How were they able to fight such a different war?[51]

Complicating any effort to generalize about the combat advisory effort in South Vietnam is the fact that U.S. advisers were not alone in their efforts to aid the ARVN. Entering the conflict in July 1962, the Australian Army Training Team Vietnam (AATTV) provided tactical guidance to the ARVN for a decade before its eventual withdrawal from the conflict, making a contribution to the war effort that has gone nearly unnoticed in the United States. While not a large commitment (the strength of the AATTV normally ran at an authorized number of fifteen officers and eighty-five warrant officers), the Australians concentrated their numbers in I Corps[52] and thus had a great influence on the operations of the 1st and 2nd ARVN divisions. It quickly became routine for both Pham Van Dinh and Tran Ngoc Hue to work with a mixed group of American and Australian advisers, a combination that sometimes led to tension but also had great strengths.

The members of the AATTV were often older and more experienced than their American counterparts, with many having seen action in previous conflicts from Korea to Malaysia. Less concerned with the possibility of fighting in a potential European or world conflict, the Australians had centered much of their military doctrine and training around small-unit warfare and counterinsurgency. Vietnam seemed the perfect place to put those skills and ideas to the test, and as such assignment to an advisory role remained quite desirable even after the arrival of the ground combat units of the 1st Australian Task Force in

Phuoc Tuy Province in mid-1966. Often with considerable experience in counterinsurgent operations and vying for a chance to serve as advisers in Vietnam, AATTV volunteers underwent an eight-week course of training at the Jungle Warfare Centre, in Canungra, Queensland, and then two weeks of cultural and colloquial language training at Military Intelligence School, in Sydney.[53] With their wealth of operational experience and their focused training, the Australian advisers often occupied a special place of importance in the units of I Corps. In the words of Ian McNeill, the official historian of the AATTV:

> The warrant officer, usually older and more experienced than the others in his group, generally came to be looked upon as the "father," his judgment often being sought by both the [American] team leader and the Vietnamese battalion commander.[54]

While their initial immersion in the byzantine structure of the advisory system in Vietnam proved jarring for many Americans, the situation was much more complicated for the members of the AATTV. Upon reaching their battalions, Australians usually found themselves isolated—not quite part of the American advisory team and often able to relate more closely to their ARVN counterparts. Having to live by their wits, Australian advisers found themselves answering to a confusing triple array of command structures—their own AATTV command, ARVN command, and the U.S. advisory team command. The Australian advisers also found themselves more often than not at the very bottom of the supply chain—not quite anyone's responsibility—and, as a result, many members of the AATTV acquired reputations as master scroungers. The system was so confusing and isolating that when ARVN units crossed paths, it often proved to be quite an occasion as their respective Australian advisers took time to seek each other out and swap stories and commiseration. Indeed, the isolation became so severe that the AATTV opened a central location, Uc Dai Loi House, in Da Nang, where advisers who were scattered throughout I Corps were encouraged to go once a month to receive their pay, gather supplies, and just be with other Australians.[55]

More accustomed to the realities faced by the military of a small nation engaged in irregular warfare, the members of the AATTV often related well to the type of conflict they found in South Vietnam.

Some Australian advisers, though, were critical of the overall nature of the MACV advisory effort and contended that the Americans were too focused on changing the ARVN and its war into something more conventional and familiar, rather than working with the situation as it existed. One Vietnamese brigadier general jokingly agreed with the view of his Australian adviser and remarked that "If the conflict were only being fought in Europe then the South Vietnamese would have won."[56] Though the Australians' emphasis on methods of counterinsurgency sometimes caused friction with their American allies, the relationships between the advisory groupings were in the main strong. The Americans often saw their Australian brethren as irascible hard chargers and hard drinkers, while the Australians very much respected the Americans' work ethic and combat ability. Though their methods were different, Australian and American advisers formed a bond among themselves and with the ARVN officers and men of I Corps.

Even in the face of considerable cultural and systemic obstacles the American and Australian advisory effort was very successful, thanks in the main to the dedication and work ethic of the individuals who took part in the often chaotic system, leaving one to wonder what level of success could have been achieved through a more organized effort that retained its original goal of training the South Vietnamese to fight their own war. Many former advisers bristle at the common perception of the ARVN as an army of incompetents and believe that MACV "never gave the Vietnamese credit for how good a soldiers [sic] they actually were" and that the United States would have "done a much better job if we had given the Vietnamese more respect and authority."[57] It is revealing that the advisers on the scene, the ones closest to both the ARVN's problems and its successes, came to the same conclusions as had Pham Van Dinh and Tran Ngoc Hue—that the focus of the American war effort should have been on the training and creation of an ARVN capable of taking over its own war, a true policy of Vietnamization of the conflict.

Although they were underappreciated and partly trained and participated in a secondary war with only minimal support, U.S. and Australian advisers succeeded against heavy odds in buttressing the battlefield ability of the ARVN. However, that success came at a steep price. The adviser controlled the all-important fire support, a force multiplier that became addictive to the Vietnamese commanders. In short, the advisers succeeded in their tasks too well, and their ARVN counterparts all too often became dependent both on their advice and on U.S. firepower support.[58]

Although the advisers were performing their difficult and rather anonymous tasks admirably and their counterparts often learned their lessons well, the American advisory effort ironically helped to create an ARVN that was unable to stand alone. ARVN soldiers and their officers were often brave and resilient, but they became overly dependent on U.S. firepower to win battlefield victories and on U.S. advisers to direct that firepower. When ARVN forces ventured into battles against sizable and determined enemy forces without the benefit of their advisers, as in the Lam Son 719 invasion of Laos, their deficiencies and dependencies quickly became apparent. With such support, the ARVN could fight well, as it did in the Tet Offensive of 1968 and in the Easter Offensive of 1972. However, eventually the United States tired of its war in Vietnam—and left the ARVN with neither advisers nor firepower support. The outcome was inevitable.

Battle at Phu Loc

As the VC and the NVA readied for their Tet Offensive, the pace of operations in the hinterlands of I Corps quickened. Critical to the communists' planning was the area around the village of Phu Loc, located along Highway 1 just north of the bottleneck of the Hai Van Pass. Though the area was already hotly contested by two resident VC battalions, in late 1967 an entire NVA regiment arrived as reinforcements, hoping to sever the critical logistic network supporting Hue City.[59] As a result, the RF/PF forces based in Phu Loc District Headquarters and the U.S. 1st Battalion, 5th Marines reported a surge in hostile contact as the VC and the NVA ambushed convoys and struck at isolated CAP platoons in preparation for their main assault.

In the early morning hours of 7 January, communist forces struck with a vengeance, attacking Phu Loc District Headquarters, the 1st Battalion, 5th Marines command post, and nearly all of the major CAP platoon compounds between Phu Loc and the Hai Van Pass. According to one U.S. Marine, "All of a sudden hell broke loose . . . it looked like ants coming over a hill or just coming through the wire towards the compound, yelling, screaming, everyone was just yelling and getting hit."[60] Attacked nearly everywhere in the district in the predawn darkness, the U.S. Marines and the South Vietnamese forces struggled to react to the chaotic situation.

Fending off heavy attacks of their own, 1/5 Marines detached platoon and company-size elements to rescue their marooned CAP platoons. In addition, a single platoon of B Company 1/5 Marines made its way to aid the besieged RF/PF forces at Phu Loc District Headquarters.[61] In need of additional reinforcements, though, the Marines called upon the Hac Bao. Departing their enclosure in Hue City aboard Marine helicopters, the Hac Bao fighters had little time to plan their attack. Surrounded and nearly overrun, Hue realized that the situation at the Phu Loc District Headquarters was dire. However, Hue had fought the communists for years and knew their tactics well. Having laid siege to a base, the VC and the NVA would expect a counterattack and have prepared ambushes along any incoming roads and around any possible helicopter landing zones in the immediate area.

As the helicopters neared Phu Loc, Hue made a difficult decision; instead of landing outside the battle and risking ambush while fighting his way in, he chose to do the opposite. Covered by a deadly Marine artillery barrage, the Hac Bao landed amid the surrounded force at Phu Loc District Headquarters. The daring maneuver caught the attacking forces by surprise, and the Hac Bao hit the landing zone safely. Struck by the audacity of the attack, facing reinforcements, and suffering from the rising application of deadly American firepower, the NVA withdrew.[62] Having lost eighty dead in and around Phu Loc, the NVA attacks quickly dissipated, though the area remained contested through the time of the Tet Offensive.[63] Tran Ngoc Hue and the Hac Bao had exhibited bravery and professionalism in battle, forging close contact with the U.S. Marines. As the action in Phu Loc died down, neither Hue nor the leadership of the 1/5 Marines realized that they would soon be locked together in one of the greatest battles of the war —the struggle for Hue City during the Tet Offensive.

While Dinh took part in a different war in which rural security was the key to ultimate victory, Tran Ngoc Hue and the Hac Bao stood as examples of what ARVN combat forces could become. They were motivated, well led, determined, and trusted by their American allies, even the vaunted Marines. After the vicious battle at Phu Loc, Coolican asked Hue about his personal bravery and his hopes for his own future. Hue's answer was simple and enlightening. He responded, "I am a soldier. I was born during the war, and I will die on the battle-field."[64] Indeed, Hue and Dinh knew nothing but war, the sad reality of South Vietnam. They had both learned much in their time in combat, and, though problems obviously remained at several levels, both believed that the ARVN was capable of ultimate victory, with reform and continued American support. Their beliefs, were about to be put to the test in the Tet Offensive, an attack that sapped American will on the homefront but served as the ARVN's finest hour.

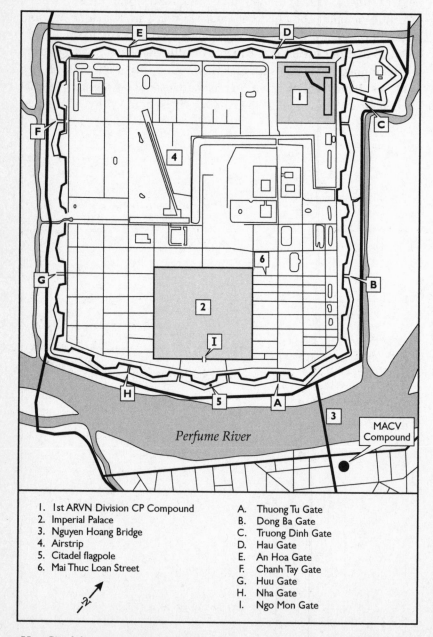

1. 1st ARVN Division CP Compound
2. Imperial Palace
3. Nguyen Hoang Bridge
4. Airstrip
5. Citadel flagpole
6. Mai Thuc Loan Street

A. Thuong Tu Gate
B. Dong Ba Gate
C. Truong Dinh Gate
D. Hau Gate
E. An Hoa Gate
F. Chanh Tay Gate
G. Huu Gate
H. Nha Gate
I. Ngo Mon Gate

Hue Citadel

4

A Time for Heroes

The Tet Offensive

THE TET OFFENSIVE was the crushingly ironic series of battles that sealed the fate of the American military effort in South Vietnam. Having devoted thousands of lives to their war of attrition, American forces had arguably achieved a great measure of success by the opening of 1968, imposing prodigious losses on communist forces. Even so, the VC and the NVA, in their revolutionary zeal, believed that ultimate victory beckoned through a military "propaganda of the deed" and that an offensive targeting the vulnerable urban areas throughout South Vietnam would provoke a mass uprising, overthrow the Saigon regime, and oust its American backers. Additionally, the communists, as they had throughout the conflict, designed their military planning with careful attention to the U.S. homefront[1] and hoped both to prey upon the fickle will of the American people and to spur antiwar elements in the United States to greater levels of protest. However, recent history also suggests that the communist leadership undertook the Tet Offensive as something of a desperate gamble—unsure if the critical morale that undergirded the NVA and VC war effort was sufficient to withstand several more years of attrition.

Tet proved to be an unmitigated military disaster for both the NVA and especially the VC. The insurgents had chosen to stand and fight, but in the end the population did not rise up and left the VC and NVA to suffer severe losses at the hands of U.S. and ARVN firepower. Driven from the cities, and with the VC smashed as an effective fighting force, the communists were forced onto the defensive and surrendered land that had been under their control for years. Apart from the physical losses suffered during Tet, the ambivalence of the South Vietnamese population forced the communists to consider the nearly unthinkable possibility that the people of South Vietnam were something more than the unwitting stooges of American imperialism. The losses and the realization that South Vietnam was more resilient than they had ever imagined led the communists to several conclusions. The war would be longer and more difficult than even they had imagined and, with the loss of so many VC cadre, would also become increasingly more conventional in nature, thus playing to the strengths of the U.S. and ARVN forces. However, even as the communists faced the specter of their own military fallibility, the will of the United States to persevere in the Vietnam War began to implode.

The critical events of 1968 are seared into the American consciousness and national psyche, painful pictures that tell the story of a war gone awry: vivid images including Westmoreland's pre-Tet confident prediction, made in November 1967, that "We have reached an important point when the end begins to come into view. . . . The enemy's hopes are bankrupt";[2] scenes of bitter fighting in the U.S. Embassy compound in Saigon; the CBS anchorman Walter Cronkite declaring that the war could not be won; Lyndon Johnson, worn down and beaten by years of war, declining to run again for the presidency; American cities on fire; and riots in Chicago during the Democratic National Convention. The disparate elements of disunity, ranging from the growth of the counterculture to dissatisfaction with a war that nobody really understood, came together powerfully in one critical moment that perhaps best defined the limitations of the American century. Historical and popular attention has focused on this most central moment of the uniquely American tragedy that was the Vietnam War, attention that seeks to explain how such an overwhelming tactical victory actually led to eventual defeat.

Scapegoats for the sorry situation abound. Westmoreland was at fault because he had never really understood the Vietnam War at all. Politicians were at fault, for they had hamstrung the valiant efforts of the U.S. military. The media were at fault for their tireless efforts to turn the American populace against the war.

Much American scholarship, though, has left a rather glaring hole in our understanding of the Tet Offensive and its place in the Vietnam War. Though the VC and the NVA often play leading roles as the story's protagonists, the ARVN and the South Vietnamese population are often consigned to the footnotes and sidebars of the history of the offensive and its aftermath. The popular historical view is flawed, for in most ways the Tet Offensive was a fratricidal affair, aimed at destroying the ARVN and provoking an uprising to oust the Americans.

The VC and the NVA realized that they could not defeat the Americans in battle; their only hope was to destroy the political and military structure of South Vietnam to present the mighty Americans with a fait accompli. That the South Vietnamese population did not rise up, that the ARVN fought bravely—more bravely than the Americans dared hope—was critical to the tactical success of the battle and portended well for the future of South Vietnam. In reality, most of the fighting and dying in the Tet Offensive, especially in the critical battles in Hue City, fell to the ARVN, a tragic victory won by a nation that did not survive to tell its own story. It was the finest hour of the ARVN, a time when both Dinh and Hue would be lauded as heroes. Not fully understanding the calamity that was befalling the United States, it was a time for South Vietnam to look forward to potential victory in its lengthy and brutal war.

Planning

Whether from desperation or revolutionary ardor, the NVA and the VC, in late January 1968, stood ready, in the words of NVA historians:

> to "mobilize the greatest effort of the entire Party, the entire armed forces, and the entire populace of both regions *to take our revolutionary war to a new and highest level of development, to employ a general offensive and general uprising to secure a decisive victory*" . . . and employ *attacks by armed forces in the principle theaters and popular uprising in the large cities and towns as the two main spearheads of the offensive.*[3]

Although the Tet Offensive struck at urban centers across the length and breadth of South Vietnam, Saigon and Hue were the logical focal points of communist attention and aggression. Saigon, the very heart of the U.S./ARVN war effort, carried a rather obvious significance, while Hue City, the historic seat of Vietnamese emperors, served in many ways as the soul of South Vietnam. The third largest city in South Vietnam, containing a population in 1968 of 140,000, Hue is divided by the meandering Perfume River, with the modern and bustling New City to the south and the older walled Citadel, which houses the Imperial Palace, to the north. In 1802, Emperor Gia Long began work on the Citadel and designed the walled imperial city to impose a sense of awe upon the Vietnamese population. Defended by a moat and by six-meter-high earth-filled masonry walls that are in some places seventy-five meters thick, the Citadel houses an entire city, jammed with streets, parks, homes, shops, and government buildings. In the southeastern section of the walled city, with its corners aligned to the four cardinal directions, stands the Imperial Palace, with walls two to five meters in height and measuring seven hundred meters to a side. In all, the massive Citadel encompasses an area of more than six square kilometers,[4] and, while it was a camera-carrying tourist's dream, it would become a rifle-carrying infantryman's nightmare.[5]

The VC and the NVA were fully aware that in a campaign meant to spark an uprising among a South Vietnamese population bedazzled by the wealth of their American sponsors, control of the Citadel would be invaluable. Raising the NLF banner aloft above the seat of Vietnamese emperors would inherit for the VC the mantle of Vietnam's glorious nationalistic past, while demonstrating the impotence of the ARVN and U.S. forces and the moral bankruptcy of the Saigon regime. The VC and the NVA also realized that a seizure of the Citadel would be of great value even if the population did not rise up in revolt. Once ensconced in the rabbit warren of defenses, towers and byways of the walled complex, the NVA and the VC would be devilishly difficult to dislodge, imposing a bloody urban battle of attrition on the ARVN and U.S. forces, a battle that would capture the imagination of the world's press and inflame antiwar ardor on the streets of the United States.

Hue City stood nearly defenseless against the coming attack. A center of both historic and spiritual significance, Hue had always been something of an open city and was only lightly defended, while the vast majority of the ARVN and U.S. forces were scattered throughout the countryside surrounding Hue and were engaged in the war of attrition. In the Citadel, General Truong and the 1st ARVN Division could call upon only the strength of a headquarters company, a small reconnaissance company, and Tran Ngoc Hue's Hac Bao. The only American presence in the city was the MACV compound south of the river, which housed a varied group of 150 U.S. advisers and MACV staffers.

During November 1967, Dinh had rotated out of Quang Dien District, leaving behind an example of pacification success, and moved to

Xuac Xu fire base some ten kilometers north of Hue City to take part in the routine of patrol and ambush in support of pacification that so typified ARVN tactics.[6] For their part, Tran Ngoc Hue and the Hac Bao, still recovering from the exertions of battle near Phu Loc, remained busy with their constant training regimen near the airstrip in the Hue Citadel.[7] As the Tet Lunar New Year neared, ARVN soldiers looked forward to visiting their families during a ceasefire scheduled in honor of the holiday. Tet is a joyous time throughout Vietnam, by far the most important holiday of the year, both a time of atonement and an opportunity to celebrate the family and village ties that bind the Vietnamese so closely to one another. The communists hoped to achieve complete surprise by launching their attack during the holiday, seizing control as the ARVN made merry. The nationwide VC and NVA buildup for the offensive, however, had attracted some unwanted attention and had led many within the American military and the ARVN to suspect that the communists would break the Tet truce. Nobody within the allied camp suspected the scale or goal of the coming Tet Offensive, however, resulting in one of the most infamous intelligence disasters in American military history.

The situation in and around Hue City was especially tense. Because of a significant rise in combat activity, General Truong was aware of an enemy buildup in his AO and believed that the Tet truce would not hold. Acting on a hunch, on 30 January, Truong made a critical decision and called off the coveted Tet leave for the soldiers of 1st ARVN Division. Although some soldiers and officers had already departed for the holiday, the remaining units and commanders were put on high alert. For his part, Truong decided to remain at his headquarters rather than spend the holiday at his home south of the Perfume River, a decision that saved his life. Not privy to Truong's decision, Jim Coolican made his way to the MACV compound in an effort to allow the hard-fighting members of the Hac Bao freedom to celebrate Tet in their own way. At the same time, Colonel George Adkisson, new on the job as General Truong's senior adviser, also returned to the MACV compound. Adkisson was well aware of Truong's assessment of the situation and knew that the NVA and the VC were up to something, and, as he reached his quarters, he slowly drifted off to sleep, troubled by a feeling of impending doom.[8]

Expecting some sort of VC or NVA action within his AO, Truong deployed his thirty-six-man Reconnaissance Company to the western approaches of the city to act as an early-warning force. The move left only the Hac Bao Company, with its six all-volunteer platoons, to defend the entire urban area of Hue City. Accordingly, Tran Ngoc Hue sent three platoons south of the Perfume River to defend strategic points there, including the province prison, and detailed two platoons to guard the nine gates into the Citadel in an effort to control access into the vulnerable city. Thus, the Hac Bao were dispersed, leaving only Hue's remaining force of fifty men to stand between the coming NVA assault on the Citadel proper and victory.

Assault on Hue City

The Reconnaissance Company almost immediately reported heavy contact with NVA infiltrators, but still the scale of the attack that broke upon the city of Hue in the predawn hours of 31 January was shocking. Initially, the NVA devoted two entire battalions and specialist sapper units to the attack on the Citadel, with the 802nd Battalion tasked with overrunning the 1st ARVN Division headquarters while the 800th Battalion occupied the residential areas of the walled city. The remainder of the NVA 6th Regiment worked to cut off Hue City from ARVN reinforcement. South of the Perfume River, the 4th NVA Regiment moved in a similar fashion on the New City, detailing its 804th Battalion both to seize much of the New City itself and to attack the MACV compound.[9]

The initial salvos of incoming artillery and rocket fire awakened Tran Ngoc Hue at his home in the northwest portion of the Citadel. It only slowly dawned on Hue that the fire was not the usual explosions of myriad fireworks in celebration of Tet but something much more sinister. Hue bundled his parents, wife, and daughter into the family bunker and prepared to rejoin his unit, stationed near the small Citadel airfield. Without a jeep for transportation, Hue commandeered his father's bicycle and pedaled toward the Hac Bao perimeter. Hue soon noticed hundreds of NVA soldiers moving in the direction of 1st ARVN Division HQ. As it became apparent that the entire city was under attack, Hue's thoughts shifted to his family; he was the father of an infant daughter; he was the senior son of elderly parents. Hue hesitated and wondered if he should return home and care for his loved ones in their time of greatest need. Hue decided, though, that his duty was with his ARVN brethren, for if his homeland fell to the hated invader his family would have no future for which to fight. Galvanized, Hue brazenly joined the marching NVA, hoping that darkness would cover his identity. After a harrowing journey, Hue finally regained the Hac Bao lines just in time to face a frontal assault by the 800th NVA Battalion.

As the NVA surged forward again and again, what amounted to a reinforced Hac Bao platoon stood firm in its defensive bunkers firing light antitank weapons (LAWs) into the massed enemy ranks with devastating effect. In fighting so difficult that even the NVA grudgingly admitted the fierceness of Hac Bao resistance,[10] Hue and his men killed fifty enemy soldiers and diverted the strength of the 800th Battalion from the airfield.[11] During the confused battle, the Hac Bao rescued two dazed American soldiers who had been caught in the crossfire and captured three NVA prisoners.[12] Tragically, as the battle raged around him, Hue learned that the platoon he had detached to defend the provincial jail was being overrun and destroyed south of the Perfume River. The last communication that Hue received from the doomed platoon leader, as he instructed his men to fix bayonets, was a request for Hue to look after his wife and seven children.[13]

The assault on Hue City had potentially devastating personal implications, for the Hac Bao and their commander were natives of the Hue area, and by the morning of 31 January they were all well aware that the attack on Hue was bigger than anything they had ever before witnessed. The VC and NVA forces were overwhelming and occupying their city, leaving Tran Ngoc Hue and his men with the realization that their homes and families had fallen into enemy hands. Grimly the men recalled that, because of their fearless nature in battle, there was a bounty on the heads of their family members.[14] Even so, Hue and his unit fought on, registering no desertions in the long and difficult struggle. In fact, the Hac Bao fighters were bothered by a problem of a different sort; they were swamped by ARVN volunteers trying to enter their ranks to fight in defense of Hue City.

Though the Hac Bao had blunted the attack of the 800th Battalion, the scant defenses of Truong's command post (CP) fell under assault by a specially trained NVA sapper unit and elements of the 802nd Battalion. A scratch force assembled from the two hundred clerks, doctors, and patients present in the CP fought a desperate, sometimes hand-to-hand struggle and drove the NVA back only after their attack had reached within sixty feet of Truong's office. There was no time to celebrate, for Truong realized that communist forces meant to overrun the entire Citadel and that his CP was their ultimate goal. The NVA would return in ever greater numbers, and unless reinforcements arrived quickly, his tiny force was doomed. General Truong immediately issued calls directing the scattered elements of the 1st ARVN Division to rush to the defense of the Citadel and Hue City. However, the offensive was so widespread that several of Truong's outlying units were already themselves under attack, and VC and NVA forces had blocked all major approaches to the Citadel.

Just before 0700, Tran Ngoc Hue received a radio communication from Lieutenant Colonel Ngo Van Chung at 1st ARVN Division HQ directing the Hac Bao to pull out of its defensive positions at the airfield to reinforce the CP garrison. Lieutenant Colonel Chung also ordered the 7th ARVN Cavalry Squadron to the CP, only to learn that the unit was itself surrounded and under heavy attack. Having overheard Lieutenant Colonel Chung's distress calls, and learning that only the Hac Bao fighters were close enough to offer reinforcement to the beleaguered defenders of the 1st ARVN Division CP, Hue leapt into action.

Realizing that the entire Citadel was at risk of being lost and that the Hac Bao fighters were vastly outnumbered, Hue rallied his men. Bellowing above the din of the continuing fighting, Hue told his small band:

> The VC and the NVA have betrayed the Tet truce and have launched an attack across the country. Because of their attack, war has come to Hue City and the situation is extremely dangerous. We have lost communication with one of our Hac Bao detachments on security duty south of the Perfume River. I do not know their fate. I don't know who among our brothers have survived. The enemy has pushed us into a corner! We must fight for our own survival, for the survival of our families, the survival of Hue City and the survival of our fatherland! Will you fight with me?
>
> His men responded with calls of "commitment," and "freedom or death!"

Tran Ngoc Hue then stated, "Now we have a very, very important mission; we must save the 1st Division HQ, which is under siege by enemy forces. We must raise this siege at any price! We must prove that we are the best of the 1st ARVN division and can defeat any foe!" Hue then shouted "Hac Bao!" as loudly as he could, and his men cried out "Hurrah, hurrah, hurrah!" in unison.

Utilizing local knowledge and the aid of civilians, the Hac Bao slipped unnoticed through the labyrinth of enemy-held streets, demonstrating a fundamental NVA weakness in the struggle for Hue City. Expecting to seize the city easily and believing that the population and even the ARVN would rally to its cause, the NVA was not prepared to face and defeat stern resistance. The few ARVN forces on hand in the Citadel and the ad hoc force defending the MACV compound south of the Perfume River would have stood little chance against a truly coordinated, continuous assault—or even against well-managed blocking positions designed to prevent the arrival of reinforcements.[15] Amazingly, though, the NVA units in the main seized only their assigned targets and hunkered down in defense instead of seizing and maintaining the initiative. Thanks in part to NVA mistakes and rampant overoptimism, then, the Hac Bao were able to approach the 1st ARVN Division HQ without incident.

The situation for General Truong and his men was dire; NVA sappers had once again penetrated through and over the wall surrounding the CP and engaged the beleaguered defenders in hand-to-hand combat. Intent on the kill, the NVA and the VC remained unaware of the Hac Bao's approach. Utilizing almost complete surprise, the tiny Hac Bao force unleashed a deadly salvo of LAW fire, destroying two NVA machine-gun nests, and burst into the CP. Fighting inside the CP was bitter and raged from room to room, but the sudden arrival of the Hac Bao resulted in a communist withdrawal.

Truong was happy to see his young Hac Bao commander, but he also realized that the crisis was not nearly over, because the cobbled-together ARVN force, still mostly made up of non-combatants, now faced off against the entire 802nd Battalion, elements of the 800th Battalion, and most of the 12th Sapper Battalion. But the NVA seemed bewildered that the ARVN soldiers were still fighting, and its attacks came in only piecemeal fashion, while the majority of the enemy force made ready to impose the reality of their revolution on the citizens of Hue City. From a position atop a tower within the CP, Tran Ngoc Hue took command of the defenders and successfully directed fire against successive NVA efforts to scale the surrounding walls. Cut off and running low on all types of supplies, the embattled force at Truong's CP held out, while so many NVA dead piled up all around that their bodies had to be soaked in gasoline and burned.

The fighting at 1st ARVN Division HQ raged for more than a day before the 1st ARVN Airborne Task Force broke through NVA blocking positions and reached the CP from the north. With the survival of the 1st ARVN Division HQ no longer in doubt, General Truong took stock of a difficult situation. NVA and VC forces, constantly re-supplied and reinforced, had taken most of the Citadel, leaving only Truong's tiny CP in ARVN hands. In many ways, the fight for the Citadel was only beginning, but Truong realized that the Hac Bao's defense of the 1st ARVN Division HQ left ARVN forces with an enclave within the Citadel, a bridgehead from which to launch their counter-offensive. Without possession of 1st ARVN Division HQ, retaking the Citadel would have been altogether more difficult, requiring an assault on the massive walls from without by main force. The retention of the 1st ARVN Division HQ was indeed so important that even NVA historians look back at failure to take the HQ as their most important mistake in the epic struggle for Hue City.[16]

The Struggle at MACV

At the tiny MACV compound south of the Perfume River, Colonel Adkisson's forebodings had proven correct when, at 0300, mortar rounds and rockets slammed into the enclosure, quickly rousing the varied group of 150 off-duty advisers, staffers, and Marine guards. Amazingly, there was something of a lull in the intense fire before a dedicated NVA sapper platoon launched its ground assault on Adkisson's hastily organized defenders. As the ground attack commenced, Jim Coolican, denied his restful Tet break from duties as adviser to the Hac Bao, made his way to the top of a sentry tower, still smoking from a direct hit from an NVA mortar round. After tending to the wounded tower sentry, Coolican began to direct high-explosive grenade fire on the NVA attackers with an M-79 grenade launcher he had had the foresight to "liberate" from the MACV armory.[17]

The fighting in the predawn hours was tense, but the Americans succeeded in driving the NVA back from the MACV compound by first light. Surrounded and in danger of being overwhelmed, the Ameri-

cans sent out a call for help and reached the 1st Marine Division forward headquarters at Phu Bai, which itself was under attack, some
eleven kilometers south of Hue City. Unaware that Hue City was cur-
rently under attack by a division-size enemy force with supplies, ammunition, and reinforcements enough to fight a long and arduous battle, Brigadier General Foster LaHue initially sent a single company of
Marines to rescue the stranded defenders at MACV.[18]

Company A, 1st Battalion, 1st Marines (Alpha 1/1), already tired
and understrength, left Phu Bai at 0830 but found its advance halted
by strong enemy contact before reaching the city proper. Company G,
2nd Battalion, 5th Marines (Golf 2/5) soon arrived to aid the stranded
Marines and, after heavy fighting, broke through to the MACV compound. Though the situation remained dire for the surrounded garrison, especially for the wounded, the immediate danger had passed.
There was no time to rest, though, for the fewer than three hundred
Marines on hand had received orders to cross the Perfume River and
link up with Truong's forces in the Citadel. Amid mounting tension between Lieutenant Colonel Mark Gravel, commander of the 1st Battalion, 1st Marines, and Colonel Adkisson, who strongly advised against
assaulting the Citadel with such a small force, the Marines moved out
across the bridge over the Perfume River. NVA forces were seemingly
everywhere, and, though the Marines struggled heroically against impossible odds, they were eventually forced to retreat.[19]

With the fighting at a stalemate, reinforcements only trickled into
the battle area of the New City, now the AO of the Marines, until 3
February, when the nature of the enemy forces they faced had become
apparent.[20] Soon brought up to a force of regimental size, the U.S.
Marines proceeded into the hell of urban warfare, in which the NVA
proved adept and resilient in a defensive house-to-house and sometimes room-to-room struggle. The Marines learned urban warfare in
difficult on-the-job training and made especially devastating use of direct supporting fire provided by 106-millimeter recoilless rifles.[21] With
great gallantry and determination, the Marines singlehandedly liberated the New City from NVA control in fighting that has rightly gone
down in Marine lore.

The goal of the Tet Offensive, though, was not to defeat the Americans directly in battle but rather to defeat the ARVN and the national
will of South Vietnam, and as such the struggle for the Citadel formed
the fulcrum of NVA and VC effort. If the ARVN had failed there, it

would have provided the NVA with a propaganda coup and could have proved catastrophic to South Vietnam's war efforts as a whole. While the Americans, typified by the Marines in the New City, fought wonderfully and were instrumental in the defeat of the Tet Offensive, the decision in the end rested with the ARVN. Had it not stood and fought, and fought well, all would have been lost.

Reinforcements for the Citadel

In the early morning hours of 31 January, Dinh's 2/3 ARVN found itself under attack on a broad frontage and reacted by concentrating its widely scattered units. With U.S. adviser Captain Joe Bolt cut off from all communication with MACV headquarters and Dinh able to receive only sporadic and partial information from the besieged 1st ARVN Division CP in the Citadel, nobody knew what was happening as the countryside erupted with enemy fire. As dawn broke, though, the scale of events became clearer, for, from their hilltop headquarters, Dinh and Bolt could see NVA forces streaming down Highway 1 toward Hue City. At noon, orders came in from Truong's CP for 2/3 to fight its way to the Citadel, but, since Truong was cut off and unable to see beyond the battle raging in his own CP, Dinh and 2/3 would have to advance blindly toward the maelstrom.

Pausing only to gather what weapons and ammunition they could carry, Dinh and 2/3 set off into the unknown, with no idea of what they would face or whether they would survive. With 20 percent of the battalion absent on Tet leave, the strength of 2/3 was already depleted. Making matters worse, one company of 2/3 had been marooned across Highway 1 and was unable to carve its way through a large NVA blocking force there and had to be left behind, while Dinh also had to assign a platoon to stand rear guard at his base at Xuac Xu, which left 2/3 with a total of only 260 men. Realizing that his small and lightly armed force could not advance down Highway 1, Dinh decided to rely on stealth and took his battalion to Hue City by moving through the surrounding rugged hill country. By midafternoon, 2/3 had reached the Perfume River and began to move east through more open ground. Suddenly a U.S. helicopter appeared overhead and flew a slow circuit above Dinh's men before lining up for a second pass. Realizing what was happening, Bolt yelled for the men to get off the road just before the helicopter, mistaking 2/3 for NVA, began an attack run. After extricating himself from the river, Bolt ran up the bank and took off his shirt and began waving his arms at the helicopter, which was lining up for a second attack. Recognizing Bolt as an American by the color of his skin, the helicopter peeled away, and 2/3 regrouped for its final push toward Hue.[22]

Upon nearing the railroad bridge just outside the city proper, 2/3 fell under RPG and small-arms fire from NVA defensive positions. Dinh threw two companies into the battle, and his men soon routed the NVA force and entered the area of Hue outside the southeast wall of the Citadel as evening fell on 31 January—the first major ARVN force to reach the beleaguered city. Having lost the element of surprise, though, 2/3 quickly came under fire from NVA defenders on both sides of the Perfume River. Using the gathering darkness to its advantage, 2/3 fanned out and advanced down the northern bank of the Perfume as far as the main Truong-Tien Bridge, where the unit fought a night engagement in a nearby open market before taking the site over as battalion CP. Having lost ten dead and numerous wounded, 2/3 ARVN fought on alone, knowing neither the location of friendly units nor the location or strength of the enemy. However, it was obvious to Dinh and his men that the situation in Hue City was dire, an awareness made worse by the fact that Dinh's wife, Duong Thi Thu Huong, and two young children and the families of most of his men were in a city now held by the NVA and the VC.[23]

The next morning, Dinh received orders to break into the Citadel itself and to advance to Truong's CP, and, as a result, 2/3 launched an assault on the Ngan Gate to the northeast of the flag tower, only to be repulsed by the determined NVA defenders. Unable to advance through the gate, the 2/3 next attempted a brazen assault over the Citadel walls. While machine gunners stationed atop nearby buildings provided covering fire, a squad of the 2/3 rushed forward with ladders. Clambering up and over the walls, the squad entered the Citadel, only to be destroyed as Dinh and the remainder of 2/3 listened helplessly as a hail of gunfire and screaming erupted from within.[24]

Since efforts to enter the Citadel through the teeth of the NVA defensive network were futile, and reinforcements had arrived to stabilize the situation at Truong's CP, 2/3 received new orders, and Dinh's men, much more used to fighting an elusive enemy in the countryside, made ready to clear enemy forces from the residential zone between

An aerial view of the southeastern portion of the Hue Citadel. 2/3 ARVN under Pham Van Dinh initially fought in the downtown area between the walls
of the Citadel and the Perfume River. To the right of the photograph is the
bridge into the Gia Hoa area of Hue City; in the center is the ruined span of
the bridge leading to the MACV Compound. Photograph VA035396, 24 June
1968, Peter Braestrup Collection, The Vietnam Archive, Texas Tech University.

the Citadel and the Perfume River. Facing an estimated company of
determined NVA defenders, 2/3 engaged in a day of bitter, house-to-
house and room-to-room fighting, sweeping through more than one
hundred buildings in the downtown area. In the ensuing two days
2/3, joined by the 3rd Battalion 3rd Regiment, next launched five attacks on the bridge over the river into the Gia Hoi District of Hue but
failed because of a lack of heavy-weapons support.

   Dinh's 2/3 was running critically low on food and ammunition
since the confused situation, bad weather, and heavy fighting had pre-
cluded helicopter resupply efforts or medevacs. In a lull in the fighting,
Joe Bolt made a dash across the Truong-Tien Bridge, as sniper rounds
pinged off the superstructure above him, to the MACV compound in

search of supplies. Inside, he found organized chaos as the Marines were under siege by a bevy of reporters who had descended upon the compound to cover the ongoing urban fighting. After scrounging up a jeepload of ammunition and C-rations, Bolt asked if any of the journalists wanted to return with him to report the ARVN side of the battle. Only the indomitable French female reporter Cathy LeRoy, who had previously been wounded while covering a battle and had also been briefly held captive by the NVA, took Bolt up on his offer and made a short foray to interview Dinh on his role in the ongoing battle.

After Bolt's return, and hoping to catch NVA defenders in the Citadel in a vise, Truong ordered the 4th Battalion, 3rd Regiment to join the fight southeast of the Citadel. Elements of the strengthened force then launched seven costly attacks against the Citadel walls, now a rabbit's warren of interlocking defenses.[25] Having failed to breach the NVA positions, it was now obvious that 2/3, now with fewer than two hundred men, along with 3/3 and 4/3, would have to find another way to join the ongoing fight in the Citadel—operations that were quickly becoming the focal point of the entire Tet Offensive and the area where the NVA had decided to make its final stand.

Counterattack

On paper, the ARVN forces within the Citadel, including the recently arrived 1st Airborne Task Force and the 3rd Squadron, 7th Cavalry, outnumbered those of the enemy, but reality was much different. Chronically short on supplies, all of the ARVN battalions at Truong's disposal were understrength, having left behind elements to hold base areas and supply lines and having taken losses in their fight to get to Hue City. They now faced nearly four well-supplied and constantly reinforced NVA battalions that were dug into imposing defensive positions and ready to resist to the last man. Additionally, the ARVN was unable to make use of the important force multiplier that so aided the U.S. Marines in their own urban nightmare in Hue, heavy direct-fire weapons. In the words of Colonel George Adkisson, "The lack of heavy direct fire weapons, particularly 106mm recoilless rifles, limited [South] Vietnamese capability in the face of well entrenched enemy and well positioned small detachments were able to stop the progress of entire companies repeatedly."[26] Already depleted ARVN units, facing the brunt of the continuing NVA military effort, had to substitute manpower for firepower in their efforts to move forward, resulting in severe casualties.[27] Still the ARVN persevered.

On 1 February, Tran Ngoc Hue and his Hac Bao accompanied three ARVN battalions and made the first concerted ARVN counterattack in the Citadel, moving along the northwestern wall in an effort to recapture the airfield. In two days of hard fighting, the units succeeded in their mission and killed more than two hundred enemy. During the fighting, Jim Coolican suddenly reappeared among the Hac Bao, having made a harrowing ride on one of the first resupply helicopters to dare make the flight to Truong's surrounded CP. Hue was surprised to see his adviser return in the midst of battle but covered his happiness with dry humor and said, "It's about time you got back. You have been gone so long that I thought you deserted."

In the next two days, reinforcements from the 1st Battalion, 3rd Regiment and 4th Battalion, 2nd Regiment fought their way to the An Hoa Gate, liberating most of the northwestern wall of the Citadel and resulting in an astounding additional 693 enemy killed in action (KIA).[28] ARVN forces now controlled the more open areas of the northern sector of the Citadel and were poised to launch attacks throughout the remainder of the city. The worst of the fighting, however, was yet to come. The NVA and the VC retained a viable logistic network running west from the Citadel, and radio intercepts indicated that the NVA and the VC had decided to hold in their sectors of the city "at all costs." Making matters worse, the ARVN now entered the narrow streets and byways of the crowded residential areas where NVA forces manned carefully planned, mutually supporting defensive positions. Although the ARVN advance ground to a halt, during the ebb and flow of battle the Hac Bao liberated Tran Ngoc Hue's own home. As his unit struggled forward, Hue assumed the worst when he saw that the structure had been destroyed, but, upon entering the charred ruins, Hue found his loved ones battered but alive, still huddled in the family bunker.

Enter the Marines

Although the initiative had passed to the ARVN in the Citadel, many of its units were exhausted, and supplies of all types, from food to ammunition, remained critically low. George Smith, on the 1st ARVN Division's advisory staff, put the situation well:

> Much of the news in the Citadel over the first week was bad. . . . By 4 February, the 3/7 Cavalry was down to . . . 40 men. The three airborne units [making up the 1st Airborne Task Force] were also badly depleted. The 7th and 9th Airborne Battalions, as well as 1/3, had each lost one of its companies in bitter fighting on 31 January before they arrived in the Citadel. The 4/2, which had been flown in from Dong Ha on 1 and 2 February, was having a difficult time covering a wide front to the southeast of the ARVN 1st Division compound. Something had to be done to put more life in the ARVN units holding on in the Citadel.[29]

With dwindling resources and reserves and his units stalled, General Truong called ever more ARVN forces to join the fight for the Citadel, including the 2nd Squadron, 7th Cavalry and all three battalions of the 3rd Regiment, which had been marooned southeast of the Citadel wall. While 2/7 fought a heavy engagement just to reach the Truong's CP, the battalions of the 3rd Regiment, including Dinh's 2/3, on 7 February made their way to the 1st ARVN Division CP on boats via the Perfume River. The week of fighting since leaving Xuac Xu fire base had been emotionally hard for Dinh, who knew only that his wife and children were lost somewhere in the inferno of the Citadel. Upon Dinh's arrival at the CP, Truong took his young commander aside and gave him the news that his family was safe. After nearly being captured, Dinh's wife had taken her young children and fled their home, some three kilometers distant from General Truong's CP, posing as refugees. Hiding among the throng of people displaced by the urban battle, the Phams stayed with friends and moved ever closer to the CP, finally reaching ARVN lines. After a tearful reunion, Dinh, like Tran Ngoc Hue before him, continued the fight.

As the ARVN fighting in the Citadel continued and reinforcements gathered, on 10 February the ARVN General Headquarters in Saigon complicated matters by demanding the return of the severely bloodied airborne battalions, part of the ARVN General Headquarters reserve, which threatened to leave General Truong critically shorthanded. Accordingly, Truong requested that the airborne battalions be replaced by units of similar strength. After some indecision, the ARVN

General Headquarters relented and promised two battalions of Vietnamese Marines. Realizing that the tenacity of the NVA defenders and the strength of their positions portended a difficult struggle, Truong pressed for still more aid. As a result of Truong's insistence, MACV and the ARVN decided to send a U.S. Marine infantry battalion to take part in the battle for the Citadel.[30]

In the predawn hours of 11 February, Major Robert Thompson, commander of the 1st Battalion, 5th Marines, which had already seen serious Tet fighting around Phu Loc, received a call to be ready for immediate redeployment. After some delay and confusion, on 12 February Thompson's Marines, accompanied by five tanks and several ONTOS vehicles, which were tracked vehicles, each armed with four of the 106mm recoilless rifles that had been found to be so valuable in the struggle for the New City, reached Truong's headquarters and prepared for battle. Truong greeted Thompson's arrival with great happiness, for the 1st ARVN Division commander realized that the battle, though destined to be difficult, was now won. The Marines, with their organic fire support, packed a much greater punch than did his depleted ARVN units, and the weather had cleared, which allowed for much more effective use of air power to aid in the coming advance.[31]

Truong planned for a two-pronged assault against the NVA-controlled areas of the Citadel that was aimed at the all-important Imperial Palace and the hated NLF banner that fluttered atop the flagpole near the southeastern Citadel wall. Truong tasked the 3rd Regiment, reliant on the power of two battalions of newly arrived Vietnamese Marines, with retaking the southwestern portion of the Citadel. Thompson's U.S. Marines were to relieve the departing ARVN airborne battalions in place and then advance toward the southeast adjacent to the Citadel wall, through some of the most densely built-up and heavily defended real estate in the tortured city.

At dawn on 13 February, the 1/5 Marines moved out to take up positions on a line that ran along Mai Thuc Loan Street from the Dong Ba Gate to the northern corner of the Imperial Palace. The relief in place of the ARVN airborne units, though, proved chaotic and deadly, for, due in part to delays and command misunderstandings, the airborne had pulled back too early and had allowed the NVA to retake several critical defensive positions. The unsuspecting Marines ran into a hail of NVA fire, which resulted in immediate and bitter fighting that focused on the Citadel wall and at the tower above the Dong Ba Gate, which had fallen to the NVA amid the confusion.

The battle heralded a week of bloody fighting for the Marines, who faced a battlefield that consisted of tiny buildings along winding and unfamiliar streets—all overlooked by powerful NVA positions honeycombed into the walls of the Citadel itself on one side and the Imperial Palace on the other. Learning the difficult art of urban warfare as they went, 1/5 advanced house by house and block by torturous block against fanatical NVA resistance and upheld the very best of Marine tradition.

Though the bulk of the fighting in the southeast fell to the Marines, they were not alone in their struggle. Aware that the territory of the Citadel was unfamiliar to the Americans, Truong attached Dinh's 2/3 ARVN to the Marines' right flank. With ranks depleted by more than eleven days of battle, 2/3 now faced its hardest fighting of the entire conflict. As the soldiers neared the frontlines to link up with the Marines, a mortar shell crashed down, blowing the legs off of one ARVN soldier, presaging a bitter struggle. In the house-to-house fighting that ensued, the NVA set up mutually supporting defensive positions in buildings that flanked the winding roads, with snipers firing from upper floors and numerous defenders in lower windows or doorways creating a deadly crossfire that converted the streets into kill zones. Lacking heavy-weapons support, 2/3 attempted to deal with such defenses by having elements of the battalion lay down covering fire while others dashed forward. In one of the first attempts to use such tactics, Joe Bolt was slated to be second to rush across the street, but no sooner had the first man in line stepped out from behind cover than he was hit in the chest by a sniper round, slamming back into Bolt and knocking him to the ground.[32]

With only small arms and no method to dislodge the snipers except to close with the entrenched enemy forces and deal with them at close range, 2/3 took heavy losses and made only fitful progress in its advance. Maddened by the mounting casualties, Joe Bolt took matters into his own hands and went to the neighboring Marines and secured the use of two 106mm recoilless rifles. Now, when taken under sniper fire, instead of launching an elaborate infantry assault on the sniper's position, the 106 simply destroyed the entire floor of the building in which the sniper had sought refuge. With the advantage of firepower,

2/3 continued its advance, but the fighting remained difficult, and fire came from every direction as NVA units sometimes reinfiltrated behind the advancing allied forces. Though it was slow learning and a difficult slog, Dinh and his men, fighting alongside the Marines, became adept at urban warfare and pressed ever closer to their goal of liberating the Citadel.

ARVN's Battle

While the 1/5 Marines, with the aid of Dinh's 2/3 ARVN, began its historic advance, it was the exclusive job of the remaining ARVN units, including the Vietnamese Marines, to clear the southwestern portion of the Citadel. Realizing that an ARVN advance to the southwest would cut critical logistic lines, the NVA reacted with great violence and on 14 February threw fresh reinforcements into a spoiling attack on ARVN lines near the Chanh Tay Gate and cut off 1/3 ARVN. Lacking in heavy direct-fire weapons, facing the brunt of enemy reinforcements, and receiving the least in the way of available air support, the ARVN's progress in the struggle was agonizingly slow. Serving in its familiar position as the divisional fire brigade, Tran Ngoc Hue's Hac Bao, along with the 2/7 Cavalry, rushed to the scene to attempt to break the encirclement. The fighting was bitter and confused, with Hue as usual leading his troops from the front. The seesaw battle lasted for two days, during which time the Hac Bao fighters were themselves surrounded, forcing Hue to call in an air strike on his own perimeter.[33]

After successfully blunting the NVA counterattack, the ARVN and Vietnamese Marines renewed their push in the southwest and within two days had reached the Chanh Tay Gate and the northwestern corner of the Imperial Palace.[34] Though progress remained slow, Truong expected the arrival soon of another battalion of Vietnamese Marines and felt that the odds in the area had shifted favorably toward the units under his command. At the same time, the U.S. Marines had taken heavy casualties, including forty-seven dead, were nearing exhaustion, and were even out of tank ammunition and shells for their 106mm recoilless rifles.[35] On their right flank, the 2/3 ARVN had lost some thirty dead, while killing fifty NVA.[36] Recognizing that the Marines and 2/3 were tiring, on 18 February, General Truong sent the

Hac Bao to help them in the final push toward the southeastern wall of the Citadel.[37]

The paths of Dinh and Hue had crossed yet again, allowing the comrades, both Truong's protégés, to work together toward the goal of ultimate victory in the most important battle of the war. The Hac Bao and 2/3 advanced side by side, their commanders for the first time sharing planning and acting as a team. Having seen constant action from the firing of the very first shots of the Tet Offensive, the Hac Bao were tired, not even having had time to change their tattered uniforms since the battle began. Upon reaching 2/3 and the Marines, though, Tran Ngoc Hue quickly demonstrated that the Hac Bao remained ready to fight. Tasked with advancing down the northeastern wall of the Imperial Palace, Hue made a startling request. "I asked Major Thompson to blow a hole in the wall [of the Imperial Palace] and my troops would rush in and kill everyone inside." Though he was impressed with Hue's bravery and the passion of his soldiers, Thompson rejected the offer, and the grinding advance of urban warfare continued.[38]

The battle for Hue City was drawing to its inevitable, bloody conclusion, and on 21 February the 1/5 Marines, the 2/3 ARVN, and the Hac Bao reached the southeastern wall of the Citadel. On the opposite flank, ARVN forces, making progress more slowly, pushed nearer to the Huu Gate, the last remaining entrance to the Citadel in NVA hands. Additionally, an offensive by the 3rd Brigade of the U.S. 1st Cavalry Division to the west of Hue City cut off the NVA from its source of supplies and reinforcements.

Isolated and facing certain destruction, the NVA again reacted with predictable fury, and, at 0630 on 22 February, it launched a surprise attack through the southwest wall aimed at exhausted elements of the 3rd ARVN Regiment and Vietnamese Marines. Again it fell to the Hac Bao to spearhead the ARVN response. Rushing from the side of the 1/5 Marines to the threatened area, Tran Ngoc Hue was disheartened to find ARVN troops fleeing in the face of the NVA attack. Threatening the fleeing soldiers with death, Hue and the Hac Bao quickly rallied the ARVN soldiers and extemporized a defensive line that halted the NVA advance in its tracks.

Hue and Coolican then called in air strikes and artillery support against enemy forces that were fatally caught in the open. After the fire abated, the Hac Bao charged forward, with bayonets fixed, into the wreckage of the smoldering battlefield. Advancing with his men, Hue could not believe his eyes; bodies, clad in new uniforms, were piled up as far as he could see, spilling forth from trenches and fox-holes and festooning bushes. Amid the devastation lay a tattered National Liberation Front flag, the forlorn symbol of the victory the VC had expected but had been unable to achieve.

Suddenly Hue received a radio transmission from an excited Lieutenant Phan Gia Lam reporting the capture of an enemy general, who sported three white stars on the collar of his uniform. It all seemed to make sense. The fresh troops, new uniforms, and a victory flag all denoted the presence of a great man. Eager to question the valuable prisoner, Hue rushed to the site. Instead of finding a communist general, though, Tran Ngoc Hue discovered that the captive was only a second lieutenant. It was the first time that the Hac Bao had ever captured an NVA soldier in his dress uniform, and they had been confused by the collar insignia. Satisfied concerning the prisoner's rank, Hue remained curious and asked why his unit wore dress uniforms and carried a flag. The dejected captive answered, "We were told that Hue City had been liberated and that we were coming here for a victory parade. The battle with your unit came as a surprise." The last NVA assault in Hue City, into which the NVA had even thrown troops meant for its victory parade, had failed, repelled and defeated by the same unit that had foiled the initial NVA assault on the Citadel nearly a month earlier.[39]

Victory

It remained for the weary and bloodied allied forces to seize the venerated Imperial Palace and the flag tower, upon which flew the hated flag of the NLF. Even this final act, though, was not without its share of revealing allied tension. As was becoming normal for the Vietnam War, a gaggle of accompanying journalists, who had identified the advance of the 1/5 Marines as "the story" of the ongoing Tet Offensive, followed the exploits of the unit with great intensity. The journalistic attention, though, was rather one-sided and began the process of marginalizing the ARVN contribution to the battle. Americans on the home front wanted to read stories about their countrymen, so there was no journalistic energy devoted to telling the story of the ARVN. In the words of Captain Jack Chase, an adviser with the ARVN 7th Cavalry:

In the first week we were [in the Citadel] the only time I saw somebody from the media was when we had just taken back the airfield.
A truck came up to cart off the bodies of some of our dead and I believe there was one photographer from the Associated Press who was
on the back of the truck. He snapped a couple of pictures but never
got off the truck. No wonder Americans think the Marines did all the
fighting.[40]

The Marine command structure was well aware of the value of the
journalistic attention lavished upon the brave actions of 1/5 Marines
in the Citadel. It was priceless positive coverage amid a series of Tet-
related military public relations nightmares that were unfolding daily
in newspapers and on television screens across the United States. The
Marines were justly portrayed as bloodied but undaunted in the grand
tradition of Belleau Wood and Mount Suribachi, persevering to victory against stalwart foes. The situation, though, could have turned
sour quickly had the 1/5 Marines been so badly battered that they had
to be relieved of their duties in the Citadel. The story could then have
transformed into one of pointless sacrifice of American lives, fast becoming a journalistic staple. As the 1/5 Marines had suffered through
the bitter fighting, Thompson had railed at higher headquarters for
aid—reinforcements, food, ammunition, permission to level the Imperial Palace—only to learn that 1/5 had to struggle onward as planned
to avoid a potential journalistic implosion. In the words of the historian Eric Hammel:

> Compounding the pressure was Thompson's certain knowledge that
> the 5th Marines commander was going to do everything in his power
> to obstruct the relief of 1/5 by Marines from any other regiment. The
> 5th Marines commander did not want a battalion from another Ma-
> rine regiment to go down in history as the liberators of the Citadel
> of Hue. Even higher Marine headquarters did not want any of the
> U.S. Army battalions then becoming available in I Corps to finish
> the job inside the Citadel. So, topping all their other priorities, Major
> Thompson and his hard-pressed staff found themselves saddled with
> the exigencies of making history.[41]

Regardless of balance of strength or motivation, it had always
been understood that only South Vietnamese forces would be allowed

to seize the culturally and politically charged ultimate objectives of the struggle for the Citadel—the flag tower and the Imperial Palace. The U.S. Marines might well have been embittered over the decision to allow the ARVN to reap the benefits won in part with Marine blood and toil, just as the ARVN worried over being relegated to an overall position of secondary importance; such is the nature of wars fought by imperfect alliances. As proud and protective of the reputation of his own unit as the U.S. Marines were of theirs, Truong believed that the glory of the final victory should be won by elements of the 1st ARVN Division, those natives of Hue City who had fought so hard to reclaim their patrimony. Accordingly, General Truong assigned the dangerous and symbolically important tasks to what he considered to be his two best units; 2/3 under Dinh and the Hac Bao under Hue.

When, on 23 February, he received orders from Truong to launch an attack on the flag tower, though, Dinh realized that the attack would likely be very difficult. Throughout the battle, the NVA had proved very adept at transforming the towers of the Citadel walls into deadly defensive emplacements, and Dinh believed that the NVA would defend the massive three-story flag tower complex to the last. Making matters worse, the men of 2/3 would have to cross hundreds of yards of open ground, under a hail of enemy fire, before reaching the outer ring of NVA defenses. Facing such a difficult task, Dinh and Bolt opted for a daring night raid, and, in the predawn hours of 24 February, select volunteers of 2/3 rushed the tower, with one company dedicated to its seizure while the remainder surrounded the structure. Announcing their advance with a fusillade of gas grenades, 2/3 stunned the NVA with the audacity of its attack. Routed, some of the defenders fought to the end in the upper level of the tower, while others leapt to their deaths. At 0500 hours, the men of 2/3 lowered the NLF banner and informed an elated General Truong of their success. Later, after sunrise, a volunteer from 2/3 climbed the battered flagpole to put the flag of South Vietnam into its place and was shot in the leg during the process.[42] As the flag unfurled in the breeze, a cheer went up from the weary soldiers across the Citadel, who realized that the month of agony in the city of Hue was at an end.

The signal honor of recapturing the Imperial Palace fell to the battered but resilient Hac Bao, who had done the most to save the Citadel from falling into enemy hands and had arguably fought the hardest to achieve its recapture. Bursts of 106mm fire from Marines' ONTOS ve-

Members of 2/3 ARVN replace the South Vietnamese flag above the Hue
Citadel. Photograph VA000472, 1968, Douglas Pike Photograph Collection,
The Vietnam Archive, Texas Tech University.

hicles silenced snipers atop the surrounding walls; then six rounds at
once vaporized the ornate gate of the palace.[43] Expecting fanatical resistance, the Hac Bao charged forward, earning the praise of an admir-
ing Major Thompson and his Marines. Tran Ngoc Hue and his men
were surprised to find an enemy bent on retreat rather than resistance
and quickly secured the seat of Vietnamese imperial authority. Fighting to the west of the Imperial Palace continued for another day, as the
Vietnamese Marines destroyed the last remaining pockets of NVA resistance. Their actions, however, were an anticlimax; the raising of the
South Vietnamese flag and the seizure of the Imperial Palace signified
the true end of the struggle for Hue City.

In an interesting postscript to the battle in the Imperial Palace,
Tran Ngoc Hue watched as a nearly naked man tottered up to surrender. He was a member of the 1st ARVN Division Reconnaissance

Company who had been cut off in the Imperial Palace by the initial NVA attack and who had survived for more than twenty harrowing days by lying submerged amid the foliage in one of the ornamental lakes and scrounging for food at night. The soldier turned out to be Pham Van Dinh's elder brother. The lives of the two comrades had crossed yet again in a very personal way in their mutual struggle to save their home city and their nation. For Hue, the incident was soon forgotten as he returned to the matter at hand. Having discovered huge stores of rice, meant to feed a conquering army, Hue allowed each of his men two bags for his family and worked to distribute the remainder among the throngs of refugees. Had he so chosen, Hue could have made a tidy sum from the rice, but he did not—and threatened to shoot any of his men if they became looters.

Rethinking Tet

Although the U.S. Marines and the ARVN in many ways fought separate battles in Hue—efforts that were sometimes charged with and complicated by issues of national and unit pride—both fought well and deserve praise. The just and warranted attention lavished on the heroic deeds of the leathernecks, though, has in part skewed the overall picture of the fighting in the Citadel, leaving the ARVN's role in the struggle nearly ignored. The commander of 1/5 Marines, Major Robert Thompson, perhaps justly perturbed after the grueling battle, continued the process begun by American journalists of marginalizing the ARVN contributions to the fighting by stating, in a press conference, that "The MACV records will reflect that the ARVN, assisted by 1/5, took the Citadel. . . . That was strictly public relations hogwash, like so much that MACV put out during the war. The 1st Battalion, 5th Marines took the Citadel. The ARVN were spectators."[44] Thus the war remained perhaps fatally bifurcated. Even in 1968, amid the ARVN's greatest victory, American units had to fight the war for the ARVN, relegating the South Vietnamese military to a position of secondary importance, though it had fought with a skill and a tenacity that were beyond American expectations. The grim irony of the situation was not lost upon ARVN men and their leaders, stung by the lack of trust displayed by their powerful ally.

Popular historical accounts of the fighting in Hue City have continued to focus attention almost exclusively on the deeds of the U.S. Marines, leaving the ARVN nearly out of the story. At the furthest extreme, Keith Nolan's *Battle for Hue* rarely mentions the ARVN at all and relegates them to a role of "mopping up behind the Marines," while accusing the ARVN of "moving from house to house in organized looting parties."[45] From the first efforts to relieve the MACV compound, the U.S. Marines demonstrated the individual bravery and the unit battle prowess that have marked the members of the U.S. Marine Corps as the finest infantry in the world. Certainly the Americans gave of themselves selflessly; the Marines singlehandedly liberated the New City south of the Perfume River and fought an epic battle in the Citadel, losing 147 killed in action.[46] In a much less heralded battle, though, the ARVN forces had actually done the majority of the fighting in the Citadel, their understrength units besting the vaunted NVA and VC in a long and bitter struggle largely without the aid of organic heavy direct-fire weaponry. During the fighting, ARVN forces lost 357 killed in action and inflicted an astounding 2,642 battle deaths on the NVA and the VC forces.[47] That the U.S. Marines fought hard and well in Hue City is beyond doubt. However, the popular view of the battle as an American struggle with a bit of perfunctory ARVN aid is invalid. In the struggle for Hue City in the Tet Offensive, it is time finally to give the ARVN its due for what was perhaps its greatest victory ever.

The Tet Offensive had dramatic consequences for the careers of Truong, Dinh, and Hue, ARVN's heroes of the hour and the victors of the Battle of Hue City. General Truong had solidified his reputation as the ARVN's best combat general, and as a result of its exploits the 1st ARVN Division received the U.S. Presidential Unit Citation. Tran Ngoc Hue won popular renown in South Vietnam as the savior of Hue City, received promotion to the rank of captain, and was awarded the coveted U.S. Silver Star for his role in the battle. For his role in the fighting, Pham Van Dinh received a U.S. Bronze Star for valor. The most famous photograph of the entire conflict, seared into the collective consciousness of the South Vietnamese people then and their expatriate communities today, depicts Dinh and his men raising the South Vietnamese flag above the battered and shell-torn Citadel. The captured moment in time remains the signal South Vietnamese image of the war, a venerated symbol of what might have been. For his efforts in the struggle, and for his image locked in time, Dinh earned national acclaim and the sobriquet "the Young Lion of Hue."

Unlike his younger comrade, Dinh, and his heroism, was somewhat more complex. While Tran Ngoc Hue received acclaim from the U.S. Marines and holds a place of prominence even in American histories of the battle, Dinh's case is different. The role of 2/3 ARVN in Tet is little known outside Vietnamese circles, and, for his part, Thompson seemingly resented the presence of 2/3 in what was, in his view, a Marine operation in the Citadel. Disdainful of the entire ARVN contribution to the battle, with the exception of the Hac Bao, Thompson reserved special scorn for the operations of 2/3, stating that "2/3 was worthless. And the . . . commanding officer was a wimp."[48]

That 2/3 ARVN was not the combat equal of 1/5 Marines is not in doubt. Dinh led a smaller, less heavily armed unit that went about its business with more caution than the Marines, in a way that Dinh felt was more suitable to the situation and to the fact that his unit was involved in a war likely to drag on for several more years. In many ways, then, Thompson's opinion reflects the standard disconnect between the competing American and South Vietnamese ways of war that stood in especially stark relief during the struggle for the Citadel. Advisers to ARVN units believed in general that their charges were underappreciated by the American military and, after serving with the ARVN, had developed a quite different view of ARVN abilities and accomplishments. Joe Bolt, who knew Dinh and 2/3 ARVN better than anyone else at the time, believed Dinh to be the best battalion commander in a division that was the best in the ARVN.[49] Far from believing that Dinh was a "wimp," Colonel George Adkisson, the senior adviser to the 1st Division, ranked Dinh among the two best ARVN battalion commanders that he had ever met and characterized Dinh as "aggressive and offensive minded."[50]

The Headquarters of I Corps Advisory Corps, Advisory Team 1, the highest advisory grouping in the corps area, singled out both the Hac Bao and 2/3 ARVN for special notice:

In the 1st Division, the performance of the 3rd Regiment and the Hac Bao (Black Panther) Reaction Company is worthy of praise. These units participated in sustained combat operations against dug-in enemy forces in the Hue Citadel during the entire period from 31 January 1968 until 29 February 1968.

A high point of the Hue battle occurred 24–25 February 1968, when the 3rd Regiment and the Hac Bao Company initiated the offensive action which cleared the Citadel. Elements of the 3rd Regiment and the Hac Bao Company cleared the west wall and the palace area. The 2nd Battalion, 3rd Regiment conducted a night attack which secured the southern wall. . . . Losses inflicted on the enemy by the 3rd Regiment and the Hac Bao Company during the period 31 January 1968 to 29 February 1968 were 1,084 NVA KIA, 22 POW's, 268 individual and 88 crew-served weapons captured. Friendly losses included 113 KIA and 67 weapons lost.[51]

Tragically, the ARVN was destined for ultimate defeat, but it basked in the afterglow of its greatest victory when its young men became heroes in 1968. Though Dinh and Hue had joined together in battle for only a short time, they would forever be linked and defined by their actions in the struggle for Hue City. No longer were the two men just General Truong's protégés; they had together seized the national imagination of South Vietnam. For his part, Hue stood unquestioned and universally admired, every inch the hero even by the exacting standards of the U.S. Marines. Dinh, however, ranked even higher in the pantheon of ARVN greatness—a man and a moment frozen in time and legend. That he had reached such dizzying heights, that he was "the Young Lion of Hue," made Dinh's eventual downfall, in 1972, even more cataclysmic.

5

After Tet

The Year of Hope

IN THE UNITED STATES, the massive tactical victory of the Tet Offensive very nearly escaped notice, lost amid the cultural and political chaos that both defined 1968 and ripped the heart out of the American war effort. To the South Vietnamese, though, the victory in the Tet Offensive was the seminal moment in their nation's short history. The South Vietnamese population had not risen up in support of revolution, and the ARVN, for all of its faults, had fought well and, with the aid of its mighty allies, defeated an all-out effort at victory by the VC and the NVA. The discovery of an estimated three thousand civilians slain in cold blood during a horrific period of societal retribution while the NVA held sway over Hue City also united the people of South Vietnam as never before and carried an obvious significance for the men of General Truong's 1st ARVN Division. Writing to his wife from 1st ARVN Division headquarters only eight days after the close of the fighting in Hue, Captain D. H. Campbell of the Australian Army Training Team, Vietnam (AATTV), provided an insight into what the slaughter meant to the ARVN:

> The atrocities that have been committed in this battle by the VC are incredible and every day reveals mass graves and the story of what happened is self evident by the condition of the bodies including many children. One can understand the hate that lets them strangle military types with wire and decorate the walls with the bodies but to bury alive whole families including the children on no stronger pretext than they refused to take up arms defies the imagination. I have always had a grudging admiration for the VC in view of what they have accomplished in the face of what was against them but any respect that I had has now gone.[1]

The bitter struggle, especially the battle to retake Hue City, had exacted a terrible toll, with the ARVN suffering two-thirds of the estimated total of twelve thousand allied casualties lost in the campaign. The extensive fighting also disrupted civilian life across South Vietnam; fleeing the urban maelstrom, some 600,000 South Vietnamese became refugees, 100,000 in the I Corps region alone. Additionally, with the strength of the allied militaries devoted to defense of the nation's cities, the VC and the NVA seized control throughout much of the countryside. The situation, though, was far worse for the Viet Cong and the North Vietnamese, who suffered a cataclysmic defeat, losing an estimated 40,000 of the 84,000 men who had taken part in the battle. In I Corps alone, Lieutenant General Robert Cushman, the III MAF commander, later estimated that allied forces had killed more than thirty thousand of the enemy, the equivalent of seventy-four infantry battalions. Marine Brigadier General John Chaisson, the director of the MACV Combat Operations Center, summarized the post-Tet situation in I Corps well in a letter home, stating that "the damage done in the cities and to the economy is staggering. ARVN will be somewhat less than effective for weeks." He then added, "there is a general tightening up of everything, and if the guys on top don't panic this could be the turning point of the war—even though he [the enemy] initiated it for us."[2]

Although major actions continued around Khe Sanh and along the DMZ, ARVN and U.S. forces planned to build on their victory and launch a nationwide offensive to push the tattered VC and NVA remnants from the densely populated lowlands and reopen the critical rice growing region to pacification and governmental control. As General Cushman later explained, the plan of action for 1968 in I Corps was to go "after the enemy first in the coastal areas in a series of short duration operations, using the mobility of our forces to fix and destroy enemy forces which had escaped from the major Tet battle areas."[3] Once the enemy was driven from the lowlands, U.S. and ARVN forces then planned to press the VC and the NVA into the highlands and perhaps even into Laos.

Severely weakened, but with an indomitable will, NVA forces, enjoying artillery support and secure logistic lines, were determined to hold their hard-won gains in the area and planned to launch further offensives in I Corps. To counter this threat, Westmoreland and his deputy, General Creighton Abrams, fed more and more troops into the area in what was the bloodiest year of the Vietnam War. Demonstrating the importance placed on operations in I Corps, by midyear MACV had concentrated more than 50 percent of all U.S. maneuver battalions alongside two of the ARVN's best divisions for the allied push in the region.[4]

Even as allied forces gathered for battle in I Corps, though, the political winds of change began to blow. Under pressure from both the political right and the left, facing a strong challenge within his own party, reeling from the media coverage of the Tet Offensive and heartbroken over the failure of his Great Society, in the spring of 1968 President Lyndon Johnson made the first in a series of decisions that heralded the end of the American involvement in the Vietnam War. With the advice of his new Secretary of Defense, Clark Clifford, Johnson rejected Westmoreland's controversial request for 206,000 additional troops, marking an end to American gradual escalation of the conflict. The spasm of presidential soul searching and decision making had a cascade effect that also included Johnson's decision not to seek reelection and the opening of difficult peace negotiations with North Vietnam.

Both the United States and South Vietnam struggled to come to terms with the post-Tet political situation—a new reality that not only portended an increased ARVN role in the conflict but also provided military planners an opportunity to reshape the Vietnam War. In March 1968, MACV proposed a scheme to enlarge and modernize the South Vietnamese armed forces to a total strength of 801,215 men by 1970.[5] Fast upon the heels of the Tet victory and an attendant upsurge in South Vietnamese national will——also while the strength of American forces remained at its height—the expansion of the ARVN stood as an opportunity to redress some of the chief weaknesses of the institution. However, the battlefield successes of 1968 served to disguise the urgency of the situation, in part causing the effort to lack real reforming zeal.

The South Vietnamese took a long view of both the process of ARVN expansion and the conflict as a whole. They drew up their own plan of force modernization, dubbed Plan Six, which centered on creating a more self-sufficient military force in the South. The plan not only contained a scheme for expansion but also concerned itself with issues of sustainability, including creation of more support units and improving military living standards and family housing. The American reception of Plan Six, though, was cool and demonstrated the more transient philosophy of a nation that was tiring of its war. Under the pressure of an impending election, Washington pressed for a more immediate solution to the problem, with Clark Clifford instructing Westmoreland on the "urgency" of strengthening the South Vietnamese military "as quickly as possible" to enable the United States to "shift the burden of the war to [the] GVN forces."

As a result of Clifford's instructions, MACV laid out a five-year plan that not only called for the strengthening of the ARVN but also assumed that a large residual U.S. combat force would remain in country to aid the ARVN in times of need. The drafters of the three-phase plan came to the conclusion that a residual force would be necessary because they assumed that even an expanded ARVN could deal effectively with only the internal insurgency, not the conventional threat posed by North Vietnam. Military logic, though, ran afoul of political reality, and in July 1968 Clifford informed MACV to prepare to substitute South Vietnamese for American ground units as quickly as possible, "to reduce American casualties and muffle domestic criticism in a presidential election year." The eventual pace and the unilateral nature of American withdrawals fatally disrupted MACV's plan, with its reliance on a residual force, and undermined the plan for true and much-needed reform of the ARVN. Instead, the eventual plans for the expansion of the South Vietnamese armed forces were more concerned with maximizing foxhole strength than with making the ARVN more self-sufficient.[6]

Optimism ran high in I Corps after the recapture of the Citadel in Hue. Decimated enemy forces seemed to be on the run, American units had relocated to the area to launch an offensive to reclaim the countryside, and the ARVN seemed poised to rebuild itself and reclaim its nationalist mantle. Amid the hustle and bustle of battles won, though, potentially fatal ARVN weaknesses remained obscured by American firepower. Shunted aside and now thoroughly an adjunct to an American war, the ARVN remained a politicized and flawed instrument of power. Ongoing struggles and discord within the American body politic, though, dictated that more and more of the conflict would soon fall to a South Vietnamese military that, in the words of Pham Van Dinh, had not yet had the chance to "grow up."

Pursuit in the Lowlands

The allied seizure of the initiative in I Corps was immediate, allowing VC and NVA units battered during the Tet fighting little time to recuperate. Though continuing operations near Khe Sanh initially grabbed most of the headlines, the push to eradicate the VC in and to retake control of the lowlands initially formed the centerpiece of what was a corps-wide allied offensive. During March and April, III MAF launched seventeen major operations of battalion size or larger and began to retake villages and hamlets that had fallen to the VC during Tet. In the southern three provinces of I Corps, communist forces in the main avoided battle and limited most of their activity to scattered guerrilla attacks, mines, and boobytraps.[7] However, in the 1st ARVN Division's area of operations, Quang Tri and Thua Thien provinces, the fighting in the lowlands remained fierce.

American and ARVN units set off in hot pursuit of NVA and VC stragglers, and for the Hac Bao the aftermath of the Tet Offensive remained especially busy as the unit engaged in a familiar routine of nearly constant action in support of the allied offensive. Although mostly engaged in battles with small enemy units, in mid-March the 1st ARVN Division received reports of an NVA battalion in the neighborhood of Thon Lang Village on the Song Bo River north of Hue and sent the Hac Bao to investigate.

Tran Ngoc Hue quickly took stock of the situation and reported positive contact with the 8th Battalion of the 90th NVA Regiment, which had taken up defensive positions within the village. Eager to push ever harder at an enemy that he knew to be on the run, Hue called in air and artillery strikes on the NVA defensive emplacements. Then, certain that nothing could have survived the maelstrom, Hue ordered his men to launch a frontal assault on the village. The NVA, though, had survived and caught the Hac Bao in a deadly crossfire as Hue's men struggled across an open rice paddy. Recognizing his mistake, Hue quickly withdrew his attacking forces, but only after heavy losses. Fighting at Thon Lang continued for two days as a somewhat chastened Hue relied more on firepower and flank movements than on audacity to make good his advance. As the Hac Bao noose tightened and the abundance of firepower made its mark, the NVA slipped away from the fighting with heavy losses. However, the Hac Bao had suffered greatly, losing forty men. For Tran Ngoc Hue, the fighting at

Thon Lang served as a warning never to underestimate the NVA. Although it had suffered greatly in Tet and the tide of the war had seemingly turned against it, the NVA would fight on, a lesson that Tran Ngoc Hue would not soon forget.

After the experience of the fierce fighting in the Citadel, Dinh and the men of 2/3 ARVN returned to Xuac Xu fire base and were reunited with both the company that had been marooned across Highway 1 and the remnants of the platoon that had been left behind at the fire base, which had fallen under NVA attack.[8] Though strengthened and resupplied, the men of 2/3 spent only a few days in base camp before returning to battle. By the beginning of March, 2/3 found itself in the familiar area of Quang Dien District, this time as a combat battalion, to work in tandem with the 2nd Brigade of the 101st Airborne, under the command of Colonel John Cushman, which had recently relocated to nearby Landing Zone (LZ) Sally.

Dinh was astonished by the condition of the district that he had left under government control only three months earlier. ARVN forces had abandoned the area to pursue the desperate Tet battle in Hue City, and, as Dinh had suspected and warned, the district RF/PF had proved no match for their battle-hardened foes. Dinh's pacification work had been for naught, because Quang Dien, like so much of the surrounding countryside, was once again infested with NVA.[9] The collapse of security in the district was so total that in March 1968 local RF/PF forces were able to maintain only three isolated outposts and control less than 5 percent of the district's territory.[10] Unlike in some areas, though, the NVA seemed determined to stand and fight for ownership of the fertile land of Quang Dien, which formed a critical part of its logistic supply system. It therefore fortified "nearly all of the villages . . . with trenchlines and bunkers."[11]

Saddened by the collapse of pacification in Quang Dien and worried about the fate of the people he had come to know as friends, Dinh was eager to get back to work in the district. His desire was equaled by that of the fiery Cushman, who tasked the U.S. 1st Battalion of the 502nd Infantry (1/502) with destroying enemy forces and their infiltration routes in Quang Dien. Heralding a new level of U.S./ARVN cooperation, for much of early March, 2/3 and 1/502 worked in tandem, sharing intelligence, base areas, and firepower. Together they went through heavy fighting centered on the hamlets Ap Dong Lam, Ap Son Trung, and Ap Pho Lai, two kilometers south of the district town. The fighting was bitter and constant, with mines, boobytraps, and company-size ambushes the norm, as allied units swept from hamlet to hamlet and drove the NVA forces from their intricate defenses. The struggle to reclaim Quang Dien had only just begun, forming the centerpiece of the critical, combined effort to wrest the lowlands of Thua Thien Province from NVA control. Already, though, the marriage of 2/3 and 1/502 had achieved great results, accounting for 247 NVA dead.[12]

On 5 April, shortly before departing for operations in the A Shau Valley, 2/3 ARVN made contact with the 12th Battalion, 4th Regiment of the NVA 312 Division east of Highway 1. Having pinned the enemy against a nearby river, 2/3, through its adviser, Joe Bolt, called in relentless artillery fire and air strikes on the exposed NVA positions. After a day of hard fighting, the remaining NVA slipped away by night, but 2/3, unaided by American ground forces, had won a significant victory, losing ten dead and forty wounded while killing seventy-one NVA and capturing numerous small arms and heavy weapons.[13] Dinh and 2/3 had made their mark on the fighting in Quang Dien. With his wealth of local knowledge, from valuable bonds of trust with the local population to familiarity with enemy infiltration routes, Dinh had proven indispensable to success in the region and had worked very closely with both the 1/502 commander, Lieutenant Colonel Bertram Bishop, and with Cushman—a cooperative relationship that was so often lacking in a bifurcated war.

In 1964–1965, Colonel John Cushman had served as senior adviser to the 21st ARVN Division deep in the Mekong Delta, allowing him a wider view of the nature of the Vietnam War. Something of a maverick in U.S. military circles, Cushman doubted the omnipotence of U.S. combat power. In his view, the NVA and the VC had survived far too long against heavy odds to allow for such a simplistic belief. Instead of accepting the pattern of shunting the ARVN aside while U.S. forces won the war in a blaze of firepower, Cushman had come to the belief that a real and seamless U.S./ARVN cooperation held the best chance for true success in Vietnam:

I knew what faced Vietnamese troops and their advisers. I was determined to help them. Much more than that, being responsible for employing the American Army's assets in this area of operations, I was determined to do all that I could to see that we operated as part of a common plan that would coordinate our operations, the operations of the ARVN 1st Division, and those of province and district forces into a single effort from this point forward.[14]

As evidenced by, and in part due to, the fruitful cooperation between 2/3 and 1/502, Cushman's first rule of operations was to work closely with the South Vietnamese. In the densely populated lowlands, Cushman realized that local territorial forces were much better equipped to discern enemy from friend and had access to intelligence from area hamlets and villages, a critical informational edge that the Americans lacked. To achieve a seamless coordination of action, the 2nd Brigade worked with South Vietnamese at all levels, from district officials to General Truong at the 1st ARVN Division CP. The high level of cooperation took several forms, including locating American battalion command posts alongside the Vietnamese district chief's headquarters.[15]

Cushman's men worked especially closely with the local RF/PF, training the Vietnamese and sometimes even integrating them into American platoons. General Truong was delighted by the prospect and the results, stating that the forces:

> worked hand in hand in almost every matter, from planning to controlling combat operations. The same spirit of dedicated cooperation prevailed between the battalion and the district staffs and among subordinate units. Cooperation was in effect so close that both staffs worked as a team and all subordinate units, U.S., RF and PF, were practically fused into a single force. The remarkable thing about this operation was that the task assigned to each element was designed to conform best to its ability to perform regardless of nationality.[16]

During operations, which involved fierce and sustained fighting, RF/PF forces selected by the district chief linked up with their American counterparts at a prearranged spot each morning. The Vietnamese troops usually then accompanied the leading element of the sweep, utilizing their familiarity with the local terrain and people and their special ability to detect mines, booby traps, and secret hideouts. The U.S. troops, meanwhile, constituted the main strike element.[17] The results of the combined effort were immediate and electric. In the words of Specialist Robert Johnson of 1/502:

With the Airborne providing the muscle and mobility, and the PF's furnishing the intelligence reports, detainee interrogation, and scouting know-how, the allies hounded the NVA in every known sanctuary in the district. "Col. Bishop used the PF's just as they should be used," Capt. Selzer said, "and he treated them with the same consideration and respect as his men."[18]

Aided by his fruitful relationship with the South Vietnamese, Cushman also invoked the second fundamental principle of the 101st Airborne Division in Quang Dien, maintaining constant and unrelenting pressure on the enemy. Utilizing local intelligence, 2nd Brigade forces swept through their AO by day, searching for enemy contact, and set ambushes by night. This tactic yielded several clashes with NVA and VC forces—short, sharp battles that, while productive, followed the same frustrating pattern that so typified the Vietnam War in which the elusive enemy took heavy losses but slipped away under the cover of darkness.

On 27 March, the 1st Battalion of the 501st Infantry (1/501), commanded by Lieutenant Colonel Wayne Procup, ran a company of the Viet Cong 810th Battalion to ground in the village of Thuan Hoa, on the Perfume River. Immediately, Procup began to arrange his forces, aided by the advice of South Vietnamese intelligence, in a ring around the village in preparation for an assault on the VC defenses. However, the approach of the abrupt tropical shift from daylight to darkness did not leave enough time for an attack. Procup knew that his chance for victory was fast slipping away and that the VC, by ones and twos, would vanish out of the trap and into the night. Frustrated, Procup requested night-long illumination of the battlefield so that he could both keep his forces in their blocking positions and hinder the enemy retreat. The flare ships arrived shortly after dark, bathing the battlefield in an eerie glow. During the night, pockets of gunfire rattled along the lines of 1/501 as isolated VC attempted to flee. At dawn, although the extemporized encirclement proved to have been imperfect and much of the enemy force had made good its escape, fifty VC had perished. Almost by chance, Cushman and the 2nd Brigade had struck upon the tactical principles that best complemented the strengths of U.S./South Vietnamese cooperation—cordon operations.[19]

Learning their new mode of operation by trial and error, 2nd Brigade utilized South Vietnamese local intelligence to discern the best

possible avenues for sweeps and places for ambushes in efforts to locate significant VC and NVA troop formations amid the villages, hamlets, and broken terrain of Quang Dien. Once one of the widely scattered reconnaissance units engaged in battle, it was a race against time
to gather allied forces at the scene before the VC and the NVA made
good their escape. The scenario of allied cooperation and the premium
placed on rapid reaction fit the strengths of the Hac Bao perfectly, and,
even as Dinh and 2/3 departed the area, Hue and his elite company
entered the fight for domination of Quang Dien.

The nearly continuous action allowed Cushman's men ample opportunity to fine-tune their tactics, and, on 21 April, C Company of
2/501 met heavy enemy contact near Thon Thanh Trung Village, seven
kilometers southeast of Quang Dien district town, which resulted in
the 2nd Brigade's fourth cordon operation. All four companies of
2/501 rushed to the scene, some by foot and others by helicopter, and
completed the cordon before nightfall. Unable to escape and pummeled by artillery fire, the NVA fought hard and beat back an assault
by A Company on the village the next afternoon. Needing more
strength to draw the noose ever tighter around the entrapped NVA,
Cushman called on the Hac Bao forces, which combat assaulted into
the area and took their place in the cordon.

Cushman and his men had perfected their craft. Foxhole positions
ringed the entire village and were no more than ten meters apart, allowing the enemy no escape paths. Light over the cordon was constant, for even a ten-minute hiatus in the illumination would allow
NVA soldiers to slither on their bellies through the rice paddies to
safety. The night regimen was difficult; every man in every foxhole
had to remain awake and alert. Any lapse would allow the resourceful
and desperate enemy opportunity to disappear. On the night of 22
April, discipline remained firm and the cordon held. The next morning, allied forces inched closer to Thon Thanh Trung against lessening
enemy fire. Preceded by an artillery barrage and air strikes, Company
A swept through the village and found only carnage. At the cost of
twelve wounded, the allied force had wiped out an entire NVA company, registering seventy-four confirmed kills and netting one very
disoriented prisoner.[20]

After their success, companies of 1/501 and the Hac Bao continued to sweep through the area looking for the enemy. The work was
slow, because each village they entered was a potential NVA strong-

point. At midday on 28 April, Tran Ngoc Hue and his men began a reconnaissance in force of the area near Phuoc Yen Village, located in a
bend of the Song Bo River south of Quang Dien district town. Even
from a distance, the scene gave Hue pause; several fresh graves dotted
the landscape, and there were no farmers in the fields. The village was
too quiet. Remembering his experience at Thon Lang, Hue ordered the
Hac Bao to approach Phouc Yen with caution, using the nearby river-
bank as cover. As the Hac Bao drew near to the village, though, all hell
broke loose. Fire of all types poured in from a prepared ambush position, fire so heavy that Hue calculated that his unit faced an entire
NVA battalion. Quickly taking stock of the developing situation, Hue
realized that his right flank was covered by the Song Bo River, while
his left flank and rear bordered on open rice paddies. Though the Hac
Bao fighters were considerably outnumbered, the threat came only
from the front. Certain that he held the advantage, Hue and his U.S.
adviser, Jim Coolican, called in smoke to gain separation from the
NVA and then directed artillery and air strikes on the enemy positions
to keep them pinned in place. Hue also passed the good news on to
a delighted Cushman. An entire NVA battalion, the 8th Battalion of
the 90th Regiment, had been located and pinned into a perfect position, surrounded on three sides by a water obstacle. Tran Ngoc Hue
and the Hac Bao had initiated what would become the classic cordon
operation.

Nearby units rushed to the scene of the developing battle, making it a truly allied affair. By dark, one company of 1/501, one company of 2/501, one company of 1/502, the Hac Bao, three PF platoons
from neighboring Huong Tra District, and forty hamlet militiamen
had joined arms to complete one of the largest and most effective cordons of the entire war. When the flare ships arrived to light the battlefield, the NVA realized that it had been trapped and reacted with
ferocity. Desperate to fight their way out of the perfect encirclement,
NVA units launched four major assaults against the lines held by the
Hac Bao and A Company 1/502. Though the fighting was chaotic, the
cordon held.

In the early morning hours of 29 April, the Hac Bao and A-1/502
moved forward in an attempt to shrink the cordon around the enemy
forces. Met by heavy fire from entrenched enemy positions, A-1/502
pulled back from the subsidiary hamlet of Le Van Thuong and called
in additional artillery and air strikes. The Hac Bao, however, achieved

Tran Ngoc Hue as Hac Bao commander. Photograph
Courtesy of Tran Ngoc Hue.

greater success and moved one hundred meters into the village of
Phouc Yen itself, fighting from bunker to bunker against fierce resistance, as Coolican directed more and more accurate fire support on the
NVA positions to their front. After a day of heavy engagement, the
cordon was sealed for the night. The following morning, the Hac Bao
again formed the spearhead of the allied advance and drove forward
into the center of Phuoc Yen—a crippling blow to NVA morale.

On the evening of 30 April, the Hac Bao withdrew from Phouc
Yen due to another operational commitment. Though the battle raged
on, the decision, won in large part by the bravery and audacity displayed by the Hac Bao, was now a foregone conclusion. At dawn on 1
May, NVA resistance began to crumble, only then allowing A-1/502
the opportunity to move forward into Le Van Thuong. A psychological

warfare team arrived and began to broadcast appeals to surrender. Among the first group of prisoners was an NVA sergeant, who took the microphone and began to tell his own men that they were surrounded and had no chance to escape. In a few minutes, ever-increasing numbers of prisoners began to surrender. Some NVA stalwarts, though, chose to resist to the last, and the cordon held for a further three days. Finally, in the early morning of 3 May, the last NVA holdouts made a final bid to escape but failed. The cordon had worked.

The results of the cordon at Phouc Yen were impressive, a battle initiated by Tran Ngoc Hue and a battle in which the Hac Bao arguably played the critical role. In the fighting, NVA forces suffered more than four hundred men killed. Even more significant, U.S. and ARVN forced captured 107 prisoners, the largest number of NVA captured in any single action to this point in the entire Vietnam War. An entire NVA battalion ceased to exist, all at the cost of only eight American and two ARVN soldiers killed.[21]

After Phouc Yen, cordon operations continued in Quang Dien and surrounding districts, with the Hac Bao again playing a critical role in achieving another spectacular success a month later, resulting in 235 enemy dead and 77 taken prisoner against only 7 total allied killed in action.[22] In a few weeks of fighting, cordon tactics and the seamless coordination of U.S. and ARVN units, best evidenced by the relationship shared between the 2nd Brigade and 2/3 under Dinh and the Hac Bao under Hue, had driven the NVA out of the coastal lowlands north of Hue City. In the words of the chief architect of the success, Colonel John Cushman, "That was how we did it in Thua Thien; work with the Vietnamese, give the enemy no rest, and encircle him at every opportunity." The physical results of the operations were astounding—28 Americans and 6 ARVN were killed in action, while 1,200—80 percent of them North Vietnamese—were killed during the cordons, and 252 prisoners—also 80 percent North Vietnamese—were taken.[23]

At a lower level, the change wrought by U.S./South Vietnamese cooperation had been no less dramatic and revolutionary, transforming RF/PF capabilities in the wake of the disasters of the Tet Offensive. Amid the increasingly cooperative structure, the RF/PF increased its commitment and involvement in battle to company level and beyond. As a result, by October 1968, 1/502 was able to deploy most of its units outside Quang Dien, leaving only a token force in the district. The results of the cooperation instilled by Cushman and his men were nothing short of astounding; growing from a tiny force able to control only 5 percent of the district, the RF/PF in a five-month period killed 215 enemy troops and took 102 prisoners, while an additional 167 enemy soldiers rallied to the ARVN. In achieving this remarkable feat, a total of 484 enemy troops put out of action, the RF/PF lost only 4 men.[24] With the NVA expelled from the area, the RF/PF forces proved capable of dealing with the remaining Viet Cong cadre, freeing U.S. and ARVN main force units to expand their actions further into the countryside and offering an opportunity for the implementation of meaningful pacification in the region.

To many South Vietnamese observers, including Dinh and Hue, who were so intimately involved in the fighting, the heightened level of U.S./ARVN cooperation represented by the struggle for Quang Dien heralded a fundamental change in warfighting. General Truong, who also paid close witness to the startling events in I Corps, later remarked that "In retrospect, combined operations were unquestionably the best approach to improve the combat effectiveness" of the South Vietnamese military, both its regular and its territorial units.[25] Especially when Americans were tiring of their war in Vietnam, the fighting in the lowlands north of Hue City stood as an example of what the Vietnam War could become, a truly allied effort in which U.S. and ARVN forces fought together, combining the best that each had to offer.

Driving into the Highlands

Even as the fighting around Khe Sanh and in the lowlands continued, allied planners turned their attention toward the distant A Shau Valley, near the Laotian border, presaging a military effort that would come to involve both 2/3 and the Hac Bao. The Americans had maintained a Special Forces camp to guard against enemy infiltration at the southern end of the A Shau until 1966, before abandoning the dangerously exposed camp and the surrounding valley to communist control. Using materials from the camp, the NVA and the VC transformed the valley into a main logistic artery of the Ho Chi Minh Trail, while the attention of MACV was focused on other areas of I Corps. After the Tet Offensive, though, allied planners became concerned that a major NVA construction effort on the "yellow brick road" infiltration route from Laos into Quang Nam Province presaged another attack on Hue City. Hoping to preempt any NVA offensive, Lieutenant General William Rosson's Provisional Corps[26] completed a plan calling for the 1st Cavalry Division and elements of the 101st Airborne in cooperation with the General Truong's 1st ARVN Division to conduct an offensive into the A Shau.[27]

Though the 1st Air Cavalry was already embroiled in ongoing fighting around Khe Sanh and the 101st Airborne's program of cordon operations continued in the lowlands, weather considerations forced the move into the A Shau, dubbed Operation Delaware, to take precedence. Dominated by seasonal monsoons, Vietnam was subject to periods of torrential downpours so heavy that they made air mobile operations impossible. The peculiar geography of the A Shau, which was inaccessible to supply operations by road, meant that only the months of April and May were suitable for any type of sustained heliborne activity, necessitating quick and decisive action in the limited window of time. Thus, on 14 April, extensive B-52 strikes began to pound the length and breadth of the A Shau preparatory to the arrival of allied ground forces.

On the morning of 19 April the 1st Battalion of the 7th Cavalry (1/7) choppered into the A Shau north of A Loui airfield (which later became known as LZ Stallion) and received heavy antiaircraft fire, while other elements of the 7th Cavalry and the 101st Airborne moved west toward the valley by ground, hoping to open a supply line along Route 547. Taken by surprise, NVA forces offered little resistance as additional allied units arrived and secured a base of operations in and around A Loui. Throughout April, increasing numbers of allied forces, including elements of the Vietnamese Airborne, arrived in the A Shau and began to fan out in an effort to destroy enemy defensive forces and their critical logistic support network.[28]

Indicative of the level of allied cooperation that was fast becoming the norm for northern I Corps, elements of Truong's 1st ARVN Division played an important role in Operation Delaware, which the Vietnamese referred to as Operation Lam Son 216. As part of the effort to reinforce the allied contingent in the A Shau, on 29 April, two battalions of the 3rd Regiment, including Dinh's 2/3, combat assaulted from the regimental base of PK-17 to LZ Lucy, one kilometer south of Ta Bat, and made immediate contact with enemy forces, with two helicopters receiving heavy damage in the landing. After the brief encounter, it quickly became clear that the NVA had chosen to flee the area, leaving ARVN and U.S. forces in the main unmolested.

For the next two weeks, ARVN forces spread out across the valley, with 2/3 operating in the central valley floor, and swept toward the south, while American forces dealt with the northern reaches of the A Shau and secured Route 547. As 2/3 moved south, it worked to construct fire support bases for ARVN artillery and uncovered several NVA stockpiles, totaling more than twelve tons of ammunition. By 10 May, Dinh and his men had reached the area of the old A Shau Special Forces Camp in the far south of the valley, the entirety of which, once sacrosanct enemy territory, had been swept and cleared. For the North Vietnamese, losses in the A Shau were heavy; they suffered 735 dead while also losing mountains of supplies,[29] crippling losses that would take several months to replace and leave the initiative in the hands of the allies.

With the weather closing in and their task complete, on 10 May, allied forces began to pull out of the A Shau. However, the popular view of events, as expressed by Ronald Spector in his book *After Tet*, that "the North Vietnamese were back [in the A Shau] in a few weeks . . . [and] American and South Vietnamese forces would not return to the A Shau for almost a year,"[30] is incorrect. ARVN and U.S. forces remained on the offensive throughout the highlands and took aim at enemy troop and logistic concentrations in Base Areas 101 and 114. The continued offensive action included additional forays into the A Shau, especially by the Hac Bao.

As the allies pushed ever harder, fierce fighting erupted in several areas of I Corps and involved two concerted NVA counterattacks aimed at stemming the tide of allied advance. Perhaps hoping that the allied command, its attention riveted in the highlands, would be caught off guard, in late April the 320th NVA Division struck toward Dong Ha. In difficult fighting, the Americans crushed the NVA onslaught, with the Americans losing 327 dead and killing or capturing 3,600 NVA. In southern I Corps, U.S. Marines launched successive offensive operations against a communist base complex on Go Noi Island and throughout the coastal lowlands, preempting an NVA offensive in the area. Shifting away from a base strategy to one of high mobility, in June the 3rd Marine Division lashed out at the 308th NVA Division north of Khe Sanh, driving ever further into the highlands and toward Laos. In August, the NVA completed the year's fury by

launching attacks on Da Nang as part of the third phase of its original
Tet Offensive planning. The American and ARVN forces in the area
persevered, crushing assault after assault, continuing a steady pattern
of battlefield victory that caused ARVN hopes to rise ever further.

Amid the fighting throughout I Corps, the 1st ARVN Division
played a considerable part, especially in conjunction with the three
brigades of the U.S. 1st Cavalry Division and elements of the 101st Airborne Division. Their combined tasks were twofold: to deny the NVA
renewed access to the rice harvest of the lowlands north of Hue City
and to launch offensive operations into the remaining NVA base areas
in the highlands. Having just fought through Tet, battles in Quang
Dien, and Operation Delaware, the 3rd Regiment of the 1st ARVN Division now undertook its most difficult and sustained operation to
date, Operation Lam Son 225, a five-month incursion into NVA Base
Area 114 in the triple-canopy rainforest in the rugged highlands west
of Hue City.

On 18 May, elements of the 3rd ARVN Brigade, including Dinh's
2/3, and the U.S. 1st Cavalry, combat assaulted into Base Area 114
in and around LZ Jose. Again having caught enemy forces off guard,
the allied units swept through a hastily abandoned NVA regimental
headquarters made up of hundreds of bunkers and containing several
tons of ammunition and a mockup of Hue City. Operations continued
against only sporadic resistance until 12 June, when 2/3 made contact
with elements of the 803rd NVA Regiment who were determined to
defend their main base area. Calling in air and artillery strikes, Dinh
and Bolt led 2/3 through three days of grueling battle, fighting from
bunker to bunker through the complex, utilizing hand grenades to destroy enemy positions from close range. The victory netted a wealth
of intelligence and captured weaponry and accounted for twenty-
six enemy killed at the cost of seven friendly KIA and twenty-two
wounded.[31]

Operation Lam Son 225 went on month after month, with the men
of 2/3 falling into a rhythm of constant patrols, ambushes and firefights as they slogged through the difficult terrain. In general, ARVN
units maintained a pattern of one month in action, followed by a few
days at PK-17 to refit before combat assaulting back into Base Area
114. Operating far from any ground support, ARVN and U.S. units
were dependent on helicopter resupply, which for ARVN units came
usually once every week. The resupply, though, was often a chaotic

and loud affair. With few available landing zones amid the tangle of the rainforest, ARVN and U.S. forces often used explosives to blow open holes in the canopy large enough to allow helicopters to land. The explosions, followed by the arrival of the aircraft, quickly caught the attention of the NVA, making resupply and medevacs especially dangerous times. On the advice of Bolt, Dinh learned to keep 2/3 constantly on the move, sending units out into the countryside in cloverleaf patterns to avoid flank attacks and leaving back ambushes to guard against any potential attacks from the rear.[32]

As the last ARVN units left the area, on 12 September, it was apparent that Operation Lam Son 225 had been a resounding success. At the cost of 74 dead, the battalions of the ARVN 3rd Brigade had accounted for 373 NVA dead and the capture of 185 individual and 31 crew-served weapons and had destroyed several tons of supplies, including two NVA hospitals and two regimental command posts. The length, arduous nature, and success of the operation proved quite impressive to American forces associated with the 1st ARVN Division and demonstrated the laudable effects of continued allied cooperation; the way forward in Vietnam seemed clear.[33]

During Operation Lam Son 225, Dinh's adviser, Joe Bolt, reached the end of his tour with 2/3 ARVN. However, certain that his place was in the field with a combat unit, Bolt was reluctant to return to a staff advisory position. After calling in favors and making some waves, Bolt received his wish and in June moved on to replace Jim Coolican as adviser to the Hac Bao, becoming the second man to advise both Dinh and Hue in battle. While Dinh's 2/3 had been involved in a constant stream of operations in the highlands, the Hac Bao, after playing its role in the cordons in Quang Dien, had fought isolated engagements across northern I Corps in its unique role as a rapid-reaction force.

Initially, relations between Hue and Bolt were somewhat strained, with each more used to the operational pace of their previous respective counterpart. After a few days of action, though, the two became both a coordinated operational team and fast friends. Bolt marveled at the new, faster pace of operations that he found with the Hac Bao, operations that could take them anywhere at any time. The two men tried to keep a close watch on divisional intelligence reports, realizing that direct orders from General Truong for the Hac Bao's employment would often follow major engagements involving ARVN units in the field or major intelligence finds. Where Dinh's operational reality had developed a grinding attritional sameness, the Hac Bao followed a more staccato routine of sharp battles, unrelated both in time and in space, battles that often knew no name and appear in no operational reports.

After receiving a call from General Truong, the men would sprint to waiting helicopters, with Hue as often as possible choosing to fly aboard a Vietnamese Air Force helicopter, beating on the side of the aged aircraft and exclaiming to Bolt, "We go now!" On one occasion, receiving intelligence that an NVA company was resident on one of the barrier islands east of Hue City, the Hac Bao combat assaulted onto the beach and swept across the island with no contact. Frustrated by the elusiveness of the enemy, Hue and Bolt sat down to draw up a plan. Nearby, Hue noticed two sticks in the ground moving. He rushed over to investigate and pulled a terrified NVA soldier from a spider hole. Operating on information gained from the prisoner, the Hac Bao cornered the concealed NVA company, killing thirteen and taking twenty-five prisoners.[34]

By July, the Hac Bao made ready to take part in another assault into the A Shau in tandem with two brigades of the 101st Airborne. After first constructing a ring of fire support bases dotting the highlands, on 4 August, the Americans, aided by two battalions of the 1st ARVN Regiment and the Hac Bao, combat assaulted into the areas near A Loui and Ta Bat. Again the NVA forces chose not to resist in defense of their logistic hub and instead relied on mines and booby traps to delay the U.S./ARVN advance. Far from being the deadly A Shau of popular history—a no-go area occupied by enemy forces as the allies stood helplessly by—the notorious valley actually yielded few contacts and little in the way of major logistics finds. After a few weeks of fruitless searching, allied forces exited the A Shau on 20 August, leaving behind minefields of their own to hinder any NVA return.[35]

As the weather began to deteriorate (including the arrival of Typhoon Bess in early September), the level of fighting decreased, although the focus of the 1st ARVN Division remained squarely on the highlands, and both the 3rd Regiment and the Hac Bao took part in Operation Lam Son 265, a three-stage operation aimed at NVA Base Area 101. Through the winter, both Dinh's and Hue's units hunted for the NVA in the jungle highlands, often in the A Shau,[36] undertaking missions that now included as a matter of routine close cooperation with American forces. The sweeps, though, yielded only sporadic contact,[37] for even in the A Shau the NVA had pulled back to Laos to recuperate from the horrific losses of the previous year. The NVA were on the run, a result achieved in large measure through allied cooperation —testament to the success achieved by the flawed advisory system in South Vietnam.

Brothers in Arms

Coming to terms with the advisory effort in Vietnam is considerably more complex than understanding its structural strengths and weaknesses and the functionality of the adviser/counterpart relationship in battle. The interactions between young Americans and Australians so far from home and their Vietnamese counterparts who were living through a lifetime of conflict were full of foibles, jealousies, love, and hate, emotions and realities intensified by the war. Although advisory relationships were intensely personal, a glimpse into the complexities of how advisers and their counterparts worked together and lived together day by day at the nexus of the U.S./ARVN war effort is instructive in terms of the real-world possibilities, both good and bad, that formed the U.S./ARVN symbiosis.

Assimilation of the advisers into their new South Vietnamese units was always a difficult prospect. ARVN officers received no training to prepare them for being advised; the constant comings and goings of the Americans, some brash and some sympathetic, were simply the way of things. For their part, armed only with their cursory advisory training and knowing only enough Vietnamese to be socially pleasant, many U.S. and Australian advisers headed straight to their new assignments immediately upon arrival in the country and were forced to rely on their wits in a strange country amid a war they did not truly understand. Some, though, were "lucky" enough to receive an additional briefing in Vietnam. After deplaning at Tan Son Nhut Airbase outside Saigon, Joe Bolt had received three days of orientation and "a sack of bullets." The orientation, though, consisted mainly of lectures on the manifest bodily perils inherent in the consumption of Vietnamese food and graphic descriptions of the various venereal diseases carried by Vietnamese women. Bolt and his cohort were aghast at what lay ahead of them and wondered how they could survive living with and among the Vietnamese, much less survive the war.

After arriving at his new unit, the incoming adviser found the world something of blur and often faced the challenge of being the "new kid" who had to replace a trusted, experienced comrade in arms. For advisers, everything was new, from the language to the terrible heat to methods and modes of operation. In such a situation, it was often the introduction to combat itself that proved to be the most jarring experience. Captain Russell Smith, of the Australian Army Training Team, Vietnam, recalled that his first combat experience took place on his fourth day in the country:

> As I stood on the edge of a paddy checking our position I suddenly felt very alone. On looking around I noted everyone had gone to ground and had no idea why; Jack Morrison [an experienced noncommissioned adviser who had taken Smith under his wing] "whispered" in a controlled roar, "Sir!! The sounds you are hearing are you being shot at and whilst standing out there you are attracting attention in Mrs. Morrison's much loved husband's direction; get the fuck out of it or otherwise she may take to you, Sir!" This was one of the times he rolled his eyes heavenwards!! I hadn't heard a thing!![38]

Advisers found that ARVN base areas often lacked the material comforts associated with the bases of their American or Australian colleagues. Captain Wally Sheppard, of the Australian Army Training Team, Vietnam, was shocked by the lack of adequate facilities on his home ARVN base camp and received some cogent advice from a more experienced colleague to go and find an American rear-area supply officer:

> Can you imagine how he feels? His gung-ho buddies and classmates are out there gathering wounds, medals and glory, while he's flying a desk! What's he gonna' tell his friends and family back home? "I was the best paper-shuffler in Vietnam!?" For a captured weapon or VC flag he'll give you the shirt off his back!
>
> It worked!
>
> For a captured AK-47, I'd get a truck-load of cement, barbed-wire and/or sandbags! Throw in a captured VC flag and I could keep the truck too! I even had a demountable ablution building delivered by a

Jolly Green Giant . . . no questions asked! It had two toilets, hot/cold water shower, its own generator, etc. No more squatting over a hole in the ground having a crap![39]

The location of the base camps, often near the imposing jungles of the highlands, presented problems in and of itself. Russell Smith recalled:

Awoke in the evening with my poncho liner moving over my lower legs—snake!!! Very quietly calling the major to wake; he did and left his bed to come alongside me and said he could see the poncho liner moving. Told him to take my shotgun (loaded with U.S. issue buckshot) and on the count of three I would leap from the bed and he could send it to God. One, two, THREE and I was out of it—BOOM, BOOM, BOOM, BOOM, BOOM —the full tube of 00 buckshot disintegrated the bed, mattress & poncho liner—no snake remains—panic —couldn't say anything as the sound of the gun within the bunker had deafened us. As we realized that it was a floor positioned electric fan that had caused the poncho liner movement 1/2 a dozen heavily armed U.S. MACV personnel burst into the bunker to see which individual had flipped and shot t'other. We were rolling around cackling with relief as bits of bedding floated in the air; later that night I discovered the ability of single malt whisky to calm frazzled nerves.[40]

Even with all of the other differences, nuances, and oddities, it was mealtime that often required the most adaptation on the part of the advisers. Though advisers normally had access to their own rations, they often ate with their ARVN soldiers in a communal setting. The staple of the ARVN diet was rice with the ubiquitous nuoc mam fish sauce, but more exotic fare was sometimes on offer. Tom Jaco, a U.S. adviser, remembers that once a month in 1970, the 54th Regiment, for which Dinh then served as executive officer, procured a puppy and tethered it outside the mess tent. For days, the men leaving the tent would feed the puppy the scraps from their plates. At the end of the month, the now rather fat puppy would disappear—heralding "puppy day" for the officers and their advisers. Aided by copious amounts of Pabst Blue Ribbon beer, the chef did wonders with the tools at hand and always produced a tasty meal, if, in Jaco's words, "you could get past the idea that you were eating man's best friend."[41]

Major Tom Jaco (left) and Pham Van Dinh (right) during their time with the 54th Regiment. Photograph Courtesy of Tom Jaco.

Beyond the physical and societal makeup of the base camps, the ARVN military culture was something that required adaptation on the part of both American and Australian advisers. One morning, Tom Jaco accompanied an ARVN regimental commander to inspect the results of an NVA night assault on a fire support base. Knowing that the commander was unhappy with the performance of his men, Jaco expected the coming encounter to be a tense affair. Upon reaching the assembled ARVN officers, who were dutifully standing at attention, Jaco watched as the regimental commander exchanged a few pleasantries before striking the offending battalion commander in the nose. The regimental commander then went down the line of officers, striking each in turn. Finally, the group went inside the command bunker for its briefing, the regimental commander and Jaco on one side of the table and the unit officers, all with bloody noses, on the other.[42]

It was the tempo and the very nature of the Vietnamese war that proved the greatest shock for many Americans and Australians alike. In some cases, the perceived difference in the war effort manifested itself only in the adviser's taking note that Vietnamese units seemed less aggressive than he had hoped. On other occasions, the differences became almost comical. Travis Kirkland, a U.S. adviser who later became adviser to Tran Ngoc Hue and the Hac Bao, was surprised to discover that, during one of his first firefights, both sides took a break from the action for lunch before resuming the battle in earnest.

On occasion, the differences between the American and the Vietnamese ways of war strained the relationships between advisers and their counterparts to the breaking point. Bob Jones, who later in his career served as adviser to Tran Ngoc Hue and the Hac Bao, at one point advised a battalion commander who routinely avoided contact with enemy forces and seemed mainly to use his position of authority for graft and to meet and woo women. Disgusted and frustrated, Jones reported the command abuses, but, because of the offender's political connections, no action was taken, a problem common in many advisory accounts throughout the conflict. In an even more amazing scenario, amid one three-day battle that he judged to be going nowhere, Travis Kirkland, exercising his authority over U.S. fire support, suspended the wasteful shelling of enemy positions in an effort to convince his reluctant ARVN counterpart to order an infantry advance. The battalion commander was horrified—and demonstrated the all-too-familiar ARVN reliance on American firepower by demanding the continuation of the barrage and stating, "If it is loud it is good." When Kirkland refused, the ARVN officer pulled his pistol and put it to Kirkland's temple. Shocked, the remaining advisory staff rushed forward and drew their weapons. The tense standoff lasted for a few minutes before cooler heads prevailed and allowed the attack to go forward with the hitherto reluctant battalion commander leading the way.[43]

Though stresses and strains, some obviously severe, were apparent within the advisory effort, by 1969, such problems were far from the norm in the 1st ARVN Division AO in northern I Corps, in part because of the quality of ARVN leadership in the division. General Truong handpicked his battalion commanders and based his decisions solely on merit, without reference to the political whimsy that so pervaded the ARVN. Truong, though, did not have absolute power within his command, and there were indeed poor, but politically untouchable, battalion commanders in 1st Division. However, in general, 1st Division was the best that the ARVN had to offer, in terms of both leadership and combat ability, which led to advisory relationships that were both productive and close, representing the advisory effort at its best. Advisers looked forward to a stint in one of Truong's battalions and especially went out of their way to seek out service with units under the command of Pham Van Dinh or Tran Ngoc Hue.

Renowned for their exploits in the defense of Hue City, both Dinh and Hue had considerable reputations as combat commanders. When U.S. Marine Captain Harvey Zimmerle became adviser to 2/3 ARVN, in September 1968, he found Dinh to be cool and calculating. Confident in his own command abilities and able to speak three languages fluently, Dinh was concerned neither with his new adviser's inability to speak Vietnamese nor with his limited time in the country; instead, Dinh cut to the chase and asked Zimmerle for a demonstration of his ability to control fire support. In response, Zimmerle calmly called in a fire mission on a nearby tree line. Satisfied with the display, Dinh and Zimmerle went on to form a productive military partnership. Only later did Zimmerle discover the source of Dinh's offhand request that first day; a previous adviser with 2/3 had incorrectly called in a fire mission on the battalion CP that had caused several friendly casualties.

Despite the excellent relationships that Dinh and Hue enjoyed with their various advisers, in many ways providing the very model of adviser/counterpart success, there were inevitable periods of tension and discord. For his part, Zimmerle was often bewildered by some of Dinh's command decisions, especially when Dinh once boarded a medevac helicopter to return to Hue City to attend a family gathering. The tension, though, was certainly not all one-sided. Working on his first night with a new adviser who was fresh to combat on a fire base near the DMZ, Hue and his men watched an outgoing mission of harassment and interdiction artillery fire. The next morning, the adviser eagerly asked Hue when he and his men would conduct a mission to assess the damage done by the artillery barrage. Hue turned and informed the young captain that there would be no such mission. The perplexed American demanded that Hue send his men out to ascertain a body count. A veteran of countless missions in the dangerous area, Hue calmly informed his new counterpart that the NVA would be ready and waiting and that he would not throw away the lives of his men to ambush or booby traps just to count up a few more bodies. Suddenly the American became quite indignant and informed Hue that the lack of a body count meant that the fire mission had been wasted. He went on to claim that it was his family back in the United

States that had paid for those artillery shells with its hard-earned taxes. How could he let that effort and sacrifice go to waste?

Though punctuated by the highs and lows that typify any complex social interaction, the relationships between Dinh and Hue and their American advisers were in the main working partnerships dominated by the desire to survive and prevail in what was to the Vietnamese a seemingly endless war. Though the Hac Bao often operated differently, being called to aid in firefights that were already under way, in general ARVN battalions and companies of the 1st ARVN Division spent much of their time engaged in search-and-destroy operations in the northern two provinces of I Corps. Sometimes the operations would support their own base camps, including PK 17, but, especially as the allied offensives of 1968 continued, the operations became more sustained and more distant from friendly territory.

ARVN units often operated in the deep bush for weeks on end; isolated and reliant on helicopters for resupply, the soldiers experienced high stress levels comparable to those of the 2/3, the Hac Bao, and their sister units engaged in a constant and steady stream of reconnaissance in force (RIF) missions, endless patrolling, night ambushes, and security operations at the fire bases that dotted the highlands of I Corps. With enemy forces on the run, the sweeps were rather hit-or-miss affairs, often resulting in no hostile contact whatsoever and only sometimes yielding a short clash with enemy units usually no larger than a platoon. However, enemy units, recuperating and refitting following the Tet disaster, lurked in base areas just across the Laotian border and could strike out at any time from their safe havens, leaving ARVN and U.S. forces acutely aware that a major battle could break out at any moment. On each patrol, everyone realized that the enemy might be hidden in great numbers in the next treeline or might be dug in on the next ridge. It was a lethal and draining game of cat and mouse.

Compared to those of their American counterparts, ARVN operations were more deliberate and had a rather rustic flair. The units under the command of Dinh and Hue were representative in that each morning the men would gather from night positions and the cook would brew some coffee and later fill the canteen of each soldier with tea, boiled to ward off waterborne diseases. The unit would then patrol until 1030, when a halt would be called for lunch, usually consisting of rice balls. Patrolling would then resume until the late afternoon, when a halt would be called to enter night defensive positions, often utilizing a double ring of defenses around the battalion CP and including several ambush positions to foil enemy probes. The cooks would then prepare the evening meal, slaughtering the chickens that the men carried tied to their rucksacks or pigs, which were carried along by the men on poles. On particularly difficult missions, ARVN soldiers sometimes supplemented their diet by hunting water buffalo, the livers of which were considered a special delicacy. The nature of the ARVN operational system made resupply day particularly raucous, as helicopters disgorged a fresh load of unhappy squawking or oinking live cargo along with ammunition and water.

The reality of participating in the ARVN war, struggling through the "wait-a-minute vines" and dense undergrowth of the trackless jungle day in and day out, chatting over dinner while surviving on the same meager rations, suffering from jungle ulcers, facing the constant expectation presented by an unseen enemy, and facing battles both large and small often gave the combat advisers and their counterparts a sense of camaraderie that belied the institutional and cultural difficulties that bedeviled the advisory system at its highest levels. For their part, both Dinh and Hue formed lasting bonds with several of their U.S. advisers, introducing them to Vietnamese culture, taking them into their homes, and even formally adopting them into their units. While in Hue City, home to several men who served under Dinh and Hue, the advisers often slept in hammocks on the porches of unit members rather than journey to their own accommodations at the MACV compound.

The adviser/counterpart relationships, though filled with the often trivial moments that define all friendships, also contained moments of bravery and heroism that typify brotherhood forged in battle. In late 1968, in the area south of Hue near Phu Bai, the Hac Bao had just completed a heavy engagement and begun a move toward the district town. Suddenly an explosion blew Hue's adviser, Joe Bolt, off his feet. Everything came to a halt, and, when Bolt came to his senses, he noticed that, while he had received only minor wounds, the man before him in the line had been blown to pieces and the two men behind him had been badly maimed. Struggling to get his bearings, Bolt heard other explosions, which meant that the Hac Bao had wandered into the middle of a minefield. Any movement meant possible death. However, there were severely wounded men who needed care, including Sergeant Weyand, a trusted member of Bolt's advisory team. Heedless of the danger, Tran Ngoc Hue sprinted through the minefield to Weyand's side and administered lifesaving first aid to his friend while awaiting helicopter extraction.

The deep bonds of camaraderie that were part of the advisory effort, and were part of the lives of Dinh and Hue, were so resilient that they endured the harshest of challenges, as evidenced in different ways by the experiences of the last U.S. advisers to serve with both men. Dave Wiseman, who had to sit by and listen on the radio as Hue's unit was destroyed in Laos, never gave up searching for his dear friend, though he had reason to believe that Hue had perished in battle. William Camper served as Dinh's last adviser and very nearly lost his life when Dinh surrendered at Camp Carroll. However, Camper feels no ill will toward Dinh and in fact still has respect for the ARVN commander whom he came to know so long ago. As part of the research for this project, several advisers sought contact with Dinh or Hue for the first time in decades, advisers who knew neither that Dinh had surrendered nor that Hue had survived the war and now lived in the United States. When the old comrades of war finally regained contact, the joy was palpable and transcended space, time, and the flow of events. The close bonds that still remain between these advisers and their counterparts—men who had been through so much and whose lives had changed so dramatically—serve as a testament to what was right about the advisory effort in Vietnam.

Elusive Victory

The year of fighting after the Tet Offensive arguably brought the United States and South Vietnam to the brink of victory in the Vietnam War. The campaign in the lowlands, typified by the remarkable cooperative action of the 101st Airborne and the 1st ARVN Division, had largely cleared the rice-growing areas of I Corps of enemy units and had done much to whittle away at the Viet Cong infrastructure in local villages—a success repeated throughout much of the country. Even the NVA historians of the conflict ruefully admit that in the fighting that followed the Tet Offensive,

Our offensive posture began to weaken and our three types of armed forces suffered attrition. The political and military struggle in the rural areas declined and our liberated areas shrank. COSVN and military region main force units were able to maintain only a portion of their forces in our scattered lowland base areas, and most of our main force troops were forced back to the border or to bases in the mountains.[44]

During the Tet fighting and the year of slaughter that followed, the Viet Cong had suffered greatly, losing the vast majority of its experienced cadre—losses that would have to be made good in part by the infiltration of NVA soldiers, a process that not only would take time but also would alter the insurgent nature of the conflict.[45]

With enemy forces for all intents and purposes driven from the lowlands, in November 1968, U.S. and ARVN forces launched an ambitious Accelerated Pacification Program aimed at making the hard-won control of the countryside more permanent and thorough. In northern I Corps, Truong's goal for the campaign was the seizure and control of 140 contested hamlets, which units under his command successfully occupied in a little over a month. Buoyed by the success, Truong raised the goal to 198 hamlets, a target that also was reached without difficulty.[46] Across the length and breadth of South Vietnam, battlefield victory begat pacification success as the total number of people and the extent of territory under GVN control surpassed expectations.[47] By the close of the year, some 76.3 percent of the population was brought within areas of government security (with control of 11.4 percent of the population contested and 12.3 percent under Viet Cong control), a proportion never before equaled.[48] Though both U.S. and South Vietnamese methods of quantifying the control of the countryside were notoriously inaccurate, the scale of the victory in the lowlands in the year after Tet was obvious to the men on the ground, including Joe Bolt, who simply remarked, "You could not find a fight in the lowlands in late 1968; the enemy was gone."

The successes in the lowlands had heralded arguably even more meaningful victories in the highlands, with U.S. and ARVN forces defeating enemy offensives and acting in cooperation to press the NVA further from populated areas and into their bases in Laos and North Vietnam. In a briefing for General Abrams, the new COMUSMACV, in

January 1969, the MACV chief of staff, Major General Elias Townsend, summed up record of allied successes:

> Two major changes since last year. The first is the degree of improvement in the maturity of the South Vietnamese armed forces. . . . And those people have been running constantly in every TAOR, all the time. . . . This constant movement finally broke the enemy and brought about this withdrawal [to Laos], uncovering of VC main forces, local forces, his caches, his pulling back to the area of sanctuaries, and enabled us to do what we've been able to do about tearing out the VC infrastructure, going back along his line of communications and tearing it up.[49]

In many ways, it seemed that an allied victory in the Vietnam War beckoned in early 1969, a time that Abrams recognized as "a moment of supreme opportunity"—an opportunity that many in the ARVN, including Dinh and Hue, realized was at hand as the ARVN, with the support of its mighty ally, came of age. However, at the same time that the tactical situation seemed so positive, the aftereffects of the Tet Offensive, years of war, government prevarication, and constant social upheaval conspired to exhaust America's collective patience with its distant war.

A New Way Forward?

On 1 July 1968, General Creighton Abrams replaced Westmoreland as COMUSMACV. While serving in his previous post as Westmoreland's deputy, though he had remained loyal to his chief, Abrams had come to believe that there was a less traditional answer to the complex problem that was the Vietnam War. As a recipient of the PROVN study of 1966, Abrams fully understood the importance of pacification. Also, according to William Colby, who served Abrams as Deputy COMUSMACV and as his principal adviser on pacification matters, Abrams took a broader view of the war than his predecessor and was more able to see the war more in its Vietnamese context rather than simply as an American military exercise.[50] Abrams believed that American strategy had artificially separated the myriad shards of the Vietnam War, from pacification to battles of attrition, when those pieces were actually part of the same hermetic whole, pieces that he hoped to gather together as COMUSMACV in his "One War" strategy. One of the central tenets of his new vision for the conflict, modeled on the success in I Corps, was that the ARVN should be more fully and completely integrated into the fighting and management of the war on all levels. In a briefing on 25 January 1969, Abrams remarked concerning cooperation:

> The 3rd Marines are now in it like this, the 101st, the 1st ARVN. That's the *best* example. *That's* where there's one war, is in northern I Corps. All us on one side and them on the other. Nobody's looking for honors. They're just all for one and one for all. It's just who's nearest. . . . And that's what we need in southern I Corps, in the lower three provinces. And we don't have that.[51]

As Abrams worked to implement his new tactical ideas, the strategic level of the war shifted with the November 1968 election of Richard Nixon as president of the United States. Having achieved electoral success in part because he had run as a peace candidate, Nixon, along with his National Security Adviser, Henry Kissinger, and his Secretary of Defense, Melvin Laird, worked quickly to devise a successful strategy for Vietnam. Nixon and his advisers realized that, though the electorate would afford the new administration a honeymoon period, the political furor over Vietnam would quickly return. The matter was so urgent that on his first full day in office, Nixon issued National Security Study Memorandum 1, which called for a revised study of the progress of the war. Building on the momentum for change, in March 1969, Nixon directed Laird to go to Vietnam to make a firsthand assessment of the conflict.

Learning from MACV staff that there had been significant improvement in the abilities of the ARVN, Laird warned Abrams that political pressures at home soon would necessitate turning over the bulk of the war to the South Vietnamese. Acting on information gleaned from his meetings at MACV and from a sense of political need, after his return to Washington Laird authored a memorandum that proposed a withdrawal of fifty to seventy thousand troops in 1969. In a National Security Council meeting on 28 March, the president and his advisers discussed Laird's memorandum. General Andrew Goodpaster, Abrams's deputy in Saigon, reported that the ability of the ARVN had increased markedly and had already led to some "de-Americanizing" of the war. Laird took exception to the term as too negative and suggested "Vietnamization" as an alternative.[52]

Both the temperament of the new COMUSMACV and the political reality faced on the homefront by the new administration conspired once again to alter the nature of the conflict faced by the ARVN. Abrams's new vision for the Vietnam War, arguably based on the acceptance of ideas that had previously been rejected by Westmoreland, foreshadowed positive changes that had been called for by younger officers, including both Dinh and Hue, for years. Abrams's vision, though, was but one element of a dynamic environment of change emanating from Washington that called for the Vietnamization of the war. The battlefield victories of 1968 and the continued ARVN improvement, then, existed in tenuous balance with a fluid tactical and strategic environment as the war reached a tipping point.

On the basis of the success achieved by the combined efforts of U.S. and ARVN forces in northern I Corps in the year after Tet, his own vision for change, and political pressure from above, Abrams developed the new "Combined Campaign Plan for 1969," which ended the division of missions between U.S. and South Vietnamese forces. To prepare the South Vietnamese for the day when U.S. troops would entirely exit the conflict, the ARVN would "learn to fight by fighting" and be integrated into the big-unit war. Drawing inspiration from the Korean War, in which Korean and American units had fought side by side and had done well, the plan called for a fuller integration of planning, combat support, and intelligence.[53] No longer would the ARVN be relegated to security duty while the Americans fought their war; finally, it seemed that the allies would fight together as one.

The new way forward represented by cooperation, though, stood in stark contrast to years of U.S. military policy during which the ARVN had been shunted aside. From 1965 to 1968, efforts to achieve actual combat cooperation had been faltering, piecemeal, and intensely individualistic, leaving the overall combat effectiveness of the ARVN marginal and its combat support assets limited. Large-scale actions against enemy main-force units, with the exception of northern I Corps, were almost exclusively planned and carried out by U.S. forces. At higher levels, the stratified system meant that most ARVN corps commanders had no real experience in formulating or carrying out operational plans of any type. At the brigade and battalion level, General Truong contended that "U.S. unit commanders were generally reluctant to participate in combined operations with ARVN units . . . derived chiefly from a prejudice against the combat effectiveness of ARVN units."[54]

Shifting away from such an ingrained system of separation would take both time and complete effort—neither of which would be forthcoming. Well-intentioned efforts at true cooperation were made, again with northern I Corps standing as the leading example of the program's potential. In several areas, "Dong Tien" or pair-off efforts placed U.S. and Vietnamese unit commanders side by side in combat.[55] However, larger operations continued to be carried out in a unilateral fashion, while multinational efforts remained the exception rather than the rule.[56]

The belated American efforts to fight a war with the ARVN rather than orchestrate two separate wars remained halting and maddeningly incomplete. The military situation had improved dramatically in the year following Tet, and the ARVN was growing in power. The opportunity, though, was to slip by, lost in political decisions to end the war in Vietnam, a South Vietnamese lack of will to reform, and American military failures to seize the cooperative moment. The ARVN remained flawed and dependent as the crisis of American withdrawal from the conflict neared, belying the hopes of Dinh and Hue. The ultimate irony is that perhaps the victories of 1968 came too late, after the indelible realities of the Vietnam War had already been set in cement.

6

Hamburger Hill

The Untold Story of the Battle for Dong Ap Bia

HOPING TO BUILD on the startling gains of 1968 through the prosecution of combined operations, Abrams planned to redouble offensive efforts against the NVA and its base areas in 1969. Although he realized that NVA forces were marshaling in Laos and that the communists might be planning a new attack of their own, Abrams called on his commanders to maintain "unrelenting pressure on the VC/NVA main force units. We must carry the fight to the enemy and complete his destruction." He then put the situation in more colorful language, stating that the coming allied offensive would "go after the enemy's machinery, crack his engine block, drain his oil, strip his gears, break his fuel lines, remove his spark plugs, and otherwise put his engine beyond repair or rebuild."[1]

As Abrams and his subordinates planned their offensive, life changed for Tran Ngoc Hue. Having proven his worth again and again as a combat leader, in January 1969, Hue received promotion to major and the command of the 1st Battalion, 3rd ARVN Regiment. Although sad to leave his beloved Hac Bao, Hue was excited to face the challenges offered by leading a larger unit. Immediately, 1/3 embarked for the continuing operations in and around the A Shau Valley, but Hue contracted a case of malaria and had to be medevaced to the hospital at Phu Bai. After a period of recovery, Hue took over command of the 5th Battalion of the 2nd ARVN Regiment, only to have the malaria reoccur, which resulted in another hospital stay. The recuperation from both bouts of malaria cost Tran Ngoc Hue a total of three months, after which, in July 1969, he assumed command of the 2nd Battalion, 2nd ARVN Regiment.[2]

As Hue recuperated from his illness, Dinh's 2/3 ARVN arrived at Phu Bai for a welcome period of refitting and refresher training. Relative inaction in a base camp provided both men a chance to reflect on

the events of the past year. Hue and Dinh, freshly promoted to lieutenant colonel, were acutely aware that the allies held the upper hand
in the struggle, and to them the next move seemed natural and indeed
simple; U.S. and ARVN forces should invade Laos and perhaps even
North Vietnam to convert their hard-won tactical successes into ultimate strategic victory. After years of struggle, both believed that the
end of the war was drawing near.

Bright, well read, and observant of current events, Dinh and Hue
were aware of a disquieting level of political unrest on the American
homefront but believed that the trouble would pass and would not
adversely affect the tide of victory in Vietnam. To South Vietnamese
observers, basing military decisions on the whim of public perception
seemed unthinkable. Dinh, Hue, and their countrymen did not believe
in their worst nightmares that their American allies would settle for
less than ultimate victory and thus void the blood sacrifice of years for
the sake of mollifying protesters in the streets at home. It was time to
strike a merciless blow, for both Dinh and Hue believed that the enemy, though battered, was using the respite in Laos to resupply and
rearm. As military victory and Vietnamization hung in the balance,
the critical hour of the war was at hand, a moment that would never
return. The chance that Dinh and Hue saw for decisive action, however, slipped away like the mirage it was, an unlimited goal caught
in the reality of America's limited war. Instead of taking the fight into
the enemy homeland, the U.S. and ARVN forces saw the optimism
of early 1969 fall to pieces, squandered in the bloody Battle of Hamburger Hill. Though undertaken amid a supposedly cooperative environment of change, Hamburger Hill was initially an American affair,
but it was also a battle in which Dinh was destined to play a central
role and a battle that interacted with the fluid reality of Vietnamization to transform the ever-changing Vietnam War yet again.

Into the A Shau

On 10 May, three battalions of the 101st Airborne Division—1st Battalion, 506th Infantry; 3rd Battalion, 187th Infantry; and 2nd Battalion
501st Infantry—along with the 4th Battalion, 1st ARVN Regiment,
launched Operation Apache Snow, which was designed once and for
all to neutralize enemy bases and communications in the A Shau Val-

ley.[3] The sudden insertion of U.S. forces into the remote valley caught the NVA by surprise, and the maneuver companies of 3/187 met light resistance, first thought only to be trail watchers, as they moved in reconnaissance in force (RIF) missions toward their objective of Hill 937 (Dong Ap Bia). The next day, following blood trails indicating where the NVA had dragged the bodies of their dead through the elephant grass, the men of 3/187 moved with ever greater caution, because the rapidly rising ground was dotted with numerous spider holes, bunkers, and even communication cables, suggesting the presence of an enemy force of great size. In the afternoon, the tension broke as the elusive NVA rained a hail of fire on Bravo Company of 3/187 from an intricate bunker complex guarding the approaches to Hill 937. Caught in a murderous crossfire, the lead elements of Bravo Company suffered heavy losses, with wounded and dead falling to the ground under fire and out of reach of their comrades. Outnumbered and outgunned, Bravo struggled on in bitter and costly fighting until all of the wounded had been recovered. Bravo then called for a medevac, but during the recovery operation a Cobra gunship inadvertently fired a salvo of rockets into friendly lines, resulting in several more casualties. As Bravo finally retreated from contact, the commander of 3/187, Lieutenant Colonel Weldon Honeycutt, received information indicating that their foe atop Dong Ap Bia was the entire 29th NVA Regiment, fresh from a refit in North Vietnam. Honeycutt, brash and confident, was pleased that an enemy force initially estimated at 1,800 men had chosen to stand and fight against 3/187 and stated, "Good. That's what we are lookin' for too—a big fight."[4]

On 12 May, the maneuver companies of 3/187 moved across the rugged terrain to determine the nature and disposition of the enemy force, for Honeycutt and his superiors had to know what they were up against in order to bring their tremendous firepower advantage to bear. Although all three of the maneuver companies came under fire, it fell to Bravo Company to move on Dong Ap Bia itself. Again Bravo ran into heavy enemy fire from a series of fortified positions along the slopes of the hill, which neither air strikes nor artillery were able to silence. After hours of hard fighting, the Americans had to withdraw from contact and dig in for the night. Although the battle was still young, a distressing pattern was already developing. During the day, U.S. forces fought bitterly to claw through enemy bunker systems and move toward the summit of Dong Ap Bia. As night closed in, the

American companies, bloodied and losing cohesion, retreated down the hill to safe areas. During the hours of darkness, the NVA forces reoccupied their old bunkers, and the battle began afresh for the same ground the next day, yielding similarly bloody and indecisive results. It was a battle more about attrition than seizing territory and as such served as a microcosm of the Vietnam War.

The following day, Honeycutt attempted to maneuver B, C, and D Companies into place for a combined assault on the hill. As they negotiated the heavily wooded stream beds, ravines, and crags of the area, though, each company became involved in heavy fighting and failed to reach its jumping-off point for the coming assault. Frustrated by continued losses (four dead and thirty-three wounded on 13 May) and lack of progress, Honeycutt was now certain beyond a shadow of doubt that "the NVA were present in considerable strength in the vicinity of Hill 937"[5] and were determined to make U.S. forces pay for the hill in blood. Regardless of the odds, though, Honeycutt and his superiors decided to press on with the assault and once again launch the weakened 3/187 into the maelstrom.

A Tedious Assault

Before moving forward, on 14 May, U.S. soldiers looked on as their air power shredded the hill with high explosive and napalm. After the spectacle, B and C Companies made their move on Dong Ap Bia from the west, while D Company moved in from the north. Faced with heavy NVA defensive fire, and slowed by a deep ravine and the loss of a medevac helicopter, Delta made little progress and had to fall back. Further west, though, Charlie and Bravo companies enjoyed more success and fought their way through shattered bunker complexes against heavy enemy fire of all types, including command-detonated claymore mines and suicide snipers who had tied themselves into the tops of the remaining tall trees in the area. In the early afternoon, two squads of Bravo Company emerged onto the crest of the battered hill, only to find yet another major bunker complex; they reported that "the top of the ridge was covered with blood, pieces of bodies and enemy dead."[6]

Having achieved their goal, but badly battered and dangerously exposed, Charlie and Bravo Companies now faced an NVA force of battalion strength, which moved in from the reverse slope of Dong Ap Bia and began to encircle the attackers. Threatened with destruction, the tired troopers of 3/187 pulled back from the hard-won summit of Hill 937. Enemy losses had been severe; a quick tally of the carnage atop Dong Ap Bia resulted in an estimate of seventy-six enemy dead. However, 3/187 had lost an additional five killed and fifty-eight wounded,[7] a slow bloodletting that necessitated calling in replacements and eventually resulted in the gutting of the battalion. As 3/187 broke contact and retreated to night positions, the NVA, drawing on its heavy advantage in numbers, again reinforced and reoccupied its bunker complexes on the slopes of Hill 937. The weary Americans faced the grim prospect of fighting for the same bunkers all over again the next day against an enemy that was ready and waiting.

The ongoing battle for Dong Ap Bia now had the undivided attention of Colonel Joseph Conmy, commander of 3rd Brigade, who arrived at Honeycutt's command post that night for a briefing. Disturbed that his 3/187 was struggling at Hamburger Hill alone, while the other allied battalions taking part in Operation Apache Snow had seen but little fighting, Honeycutt gave Conmy a soldier's account of his perception of the situation:

> Joe, this fight is getting awful rough. . . . I don't know how many of the bastards are up there, but I know there's a helluva lot of them. The bastards have got heavy weapons. They've got communications. They're dug in. They've got a defense in depth, and they're movin' fresh troops up those draws from Laos every night. Every night, and I don't have the manpower to stop them. We're in a goddamn fight here, Joe—and I mean a fight! . . . Joe, we've got to get some help out here. . . . The 506th has got to get their asses in gear and get involved in this fight.[8]

Conmy agreed with Honeycutt's appraisal of the situation and told the 3/187th commander that 1/506 was moving in the direction of Dong Ap Bia as support and that the ARVN were preparing to move, as well. The news did little to cheer Honeycutt, who realized that 1/506 was too distant to provide any immediate aid.

On 15 May, with A Company relieving C Company, 3/187 launched another major assault on Hill 937. By this time, the constant bombardment of the hill had transformed the ground into a twisted wreckage of shattered trees, making the terrain nearly impassable in places. Bravo Company faced the heaviest fire and requested helicopter support to make good its advance. The gunships, though, came in from the wrong direction and, instead of hitting the enemy bunker complex, mistakenly fired their rockets at the command element of Bravo Company, killing two and wounding fourteen. Later in the day, enemy RPG rounds detonated in the battalion command post, wounding several, including Honeycutt himself.

Enemy forces, still estimated at a full regiment, fought tenaciously and with great skill from a series of bunkers arranged in concentric rows, which afforded maximum utilization of the difficult terrain and left U.S. forces to face small-arms fire, mortar barrages, claymore mines, machine-gun fire, and massed infantry counterattacks. The NVA also used its position further up the slope to its advantage and rolled grenades down the hill into the advancing American ranks. Amid the chaos, A Company moved to within seventy-five meters of the top of the hill, but heavily engaged B Company failed to keep pace. Realizing that his lead elements were again exposed and vulnerable as the NVA maneuvered on their flanks, Honeycutt reluctantly gave the order to withdraw from contact to the lines occupied the previous night. The steady losses had taken their toll, with A Company reporting one hundred men ready for action, while B Company had been reduced to only sixty-five effectives.[9] As a result of the scale of the fighting and the level of loss, Conmy decided that any further attacks on Dong Ap Bia would have to wait until 1/506 arrived to take the pressure off the bloodied and weakened 3/187.

Reinforcements

Because of the overall strength of the NVA in the area, it took 1/506 two days to make its way into position to take part in the attack on what had become known as Hamburger Hill. The delay was frustrating for the impatient Honeycutt but came as a welcome respite for his troops. Finally, massive air strikes and artillery preparation on the morning of 18 May heralded the two-battalion advance on Hamburger Hill. After the devastating fire, a tear gas barrage ensued—but affected the attacking forces of 3/187. Fire was quickly adjusted, but then the prevailing wind blew the gas harmlessly into Laos, the gas therefore having achieved nothing. Even so, by midmorning, A and D Companies of 3/187 had moved under the cover of the artillery barrage to their start points some two hundred meters below the crest of the hill. To the south, though, 1/506 met heavy resistance and advanced slowly, taking fire from bunkers on all sides, which left the battered 3/187 once again alone and exposed in the final stages of its assault.

Delta and Alpha Companies of 3/187 made good initial progress and again advanced to within seventy-five meters of the top of Hamburger Hill but then fell under heavy fire from unseen NVA lurking in a complex of bunkers and in the few remaining trees. Claymores roared their deadly greeting, and satchel charges whirled in amid the cacophony of small-arms fire. In addition, mortars on the east side of the hill had zeroed in on Delta and rained down a steady stream of shells. The battle raged for more than half an hour, during which time all of D Company's officers received wounds, leaving an NCO in command of a company that had been reduced to a total of only fifty-seven men who were able to fight. Though A Company had fared somewhat better, the situation for D Company was desperate; yet they were so close to the top of Hamburger Hill! Feeling that victory was near, Honeycutt ordered the beleaguered troops to hold fast and sent C Company forward with badly needed ammunition and supplies.

Though 1/506 still lagged behind and his units had taken heavy losses, Honeycutt remained positive that the arrival of C Company would make the difference and that Hamburger Hill would fall. He was so sure of impending success that he headed toward the front lines to be with the forward elements of his command when it achieved the historic victory. Suddenly, though, the sky erupted in a downpour, making matters immeasurably worse. The tortured hillside now became a wilderness of mud, three feet deep in some places, that made forward movement nearly impossible and grounded air support. Realizing that he could not order his men further in such conditions, Honeycutt reluctantly ordered his troops to fall back, and 3/187 made its way back down Hamburger Hill into defensive night positions. 1/506, which had not made nearly as substantial gains, also had to withdraw.

The struggle for Hamburger Hill had already been long, bitter, and quite costly. The losses were greatest for 3/187, which had been in the battle nearly eight days. Though replacements had arrived during the battle, most were raw recruits. The true key to the fighting strength of 3/187 lay in the number of veterans who remained from the outset of Operation Apache Snow, which puts the ferocity of the fighting at Hamburger Hill into perspective. Since the beginning of the operation, Alpha and Bravo Companies had lost nearly 50 percent of the men on their original rosters, while Charlie and Delta companies had lost nearly 80 percent.[10] A better-known account of the price paid by 3/187 appeared in an AP story filed by the reporter Jay Scharbutt, who had interviewed Honeycutt and several 3/187 troopers. Scharbutt was fascinated by the ebb and flow of the battle and saw the fighting as illustrative of the Vietnam War. His widely circulated account of the battle helped to reignite lingering controversy on the American homefront with its graphic accounts of the seeming futility of the fighting:

> Paratroopers came down from the mountain, their shirts dark green with sweat, their weapons gone, their bandages stained brown and red from mud and blood. Many cursed their hard nosed Battalion commander, LTC Honeycutt, who sent three companies Sunday to take the 3,000 ft mountain just over a mile east of Laos and overlooking a shell pocketed A Shau Valley. They failed and suffered. "That damn Black Jack [Honeycutt's call sign] won't stop until he kills every one of us," said one of the 40–50 Airborne Division troopers wounded. Honeycutt, 38, of Columbus, GA, had been given an order: take the mountain.[11]

Reorganization

As casualties mounted and political storm clouds gathered, Major General Melvin Zais, commander of the 101st Division, rather belatedly decided to gather reinforcements for a climactic four-battalion assault on Dong Ap Bia. Considering the new American focus on allied cooperation, the ongoing fighting seemed the perfect occasion to involve the ARVN in a truly major battle, and General Truong received word to prepare one of his best battalions for action at Hamburger Hill. For this most important mission, Truong chose 2/3 ARVN.[12] However, the battle, sometimes heralded as the apogee of U.S./ARVN cooperation, actually revealed the weaknesses and flaws of the cooperative system, a basic yet powerful answer to the problems of the Vietnam War, but an idea that was proved by Hamburger Hill to be both belated and shallow. The ARVN had not been included in any of the major planning for the battle and came to the battle late, and the relationship between 2/3 and their American allies proved contentious. When the test came, the war in Vietnam remained an American war.

The plan developed by Zais and his staff for the final assault on Dong Ap Bia called for a coordinated attack on the hilltop from all directions by 1/506, 2/501, 2/3 ARVN, and 2/506, which was slated to relieve Honeycutt's battered 3/187. When Honeycutt learned of the decision to replace 3/187, he was livid. His unit had done most of the fighting and, he believed, deserved the accolades that came with final victory, and, when Zais visited Honeycutt's headquarters, the commander of 3/187 made his opinion clear. Honeycutt informed Zais that the decision to relieve 3/187 "stunk." "After all the fighting this battalion has been through, after all the casualties we've taken, if you pull us out now, it will forever be viewed as a disgrace by everyone in the division." Honeycutt then assured Zais that 3/187 could take the top of Dong Ap Bia with only one additional company. Contending that only bad luck and bad weather had stymied 3/187 in its previous attempts at the summit, Honeycutt said:

> General, if there is anybody that deserves to take that sonofabitch, it's the Rakkasans [the nickname of 3/187]—and you know that as well as I do. And there just is no goddamn way in hell I wanna see . . . the 2/506th come in here and take that mountain after all we've been through. And if it ain't gonna be that way, then you just better fire my ass right now. Right this minute![13]

Persuaded by Honeycutt's emotional appeal, Zais allowed the brash leader and the weary troopers of 3/187 to have their chance at victory. The fight for Hamburger Hill had become a defining moment of the entire conflict. U.S. policy in Vietnam and the reputation of the American military were on the line, splashed across newspaper headlines for all to see. American forces had to take Hamburger Hill to vindicate U.S. policy. A perfect conclusion to the battle entailed the battered but resilient 3/187 breaching the enemy lines and rushing to victory on the bloody hilltop, not any other U.S. unit and certainly not the ARVN, objects of scorn and ridicule in the United States. Such a scenario would be a public relations nightmare and a blow to American morale.

For the allied units involved in the planned assault on Hamburger Hill, 19 May was a day of movement and preparation. Honeycutt and 3/187 received the support of A Company of 2/506, and, under the cover of heavy preparatory fire, the units moved into their attack positions tight against the enemy's main defenses for the combined assault, scheduled for the next day. To the southwest, 1/506 met considerable resistance but also reached its attack positions some two hundred meters from the top of the hill. To the northeast, 2/501 choppered in and moved toward Dong Ap Bia, leaving it the longest distance to traverse in the attack. 2/3 ARVN hit the ground to the southeast of Dong Ap Bia early in the afternoon of 19 May and made its way to its jump-off point for the main assault without incident. Dinh's unit would have one of the longer lines of advance, beginning its assault some five hundred meters below the crest of Hamburger Hill.

Was Hamburger Hill Worth It?

The story of the fall of Dong Ap Bia is both celebrated and controversial in the United States. Was assaulting and taking Hamburger Hill by brute force while suffering heavy losses truly necessary, or would massive air strikes have accomplished the same result? In that sense, Hamburger Hill serves as a microcosm of the entire American war in Vietnam. The celebrated part of the battle is also well known in American sources ranging from military documents to popular film. Pushed to the brink of its endurance by its seemingly heartless commander, 3/187 harnessed its waning strength for an epic push to the top of the shattered hilltop against fanatical but, in the end, futile enemy resistance. The other allied units straggled up the hill only after the enemy had broken and began retreating into Laos.

The story, though stirring and compelling, is false; the men of 2/3 ARVN, not 3/187, were the first to achieve the summit of Hamburger Hill. The true story, though common knowledge among South Vietnamese, is little known in the United States, intentionally forgotten as an embarrassing episode in one of America's crucial battles of the war.

The Traditional Story

According to accepted historical tradition, on 20 May at 1000 hours, following the most intense and effective artillery barrage of the entire battle, one ARVN and three U.S. battalions moved forward into the final assault on Dong Ap Bia. 1/506, encountering very stiff resistance, barely reached the southern edge of the hill by midafternoon. 2/501 met no enemy resistance in its drive to the northeast and halted in a blocking position below the crest of the hill. Beginning at 0942, 2/3 ARVN reported that it was receiving friendly mortar fire,[14] a real risk when units are attacking a target from all angles. Once the fire ceased, 2/3 met little enemy resistance in its advance. Even so, after losing two U.S. advisers to wounds, some of the ARVN troops fled.[15] After being rallied by their officers, the ARVN forces finally moved forward and fought well, and at 1230 they reached the top of Hamburger Hill.

The brunt of the battle, the story goes, fell to the troopers of 3/187, who, augmented by the strength of A Company 2/506, moved forward cautiously. In what seemed a ghostly calm, the men advanced through the first major bunker complex, one that had caused so much suffering in the past, without incident. Some of the men dared to hope that the NVA had held true to past form and slipped off in the night and that the battle had come to an end. As 3/187 neared the second bunker complex, though, the NVA struck at point-blank range. Enemy fire poured in from all directions, and the slope of the hill was so steep that the NVA again rolled grenades into the American lines. Urged on by Honeycutt, 3/187 pushed through the last remaining enemy defenses, and, at 1144, C Company, which had suffered so much in earlier battles, reached the crest of Hamburger Hill. NVA forces launched furious counterattacks to push the invader back, but the other companies of 3/187 closed in and secured the lodgment atop the hill.

From this point, the level of enemy resistance varied. Some units that still occupied bunker complexes on other parts of the hill fought on, other NVA soldiers chose to die sacrificially, and many others simply fled. For hours, the four allied battalions on Hamburger Hill searched out the last remaining pockets of NVA resistance and also discovered sizable weapons caches, including 152 individual and 25 crew-served weapons, 75,000 rounds of ammunition, and 10 tons of rice. The NVA had chosen to stand and fight on Dong Ap Bia and had paid dearly, suffering an estimated 633 dead. American losses were also heavy, numbering 70 dead and 372 wounded. Although mopping-up operations in the area continued for a further seventeen days, the beleaguered victors of 3/187 departed Dong Ap Bia on 21 May for a well-earned rest at Eagle Beach, on the South China Sea. The battle had been won, but lingering questions remained about the value of the struggle and its attendant suffering. What was beyond doubt, though, was that the valiant 3/187 had achieved its goal. Their seizure of Hamburger Hill had validated a long and brutal struggle.

Unsung Heroes

The use of new evidence, coupled with a fresh look at existing sources, allows for a retelling of the capture of Dong Ap Bia that incorporates the South Vietnamese perspective. 2/3 ARVN departed on helicopters on the morning of 19 May toward Fire Base Curahee, while Dinh and his adviser, Major Harvey Zimmerle, USMC, undertook an aerial reconnaissance of possible landing zones nearer Hamburger Hill.[16] Just after 1300, 2/3 air assaulted into its landing zone and lost only two men, who tumbled into a nearby bomb crater and broke their legs.

Once on the ground, the 2/3 quickly made its way toward its line of departure for the upcoming assault, sent out reconnaissance patrols, and prepared defensive positions for the night. Realizing that the enemy was all around, 2/3 moved again under cover of darkness to another defensive position and did not allow the men to light cooking fires. The precaution seemingly paid off, but Dinh and Zimmerle soon realized that the coming assault of Hamburger Hill was fraught with danger. As 2/3 ARVN scouted the terrain, Warrant Officer Max Kelly, a normally stoic adviser from the AATTV with a wealth of knowledge gained in stints in World War II and Korea, put the thoughts of all into words by stating that the hill "was knocked around to buggery."[17] What had been a hill topped with triple-canopy rainforest was now a smoldering tangle of fallen trees, shell craters, and mud, grim testimony to the ferocity of days of fighting. If this were not bad enough, Dinh and Zimmerle knew from reading reports of the battle that the NVA, which "had knocked the shit out of" 3/187,[18] was dug in amid the desolation and was determined to stop the assault at all costs.

Another area of concern was ARVN communication with the

The treacherous terrain of Hamburger Hill. Slide VAS030265, August 1969, Elwin C. Vanderland Collection, The Vietnam Archive, Texas Tech University.

three U.S. battalions. Friendly forces surrounded Hamburger Hill and planned to attack from all sides, markedly increasing the possibility of friendly fire casualties as the battle progressed. Additionally, the ARVN soldiers worried that in the heat of battle they might be mistaken for NVA. Zimmerle assigned advisory teams, which included Lieutenant Jimmy R. Gibson, Gunnery Sergeant Paul A. Henry, Sergeant Bertram A. Carr, and Private First Class Billy W. Campbell, to the companies on the ARVN right and left flanks to maintain radio contact with neighboring friendly units and had all ARVN forces wear red and gold identifying shoulder straps.[19] Though reasonable precautions had been taken, Dinh and Zimmerle knew that the coming day still entailed a heavy risk of casualties from friendly fire.

Dinh chose to move 2/3 to its line of departure under the protective cover of darkness and, once in place some five hundred meters below the crest of the hill, became quite concerned because the ARVN avenue of advance lay across open ground, which afforded the NVA a clear field of fire. Fearing heavy losses Dinh made a fateful decision and chose not to wait until the proposed assault time. Instead, in the half-light Dinh sent a reconnaissance force, the 3rd Company, under his trusted Lieutenant Tuan, up a dry creek bed toward the top of Hamburger Hill.[20] Dinh hoped that the audacious move would catch even the watchful NVA by surprise and thus save the lives of his men and the soldiers of the three attacking U.S. battalions. If NVA forces were waiting and caught his men in the creek bed, their lives would be in peril; it was a do-or-die mission.

The NVA had not expected an attack along Dinh's line of advance and had devoted only minimal manpower to the defense of the area. Moreover, the night attack did not allow time for the few defenders present to man their bunker complexes. Through a combination of luck and skill, Tuan's men moved quickly through an undefended route to the summit of Hamburger Hill—one that had waited, untried and untested, while 3/187 had toiled for day after agonizing day further west. Once Dinh learned of Tuan's success, the remainder of 2/3 moved forward quickly against only sporadic resistance from the stunned NVA. As 2/3 neared the crest of the hill, though, "all hell broke loose," as a heavy wave of NVA small-arms fire tore into the leading elements, forcing them back.[21] Contrary to the Western accounts of the battle, no U.S. advisers were wounded, and the ARVN did not flee; instead, Zimmerle calmly called in a new artillery strike and "walked" it over the top of Hamburger Hill, and 2/3 advanced in its wake. Around 1000 hours, while 3/187 began to batter through heavy enemy resistance, 2/3 ARVN reached the crest of Hamburger Hill, compromising the enemy defensive positions.

King of the Hill?

Once atop Dong Ap Bia, 2/3 alerted the adjacent U.S. units to its presence and moved to aid 3/187, which was still engaged in bitter fighting with the main enemy force.[22] According to Honeycutt's operational orders, Zimmerle popped a purple smoke grenade to mark his location, but within seconds friendly artillery fire began to rain down on 2/3's position.[23] The advance of 2/3 ARVN had occurred before the scheduled attack and had been so fast that it caused confusion for the surrounding friendly units. After a short time, incoming fire ceased as

Zimmerle straightened out the communication problem, and 2/3 further consolidated its position on the crest of Dong Ap Bia. Then a second call came in to Zimmerle to mark his position with smoke. Fearing another friendly fire incident, Zimmerle refused and informed the circling command and control helicopters that they could fly low and identify 2/3 troops by their red and gold shoulder straps. Kelly added that 2/3 would be easy to recognize because he was the only soldier in the area wearing an Australian bush hat.

As Dinh and Zimmerle worked amid the enemy bodies to call medevacs for their own three killed and five wounded, the command-and-control helicopter carrying Colonel Joseph Conmy, commander of the 3rd Brigade, circled above the battle. By Conmy's side sat Lieutenant Colonel Cecil Fair, the U.S. Senior Adviser to the 3rd Regiment of the 1st ARVN Division, and Colonel Phan Van Hoa, commander of the 3rd Regiment of the 1st ARVN Division. The chopper circled low while the battle raged, working to direct the struggle and keep track of friendly units. While Conmy dealt with U.S. forces, Fair remained in contact with Zimmerle and watched the quick progress of 2/3 to its objective. Fair then reported to Conmy that the summit of Dong Ap Bia was in friendly hands and that 2/3 awaited further orders.

Fair was soon shocked to receive a new directive from Conmy, who told him "to get your people off the hill, because we are going to fire an artillery preparation on top of the hill." Fair could not understand the order, and Colonel Hoa was so frustrated that he "almost jumped out of the helicopter." Fair reminded Conmy that there was a full ARVN battalion atop Dong Ap Bia that could launch an attack on the rear of the enemy forces locked in battle with 3/187 and requested that he adjust the fire plan accordingly. Conmy refused Fair's advice and said, "if your guys are not out of there they are gonna get blown all to hell."[24]

On the ground below, Zimmerle received the order to abandon the crest of Hamburger Hill. Incredulous but in receipt of direct instructions, Dinh and his advisers did what they were told. Shortly after Dinh and his men moved away, the leading elements of 3/187 broke through the NVA defenses along their line of advance, moved to the summit of Dong Ap Bia, and took their place in history as the victors. An hour and a half later, 2/3 returned to the top of Dong Ap Bia for a short period before moving southwest to conduct RIF operations in the A Shau Valley. In so doing, Dinh, Zimmerle, Kelly, and the men of 2/3 ARVN marched away into obscurity.

After the close of the battle, Fair was "fighting mad" that the opportunity presented by the seizure of Dong Ap Bia by 2/3 ARVN had been missed. He went to see Colonel Harry Hiestand, the Senior Adviser with the 1st ARVN Division, and asked him why such a seemingly wasteful order had been given. Hiestand informed Fair that the decision had come from the very highest levels and did not concern him. When Fair pressed the matter, feeling that 2/3 ARVN had not received its due, Hiestand became stern and replied, "Hush! Just forget about it! Don't talk about it no more!" Hiestand's reaction confirmed Fair's suspicions. 3/187 had fought long and hard for Dong Ap Bia, and the glory of the victory had to be theirs. Reluctantly, Fair kept the truth of Hamburger Hill secret for more than thirty years.[25]

Hamburger Hill had been a long and very difficult struggle. It had also been an American struggle. It was a battle that the ARVN joined as an afterthought. The battle was already controversial and costly enough; better simply to have 3/187 earn its just reward than have the ARVN stumble onto the summit. There would be no active cover-up regarding events at Dong Ap Bia; nobody was coerced into making false statements about who reached the top of the hill first, and, indeed, in the confusion of battle, only a select few even knew that 2/3 ARVN had been the first to achieve the summit of Dong Ap Bia. A heroic mythology grew around the story of Hamburger Hill, and the deeds of 2/3 ARVN do not appear in any of the official U.S. combat after-action reports for the battle. Another important source, the after-action report filed by Cecil Fair, is missing. The story of 2/3 ARVN remained safely hidden, buried in the minds of the few U.S. advisers who had been on the scene that day. For years, these men watched as books and movies about Hamburger Hill came and went, while the only Vietnamese faces ever seen in the battle were those of the enemy. Warrant Officer Kelly knew the reality of the situation and put his mounting frustration into simple words:

> They didn't want the bloody ARVN to be up there. . . . They'd been up there about 10 days getting hell beat out of them and then along comes an ARVN battalion late and gets to the top of the hill. Takes the gloss off it doesn't it?[26]

Who Took Hamburger Hill?

Ultimately, Hamburger Hill remains a contested story with divergent opinions and memories—very much like the Vietnam War itself. Despite the testimony of Zimmerle, Fair, and Kelly, other very credible witnesses—ranging from Conmy to Honeycutt—contended in their after-action reports that 3/187 was the first unit to reach the top of Dong Ap Bia. To this day, Honeycutt contends vehemently that 3/187 achieved the final victory. In a brief phone interview, I informed him of Dinh's claim and he told me that "There were no goddamned ARVN within a mile of that goddamned hill" and offered personally to set Dinh straight on the matter if the two ever met.[27]

In what was a case of one person's word against another, I continued the search for more evidence and witnesses. I realized that General Ngo Quang Truong would be an unimpeachable source, but I knew that scheduling an interview with him would be a long shot at best. Truong was notoriously reclusive and close-mouthed about his experiences in the Vietnam War and consistently refused to tell his story or to weigh in on the controversies surrounding the war.[28] While in Washington, DC, to interview Tran Ngoc Hue, I learned that General Truong lived in the area and convinced Hue to set up a meeting with him. Living in a quiet suburban home, General Truong was a gracious host and was quite happy to learn of my interest in the ARVN. We spoke of the lives and careers of both Dinh and Hue while the general showed me maps and pictures of the war. Eventually, I asked if Dinh had indeed reached the top of Hamburger Hill first. General Truong went silent and gazed at me for a long while. After the awkward silence passed, Truong looked away and simply said that he did not want to get involved in any controversies.[29] The conversation then moved away to other, less troublesome topics. However, the look on General Truong's face, together with his comment, said volumes. He could have put the matter to rest simply by asserting the accuracy of the popular portrayal of the battle. Instead, he let the matter go—too genteel and too refined to cause trouble and pain for his former American allies.

I still had a need to find hard, documentary evidence—a historian's "smoking gun." Finally, after years of searching and having concluded that no such document existed, I found it by luck, buried in a pile of Miscellaneous Records on the fighting at Hamburger Hill. In a one-page document produced at the Headquarters of the United States Military Assistance Command, Vietnam, on 22 May 1969, Colonel Wilson C. Harper, Chief of the Command and Control Division, reported:

On 19 May, 1969, 2/3 ARVN conducted combat assault on LZ YC324976 and began moving to positions to the southeast side of Hill 937, in preparation for four battalion attack on 20 May 1969. Three battalions from 3rd Airborne Brigade, 101st Division progressed to multi-battalion attack which began 201030H [20 May 1030 hours]. Advance of 2/3 was extremely rapid due to use of high speed trail and light enemy resistance. They were the first to reach the top of Hill 937 and assaulted positions vicinity YC327980. The 3/187 was meeting heavy resistance on their axis of attack. The 2/3 ARVN went to assist by moving N along Hill 937 and relieving the pressure. However, friendly fire from 3/187 prevented 2/3 ARVN from moving close. The 2/3 ARVN then moved on reverse slope of the southeast side of the hill.[30]

The document is further corroborated by evidence from the recently released *The Abrams Tapes, 1968–1972*, which contains the following quotation from a MACV command meeting on 21 May 1969:

They got up to the crest of the hill, as a matter of fact ahead of the artillery preparation that was going in. The resistance was on the west slope—the 3rd of the—3/187. And they then had to back Dinh's battalion off the top of the hill so they could put the artillery in on the reverse slope. So then he—it was an hour and a half later when he got *back* on top of the hill and *met* them. He was there to meet the 3rd of the 187th. So the facts are the first people to the crest was [sic] the ARVN.[31]

The evidence is overwhelming. 2/3 ARVN was the first unit to the top of Hamburger Hill. Everyone knew it—from Dinh himself to Abrams in Saigon. But 2/3 had been ordered off of the hill, and the victory went to 3/187. Rather than engaging in an active cover-up, the truth of the matter simply went unrecorded and unreported. That commanders at all levels turned their faces away from the matter is very revealing. American forces were in the war to defend South Vietnam. Americans called for the South Vietnamese to stand and fight, to give more, and to join U.S. forces in the "big-unit war." However, when the South Vietnamese had the audacity do what the Americans asked, to play an important role in battle—an American battle—it had to be swept aside and forgotten. Such was the fragile nature of the American ego and national will.

Postscript

The NVA paid a high price at Dong Ap Bia but succeeded beyond its wildest dreams, for the growing public and governmental pressure in the United States tipped the strategic balance of the war. Under siege amid the growing political fallout from Hamburger Hill, Nixon visited Vietnam on 30 July, instructed Abrams to avoid further American casualties in battle, and forcefully reiterated his earlier decision that MACV should concentrate on readying the South Vietnamese to assume the burden of the war. During the same month, Laird announced the policy of Vietnamization to the world.[32]

Hamburger Hill was the last battle of its kind in the Vietnam War. Before Hamburger Hill, the United States had been involved in an incremental buildup over years, while the ascension of Nixon to the presidency had done much to dampen the antiwar furor on the American homefront. However, Hamburger Hill reignited the protests, and the political pressure became so great that Nixon opted to make his decision for Vietnamization public and to begin a withdrawal of American forces from the conflict, a withdrawal based on political considerations in the United States rather than on the military needs of South Vietnam.

The results of Hamburger Hill were simple and chilling. The American people were losing patience with their war in Vietnam and were calling for the return of their husbands and sons from the distant battlefields where they were fighting in defense of South Vietnam. The period following the Tet Offensive had reached a horrifying conclusion. To Dinh and Hue, it should have been the great year in which U.S. and South Vietnamese forces cooperatively took the war into enemy sanctuaries in Laos and North Vietnam, which they believed would lead to victory. Instead, it was a year in which the enemy gained the upper hand in the war of wills, in part due to fighting over a desolate and essentially worthless hilltop.

7

A War Transformed

Vietnamization, 1969–1970

AS AMERICAN POLITICAL and military leaders made critical strategic decisions in both Washington and Saigon during the summer of 1969, a deceptive calm fell over I Corps. In the wake of Hamburger Hill, communist strength throughout the region south of the DMZ was at a low ebb and included only five NVA regiments and two VC regiments in Quang Tri and Thua Thien provinces, the equivalent of twenty-four VC and NVA battalions in Quang Nam Province, and twelve VC and NVA battalions in the southern provinces of Quang Tin and Quang Ngai. Facing the considerable might of the allied forces concentrated in I Corps, the VC and the NVA contented themselves with attacks by fire while they rebuilt from their losses of the previous year.[1] The lull in the fighting, though, was illusory. Major General Raymond Davis, commander of the 3rd Marine Division, understood the reality of the situation and noted that the forces under his command and the ARVN were "now in a posture where we totally control Quang Tri Province." "However," he added, "we cannot lower our guard or decrease our forces one iota so long as the enemy retains his total sanctuary in Laos and in and above the DMZ."[2]

Following a trend set by Johnson and McNamara in the aftermath of the Tet Offensive; Nixon, Kissinger, and Laird had realized that political support for the Vietnam War had waned. As a result, the United States did "lower its guard" and greatly decreased its force level along the DMZ and the Laotian border. Instead of being marked by increasing vigilance against a resurgent foe, the year after Hamburger Hill was dominated by the increasingly rapid withdrawal of American forces from and public interest in South Vietnam. As the process began, neither Dinh nor Hue despaired of victory, but both remained frustrated that the opportunity that seemed to beckon for a quick decision had evaporated and that the war instead remained as it always had been; a long, difficult, grinding match with a determined enemy. But their confidence remained high, for they believed, no matter what rumblings emanated from Washington, that America would not simply abandon South Vietnam after so much sacrifice. They also believed that their own government and nation would strengthen and reform, especially as the younger generation, their generation, came of age. Dinh and Hue remained dedicated to the cause of South Vietnamese independence and eager to fight for their country. Nevertheless, as the war transformed around them yet again, the optimism of the post-Tet period gave way to grim realism and fierce determination.

A False Dawn?

The tide of victory after Tet had in some ways obscured the myriad weaknesses that still existed in the South Vietnamese state and its military—weaknesses veiled by American firepower. Just as the Americans had failed to achieve outright military victory, the leadership of South Vietnam had not seized the "supreme opportunity" provided by the victories of 1968–1969 to instill meaningful reforms meant to perpetuate the momentary strength of the South Vietnamese position. President Thieu instead had used Tet to launch a purge of his political enemies—specifically the province chiefs who were loyal to Nguyen Cao Ky.[3]

Although Thieu had achieved a great measure of power, political machinations at the highest levels continued within the South Vietnamese government for the remainder of the conflict, maneuverings that had an adverse effect on both the ARVN and the state. Military appointments, especially at corps and division levels, remained as they had been, the plaything of the political leadership, awarded for loyalty rather than military ability. While many of its leaders concentrated on their collective political futures, critical training programs for the ARVN lagged, while pay rates and amenities for the soldiers dipped alarmingly.[4] For members of the ARVN, including Pham Van Dinh and Tran Ngoc Hue, the lack of true reform remained a source of real concern, one that they still hoped would be cured by ultimate military victory. For others, the failure of the South Vietnamese leadership to take the obvious steps necessary to form a stronger state and military were depressing and obvious. "After all these years of war," an American journalist remarked in 1970, "the Saigon government remains a network of cliques, held together by American subsidies, a group of people without a coherent political orientation, bent on their own survival."[5]

On the local level, political duplicity cloaked the pacification successes of the post-Tet period in a mantle of complacency. Though the security posture of I Corps had risen to an astounding 93.6 percent in 1969,[6] the success did not necessarily mean that government programs were any more efficient or that the RF/PF had risen to a uniform standard of ability. Political sleight of hand also played a significant role in the encouraging rural picture. The Hamlet Evaluation System (HES) served as the standard measure for illustrating the GVN's control of the countryside. Although its veracity had long been held in doubt, the HES rated hamlet security on a sliding scale from A (government controlled) to E (VC controlled). In early 1969, the Thieu government directed a change in the system so that A, B, C, and D hamlets, which had obviously included a great many locales that were previously considered contested areas, would now be listed as under government control, and the E hamlets would be dubbed "hamlets not yet fully controlled by the government." The blatantly political step instantly transformed the pacification picture and caused great consternation to American operatives, who realized that "contested areas and Viet Cong–controlled hamlets remained in the countryside, if not in the official South Vietnamese vocabulary."[7]

Government trickery notwithstanding, great strides had been made in local security,[8] and even the NVA recognized that ferocious fighting had led to "rapid pacification operations in the rural lowlands."[9] Still, MACV remained acutely aware that the gains were fragile. As late as 1970, Abrams complained that only around 50 percent of the RF/PF were effective in a true military sense:

Freedom is a gift. Paid for by the government! And they're [South Vietnamese rural civilians] not involved in it! It's somebody else that's supposed to do that, and if the PF won't do it, then the VC'll do it. But they're [South Vietnamese rural civilians] not in it! If they were in it, they'd be telling the PF about who was coming, or the kids would be telling them about the VC out looking by the water buffaloes, and so on.[10]

In perhaps the critical moment of the war, tragic flaws of leadership and will, flaws at once both intrinsically Vietnamese in nature and imposed by an American system of warfighting, retained an upper hand over the potential for reform.

The ARVN, more than any other organ of the South Vietnamese state, had demonstrated the most progress in the period since the Tet Offensive, playing an ever-greater role in the prosecution of the conflict in tandem with the U.S. military. Abrams and the American military establishment rightly lauded the ARVN for its accomplishments but were disturbed by a CIA report on ARVN capabilities in December 1968, which attributed much of the ARVN's success to increased U.S. fire support, without which "the South Vietnamese military establishment would crumble rapidly under a heavy Communist assault." The report contended that Saigon's inability to take over a greater portion of combat duties stemmed from "the long-standing lack of effective leadership, an inequitable selection and promotion system," aggravated further by "low pay scales and . . . widespread corruption, political favoritism, and privilege-seeking that are rife within the military establishment."[11]

Abrams attacked what he termed the CIA's "distorted picture" of the military reality of South Vietnam. He retorted that none of the Vietnamization programs were designed to let the South Vietnamese "go it alone."[12] However, the grim reality was that the U.S. withdrawal from Vietnam would be fast and complete and the ARVN, wedged as it was between the weakness of its own national leadership and the American desire to quit the conflict, would in fact be left to "go it alone." The tide of victory after the Tet Offensive had been too weak and the veneer of change within the South Vietnamese state and military had been too thin to stand such a test.

A Changing of the Guard

Even as the forces of change gained momentum, all across I Corps, and indeed throughout South Vietnam, the tide of allied victory continued seemingly unabated. In northern I Corps, American and ARVN forces launched successive operations in and near the A Shau and around the Laotian salient, while further south the allies pressed ever further into the Vietnamese hinterlands to keep enemy forces away

Lieutenant General Robert Cushman, commanding general III MAF (left), and General Creighton Abrams, who later became COMUSMACV (center). Photograph VA035377, 16 July 1967, Peter Braestrup Collection, The Vietnam Archive, Texas Tech University.

from Da Nang. The successive offensives met with little overall resistance, as the NVA and the VC reverted to a policy of small-unit guerrilla actions and attacks by fire while they rebuilt their forces. Continued success, though, masked the fact that the war was actually at a critical point, for while the NVA struggled to recover from its grievous losses, U.S. forces began their withdrawal in earnest, leaving more and more of the fighting to a flawed ARVN.

Across South Vietnam, U.S. withdrawals resulted in a scramble by the ARVN to cover areas that had been previously guarded and patrolled by American forces,[13] but the situation was most severe in the provinces of I Corps. The drawdown of the massive U.S. commitment to I Corps actually began in late 1968, when Abrams shifted the 1st Cavalry Division south to III Corps. The overall program of Vietnamization began in June 1969, when MACV met President Nixon's initial goal of reducing forces in Vietnam by fifty thousand by deciding to withdraw the 9th Division from the Mekong Delta and the 3rd Marine Division from its outposts along the DMZ. Abrams commented that he chose the 3rd Marine Division "because it would be leaving the area to the 1st ARVN Division, recognized by all as the strongest and best ARVN division; and finally, because northern I Corps has one of the best security environments in the country for the people."[14]

The withdrawal of the 3rd Marines, which began in the fall of 1969 and was complete by November, had wide-ranging repercussions. The 1st ARVN Division, along with the 101st Airborne and the 1st Brigade of the 5th Mechanized Division, had to reshuffle its forces in order to defend Quang Tri and Thua Thien provinces. The important task of standing guard along the DMZ fell to the 1/5 Mechanized and the newly formed ARVN 1st Division Forward, under the command of Colonel Vu Van Giai at Dong Ha, which consisted of the 2nd Regiment of the 1st ARVN Division and a single brigade of Vietnamese Marines.[15] Without the American Marines, the allies had to constrict their defensive lines eastward to Firebase Fuller and ceded the western highlands along the Laotian border, including the A Shau Valley, to enemy control.

As the U.S. Marines completed their withdrawal, Colonel Giai visited the 3rd Division CP for a farewell dinner where Marine commander Major General William Jones wished Giai good hunting. For his part, Giai was acutely aware that the departure of the U.S. Marines meant that the few remaining forces could neither withstand a direct enemy attack nor interdict enemy infiltration into and through the western highlands.[16] The gains of 1968 and 1969 in the highlands, won through blood and sacrifice on the part of Americans and South Vietnamese alike, were lost, signaling the beginning of a new chapter in the long conflict.

Along the DMZ

Shortly after his success at Hamburger Hill and his promotion to lieutenant colonel, Pham Van Dinh took over duties as operations officer at 1st Division Forward at Dong Ha. In his new position, Dinh served on Colonel Giai's staff and worked to convert operational orders into reality in the defense of the DMZ. The two men worked closely together, with Giai taking Dinh under his wing. His new position afforded Dinh a much broader view of the conflict. Although removed from combat, Dinh was happy with his new assignment, which was an important step in his career.

Giai and Dinh at 1st Division Forward initially worked with the U.S. Marines as they made their withdrawal, but by September the defense of the central DMZ fell entirely to the 2nd Regiment.[17] Reliant on a weaker force to defend the most threatened real estate in South Vietnam, Giai developed a system in which the five battalions of the 2nd Regiment were in constant motion, rotating through the fire bases from A2 to Camp Carroll, on perpetual guard against NVA infiltration. Giai stressed the active schedule in order to keep his troops on their mettle and to avoid allowing them to settle into an overly comfortable defensive posture. Every three months, one of the battalions rotated into Dong Ha to perform base security, and to regroup and rest.[18]

Having recovered from his reoccurrence of malaria, in July 1969, Tran Ngoc Hue joined his new command, the 2nd Battalion of the 2nd Regiment, while it was on fire base A2 along the DMZ. With his unit under the command of 1st Division Forward, Hue once again found himself working closely with Pham Van Dinh. Though the paths of the two ARVN comrades had crossed yet again, Dinh witnessed the struggle for the DMZ at a strategic level, while for Tran Ngoc Hue the fighting was intensely personal. For nearly a year and a half, 2/2 cooperated with the other battalions of 2nd Regiment and rotated through assignments that concentrated in and around firebases Sarge, Fuller, and Khe Gio, which guarded the northwestern edge of the allied defensive line.[19] Aided by an array of high-tech sensors, the battalions of the 2nd Regiment normally left a single company on their respective fire bases while other companies patrolled first to detect and then halt any enemy infiltration.

The battalions of 2nd Regiment during the second half of 1969 and through the end of 1970 generally characterized combat activity along the DMZ as light. Although they avoided clashes of large units, the NVA made life along the DMZ as bloody as possible for the South Vietnamese and hoped to impose upon the ARVN a morale-sapping war of attrition. Dotted with spiderholes, interlocking defenses, and infiltration routes, the DMZ was a moonscape of desolation and was familiar ground to the experienced NVA. Although ARVN sweeps rarely netted contact with large units, every hedge, every slight rise, every shattered building had the potential to hide an ambush. The ubiquitous mines and booby traps took a horrible psychological toll, their explosions suddenly blowing off soldiers' limbs while providing no target for retaliation. ARVN patrols were tense affairs, with death or dismemberment lurking around every corner—patrols that often resulted in casualties but rarely led to any discernable gain.

The NVA kept up relentless pressure on the ARVN and U.S. forces along the DMZ through attacks by fire, a problem not faced by any other allied soldiers in the whole of South Vietnam. Artillery from the north side of the Ben Hai River, no longer subject to U.S. bombing, was within easy firing range of the stationary ARVN bases and pounded away with seeming impunity. Additionally, small teams of NVA mortarmen often slipped to within range of an ARVN base, fired a few well-directed rounds, and then moved away before South Vietnamese forces could retaliate. Attempting to utilize uncertainty as a weapon, the NVA followed no real pattern in its shellings. Some days were quiet, while on others only a stray rocket impacted on any given ARVN fire base. More commonly, a few shells hit the fire bases each day, vastly complicating the simple tasks of daily life. On seemingly random days, though, hundreds of artillery shells, mortar shells, and rockets poured in and caused heavy casualties and massive destruction.[20]

On rarer occasions, NVA forces launched direct attacks on exposed ARVN forces. Elite and highly trained sapper units specialized in using stealth to breach complex defensive networks at night and in using maneuver and firepower to cause maximum damage at minimum cost while sowing chaos and fear. Wearing dark clothing and with their skin blackened, sappers used bamboo mats to cross over barbed wire entanglements. Once inside ARVN defenses, the sappers invariably struck at the command bunkers and brandished satchel charges as their weapon of choice. In late 1969, Tran Ngoc Hue and 2/2 occupied Fire Base Sarge, with an outlying company under Captain Ton Huyen Trang stationed at Camp Carroll North. In the dead of night, a squad of North Vietnamese sappers penetrated the defenses of Carroll North, overran part of the base, and killed the company commander. In a confused and sometimes hand-to-hand battle, Hue's men eventually proved victorious, called for medevacs, and cleared away the enemy dead.

As usual, American and Australian advisers shared in ARVN's

war. U.S. Army Captain Gordon Greta joined 2/2 as an assistant adviser while it was stationed at Camp Carroll. With no advisory training, Greta found himself in a new world, forced to communicate with his Vietnamese counterparts under fire by drawing pictures. After a short time of adjustment to the South Vietnamese culture and to the reality of war along the DMZ, Greta remained surprised by the level of constant danger represented by incoming fire and by the fact that he could sometimes see the North Vietnamese atop their own fire bases across the DMZ. What was new and frightening to Greta, though, was just a part of everyday life for the men of the ARVN, who went about their work amid the shelling as normal. Impressed by the level of tenacity he found in the ARVN, Greta came to have a deep respect for Hue and his men.

Like many Americans, Greta marveled at the diminutive stature and the stamina and strength of the typical ARVN soldier. In their constant patrolling, Greta often found that he had great difficulty keeping pace with a ninety-pound ARVN soldier who carried a thirty-pound radio strapped to his back. The near-constant action faced by the ARVN soldiers and the aplomb with which they greeted their difficult lives convinced Greta that these young soldiers were the best and bravest people that he had ever met.[21]

In the spring of 1970, Major David Wiseman USMC took over as Tran Ngoc Hue's senior adviser. Wiseman was new to Vietnam, while Hue was welcoming yet another in a seemingly never-ending advisory revolving door. Wiseman recalled:

When I got to MACV in Hue, everyone warned me what a problem Harry [Tran Ngoc Hue] was . . . and how he expected his advisers to go everywhere with him. Those of us who were any help to Harry found him fiercely protective of us . . . particularly when he realized that we weren't going to sneak into Dong Ha every chance for American chow and hookers. Harry was a warrior and a devout family man—those of us who also were . . . well, we got along fine. I can't remember such a quick bonding and immediate rapport ever in my life before or since then.[22]

Wiseman and Hue became very close comrades of war, a friendship cemented by the reality of combat along the DMZ. On one occasion at Fire Base Fuller Hue, Wiseman and several ARVN soldiers were entombed as their bunker collapsed under enemy fire.[23] After being buried for a few hours, covered by earth, body parts, and the ubiquitous rats that inhabited the filth of the base, Hue escaped, located the unconscious Wiseman, and extricated him from the remains of the bunker.[24]

After the conflict, Wiseman recounted that his friendship with Hue carried even into their family relationships:

> Whenever one of our wounded troops was sent back to the field, he would drop by Harry and Cam's [Harry's wife] house before coming back. Cam would send some mail and always sent me some Vietnamese meat treats wrapped up in banana leaves to keep them fresh. When we had our one week back from the field, Harry would always drag me home with him. I used to try to talk to his mother. She taught me how to chew betel nut, which caused a rush through your upper body that made it hard to raise your arms. One of the happiest things I was able to do was to get an old Navy friend . . . to send me a Japanese three burner cooking stove that ran off propane for his mom.[25]

The very closeness of Hue's relationship with Wiseman eventually saved his life.

Return into the Highlands

While, in many areas of I Corps, 1970 remained a bloody, small-unit game of cat and mouse, the situation was quite different in the highlands of Thua Thien Province. Because American withdrawals had forced the allies to cede control of the western border region, communist forces had engaged in a steady buildup in the area, repairing roads and massing supplies in what appeared to be preparations for a renewed offensive into the lowlands around Hue City. Worried both by NVA activity and by the continuing constriction of ARVN defensive lines, General Lam, at I Corps, and General Truong agreed that it was of the utmost importance to once again project ARVN power into the area near the A Shau Valley, the site of so much bitter fighting only a year earlier.

The plan, based on the use of ARVN forces with significant aid from the 101st Airborne—a reverse of prior forays into the region—first called for the construction of a network of fire bases in the western highlands near the A Shau and Da Krong valleys. The fire bases, aided by a screen of electronic sensors, had the same goal and mission as the fire bases along the DMZ, both to interdict communist infiltration and to stand against any major NVA offensive actions. However, while the NVA chose to stay on the defensive throughout the remainder of I Corps, it reacted with great violence to the renewed ARVN/ U.S. presence in the highlands and touched off one of the biggest battles of the year.

On 31 May 1970, the 2nd Battalion, 54th ARVN Regiment air assaulted into the area of what had been the U.S. Marine base of Tun Tavern at the entrance to the Da Krong Valley, some seventy kilometers west of Hue and only seven kilometers from Laos. The base was to form the lynchpin of the ARVN/U.S. defensive line in the area. Hoping to catch enemy forces off guard, 2/54 relied on speed to hit the ground, push out reconnaissance elements, and construct a defensive perimeter before the NVA could mass for a possible counterattack. Impeded by only sporadic mortar fire, the troops' efforts to establish the fire base initially went well, though deteriorating weather conditions slowed work considerably. However, in the predawn hours of 2 June, Tun Tavern came under heavy mortar attack, which Captain Bill Deane, an AATTV adviser, realized was preparatory to an NVA infantry assault on the ARVN lines. Deane, whose company was out on reconnaissance duties, immediately made his way back toward Tun Tavern.[26]

Before Deane reached his goal, though, elements of the 66th NVA Regiment launched a massive assault on the fire base. The attackers broke through the ARVN defenses and overran part of the battalion area as the battle degenerated into a confused foxhole-to-foxhole and hand-to-hand struggle. The situation was so desperate that a helicopter gunship arrived on station and poured fire directly into the tangled mass of combatants atop the fire base. By the time Deane's company arrived, the NVA attacking force had retreated after suffering heavy casualties. The defenders had held but were in a precarious position—exposed to NVA mortars, isolated, and subject to another infantry assault. Soon the situation got even worse when a direct hit from a mortar shell injured all but one of the ARVN battalion officers, leaving Deane, one of the few surviving advisers, in command at Tun Tavern.

Events on Tun Tavern soon spiraled out of control. In his after-action report, Deane described:

> [t]he disgusting eagerness of the ARVNs to medevac themselves, (officers and men) after they had received the slightest wound, and their complete disregard for the needs of more seriously wounded soldiers. By the time the first dustoff arrived, about 20 seriously injured, some of them with limbs missing, were lying on stretchers or ponchos beside the helipad. By the time the advisers had helped WO Birdie on board [a badly wounded AATTV adviser] and had returned with a stretcher borne U.S. soldier, the dustoff was crowded with ARVN soldiers who had been able bodied enough to board the dustoff of their own accord, while those more handicapped were unable to get help. In the event, the wounded U.S. soldier had to be thrown across the ARVNs already sitting on the floor, and died on the return trip.[27]

As the dustoffs came and went, the NVA responded with accurate mortar fire, which limited the helicopters' time on the ground. With only two advisers and a single ARVN officer, who desperately wanted to board a medevac, the situation continued to deteriorate. Soldiers even feigned injury by smearing the blood of their compatriots on themselves, which forced Deane to inspect wounds to make sure they were genuine before he allowed soldiers to board the helicopters. Morale had plummeted to dangerously low levels, command was inadequate, and the soldiers atop Tun Tavern were more of a rabble than a coherent military unit.

General Truong, aware that the situation at Tun Tavern was precarious, contacted Colonel Giai at 1st Division Forward and requested that Lieutenant Colonel Pham Van Dinh be transferred to the 54th Regiment to act as its executive officer and that Dinh take over immediate command at Tun Tavern. It was a dangerous assignment, one that many ARVN officers would have found a way to avoid. Heedless of the dangers, Dinh boarded the next available helicopter and made his way to the fire base, determined to set things right.

With morale hitting rock bottom, Deane learned that Dinh was coming to take charge. Not knowing what to expect from the new officer, Deane did not have high hopes. He recalled:

He [Dinh] arrived looking resplendent in a fresh uniform, colorful scarf[,] carrying a swagger stick, his chopper attracting the obligatory couple of mortar rounds, I met him at the pad and brought him back to the shallow shell scrape that Capt Pat McCann USMC and I were more or less cowering in. We beckoned him in but he said "No way," looked around him and said "A bit of trouble here." He then set off by himself to check out the position. . . . [Later Dinh] returned and again stood on the lip of our shell scrape looking around. He was an obvious and distinctive target for the mortars that had been harassing us all day and within a minute or so a round landed near him, wounding him badly in the arm.[28]

Now a casualty himself, and having served as executive officer of the 54th Regiment for only a few hours, Dinh was placed on the next chopper out and spent a month in the hospital recovering from his injuries, marking the seventh time he had been wounded in combat. Whereas other ARVN officers had folded under pressure, Dinh had refused even to take cover, to the amazement and consternation of his momentary Australian colleague.

General Truong decided that holding the fire base would be prohibitively expensive, and, by the evening of 3 June, Tun Tavern had been evacuated. The fighting had been brutal, and of the roughly four hundred ARVN soldiers dedicated to the battle, sixty-five had been killed and ninety had been wounded.[29] The failure at Tun Tavern, though, did not put an end to the ARVN/U.S. efforts in the highlands, as several battalions continued their sweeps through the area while others constructed and manned several other fire bases.

The NVA, anxious to protect its lifelines in the area, kept up pressure against the allied units, which were isolated and occupied the far end of the U.S./ARVN supply chain. In July, NVA forces massed against the 101st Airborne Division's Fire Support Base Ripcord. Under heavy fire and engaged in fierce hilltop battles against their determined foes, U.S. commanders eventually chose to abandon Ripcord, making the action there one of the last major ground battles involving U.S. forces in the Vietnam War. Finally, the NVA began major operations against Fire Base O'Reilly, occupied by elements of the 1st ARVN Regiment. After the loss of Tun Tavern and Ripcord, Truong knew the symbolic value of holding firm and remarked, "They will not take

O'Reilly. If we lose O'Reilly we lose everything we have been trying to accomplish for the last ten years."[30] Pressing all four battalions of 1st Regiment into a forward defense of O'Reilly, the ARVN defenders held out until the onset of the seasonal monsoon ended chances of aerial resupply. The defense of O'Reilly, amid a long-running and brutal series of battles, stood in stark contrast to that of Tun Tavern and indicated both the ARVN's capabilities and the uneven nature of ARVN command and success.[31]

In the Lowlands

After his recuperation in the hospital, Dinh relocated to Fire Base Anzio, south of Hue City, to take over as the Executive Officer (XO) of the 54th Regiment on a permanent basis. Dinh's quick rise through the command ranks continued, but in his new position he served in the main as the commander's assistant and was not involved in the routine of tactical planning. As was so often the case, Dinh's commander, Colonel Huan, wanted there to be a clear delineation of duties and made sure that the XO knew his place. Perhaps Dinh's position of stardom within the ARVN was responsible for what might be termed a clash of personalities in his new slot. The U.S. senior adviser to the 54th, Major Tom Jaco, who, like most Americans in northern I Corps, knew of Dinh's reputation even before his arrival at Anzio, witnessed the level of Dinh's fame. When divisional commanders arrived at the 54th's CP, they went to Dinh first, not to the commander of the unit. While his superiors treated him with great and obvious affection, the soldiers stood in awe of Dinh as a true hero; in Jaco's words, to the common soldier and to the man on the street, Dinh simply "represented hope."[32]

While Dinh served as its XO, the 54th Regiment normally worked in and around fire bases Anzio and Roy and guarded the lowlands south of Hue City from NVA infiltration and attack. Sometimes, though, the battalions of the 54th served in other AOs, and both worked with units of the 101st Airborne Division in the highlands and reinforced ongoing operations as far north as the DMZ. On one such occasion, in late August 1970, Dinh led a forward command element of the 54th into an ongoing battle around My Chanh Hamlet against units of the 318th NVA Battalion that had taken up residence in the

Pham Van Dinh enjoying a short break from the military routine aboard his motorbike. Photograph Courtesy of Harvey Zimmerle.

area. In the fighting, the 2nd Battalion of the 54th Regiment lost four dead and accounted for ninety-eight enemy killed in action.[33]

In general, though, contact for the 54th remained "light" as the various battalions in the regiment worked to shield the pacification successes of the lowlands.[34] Morale in the regiment was high, and Jaco remembers the time as "sometimes kind of boring because there was not a lot of action."[35] Dinh and the men of the 54th engaged in much the same existence as the men of Tran Ngoc Hue's 2/2 who served along the DMZ, an existence of sweeps, ambushes, booby traps, and attrition. Within this reality of warfare, and even in his truncated position of authority, Dinh was seen by Jaco and the other advisers as a true leader who cared deeply for his men and his nation, who inspired his men in battle, who did not shun danger, and who was simply a "soldier's soldier." Even the senior adviser to the 1st ARVN Division, Colonel Ben Harrison, had cause to recognize Dinh's combat ability and leadership and knew that the young Vietnamese officer was destined for great things.[36]

While serving in what was in essence a noncombat staff position, Dinh demonstrated leadership abilities of a different kind. ARVN units typically operated from base areas that included ubiquitous "family camps," which were thriving communities full of the wives and children of the nearby ARVN soldiers. Often existing on the verge of destitution, the shantytowns were sometimes shocking to new advisers but were central to the morale of the ARVN fighting men. While, to some less able ARVN commanders, family camps were nothing but a nuisance, officers such as Dinh and Hue saw them both as a fundamental reality of life and an opportunity to have a positive influence. Upon his arrival at the 54th, Dinh learned that the men of his unit could not afford adequate education for their children on their meager pay. Incensed, Dinh chose not to accept the situation as a sad part of ARVN life but instead worked with Jaco to found a school for the regiment's main family camp near Phu Bai. The two struck deals with several Vietnamese and American units for supplies, and Jaco succeeded in having the nascent school adopted by his old high school in the United States. After months of toil, the school, which catered to forty students, became a reality, and morale within the 54th soared.[37]

On a broader front, Dinh witnessed the South Vietnamese government's most recent attempts at reform, including the continuation of pacification programs and the introduction of the "Land to the Tiller" program. While far from perfect, the reforms seemed to Dinh to be steps in the proper direction, steps that gave him great hope. However, they were imperfect measures that would take considerable time to achieve their ultimate intended impact, time that both Dinh and Hue realized was rapidly slipping away.

The Future of the ARVN

Although there were dramatic differences between units, in 1969 the morale of the U.S. military in Vietnam began its well-chronicled slide. The author Keith Nolan remarked:

> The 1969 Summer Offensive was unlike many Vietnam campaigns only because of its mood. It was the first major engagement after the announcement of U.S. withdrawals. A new slogan was heard: Why be the last man killed in Vietnam? . . . They [American soldiers] knew they were leaving, and they knew the job wasn't done. A spiritual malaise began to affect the entire war effort. "Nothing much of any-

thing was decided by the summer campaign," commented SP4 Bob Hodierne, U.S. Army combat photographer. . . ."It, in fact, could be seen as painfully typical of the whole damn experience. Pain, death, little private acts of heroism and cowardice, individuals changed forever, and when it was done—what? As the GIs said, 'Fuck it, it don't mean nothing.' "[38]

As in the U.S. military, reactions to the changing war within the ARVN were mixed. After the fight at Tun Tavern, Captain Bill Deane, an AATTV adviser, felt that 2/54 became much less aggressive. Deane recalls that, while the battalion remained active in nearly constant search operations, when the unit stopped on a trail to set a night ambush, ARVN soldiers often defecated on the trail on either side of their position, presumably to warn away and avoid meaningful contact with any enemy forces that did not know of their presence.[39] In the view of Tom Jaco, senior adviser to the 54th Regiment, though, the regiment itself and the 1st ARVN Division as a whole remained quite competent and actually had fewer morale problems than many of the American units in the area.[40]

That the war was difficult and trying for American soldiers who had arguably been rejected by their own nation is beyond doubt. That the ARVN was flawed and cannot accurately be compared to American units, and that 1st ARVN Division does not represent the entirety of the ARVN experience is also beyond doubt. However, America was a mighty nation not threatened by imminent takeover. American soldiers in the main served only a single year in combat before returning to "the world." Tran Ngoc Hue, Pham Van Dinh, and their men had no such luxuries. Dinh was nearing his tenth year of war, and Hue was in his eighth, and yet the conflict continued even as hope of victory began to wane. If it is understandable that the reality of a war transformed hung like a pall over American soldiers, what of the ARVN? That the South Vietnamese, for all their faults, persevered is a strong reflection of their ability and strength, a strength that their advisers knew firsthand. Gordon Greta had become quite close to Tran Ngoc Hue and the men of 2/2 amid the strains of war. He could not shake the feeling that these men who saluted him and showed him deference—men who had been fighting for their country for years with only the prospect of fighting for years to come while Greta looked forward to a trip back to his world within a year—were the true heroes of the war. In his words, Greta felt that he "was not fit to polish their boots."[41]

The grim reality of the new mathematics of the Vietnam War was obvious to the planners of MACV. In response to questions from incoming president Nixon in early 1969, the four corps senior advisers and Abrams himself stated unequivocally that the ARVN, as matters stood, was unable to stand alone against either the Viet Cong threat or an invasion by the North Vietnamese, much less face both threats. Taking the pace of modernization and Vietnamization into account, Abrams predicted that by 1972 the ARVN would be able to stand against the VC but that even then only the continued participation of U.S. ground forces would allow the ARVN to fend off an NVA threat. Over Abrams's continued objections, though, withdrawal planning intensified—withdrawals that most American commanders realized would seal the ARVN's fate.[42]

The consequences of the continued withdrawals were most obvious to the personnel of I Corps, who existed under the perpetual threat of NVA attack. Ben Harrison, in his position at 1st ARVN Division, knew that the ARVN soldiers in I Corps were up to the task of defending their population base in the lowlands but did not have the strength to take on the NVA in the border areas. Tom Jaco, at 54th Regiment, put the situation as it existed in 1970 best when he remarked:

> The ARVN [in 1970] was dependent on the United States—dependent on advisory groups, dependent on support; air support, fire support, medical support . . . we could teach them how to call upon that support, but if it was not there to be called it would not do them a heck of a lot of good.[43]

The loss of initiative in the war as the enemy built up its forces was palpable to Tran Ngoc Hue as he watched the allied line along the DMZ constrict while the bloody war of attrition continued. If the worst-case scenario of a quick, unilateral, and complete American withdrawal came to pass, he realized, neither his government nor his military was yet ready to bear the responsibility of the entire war. Hue knew that the ARVN, created for and thriving in its niche role alongside the mighty Americans, needed time to prepare for the new challenges that lay ahead. As usual, Hue was ready and eager to do his part in enabling the ARVN to ready itself for the future—but his time in the war was about to come to an end.

For Pham Van Dinh, the reality presented by events of 1969–1970 was starker. While he had fought hard and well, Dinh had also watched with joy as the allies followed up their Tet victory with a campaign that had reclaimed the lowlands and even hounded the enemy into Laos. Just as victory seemed to beckon, though, U.S. will had imploded, and the withdrawal of American forces began. As the fighting continued, Dinh watched with increasing concern as the allies pulled back ever further and ceded to the enemy areas for which the ARVN and U.S. forces had struggled and bled. Dinh, like Hue, was painfully aware that, without U.S. support, the ARVN would be unable to survive. Yet, it appeared that American forces were leaving the conflict before the job was complete and abandoning the ARVN to its fate.

At the end of 1970, the fears of commanders from Abrams to Hue and Dinh were just that—fears. The United States was quitting the conflict, that much was certain. However, questions remained. Few South Vietnamese believed that the worst-case scenario—a complete American exit from the conflict—was imminent. Surely the United States would continue its support of South Vietnam in some meaningful way after the investment of so much time and sacrifice. Given that hope of continued U.S. support, both Dinh and Hue believed that the ARVN could fight on; after all, the ARVN had learned much and was fighting well. With the requisite time, the ARVN would fix its faults. The two comrades knew, though, that if the test came too quickly, the ARVN would fail. These suspicions became reality in Operation Lam Son 719.

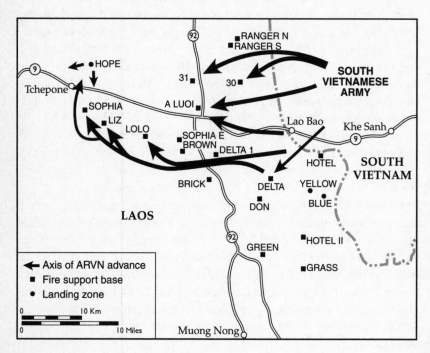

Lam Son 719

8

Shattered Lives and Broken Dreams

Operation Lam Son 719

WHILE VIETNAMIZATION ALTERED the strategic reality of the war in I Corps, the major military event of 1970 took place further to the south. For years, U.S. and South Vietnamese military leaders alike had longed to mount major operations against the communist base areas and supply lines just across the border in Cambodia, uncomfortably near Saigon. Political expediency, however, had always trumped military need, but, in March 1970, the advent of a new Cambodian government, under the pro-American general Lon Nol, presented U.S. and ARVN forces with a tactical opportunity, while communist threats to the fledgling Cambodian government provided a political need for major cross-border actions.

While the Americans wrestled with issues of a potential political backlash against any move into Cambodia, it was the ARVN that on 14 April initially answered Lon Nol's pleas for military help. In the area of the Angel's Wing, ARVN forces of III Corps launched Operation Toan Thang 41, which aimed at the disruption of Base Area 706. Facing only light NVA resistance, ARVN operations in Cambodia spread both north and south and achieved marked success at only minimal cost in lives and materiel. One three-day operation in the Parrot's Beak area of Cambodia was indicative of the ARVN level of success; it accounted for 1,010 enemy dead and 204 prisoners at a cost of 66 ARVN dead and 330 wounded. NVA materiel losses included one thousand individual and sixty crew-served weapons and more than one hundred tons of ammunition.[1]

With their morale buoyed by their successful incursions into enemy-held territory in Cambodia, on 1 May 1970, ARVN forces were joined in battle by American ground and riverine units in Operation Toan Thang 43. Aiming to take back the initiative from the communists, to shock the NVA logistic system, and to forestall any major enemy offensives, both ARVN and U.S. forces made rapid progress. Though it arguably achieved substantial gains, the joint operation was strictly limited in time and scope, and by 29 June all U.S. forces had withdrawn back into South Vietnam, while thirty-four thousand ARVN troops remained in Cambodia for another month to search for and destroy NVA supply caches.

The various operations that collectively made up the Cambodian Incursion accounted for more than eleven thousand NVA dead, shocked the communist logistic system in Cambodia, and destroyed enough supplies to support enemy actions in the area for a full six months.[2] At a strategic level, the results of the Cambodian Incursion were much more mixed, having caused a furor of protest in the United States, which was partially responsible for Nixon's choice to accelerate the speed of the withdrawal of American forces from Vietnam. At a tactical level, taking the battle beyond the borders of South Vietnam and striking the NVA in its base areas proved a tonic for ARVN morale. Even so, little more than twelve South Vietnamese battalions had been involved in Cambodia at any one time, and the NVA response to their presence had been negligible. The true test of Vietnamization was yet to come.[3]

With the destruction of the Cambodian base areas, the allies rightly surmised that the NVA was now dependent upon the Laotian branches of the Ho Chi Minh Trail and hoped that an offensive aimed at the logistics hub near the deserted village of Tchepone might fatally disrupt NVA operations. Although such an operation was fraught with difficulties that ranged from rugged terrain to nagging issues of ARVN command efficiency, the results of the Cambodian Incursion suggested that the NVA would not resist the attack in a meaningful way. However, the NVA too had recognized the value of its Laotian logistic system and was determined this time to stand and fight.

It was ironic to many South Vietnamese observers that the Laotian invasion did not come as the logical culmination of the military successes of 1968, when the communists were on their heels and the battle might have been decisive. Instead, the operation came only after Vietnamization had reduced the American troop presence in Vietnam from ten divisions to six, after the June 1970 passage of the Cooper-Church Amendment had limited the actions of U.S. forces to the geographic confines of South Vietnam, and after the NVA in Laos had been afforded two more years of time to prepare the battlefield. Instead of U.S. and ARVN soldiers marching in lockstep at their peak of military success, the ARVN walked alone into a trap.

Planning

The impetus for Lam Son 719 seems to have come from the White House, which pressed the idea of a cross-border invasion on MACV as early as August 1970. By December, the pressure on Abrams, who realized the difficulties inherent in such an operation, rose considerably with the receipt of instructions from Admiral John McCain, Commander-in-Chief Pacific Command, which stated, "I recognize that this operation [into Laos] may present many problems to you and the RVNAF . . . and request that you immediately initiate necessary action for the preparation of this plan."[4]

In early January 1971, Abrams called on Lieutenant General Cao Van Vien, head of the South Vietnamese Joint General Staff (JGS), and suggested an operation into lower Laos. Vien, who had long been a supporter of such an operation, took the news to President Thieu. A grim reality formed the basis of part of the Thieu regime's eventual decision to support an invasion of Laos; in early 1971, the United States presence in South Vietnam was still substantial enough to offer meaningful support for such a large-scale operation. However, ARVN planners believed that, "If the offensive were deferred, U.S. support would no longer be as adequate and as effective."[5] No matter what the odds or difficulties, if an invasion of Laos did not take place in 1971, it never would, because of the increased pace of the American withdrawal.

Both the failures and the successes of Lam Son 719 can be seen as the result of the bifurcated U.S./South Vietnamese war experience. The ARVN that planned and carried out the invasion of Laos in 1971 was exactly the military force created by the Americans and perpetuated by the South Vietnamese, a military force built imperfectly on the American model, not a South Vietnamese model. The ARVN was trained to act as an adjunct to the American war effort and as such was used to operating in small units against a local enemy, while the Americans fought the "big-unit war." It was a military force that had become dependent upon advisers and the firepower they provided and that fought long and well in the war as the Americans had defined it.

Suddenly, though, the ARVN embarked on a multidivisional campaign in the biggest battle yet of the "big-unit war." The ARVN indeed had great strengths that would shine through in the pivotal campaign. However, the ARVN also had glaring weaknesses, which it had not yet had the time or the inclination to overcome—weaknesses that reflected the flawed nature of the U.S./South Vietnamese symbiosis.

In mid-January, Vietnamese Joint General Staff representatives took their initial scheme for a Laotian incursion to General Lam at I Corps, which left only three weeks to prepare and plan for such a massive undertaking. Because of the desire to achieve the utmost secrecy, ARVN and I Corps leadership compounded the error by waiting until the last possible moment to inform participating units of their roles in the invasion. The South Vietnamese Airborne Division, slated to play the most important and complex role in the drive to Tchepone, received detailed guidance from I Corps only on 2 February, which left it barely six days to carry out its divisional operational planning.[6]

To the ARVN, having served so long as an adjunct to the American war, the experience of planning an operation of such massive proportions was new.[7] Additionally, neither the Americans nor the South Vietnamese proved able to see much beyond the strategic reality that had been a part of their war for so long and translated tactics that had proven successful in South Vietnam into Laos, where they had much less operational relevance. Though the planners rightly stressed speed and surprise, the invasion was overly reliant on the formation of static fire support bases, a staple in the fighting in South Vietnam, bases that would both tie down considerable ARVN forces and become tempting targets for NVA counterattacks. Most important, ARVN planning rested on a fatal expectation that the NVA would react as it had in Cambodia and not vigorously contest the battlefield.[8] In the end, then, the planning for Lam Son 719 was rushed, based on an imperfect strategic understanding of the situation, and overly reliant on NVA compliance. In the words of Major General Nguyen Duy Hinh, the ARVN chronicler of the campaign:

Planning and preparations for the offensive were another major area that needed improvement. The operational plan for Lam Son 719 was adequate only so long as the operation progressed smoothly and ARVN forces were able to hold the initiative. It should have taken contingencies into full consideration and been able to respond to them with resourcefulness.[9]

Phase I of the plan for Lam Son 719 called for U.S. forces and elements of the 1st ARVN Division, in what was known as Operation Dewey Canyon II, to open Route 9 up to the Laotian border, reoccupy Khe Sanh as a forward operations base, secure lines of communication, and make diversionary moves toward the A Shau Valley. In Phase II, elements of the South Vietnamese Airborne Division, supplemented by the 1st ARVN Armored Brigade, were to advance down Route 9 toward objective A Loui, nearly halfway to Tchepone. Airborne and ranger forces were to helicopter in and secure fire bases and landing zones north of Route 9, while battalions of the 1st and 3rd Regiments of the 1st Division performed a similar task on the Co Roc plateau in the south to guard the flanks of the ground assault. Airborne and armor units would next sweep into Tchepone and choke off the enemy logistics flow until the rains came in early May. In Phase III, elements of the 1st ARVN Division would drive south down Route 914 and destroy the major communist logistics hub at Base Area 611 before returning into South Vietnam via the A Shau Valley. If the complex and ambitious offensive achieved its goals, it would cripple the NVA logistic structure and potentially derail NVA planning for years.[10]

The terrain of the region was a central limiting factor on the scope of the offensive. Route 9, the main avenue of advance, situated in the Xepon River valley with the river to its immediate south and mountains to the north, was a single-lane dirt road so badly damaged by the ravages of war that it was impassable in many places. Ground forces, though, would be confined to the road by the nearness of the river and mountains. Thus, repair of Route 9 became central to the operation's success. Rising hills and heavy vegetation restricted operations north of the Xepon. To the south, the Co Roc escarpment, a rectangular plateau about four kilometers long, and another ridgeline further west with jungle covered peaks, dominated Route 9 and the valley floor. The nature of the landscape thus made the course of the ARVN advance fatally predictable, for the NVA realized that South Vietnamese forces were obliged to occupy the prominent hills and crags both north and south of the Xepon for Lam Son 719 to stand a chance of success.[11]

Initially, it seemed that both Dinh and Hue would act only as interested observers as Lam Son 719 ran its course.[12] Dinh's unit, the 54th Regiment of the 1st ARVN Division, remained tasked with the security of the lowlands south of Hue City. Further north, it fell to the 2nd Regiment of the 1st ARVN Division, including Hue's 2/2, to continue interdiction operations along the DMZ, while providing security for Route 9. Even though they were distant from the campaign's epicenter, it became obvious to both that the veil of secrecy to which operational planning time had been sacrificed had failed. Dinh was concerned that civilians and reporters alike, seemingly everyone in I Corps, were buzzing about the impending invasion long before its launch date. During operations in Laos, captured enemy soldiers confirmed Dinh's fears that the NVA had been preparing for a potential ARVN invasion aimed at Tchepone since October 1970 and were thus in many ways better prepared for the coming battle than their ARVN foes.[13]

ARVN estimates of enemy forces in southern Laos included three infantry regiments, an artillery element and the Binh Tram logistic units that manned and operated the Ho Chi Minh Trail, a total enemy strength calculated at twenty-two thousand, made up of seven thousand NVA combat troops, ten thousand men belonging to logistic units, and five thousand soldiers from the Pathet Lao (the NVA's Laotian allies). Estimates also contended that eight additional NVA regiments were near enough to the area to join the battle in southern Laos within two weeks. However, the estimates of enemy forces in the area of the invasion proved to be far too low. A North Vietnamese history of the battle contends that, in February, NVA defensive forces in southern Laos numbered sixty thousand troops consisting of five divisions, two separate infantry regiments, eight regiments of artillery, three engineer regiments, eight sapper battalions, six anti-aircraft regiments plus rear service and transportation units.[14] While North Vietnamese figures are notoriously inaccurate, it is obvious that the ARVN estimates of NVA strength and the concurrent Allied hope that enemy units would retreat in the face of battle were seriously flawed. In the mountain rainforest that they had occupied and prepared for years, the NVA, numerous, waiting, and well prepared, held nearly every advantage against the ARVN forces, which would be fighting out of their element.

Making the job of the ARVN in Laos even more complicated was the fact that the Cooper-Church Amendment also forbade participation by U.S. advisers in operations outside the geographic confines of South Vietnam, which meant that ARVN forces would go to battle without the conduit to U.S. firepower upon which they had been dependent for so long. Realizing the inevitable, as a part of the broader Vietnamization process, U.S. and Australian advisers had begun to give their counterparts lessons in calling fire support in English. However, the lessons were haphazard, and most advisers believed that their counterparts lacked both the basic language skills and the technical jargon required to be effective and intelligible to pilots in the fast-paced, adrenaline-drenched world of combat air support,[15] a weakness that would play a critical role in coming events.

Invasion

The preliminary phase of the operation got under way on 30 January, when lead elements of the 1st Brigade, 5th U.S. Infantry Division attacked west from Fire Support Base Vandegrift along Highway 9. Against only sporadic NVA resistance, by 3 February, U.S. forces had reopened Khe Sanh as a forward base, pushed to the Laotian frontier, and made their planned diversionary moves toward the A Shau Valley. Next, during a pre-invasion deployment phase, select ARVN units of I Corps, including the 1st Armored Brigade, the 1st Ranger Group, two regiments of the 1st ARVN Division, and two engineer battalions, along with the South Vietnamese Airborne Division and the 258th Marine Brigade, made their way to the border area in preparation for their roles in the invasion.[16] ARVN and U.S. forces carried out Phase I of Lam Son 719 with much success and against only minimal opposition, allowing for further hope that the coming cross-border operation would surprise the NVA and overcome its will to resist.

In the early hours of 8 February 1971, eleven sorties by B-52 bombers announced the ARVN invasion of Laos. Supported by air strikes and artillery preparation, at 1000 hours the 2nd Troop of the 17th Armored Squadron crossed the border with ARVN soldiers, jubilant after so many days of waiting, waving to reporters from atop their armored vehicles. Eventually the ground thrust consisted of the 1st Armored Brigade (11th and 17th Armored Squadrons), reinforced by the 1st and 8th Airborne Battalions, which were to provide cover while the 101st Combat Engineer Battalion and a platoon of bulldozers restored the single lane road that was to serve as the ARVN lifeline. Ahead of the column and on the mountain slopes to the north and the south, helicopter gunships provided cover by attacking NVA defensive positions.[17]

To the north of the ground advance, the 2nd Airborne Battalion air assaulted into the area of Landing Zone 30, some ten kilometers north of Route 9, while the 3rd Airborne Battalion seized Landing Zone 31, to provide flank support. Further north still, the 21st Ranger Battalion air assaulted into the area near what eventually became Ranger South. To the south of Route 9, the 4/3 Infantry Battalion seized Landing Zone Hotel, which dominated the Co Roc escarpment, while, four kilometers further south, 1/3 and 2/3 (Dinh's old unit) established themselves against spotty NVA resistance near Landing Zone Blue. Though to the north and south ARVN flanking forces had achieved all of their objectives in their efforts to guard the ground advance, the Armored Task Force was delayed by the poor condition of the road and by the end of the day had advanced a scant nine kilometers.

On the second day of the operation, inclement weather set in, which prohibited any further air assaults and hampered the all-important repairs to Route 9. On 10 February, the weather improved and allowed the offensive to continue. In the north, the airborne and rangers worked to consolidate their gains and searched for enemy troop concentrations. Ominously, perhaps, contact with the NVA remained light, which led some to believe that the enemy was protecting his assets and gathering his forces for a massive counterattack.[18] To the south, the 1st ARVN Division expanded its area of operations further west, with 4/1 Infantry Battalion seizing Landing Zone Delta, some ten kilometers west of LZ Hotel. The greatest success of the day, though, fell to the ground element of the assault. By early evening, the armored column joined with the 9th Airborne Battalion which had air assaulted into objective A Loui at a critical road junction twenty kilometers inside Laos and roughly halfway to the ultimate objective of Tchepone. Although the advance had fallen behind schedule, losses remained light, and the ARVN strength in Laos had reached 7,500 men. However, the day had also witnessed a disaster. A VNAF helicopter on its way to Ranger South had been shot down, killing the G3 and the G4, the chief planner and the chief logistician, of I Corps, who carried copies of the plans for the operation—plans that now had presumably fallen into enemy hands.

For the next few days, ARVN troops fanned out on both flanks in search of NVA supply caches and worked to strengthen their defensive posture. At the same time, reinforcements continued to arrive throughout the campaign area, and ARVN strengh eventually reached a total of ten thousand men and including thirteen infantry battalions, two ranger battalions, two artillery battalions, and one engineer battalion. Although the search for supplies netted some notable successes, especially in the south, disaster loomed, for at A Loui, though faced with minimal resistance, the all-important ground advance had inexplicably lurched to a halt, and, in the words of the U.S. Air Force historian of the operation, "The ARVN drive to Tchepone temporarily lost its westward momentum as the units searched for caches by day and defended their fire support bases by night."[19]

The halt at A Loui was an inexcusable failure in command. The only hope for ARVN forces, badly outnumbered and deep in enemy-held territory, was to maintain the initiative through speed of movement. Nonetheless, the ARVN advance stagnated, at the order of President Thieu himself because of his politically driven desire to hold down casualties among his loyal airborne forces. Intensely frustrated by the delay, Abrams fumed at Generals Vien and Lam to have their forces move forward quickly to avoid giving "the enemy both time and opportunity to organize his reaction in a more effective way."[20] After nearly a week of wavering, Lam finally decided to have the 1st ARVN Division move out to establish fire support bases further west along the southern bank of the Xepon River to cover a renewed airborne and armor ground movement toward Tchepone, a process slated to take five days. However, the ARVN's opportunity had passed.

NVA forces undertook a rapid process of reinforcement and concentrated their strength near the static and thus vulnerable ARVN fire bases to the north and south of Route 9. The bulk of the NVA 70B Corps, made up of the 308th, the 304th, and the 320th Divisions, augmented by a tank regiment, gathered north of Route 9 near the bases of the ARVN airborne and rangers. Fewer communist forces gathered in the south, where the 2nd NVA Division, eventually joined by the 324B Division, put pressure on the fire bases of the 1st ARVN Division. The prospect of facing ever-growing numbers of the enemy seemed an

South Vietnamese soldiers search a trail area in Laos during Operation Lam Son 719. Photograph VA002287, 1971, Douglas Pike Photograph Collection, The Vietnam Archive, Texas Tech University.

opportunity to MACV, an opportunity for a crushing victory. In a mid-February briefing, Abrams heard that "The real significance of that Lam Son operation . . . is the enemy has everything committed, or en route, that he has. . . . So if they're hurt, they're going to be beat for a long time."[21] It remained to be seen whether the ARVN was up to the task.

NVA Counterattack

On 17 February, having lost a week of precious time since the halt at A Loui, bad weather hampered renewed ARVN efforts to advance, even as the NVA counterattacked the more isolated ARVN fire support bases. After subjecting the exposed positions of the 39th Ranger

Battalion to a punishing artillery barrage, multiple battalions of the NVA 308th Division launched a ground assault on Ranger North. Ominously, the attacking forces were quite obviously troops newly arrived from North Vietnam, carrying new weapons and wearing fresh clothing. Several of the surrounding ARVN defensive outposts fell quickly, but, with the aid of substantial U.S. air support, Ranger North momentarily held in hand-to-hand fighting. By the evening of 20 February, though, contact was lost with the commander of the 39th Ranger Battalion as massed NVA forces poured through the ARVN perimeter. Forced to abandon their positions, the surviving defenders made a harrowing journey through enemy lines to join with the 21st Ranger Battalion at Ranger South. The soldiers at Ranger North had fought bravely and well in the face of overwhelming odds. The results of the struggle were grim, with 39th Ranger Battalion being rendered combat ineffective, having suffered 178 killed and 145 wounded, which left just 100 men able to continue the struggle—the human cost of a plan gone awry. The rangers, though, had exacted a fearsome toll on their NVA tormentors, accounting for an estimated 639 enemy killed in action.

As the firefights raged around Ranger North, President Thieu visited I Corps and learned of the worsening situation. In the presence of the ARVN division commanders, Thieu counseled caution to General Lam and suggested that the move west toward Tchepone once again be put on hold to allow for the expansion of search activities to the southwest into NVA base area 611. As a result, what had been meant as a lightning-quick operation that would seize and hold the initiative further stagnated and turned into an attritional slugfest, something for which the ARVN was unprepared.

For the next three days, during a lull in the fighting, as the NVA repositioned its forces, the varied elements of 1st ARVN Division, which had been spared the worst of the carnage, continued to move south and west, opening Landing Zone Brown and Fire Support Base Delta I, in search of NVA supply dumps and oil pipelines. The storm, though, broke once again on 25 February as NVA forces launched a generalized offensive against ARVN positions throughout the area of the operation. In the south, NVA assaults centered on Fire Support Base Hotel II and preempted further sweeps and troop movements in the area by 1st ARVN Division. However, the NVA again focused its most intense efforts in the north, in an attempt to build on its earlier successes. Realizing that Ranger South was isolated and vulnerable, General Lam made the difficult decision to evacuate the base under fire. With the flank support provided by the rangers gone, the ARVN airborne at Fire Support Bases 30 and 31 now faced the brunt of the furious NVA attack.

NVA forces moved in as close as they could to both bases, both to negate the use of U.S. air power and to use their own antiaircraft weapons to cut off the ARVN bases from helicopter resupply. At 1100 hours on 25 February, NVA artillery fire rained down on FSB 31, while U.S. helicopters and fixed-wing aircraft scrambled to locate and suppress the sources of the bombardment. It quickly became apparent, though, that FSB 31 had been completely surrounded by a massive enemy force, one that for the first time included tanks. At the critical moment when the NVA ground attack began to roll forward, antiaircraft fire struck a U.S. F-4 aircraft and forced the pilot to eject. Following standard procedure, the U.S. forward air controller on the scene shifted his attention to the rescue of the downed pilot, which left no air cover for the beleaguered defenders of FSB 31 in their time of greatest need.

Having recognized the serious nature of the situation, General Lam ordered the nearby armor, still languishing in the area around A Loui, to set out cross-country in an effort to relieve the pressure on FSB 31. Even such a simple order, though, had difficulties making its way through the dysfunctional ARVN command system. The armor was under the control of Lieutenant General Du Quoc Dong, the commander of the Airborne Division, who was equal to General Lam in rank and who was unhappy to find himself subordinated to Lam for operations in Laos. A firm friend of President Thieu, General Dong did not even condescend to attend I Corps briefings during the campaign. Reluctantly, General Dong initially instructed Colonel Luat, in command of the 1st Armored Brigade, to comply with Lam's wishes, and the tanks and armored personnel carriers (APCs) of the 17th Armored Squadron rumbled slowly northward, only to meet an NVA ambush. Although the fighting was heavy, with the ARVN losing two tanks and an APC, General Lam instructed the armor to continue its relief mission. From his own HQ, though, General Dong ordered the armor to remain in place, some eighteen hundred meters short of its goal. The command breakdown sealed the fate of the defenders of FSB 31; in the words of the historian Keith Nolan:

The 3rd Airborne Battalion was truly alone in their fight against a well-coordinated tank and infantry assault, the USAF having forsaken them for their own comrades, the ARVN armor having halted in place to wait and see. The only aircraft above Hill 31 was a helicopter with several airborne advisers aboard. It dipped down to fire an M-60 ineffectually against the surging attack.[22]

Taking advantage of the disappearance of U.S. air power, the NVA closed in on three sides, armor from the northeast and infantry from the northwest and the south. By early evening, NVA armor penetrated the base defenses, and the ARVN paratroopers responded with small-arms fire and LAW rockets, which took a fearsome toll on the attackers. However, enemy infantry soon overwhelmed the defenders and swarmed through the ARVN trenches,[23] and the 21st Airborne Battalion artillery commander sent out a last message calling for fire directly on his position, as the NVA dug into the roof of his bunker. Amid the confusion, a number of paratroopers managed to break out of the encirclement and moved south to link up with the stalled armored force, but a total of 135 ARVN soldiers were killed or captured, and another critical support base had fallen to the enemy. Again, ARVN soldiers had fought bravely and well, inflicting 250 KIA on the NVA, which also lost eleven tanks in the bitter fighting, fighting in a tactical situation made immeasurably worse by command weaknesses that had once been obscured by the ARVN's normal role as an adjunct to the American war but that came into stark relief as the ARVN's leadership struggled to come to grips with the big-unit war.

Fighting Alone

As I Corps commander, General Lam was a first-rate politician but an inept combat leader. Affable, genial, and so addicted to tennis that he even took breaks amid battle for his afternoon matches, General Lam spent little time at the forward command areas and exerted little true tactical control over events in Laos.[24] General Lam enjoyed close political ties to President Thieu, and the two men often worked together in making battlefield decisions regarding Lam Son 719, decisions more closely linked to political considerations at the presidential level than to the realities of events that confronted the troops in Laos.[25]

I Corps also suffered from tactical shortcomings born out of the realities of having been shunted aside as part of the American war for so long. Colonel Ray Batterall, who worked with the ARVN at I Corps Forward at Khe Sanh, noted that never before had I Corps really worked as a coherent unit. Also, with the bulk of their forces historically spread across the countryside in support of pacification, General Lam and his subordinates had in the past dealt only with logistic and administrative matters and had left tactical planning to the Americans. Lacking experience, then, in battlefield planning, General Lam, looking ahead to the invasion of Laos, faced a "nearly insuperable array of new challenges." Batterall concluded that the corps headquarters was deficient in all areas and did not even truly grasp "the responsibilities inherent in attachment, the differences between a zone of action and an axis of advance, or the full meaning of the word 'secure.'"[26] If these problems were not enough, the loss of the I Corps G3 and G4, the chief planner and the chief logistician for the offensive, so early in the battle only muddled the tactical situation even further and crippled the ability of I Corps and its subordinate units to react to a fast-changing and difficult situation. Command and control sometimes broke down completely, and, in the words of ARVN Major General Nguyen Duy Hinh, "During the operation, there were several instances in which division commanders lost control of their units. Even the I Corps commander sometimes did not know the major events affecting his divisions."[27]

Apart from a lack of tactical experience, the political machinations of the upper echelon of ARVN command, from meddling on the part of President Thieu to petulance on the part of subordinate commanders, were a source of befuddlement to American observers. Tom Jaco, who witnessed events from his new position as deputy adviser at I Corps Forward in Khe Sanh, was stunned to find a situation with "more political intrigue than you can ever imagine." As the armor sat in place "without a clue" and the Vietnamese Marines later acted bravely but independently, Jaco watched in horror as "command and control fell apart," sacrificing the lives of brave ARVN soldiers to ineptitude and political infighting.[28]

To the members of the ARVN, the failure of the command structure during Lam Son 719 had devastating implications. In a postwar study of the operation, Major General Hinh reflected:

The most important problem to be solved was insubordination on the part of general reserve unit commanders who like many other generals considered themselves to be pillars of the regime. The I Corps commander apparently bowed to the political powers of these generals and this adversely affected his conduct of the operation. The unsubmissive attitude of the Marine and Airborne Division commanders was actually inexcusable in that they placed themselves above the national interest and let their personal pride interfere with the task of defeating the enemy. For the operation to succeed as planned, the problem of effective command had to be satisfactorily solved above everything else because it affected the relationship between subordinate staffs and the control of the operation itself. At least, the I Corps commander should have been given the authority to require that his orders be strictly carried out.[29]

U.S. air power was critical to the successes achieved during Operation Lam Son 719. It was the actions of U.S. helicopter pilots, who braved their own personal hell in a stream of missions into and out of stricken ARVN bases while facing constant enemy fire, that made the ARVN operation and the survival of the ARVN soldiers themselves possible. Additionally, during the cross-border operation, B-52s flew some 1,280 sorties, about 30 a day every day for the whole period, while tactical aircraft flew more than 8,000 total attack sorties.[30] However, the reliance on U.S. air support had profound drawbacks, as, in the opinion of General Hinh, the ARVN became overly reliant on American firepower:

Another shortcoming of ARVN units at battalion and lower levels was their failure to maneuver when being engaged. After the first contact, they tended to stop and wait for support rather than conduct probes and maneuver to attack or close in on the enemy. This shortcoming indicated a need for additional training for small-unit leaders.[31]

Although U.S. air support was plentiful enough that the ARVN remained tactically addicted to it, it was sometimes hard to access. Because of a host of problems, including a shortage of Forward Air Controllers (FACs) devoted to the support of the Airborne Division, a convoluted command structure, and language difficulties, air support had faltered badly during the final NVA assault on FSB 31, which led Colonel Arthur Pence, the U.S. adviser to the ARVN Airborne, to lodge a formal complaint. In part because of his protest over the affair, Pence was replaced as adviser to the ARVN Airborne by Colonel Benjamin Harrison, who also served as senior adviser to the 1st ARVN Division. The trouble, though, did not end there, for Harrison went on to lodge his own written complaint with XXIV Corps concerning the control and usage of air power, after which the situation was taken under much better control.

Even after the systemic changes made in the wake of FSB 31, problems still existed in the link between the ARVN and its lifeline of air power support. In the heat of battle, the few ARVN who could speak English often found it difficult to get their points across adequately to their American allies aboard the FAC aircraft. The situation was even worse in ARVN units that had taken heavy casualties and thus were unable to produce anyone able to speak English. Ben Harrison put the human cost paid by the ARVN by fighting without its advisers into stark perspective:

> The ARVN could scream and cry, but by not having their advisers with them they could not transmit the true nature of the situation across to the Air Force as well as their adviser would have. . . . [In situations which] normally a U.S. adviser would have raised all kinds of hell . . . [the ARVN often could not get their point across and] got their asses shot off by the NVA and couldn't get any tactical air support.[32]

Retaking the Initiative

As the ARVN command machine sputtered and coughed, the NVA continued to press its newfound advantage. South of Route 9, the 1st ARVN Division, less reliant on static defenses, faced increasing resistance, with 2/3 ARVN becoming surrounded by an entire NVA regiment near Landing Zone Hotel II. Fighting a running battle with a vastly superior enemy force, Dinh's old unit acquitted itself well and, through use of its own organic firepower and excellent air support, blasted its way through enemy lines and escaped to the north.

Lieutenant General Hoang Xuan Lam, commander of I Corps, talks to reporters during Operation Lam Son 719. Photograph VA002291, 1971, Douglas Pike Photograph Collection, The Vietnam Archive, Texas Tech University.

Although the encroaching might of the NVA forced the closure and evacuation of Hotel II, the 1st ARVN Division continued to live up to its sterling reputation as the best unit in the ARVN. While other units became enmeshed in political bickering, the actions of 1st ARVN Division earned praise from its U.S. advisers for demonstrating "outstanding fighting ability, inspirational leadership, and sound tactics."[33]

With the ARVN advance stymied, President Thieu once again intervened and directed General Lam to relieve the embattled Airborne Division with elements of the Vietnamese Marines, a relief to take place while entire formations of the airborne remained surrounded and under heavy fire. Worried by the prospect that his most politically loyal formation would suffer further grievous losses, President Thieu had asked the impossible. Alarmed, on 28 February, General Lam journeyed to Saigon with his own suggestions regarding how to save the situation.

Both men realized that the ARVN offensive, which was now a matter of national pride, had degenerated into bitter and costly fighting only halfway to its ultimate objective. General Lam believed that the offensive, and thus the reputations of its architects, could be salvaged and suggested that the airborne remain in place while the 1st ARVN Division, which had acquitted itself so well, continued the drive to Tchepone, utilizing a daring series of heliborne leaps. Thieu approved the risky plan, which involved the projection of ARVN forces, now totally reliant on helicopter insertion and supply, further into the midst of the massive enemy buildup even as the fighting north and south of A Loui continued to rage.

To Major General Pham Van Phu, who had recently taken command of 1st ARVN Division upon the elevation of General Truong to the command of IV Corps, and to Colonel Vu Van Giai, in command at 1st ARVN Division Forward at Fire Support Base Delta I, the attack on Tchepone seemed fraught with danger. In Giai's mind, Tchepone was nothing more than a symbolic target, reminiscent of Hamburger Hill. The town itself was ruined, and the NVA had long since moved its most sensitive supply caches out of the town itself into the surrounding hills and jungles. Colonel Giai suspected that the NVA, though it could not know the timing or mechanism of the coming attack, was ready and waiting around Tchepone and that ARVN forces would walk into a trap. For this reason, both Colonel Giai and General Phu suggested a lightning raid, getting in and out of Tchepone by utilizing the speed of helicopter transport, before NVA forces could react.[34] Their planning was approved, which left the ARVN a chance to salvage a stunning victory from under the very noses of the NVA.

The new assault plan resulted in a considerable shuffling of forces, and, on 3 March, elements of the Vietnamese Marine Division took over responsibility for much of the eastern area of operations south of Route 9, freeing the 1st Regiment of the 1st ARVN Division for its part in the renewed offensive, a series of combat assaults designed to seize critical points along the escarpment to the west. Correspondingly, along the DMZ, American forces expanded their area of operations, which allowed the reassignment of 2nd Regiment of the 1st ARVN Division. The ARVN regiment, including Tran Ngoc Hue's 2/2, made its way to Khe Sanh to play its role in the ongoing battle, the assault on Tchepone itself.

While Hue and his men made their preparations, the situation in Laos grew even more alarming as the NVA assaulted the 2nd Airborne Battalion at FSB 30. While a tenacious defense and lavish air support momentarily held the encroaching NVA at bay, by 3 March, all of the artillery pieces on the base had been damaged and helicopter resupply had become increasingly perilous. As a result, General Lam ordered the 2nd Airborne Battalion to abandon its position. At the same time, the 17th Armored Squadron, which had earlier pushed to the north to aid the defenders of FSB 31, became engaged with a sizable enemy force and lost one hundred killed and ten armored vehicles.

As the NVA noose tightened north of Route 9, the 1st Regiment of the 1st ARVN Division began its move to the west, heralded by the 3rd Battalion, 1st Infantry Regiment's combat assault into what became Fire Support Base Lo Lo, atop the highest peak of the southern escarpment, some thirteen kilometers southeast of Tchepone. Though there had been heavy preparatory air strikes, the 3/1 helicopter landings met with strong enemy anti-aircraft and small-arms fire. Having long expected a landing on such an obvious target, NVA forces had prepared well, digging into the surrounding hillsides. Heavy fire postponed landings at FSB Lo Lo twice, while additional air support pummeled the NVA defenders. Finally, 3/1 touched down at FSB Lo Lo at the price of eleven helicopters shot down and forty-four others hit by gunfire.

As the infantry moved out from Lo Lo, 4th Battalion, 1st Infantry initiated operations at Landing Zone Liz. Supported by heavy air strikes, the landings at LZ Liz met with less resistance, which allowed 4/1 to sweep out of the LZ quickly. The tempo and effectiveness of the ARVN assault continued on 5 March with attacks by the 4th and 5th battalions of the 2nd Regiment on Landing Zone Sophia, just four and a half kilometers southwest of Tchepone. By nightfall, LZ Sophia had eight 105mm howitzers in place, while 4/2 pushed to the north and seized a crossing over the Xepon River. While the NVA had been prepared for the initial shift of ARVN lines westward, the speed of the renewed advance, coupled with effective air support, had caught the defenders by surprise. All was ready for an assault on Tchepone itself, but speed remained critical as NVA forces began to mass against the new threat.

Strike on Tchepone

By 5 March, Tran Ngoc Hue was well aware of the successes and failures of Lam Son 719, having followed the ebb and flow of the battle with great interest. He also knew that his battalion, along with the 3rd Battalion, 2nd Regiment, would lead the final assault on Tchepone. While he had great hope that the attack would succeed, especially given the successes of recent days, Hue could not shake the feeling that he was walking into a trap. Because his wife, Cam, was caring for their two-month-old daughter, Hue decided not to tell her that he was going to Laos lest she be overcome with fear. The night before the battle, Hue had one last dinner with his U.S. advisers, Dave Wiseman and Gordon Greta, who expressed their frustration at not being able to accompany 2/2 into Laos. As the meal ended, Hue turned to Wiseman, his dear friend and comrade in war, and asked if he would adopt his children. Stunned, Wiseman asked Hue how he could make such a request. Hue did not provide an answer but instead once again asked Wiseman for his word. Realizing the danger that Hue would soon face and the difficulty of leaving his young family alone to their fate, Wiseman agreed.

The next morning, 120 helicopters assembled at Khe Sanh to carry 2/2 and 3/2 into Landing Zone Hope just north of Tchepone in what was the largest airmobile operation of the entire Vietnam War. Benefiting from a massive aerial bombardment and total surprise, the helicopters approached LZ Hope against only minimal resistance. Captain Rich Johnson piloted the first helicopter into Tchepone, leading a long line of troop carriers that landed on the tiny LZ one at a time. By early afternoon, the trooplift was complete, and, remarkably, only one helicopter had been damaged by enemy fire. The ARVN infantry quickly fanned out from its LZ and moved into Tchepone, attaining the ultimate goal of Operation Lam Son 719.

After receiving a promotion to lieutenant colonel on the spot, Hue and the troops of 2/2 and 3/2 searched the area in and around Tchepone for three days unmolested and destroyed several substantial supply caches. The finds, though, were not of the magnitude that the ARVN high command had hoped, since the NVA had removed most of its supply dumps to the west of the ruined town. Instead of pushing further west in search of supplies, Tran Ngoc Hue received orders to cross the Xepon River south of Tchepone and join with ARVN forces at Fire Support Base Sophia. Wary of the continued NVA buildup in the region, President Thieu and General Lam had made the decision to withdraw their forces from Laos after having achieved only a token capture of Tchepone.

The decision to withdraw so far ahead of schedule was both controversial and flawed. At MACV, Abrams advocated seizing the moment and remarked that the NVA:

> must be stopped . . . and a major battle, which might even be the decisive battle of the war, must be won. I urged the employment of the 2nd ARVN Division in Lam Son 719 now. Politically, psychologically and militarily, President Thieu can accept nothing less. We have the resources to do it.[35]

President Thieu and General Lam, though, contended that the ARVN forces in Laos were in mortal peril and that even the addition of the 2nd ARVN Division would not be enough to ensure victory. The only reasonable course of action was an orderly withdrawal to conserve as much of the committed force as possible. Military concerns, though, were in actuality only secondary; the ARVN had reached its psychological goal, and the reputations of its political masters presumably had been saved. In the words of ARVN Major General Hinh, "It was apparent that President Thieu had decided, at the outset, that once Tchepone had been entered . . . the withdrawal would begin without delay."[36]

The withdrawal, though, was not the rapid conclusion to a successful raid that had been planned and envisioned by Colonel Giai. He had hoped that once the units of 2nd Regiment had accomplished their tasks around Tchepone, they would be helififted out to Khe Sanh, beginning a west-to-east pullback of committed ARVN forces. Instead, reinvigorated by victory, General Lam had a new scheme that called for the units of 2nd Regiment to pull back to an area nine kilometers south of A Loui, near Landing Zone Brown, to take part in further raids on NVA supply caches along Route 914, operations slated to take nine to ten days. Only then would the ARVN units withdraw, beginning with Fire Support Base Lo Lo and working progressively eastward. Thus, ARVN high command had not opted to remain in Tchepone in an effort to fight a decisive battle. Neither, though, would the ARVN execute a rapid withdrawal before the NVA once again marshaled its forces. Instead, Thieu and Lam had decided upon an unsatisfying and dangerous middle path—ARVN units, reliant on helicopter support, would loiter in and around base areas to the south of Route 9 and conduct operations into the heart of the area of a renewed and massive NVA buildup.[37]

Disaster in the South

Although the NVA had been prepared to fight in defense of its critical logistic area, Operation Lam Son 719 had not been a trap planned for the unwary ARVN in the strictest sense of the term. ARVN delays and mistaken command decisions, however, had made it so. Overwhelmed by politicized decision making and the tactical problems of conducting a large-scale conventional attack, the ARVN had neither pressed its initial advantages nor made good its exit before disaster loomed. Despite heavy losses, including an estimated three thousand killed in action, the NVA had continued to replenish and build on its combat strength in southern Laos, in Abrams's words, "committing everything he had" to the ongoing battle.[38] The additional forces, including five infantry regiments plus supporting armor and artillery, concentrated against the increasingly isolated and vulnerable units of 1st ARVN Division south of Route 9.[39] Even as the NVA gathered to administer the coup de grace, on orders from I Corps several ARVN battalions maneuvered ever further to the south in search of caches, moves that took them deeper into the area of the NVA buildup, a situation tailor-made for disaster. Although General Lam at I Corps was slow to recognize the desperate nature of the situation, the men on the ground realized that the NVA were closing in for the kill, and 1st ARVN Division soon found itself fighting for its life.

The climactic battle began to take shape as NVA forces surrounded ARVN soldiers of the 1st Regiment around and atop Fire Support Base Lo Lo. On 14 March alone, two hundred rockets and one hundred artillery rounds rained down on the FSB, halting any attempts at helicopter evacuation or resupply. With the 4th Battalion, 1st Regiment acting as rear guard, the remaining units attempted to break out to the east. While 1/1, 2/1, and 3/1 moved out of the inferno, 4/1 fought a running four-day battle against two entire NVA regiments. Supported by waves of air power, and persevering in the face of NVA loudspeaker appeals for their surrender, 4/1 valiantly fought on and enabled the withdrawal of its sister units.

Out of ammunition and pressed into a perimeter only sixty meters in diameter, the eighty-three survivors of 4/1 faced destruction, and their rescue was indicative of the bravery of the American helicopter pilots. Circling above the battlefield in his Cobra attack helicopter all afternoon and having expended all of his ammunition, Captain Keith

Brandt stayed in contact with the sergeant now in command of the remnants of 4/1 and volunteered to lead an extraction flight of Huey slicks, under Captain Rich Johnson, to the stricken unit. Swooping low over the battlefield, Brandt's helicopter had its hydraulics shot away by enemy fire and crashed into the trees below. As his helicopter hurtled toward the earth, Brandt sent one last radio transmission to Johnson: "I've lost my engine and my transmission is breaking up. Goodbye. Send my love to my family. I'm dead." Out of ammo and low on fuel, Brandt could have left the battlefield; he instead chose to remain behind to direct the extraction of men he did not even know. Such was the nature of the American helicopter pilots in Operation Lam Son 719.[40]

Having just witnessed his friend's death, Johnson pressed on with his mission. As fire popped all around his aircraft, amazingly including mortars being used as direct fire weapons, Johnson made his descent. The ARVN soldiers were in a small clearing in the trees, leaving Johnson only a "hover hole," which he had to enter with great care and agonizing slowness. When he touched down, desperate South Vietnamese soldiers surrounded his craft, all wounded and all knowing that his would likely be the only helicopter that came to their rescue. As the mad rush to board his helicopter began, Johnson's craft took several hits—from *above*—NVA 50-caliber machine guns were firing on his helicopter through its rotor blades from the surrounding hills. Finally, Johnson got his helicopter back into the air, with twenty-five ARVN survivors on board. As he looked back into the craft, Johnson saw utter carnage; all of his passengers were wounded, and the soldier nearest him had a gaping hole in his head where his eye had once been.

Once airborne, with ARVN soldiers even hanging from the helicopter's door guns, the helicopter began to redline; it would not be able to continue its flight with all of the weight on board. Johnson knew then that "it was either all of us were going in [to crash] or some of us were going in." Johnson gave the difficult order to push the four ARVN soldiers who dangled from the guns off the craft, at a height of two hundred feet. Finally, Johnson's wounded bird made it back to Khe Sanh, with twenty-one ARVN survivors as well as his own crew of four. While scenes such as the return of Johnson's chopper made international headlines and perpetuated the myth of ARVN cowardice, Johnson and his comrades knew the reality of the situation. ARVN soldiers, who had already seen a lifetime of war, "had looked around and, hell, he's the last son of a bitch on the ground and he's not going to be left behind. I'd jump on the skid too. And so would you."[41]

A Warrior's Fate

As 4/1 was being ripped to pieces, Tran Ngoc Hue's 2/2 moved by helicopter to Landing Zone Brown to take part in the search for enemy supplies in the Cua Tung area. Before it could move out on its new mission, though, Hue's unit joined battle with NVA forces that had surrounded 3rd Battalion, 3rd Regiment just south of LZ Brown. With the aid of air support, the ARVN units broke the enemy cordon, and the NVA momentarily retreated to regroup. For the next three days, 2/2, along with 5/2 and 4/2, fought off NVA probes and covered the withdrawal of 3/3 and 4/3 from the battle area. After the extraction of the friendly forces, 2/2 continued its mission to search for enemy supply dumps but fell under ever-increasing NVA attack. Belatedly realizing that the 2nd Regiment faced destruction, General Lam decided to quicken the extraction operations and finally to forgo the now futile searches for NVA caches. Even so, priority for extraction went to the units fighting north of Route 9 and the ground element near A Loui. Hue and his men would have to fight on.[42]

Directed to make their way to FSB Delta I, by 19 March, 2/2, 3/2, and 4/2 were all in heavy contact with enemy forces. Despite 686 helicopter gunship sorties, 246 tactical air strikes, and 14 B-52 missions, the NVA pressed the attack in a bid to annihilate the now surrounded units. Run to ground, and facing desperate odds, the battalions of 2nd Regiment took up defensive positions and could only hope for helicopter extraction.

Cut off by vastly superior enemy forces and unable to reach FSB Delta I, Hue had his men dig in atop Hill 660 and throw out defenses to stem the attacks that he knew were coming. Unbowed, Hue called for all of the air support he could get, including B-52 strikes, even though the NVA lines were so close that shrapnel from those strikes rained down among his own men. Heedless of their losses to air power, NVA infantry units poured forward in the assault, covered by artillery fire, mortars, and flame throwers. Facing certain death, Hue requested air extraction, and, in the early afternoon of 20 March, troop ships arrived on scene and, beginning with 3/2, heroically attempted to lift the beleaguered ARVN infantry to safety. However, even though U.S. air power on that day alone had mounted 1,388 gunship sorties, 270 tactical air strikes, and 11 B-52 missions, NVA fire remained so heavy that twenty-eight of the forty helicopters used in the lift were hit and rendered unflyable; 2/2 and 4/2 would have to remain behind alone at the western side of the dwindling ARVN line.

Running so low on supplies that men drank their own urine, 2/2 neared the end of its ability to resist. Still the men fought on, as Hue barked orders and called down protective fire. While Hue was on the radio working to control air support, his world suddenly went black; the explosion of a mortar shell peppered him with red-hot shrapnel in the leg, arm, and face. The wounds were so bad that his men thought that he had died and affixed an identity tag to his foot so that his body could be recovered after the fight. Gradually, though, Hue regained consciousness and, through the fog of pain, heard the NVA on the radio announce its intention to launch a final assault to obliterate the remnants of his battalion. At the same time, the call came in from the ARVN command for 2/2 to attempt a breakout. As his men prepared to carry him away, Hue knew that he would only hinder their progress and requested to be left behind, to give them the best chance to be able to return to their families. Tearfully, Hue's XO, Captain Nguyen Huu Chuoc, agreed, saluted his fallen leader, and led the ragtag survivors of 2/2 in their breakout attempt even as the final NVA assault began.

In total darkness, and amid chaotic, hand-to-hand fighting, Captain Chuoc and some sixty ARVN soldiers made their way to safety and were picked up by helicopters the following day, all that remained of the once proud 2nd Battalion, 2nd Regiment. Unable even to stand, Hue watched helplessly as the victorious NVA swept across his position. A single NVA soldier made his way to where Hue lay slumped against the stump of a shattered tree; upon reaching Hue's position, the enemy soldier opened his eyes wide—he had stumbled across a special prize, an ARVN battalion commander. Hue asked his captor to shoot him, but he politely refused and instead took Hue away for questioning by nearby officers. Hue's next interrogator was an NVA colonel who hailed from Hue's own home village of Ke Mon. The colonel knew Hue and his reputation well—the legendary commander of the Hac Bao, the man who had saved Hue City—and informed Hue that General Giap himself would want to meet him and would have special plans for his future.

Hue's new life as a prisoner of the hated communists began with a harrowing journey up the Ho Chi Minh Trail and into captivity. Though the NVA desperately wanted Hue to survive, they had no medicine with which to treat his extensive wounds and only washed them in salt water. The ARVN soldiers captured with him, his loyal comrades in arms, physically carried Hue on the journey up the trail. Slowly his men trudged, from Binh Tram to Binh Tram, the NVA logistics points set one day's march apart on the trail, and made their way northward. The column moved only at night to avoid U.S. air strikes along the trail and were not allowed inside the Binh Tram areas but instead had to make camp in the surrounding jungle under constant guard. All the while, Hue was very thirsty because of his considerable loss of blood; unable to eat the meager rations of rice and sugar that the NVA offered, he hovered near death.

For Hue, the agonizing journey was "his time in hell," as insects and worms invaded his open wounds and slowly ate the flesh from several of his mangled fingers. As his body was consumed, Hue screamed out day after day as his men looked on in horror. Expecting death at any moment, Hue thought again and again of his young family. It was the ultimate sadness that his life with them, his beloved wife and children—who did not even know if he was alive or dead—was over. All Hue could do was put his future and that of his loved ones into God's care.

Once the procession reached North Vietnam, Hue finally received medicine for his wounds, but he lost several of his fingers. Shifted to trucks, Hue and his men made their way to Vinh, where they were met by crowds of civilians who cursed, spat, and pelted them with rocks. After being paraded through the streets, the prisoners of Lam Son 719 were herded onto trains for the final journey to Hanoi, where Hue entered Hoa Lo Prison, the infamous Hanoi Hilton. At age twenty-nine, Hue faced the prospect of life in prison. He was a prisoner for thirteen long years.

For Tran Ngoc Hue's advisers, the destruction of 2/2 came as a terrible blow. Wiseman and Greta felt a rage born of helplessness as they listened on the radio as 2/2 was surrounded time and again and eventually "welcomed back the 26 . . . soldiers who survived."[43] As the stragglers reached Khe Sanh, some lucky enough to arrive by helicopter while others made their way back to South Vietnam on foot, neither Wiseman nor Greta was able to gather any conclusive evidence concerning Hue's fate. Someone had seen Hue lying dead; someone else had seen him carried away aboard a litter. Amid the chaos of the ARVN retreat, nobody knew. It was a crushing blow; the unit had been there one day and the next had simply ceased to exist, and the fate of its young commander was unknown. The "complete fucking disaster" of Lam Son 719 left Greta disconsolate. Without a unit to advise, Greta turned to drink and has no further recollections of his tour in Vietnam save for the surreal moment when a recruiter tried to get him to reup for another year. For Dave Wiseman, the events of Lam Son 719 were even more personal; now he had a special responsibility and tie to Hue's young family. Not willing to accept that Hue was dead, Wiseman would search for his comrade for years, eventually making good on a promise born of battle.

Aftermath

After Hue's capture and the extraction of the remnants of 2/2 and 4/2, NVA attacks continued unabated against the ARVN forces that remained in Laos. To the south, the NVA massed against the fire support bases now in the hands of South Vietnamese Marines. For three days, events followed a now familiar pattern, with NVA surrounding and attacking first FSB Delta and then FSB Hotel. After fierce fighting, where the defenders served as a rearguard for the retreating armored column, the Marines eventually abandoned both bases, amid severe command confusion at the highest levels, and pulled back to Khe Sanh. In the north, the remnants of the ARVN armored column, which had originally planned to make a lighting penetration to Tchepone, limped back down Route 9, under heavy fire and continual threat of ambush. The operation so completely unraveled that in the end the armor could not even retreat down the tortured roadway that planners had once hoped would serve as the lifeline to victory; instead, it had to make a diversion through the broken terrain around the Xepon River to avoid enemy attacks. On 23 March, the armor made good its escape from Laos, having lost twenty-one tanks, twenty-six APCs, thirteen bulldozers, two road graders, two trailers, and fifty-one other assorted vehicles.[44] On the following day, the last elements of the South

Vietnamese Marines exited Laos, and Operation Lam Son 719 had come to an end.

In many ways, the invasion of Laos represented what was good and right about the ARVN, which after years of being sidelined was able to extemporize an operation outside its national borders in an area where the NVA held virtually every advantage. During the operation, ARVN units and soldiers fought hard and well, exemplified by the experience of 2/2 ARVN under the sterling leadership of Tran Ngoc Hue. Incidents of bravery abounded during Lam Son 719, bravery that went unreported then and remains unchronicled by Western historians to this day. During the fighting, the ARVN, aided by the might of U.S. air power, forced the NVA to pay a fearsome butcher's bill for the retention of its base areas in Laos, doing great damage to the Laotian logistics network and inflicting some thirteen thousand battle deaths on the NVA.

The results of the campaign, though, were far less than had been expected and did not prevent the NVA in just a year's time from undertaking its massive Easter Offensive. In Lam Son 719, ARVN units suffered nearly 8,000 total casualties and an estimated 3,800 KIA, representing a loss rate of 45 percent of the total force allocated to the operation. In support of Lam Son 719, U.S. forces lost more than one hundred helicopters and seven fixed-wing aircraft. That the operation had started on such a high note but bogged down under the weight of ARVN's own command problems and tactical inefficiency, which resulted in only a token raid on Tchepone and the seeming sacrificial waste of so many good men during the withdrawal phase, was especially galling to American and Vietnamese observers alike.

Both the strengths and the weaknesses of Lam Son 719 foreshadowed the future of the conflict in South Vietnam. The operation proved that the ARVN indeed had great potential and was coming of age; however, the multiple command failings of the ARVN and the resiliency of the NVA indicated that the ARVN was not yet ready to shoulder the burden of war alone. Major General Hinh put into words the problem that vexed so many but was only rarely stated aloud:

The question posed at the time appeared to be whether the RVN, without U.S. presence and support, could meet the challenge posed by the enemy's continued expansion and development.[45]

Lessons from Laos

Controversy dogged Lam Son 719 from the very inception of the operation and continued unabated after its conclusion. The media, feasting on a steady diet of compelling images generated by the withdrawal, portrayed Lam Son as an inglorious failure, while U.S. and South Vietnamese political and military leaders trumpeted the invasion of Laos as a costly but important victory. The historical truth, as is so often the case, lies between the two reactive extremes. The ARVN, constructed to fit neatly into the American matrix of the Vietnam War, had exhibited exactly the strengths and weaknesses expected of a military that had been shunted aside into a backwater of its own war for so long and then suddenly been thrust into the fully fledged reality of the "big-unit war."

Although the Thieu government relentlessly pushed its perspective of Lam Son 719 as a great victory, the South Vietnamese people, tired from endless years of war and awaiting a now inevitable American withdrawal, took the results of the operation with more skepticism. In the words of ARVN's chronicler of the battle, Major General Hinh:

> Despite official claims of a "big victory" and mass demonstrations to celebrate the "lower Laos victory," the people still were shocked by the severe losses incurred. Perhaps the greatest emotional shock of all was the unprecedented fact that ARVN forces had to leave a substantial number of their dead and wounded. It was a violation of beliefs and familial piety that Vietnamese sentiment would never forget and forgive. This came as a horrendous trauma for those unlucky families who, in their traditional devotion to the cult of the dead and their attachment to the living, were condemned to live in perpetual sorrow and doubt. . . . Was it a victory or a defeat? Popular sentiment seemed to be aroused by the dramatic accounts and personal feelings of the I Corps troops who returned from Laos. Almost without exception, they did not believe that they were victorious.[46]

Lam Son 719 had a particularly devastating effect on the military and civilian population of I Corps. The heavy losses, due in the minds of many to command inefficiencies, were especially hard to bear for the soldiers themselves and caused morale in the 1st ARVN Division to drop at what proved to be a critical time. Even at the highest levels across I Corps, U.S. advisers noticed a palpable depression among ARVN commanders. When asked about the morale of 1st ARVN Division following Lam Son 719, General Vu Van Giai, who would command the ill-fated 3rd ARVN Division during the Easter Offensive the following year, simply stated, "Yes, the morale of 1st Division was damaged after Lam Son 719. I suffered the consequences of this in 1972."

In his position as XO of the 54th Regiment, Dinh was well placed to witness the progress of Lam Son 719. While the 54th continued its own operations south of Hue City, Dinh listened on the radio, gathered newspaper reports, and gleaned information from ARVN command meetings as the operation ran its course. Even at his rank, Dinh was aware of the command gaffes, delays, and outright insubordination that defined the invasion, and he listened, stunned, as ARVN units paid the human price for inefficiency. He followed the story of the destruction of the airborne and the rangers. Most important, though, he learned of the slow death of so many units from his own 1st Division. He listened as 2/3, his old unit—his beloved men—was battered so badly that it had to be withdrawn from battle. He also listened as 2/2 was destroyed and his comrade Tran Ngoc Hue was lost. Though he also knew well the massive damage inflicted on the NVA, Dinh had never before witnessed "such a spectacle," and he drew the depressing conclusion that the operation was a "big defeat." In something of an emotional epiphany, Dinh, like so many of his ARVN comrades, came to believe that the brave men lost in Laos were part of "the sacrifice of a fine army for political purposes and vanity."

As Lam Son 719 drew to a close, Dinh and 2nd Battalion, 54th Regiment made their way to Khe Sanh to act in support of the ARVN withdrawal.[47] In his new position, Dinh watched as the stragglers of the 1st ARVN Division made their forlorn way to safety in South Vietnam. Next, it fell to Dinh and his men to close the ARVN forward base at Khe Sanh, destroying what was left there before exiting the area in a ground convoy bound first for Dong Ha. Along the way, Dinh witnessed one of the most disturbing sights he would ever see— women, children, and old men, dressed in white, the traditional color of mourning, crowded in on the procession of military vehicles. Weeping, collapsing to the ground in grief, and sometimes screaming their frustration to the skies, the throngs beseeched Dinh and his men to give them information on their fallen loved ones. In Vietnam, the dead must receive proper burial, lest their restless souls be condemned to wander the earth for eternity. Families must know the day and hour of their loved one's death so that they can celebrate their departure and honor their memory every year. For these grieving widows, fathers, and children, though, there would be no peace. It was a fundamental violation of what it meant to be Vietnamese.

Lam Son 719 was a critical moment in the life and transformation of ARVN hero Pham Van Dinh, the nexus of a disturbing reality that had been forming since the aftermath of the Tet Offensive, when the perceived opportunity for decisive victory had passed, replaced instead by Vietnamization. Dinh had retained his great hope even as the Americans began their exit from the conflict, in the belief that their withdrawal would be slow and measured and as the ARVN came of age and readied to fight its own war. Lam Son 719, though, shone a bright light on the process and demonstrated that Dinh's beloved ARVN was not yet ready to shoulder the burden of war. To Dinh, perhaps the greatest lesson of the invasion of Laos was that, while the ARVN fighting men and their junior officers fought well and hard, their leadership at the highest levels remained politicized and unsound. Dinh's greatest hope was that the leadership problems exhibited so clearly in Lam Son 719 would galvanize the ARVN to make more rapid changes and to fully redress the rot of politicization. There were signs of hope, including General Truong's elevation to the command of IV Corps. The young patriots, the leaders of what Dinh hoped would be a new age, were rising in power. If the Americans stayed the course for a while longer, Dinh thought that the process of reform might be completed. The war was becoming a race between the speed of American withdrawal and that of ARVN reform. It was a race that Dinh realized the young patriots had to win. The alternative—facing the NVA again in pitched battle with the same leadership in control and facing the same mistakes without the security blanket provided by the presence of U.S. ground forces—was too grim to contemplate.

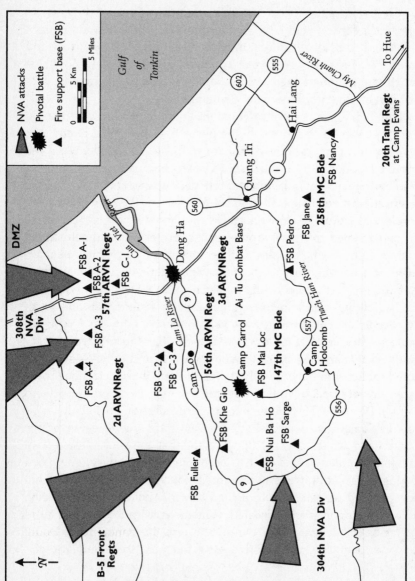

Easter Offensive

9

The Making of a Traitor

IMMEDIATELY AFTER THE conclusion of Operation Lam Son 719, President Nixon proclaimed, "Tonight I can report that Vietnamization has succeeded." He then announced an acceleration of the U.S. troop withdrawal process, with an additional 100,000 troops slated to return to the United States by November 1971, and promised his war-weary constituents that "American involvement in Vietnam was coming to an end."[1] The complex military legacy of the ARVN performance in Laos, demonstrating at once both great potential and critical dependencies, nearly faded from view amid the bright light of political expediency, for, regardless of the pace of South Vietnamese reform, regardless of the overall ability of the ARVN to survive, America was quitting South Vietnam.

An eerie military calm set in across South Vietnam for the remainder of 1971. Bearing out U.S. intelligence estimates, the NVA remained in a defensive mode, and, although the ARVN launched several offensive operations within its borders, contact with NVA units remained slight. With the NVA avoiding battle and the VC nearly eradicated, the situation was so peaceful that former Marine colonel Robert Heinl observed, "If successful pacification is the yardstick, the war in Vietnam is already settled. We have won."[2] Throughout the countryside, the indicators of success were everywhere; pacification indeed flourished, the "Land to the Tiller" program distributed land to those who had none, and rice production soared with the continued use of a high-yield hybrid dubbed "miracle rice."[3] In part, the tranquility in South Vietnam was a result of the ARVN/U.S. successes of Operation Lam Son 719, which had sorely depleted NVA stocks and manpower. However, the communists had an ulterior motive for their quiescence: realizing the political reality that undergirded American policy, the primary NVA aim was to avoid any action that carried the risk of slowing the U.S. withdrawal.[4]

Perhaps the NVA need not have worried, for the drawdown of American forces in Vietnam continued to gather a rather unseemly momentum and was the force behind a strategic restructuring of the entire conflict. From a high of more than 500,000 troops in South Vietnam in 1968, by May 1971 U.S. strength in theater had been slashed by half, and in terms of combat units more than 70 percent of American maneuver battalions had been withdrawn. Even as it became clear in late 1971 that the NVA had recuperated from the Cambodian and Laotian incursions and was building up for a renewed offensive, the United States countered with an announcement of the pending redeployment of an additional seventy thousand troops, which by April 1972 left only sixty-nine thousand American servicemen in Vietnam and no units of divisional size.[5] The disengagement process also involved a reduction in combat support elements, including command and control communications systems, which significantly reduced the ARVN's ability to react to any major NVA attack.[6]

Although the withdrawals succeeded in both cutting the number of U.S. casualties and limiting the political fallout of the war on the American homefront, they presented clear tactical problems to the wounded and overstretched ARVN, especially in I Corps. General Truong put the difficulty of dealing with the emerging change and growing threat well:

By March 1972, almost all U.S. combat units had redeployed from MR-1 [I Corps]. The single remaining unit, the 196th Infantry Brigade, was standing down and conducted only limited operations around Da Nang and Phu Bai airbases, pending return to the United States. Ground combat responsibilities were entirely assumed by ARVN units with the support of U.S. tactical air, naval gunfire and the assistance of American advisers. In the area north of the Hai Van Pass, where 80,000 American troops had at one time been deployed, there were only now two ARVN infantry divisions supported by a number of newly-activated armor and artillery units. Total troop strength committed to the defense of this area did not exceed 25,000.[7]

In accordance with the policy of withdrawing combat forces, both the Americans and Australians began a swift and relentless drawdown of combat advisers serving with ARVN units. With the exception of airborne advisers and some teams in I Corps, MACV closed out all battalion advisory teams by June 1970 and began to phase out regimental advisory teams in September. At the highest level, the advisory drawdown was reflected in the reorganization of corps advisory headquarters into regional assistance commands. In the field and in training slots, though, advisers simply disappeared, which left most ARVN battalion and regiment commanders without their familiar conduit to U.S. firepower, upon which they had long been dependent.[8] While it might have been argued that the withdrawal of allied ground forces was warranted because of the improved military situation, the same cannot be said of the drawdown of advisers. Although some ARVN units were fully able to stand alone, the events of Lam Son 719 indicated that much of the ARVN still sorely needed advisory support. Because the United States expected the ARVN to shoulder more of the burden of the conflict, the continued presence of advisers at all levels was more vital than ever.

In a tactical sense, the ARVN tried as best it could to make do after the exit of American forces. The task, however, was especially difficult in I Corps. The Australian historian Ian McNeill explained:

> Despite the relative lull in operations initiated by the enemy, I Corps in 1971 had the air and urgency of a nest of ants before the storm. Roads were filled with military traffic as American, Korean and South Vietnamese troops and stores changed locations; ARVN units which had moved once to occupy the void left by departing U.S. forces had to move again as the withdrawal continued; troops ordered to part-occupy the abandoned, sprawling U.S. bases arrived to find them already stripped by grasping and corrupt contractors; new units were being created and new formations were organized out of the reshuffling of existing units. Former, well established operating patterns and familiar areas of responsibility, for Territorial Forces as well as ARVN, no longer existed.[9]

In an effort to offset the withdrawal of U.S. forces, MACV and the military leadership of South Vietnam embarked upon Phase III of the RVNAF Improvement and Modernization Program, which had begun in the wake of the Tet Offensive in 1968. The program had met with remarkable success, expanding total South Vietnamese military strength from 650,000 to nearly 1.1 million in only five years. Within the impressive catalogue of military might, the ARVN had expanded to more than 400,000 troops, while the Territorial Forces had risen in strength to more than 500,000 men. Both the ARVN and the Territorial Forces also received new weaponry, eventually including 175mm artillery pieces, M-48A3 tanks, and TOW wire-guided antitank missiles. The South Vietnamese Navy and Air Force also saw similar expansions and upgrades in equipment, with the staple of the South Vietnamese Air Force, the outdated A-1 Skyraider, gradually replaced by the A-37 and F-5A jet fighter-bombers.[10] Training of the expanded military forces of South Vietnam also improved and centered on the strengthening of areas of weaknesses exhibited during the Laotian incursion, including coordination of fire support, airmobile operations, and logistical support.[11]

Though the Improvement and Modernization Program netted great gains in terms of raw military numbers, the situation in South Vietnam in many ways worsened as other important programs fell by the wayside and economic turmoil beset the nation. As the U.S. soldiers returned to "the world," the money they normally spent in country, a substantial source of hard currency that propped up the weak South Vietnamese economy, disappeared. The Republic of Vietnam earned $403 million in 1971 but just $213 million in 1972, while direct U.S. economic aid dwindled rather more gradually, falling from $575 million in 1971 to $454 million in 1972.[12] Inflation picked up steam as the South Vietnamese economy slowly imploded, and ARVN soldiers, whose pay failed to keep pace with the upward price spiral, fell ever further into economic despair. Making matters worse, efforts to house military dependents, so important to ARVN morale, collapsed and created a crippling housing shortage, which left the families of many soldiers to live in squalor.

Amid the economic turmoil and low morale, ARVN desertion levels remained uncomfortably high, with 140,000 men deserting their units during 1971 alone. Considering the social and family difficulties inherent in military service in the ARVN, the South Vietnamese government chose in the main to overlook the desertions, which were after all only one symptom of a system that was becoming more dysfunctional. In 1971, when General Truong, then in command of IV Corps, cracked down on desertions, he received instructions to desist, because his successful efforts only took the deserters out of the family agricultural plots to which they had fled and upset the delta rice harvest.[13]

For a military that had so long been shunted aside by and dependent on its mighty American ally, it is not surprising that the critical problem within the ARVN remained one of leadership. At the lowest level, restrictive ARVN policies limited the number of potential officers for a military force that was expanding rapidly, leading to a chronic shortage of qualified company- and battalion-level leaders. At the highest levels, though MACV railed against the continued incompetence demonstrated by some division and corps commanders in the wake of Lam Son 719, meaningful change was slow in coming. Even the generals themselves admitted that something had to be done. General Vien wrote after the war that:

> the problem of leadership should have been reviewed especially at corps and division levels. The appointment of general officers to these key command jobs should have been devoid of political considerations and based entirely on military professionalism and competence. . . . Military discipline should have been strictly enforced even with general officers especially when the conduct of a major and decisive operation was at stake.[14]

Beneath the surface of military calm, boiling undercurrents of uncertainty eroded strategic reality and left the ARVN at a critical juncture. The Americans were leaving, even as the NVA girded itself for a renewed onslaught. The ARVN had built to prodigious levels of strength and had won great, if unheralded, victories, but it retained substantial flaws that the leadership of the nation seemed unwilling fully to address. For the soldiers of I Corps, especially the battered 1st ARVN Division, which in the absence of its American allies alone stood guard over the bloodiest and most threatened real estate in South Vietnam, the gathering storm clouds seemed especially dark. To Pham Van Dinh, it appeared that the race between the speed of American withdrawal and that of ARVN reform was being lost. Dinh was by no means alone in his grim assessment. As what had been unthinkable became all too real, many in the ARVN began to lose hope. Lieutenant Colonel William Camper, who had served as an adviser to the 1st ARVN Division from October 1964 to March 1965, returned for another tour in 1971, serving as Dinh's final U.S. adviser during the war. With service at both extremes of American involvement in the Vietnam War, Camper was in a unique position to observe the changes in the

ARVN and reported that "Vietnamese morale after the U.S. Forces withdrew dropped. They felt that we had abandoned them. I think this permeated every echelon from the lowest soldier to the generals."[15]

Regardless of Dinh's nagging doubts and the loss of so many friends in battle, it was back to the business of war as usual after Lam Son 719.[16] Several units within the wider 1st ARVN Division had suffered greatly in the Laotian incursion, and in the most severe cases—including Tran Ngoc Hue's 2/2—battalions were rendered combat ineffective and had to be taken off line for complete overhauls. The damage was indeed so bad that some outside observers believed that the entire 1st ARVN Division was no longer combat ready.[17] Although he was mindful of the fragile state of some of the units under his command, Major General Pham Van Phu, commander of the 1st ARVN Division, determined to remain aggressive, both to build on the tactical opportunity provided by the battering of NVA forces in Laos and to rebuild the confidence of his own men.

Because it remained at full strength, the 54th Regiment played an enhanced role in the ongoing security operations in both Thua Thien and Quang Tri provinces. Without missing a beat, the various battalions of the 54th shifted from their operations in support of the Laotian incursion to action in operations Lam Son 487 and 720. The basic concept of the renewed operations was familiar: to deny enemy infiltration into the pacified areas of the lowlands. However, within the rubric of Lam Son 487 and 720, the 54th Regiment undertook a bewildering array of additional assignments. It was actually a rarity for battalions of the 54th to guard their own area of operations around Fire Base Anzio. Sometimes the battalions drew rather plum assignments, including guarding the Hue Citadel. More often than not, though, the units of the 54th Regiment found themselves engaged in some of the most dangerous work in all of I Corps.

After the withdrawal from Laos, 1/54 and 4/54 launched search-and-destroy operations near Khe Sanh and made only light contact in search of NVA stragglers. The 1st Battalion then moved on to operations in the Da Krong Valley and again faced little resistance from an enemy force bent on avoiding battle and recuperating from recent heavy losses. During May and June, 1/54 and 4/54 launched incursions into the northern reaches of the A Shau Valley, resulting in sharp clashes that indicated that the communist recovery was well and truly under way. Although the 54th Regiment and the remainder of the 1st

ARVN Division fought hard, they could not sustain the pace. As more and more American units left I Corps, the tactical implications of the withdrawal became clear. The 1st ARVN Division could not defend the entirety of northern I Corps alone; one battered but resilient ARVN division could not take on the job that had once been the purview of eighty thousand of the United States's finest soldiers and Marines.

The operations of the 54th around Khe Sanh and in the Da Krong and A Shau valleys were of great symbolic importance: they were the final allied operations ever in those areas, the forbidding and legendary scenes of some of the hardest fighting of the entire Vietnam War. Unable to defend everything, 1st ARVN Division constricted its lines and once again ceded control of the western highlands of I Corps to the NVA. By late June, elements of the 54th Regiment found themselves defending the area around Fire Base Fuller, one of the lynchpins of the new defensive bastion, while resurgent communist forces built their strength, reassumed their positions in the highlands, and began to exert pressure on the new ARVN line.[18]

Pham Van Dinh found the developing situation immensely frustrating. The ARVN had lost so many good people in efforts to push the NVA out of I Corps—twice—and had been so near victory. Now the land that had cost so much in blood, where once he could ride in an open jeep all the way to Khe Sanh in peace, was again in the hands of the enemy. In the previous pullback from the west, substantial American forces had remained in South Vietnam, but now the retreat carried a disheartening air of permanence. How was South Vietnam alone to regain its lost territory and push the North Vietnamese out once again? As U.S. support for the war waned, the tactical reality presented by the new phase of the conflict pressed hard on Dinh and caused him to think for the first time that South Vietnam might actually lose its struggle for survival.

The Creation of the 3rd ARVN Division

The deteriorating military situation in I Corps forced the hand of the often reluctant South Vietnamese government to provide reinforcements for the beleaguered 1st ARVN Division. One option involved grouping together existing ranger battalions into a coherent division, but the scheme was dropped instantly because of the overwhelming political problems presented by such a command reshuffle.[19] Another alternative to buttressing the ARVN's defensive posture along the DMZ involved shifting northward an already existing division, an option mooted due to continued ARVN immobility. General Truong remarked:

> Making a permanent shift in deployment of an ARVN division was a major undertaking, since it involved relocating thousands of families as well as soldiers and equipment. It took seven months to complete the move of the ARVN 25th Division from Quang Ngai to Hau Nghia.[20]

In the end, the South Vietnamese high command created an entirely new formation—the 3rd ARVN Division. However, the 3rd was new in name only and involved not a callup of fresh troops but rather a reshuffling of existing battalions and personnel from other units. The 2nd Regiment of the 1st Division, including Tran Ngoc Hue's old unit and much of General Giai's command at 1st Division Forward, shifted wholesale into the 3rd Division. The first three battalions of the 2nd Regiment remained in place, while the 4th Battalion became the 1st Battalion of the newly formed 56th Regiment of the 3rd Division and the 5th Battalion became the 1st Battalion core of the 57th Regiment. The 4th Battalion of the 51st Regiment outside Da Nang became the 2nd Battalion of the 56th, while the 2nd Battalion of the 6th Regiment of the 2nd ARVN Division became the 2nd Battalion of the 57th. Thus, the 2nd Regiment of the 3rd Division came in as a complete and coherent unit that, while it had suffered greatly in Lam Son 719, had acquired considerable experience in northern I Corps. The core battalions of the new 56th and 57th regiments were also veteran formations but had no experience working together within their new units.

There were, however, problems within the experienced core units of the 56th and 57th regiments. Colonel Donald Metcalf, who became the senior adviser to the 3rd Division, remarked:

> I would say that it is no secret that . . . [3rd Division] got a lot of people that were not performing well where they came from and were sent down the road to be assigned to the 3rd ARVN as a means of getting them off their books. Now how much of this can you really take in a division before beginning to impact on its performance? I

would say that the five battalions of the 2nd Regiment were essentially intact. They came from the 1st ARVN Division in that manner. But, I would believe that the 2nd ARVN Division kind of loaded its battalion. They asked for volunteers in the 2nd ARVN Division who wanted to go to Quang Tri again. It was so negligible that they eventually had to put a battalion together. They sent it to Dong Dong training center and within ten days half of the battalion had deserted back to Quang Nghai.[21]

The 3rd battalions of the 56th and 57th regiments were entirely new formations, cobbled together out of a mixture of RF/PF forces and hard-core ARVN deserters. Facing a new and daunting situation, the transformed territorial troops were often less than eager to serve in their new capacity. Colonel Metcalf commented:

Unfortunately the two 3rd Battalions of the 56th and 57th were . . . well, when you send for quotas of a thousand RF or PF or PSDF [People's Self-Defense Force], what do you get? You get that person that can best be spared, so we had two battalions of this type.[22]

In the case of the deserters, nearly seven hundred mainly parceled to the 3rd battalions of the 56th and 57th regiments,[23] "military police had gone to see them in prison and asked them, 'Do you want out?' and offered them the chance to join the ARVN again along the DMZ."[24]

The new division lacked critical equipment and had no logistic structure whatsoever, but, more important, it needed a command structure of its own. However, it was difficult to find someone who was willing to take on the difficult task of commanding the patchwork formation; the risk of failure was just too high. After considerable wrangling, Major General Vu Van Giai agreed to become, in his words, "the unlucky commander of this newborn division, the division that nobody wanted."[25] In his search for experienced subordinates, General Giai turned to his old protégé, Pham Van Dinh, to lead the 56th Regiment. Although he realized that command of a unit of such varied abilities would be difficult, Dinh looked forward to facing a new challenge and accepted Giai's offer.

Technically created on 1 October 1971, the 3rd Division remained a work in progress; as veteran units sorted out their new arrangements, newer units underwent hurried training and commanders at all levels struggled with the vital minutiae of logistics and tactical deployment. As a new and untested unit, 3rd ARVN became the recipient of much attention from the dwindling U.S. advisory effort and was eventually placed under the rubric of Advisory Team 155. In one of their first reports on the abilities of the 3rd Division, U.S. advisers were impressed with the senior leadership team that Giai had assembled, terming them "both experienced and extremely capable." And though the advisory team found much that was laudable about the division itself, they also noticed its distinct weaknesses and, in a report to advisory team headquarters, remarked:

> The desertion rate for 3rd Division units remains unacceptable, but it appears that little can be done at present to lower it. The primary causes appear to be that large numbers of the Division's new personnel are not native to this part of the country, and are in fact from the III Corps and Saigon areas, having been brought here by the buildup requirements of the new units. 3/56 and 3/57 Bns are composed largely of federalized RF and PF personnel who are presently disenchanted at the prospect of being full time soldiers.[26]

General Giai was particularly upset by the continued endemic desertion, a problem compounded by communist aid extended to the deserters in the form of an underground railroad of safe houses designed to aid fleeing soldiers in their return south.[27]

There now existed three ARVN divisions, along with a variety of supporting units, in I Corps. The 2nd ARVN Division guarded the three southern provinces of I Corps, while the veteran 1st ARVN Division defended the western approaches to Hue City. It fell to the inexperienced and undermanned 3rd ARVN Division to stand along the DMZ and the highland approaches from Laos—the most difficult job in the ARVN. The task was indeed so difficult that the 3rd ARVN Division was reinforced by two brigades of Vietnamese Marines, who located much of their force around Fire Base Mai Loc to guard the southwestern portion of the 3rd ARVN Division line of defense. Even with these reinforcements, General Giai and Pham Van Dinh considered the decision to put the 3rd ARVN Division in the crosshairs of the NVA at best a dangerous gamble. It was common knowledge among the ARVN commanders on the spot, their American advisers, and indeed the NVA that the 3rd ARVN Division was not up to its considerable task; only the upper-echelon ARVN leadership seemed unmoved, ready to accept military risk to avoid the political problems of a more comprehensive answer to the problem of DMZ defense.

The U.S. advisers to 3rd ARVN Division put the situation bluntly in their report:

> The mission of the 3rd ARVN Division is to: "Conduct offensive operations against the enemy; to locate and destroy enemy forces, base areas, and lines of communications; prevent enemy infiltration throughout the DMZ and the Laotian border; coordinate military activities to support local forces, organize a defensive system, and enlarge the fixed encirclement lines; protect the main roads, natural resources, and military equipment." The division's mission statement outlines tasks which would be ambitious even for a corps size organization. The fact that a division is being formed in the shadow of the enemy homeland is also extremely ambitious. The 3rd Division is not now, or will it be in the foreseeable future, strong enough to meet all the requirements of its mission statement. As a result the division must be considered over committed.[28]

General Truong also put the dilemma that faced 3rd ARVN Division well in his postwar chronicle of the Easter Offensive:

> What then caused the demise of this division? To put it briefly, the 3rd Division failed because it was overburdened. For the defense of the DMZ area, this unit had taken over the combat responsibilities formerly assigned to nearly two U.S. divisions, the reinforced 3rd Marine Division and the 1/5 Brigade (Mechanized). . . . How could such a defense hold in the face of the strongest, concentrated enemy offensive of the war?[29]

The 3rd ARVN Division arrived along the DMZ in dribs and drabs after its October 1971 activation date. While some battalions continued their unit training at Phu Bai, more experienced units, including the 2nd Regiment and the 1st battalions of the 56th and 57th regiments, took their places along the DMZ both to guard against infiltration and to learn to act within their new regimental and divisional structures. NVA action, with the exception of intermittent shelling of the ARVN bases, remained light, which allowed units of the 3rd ARVN Division to launch successful minor operations and to find their confidence. By December 1971, morale rose as 1/56 and 4/2 launched the 3rd ARVN Division's first ever multibattalion operation, the planning and execution of which were termed "exceptional."[30] In truth, the 3rd ARVN Division was no worse than any other division in ARVN; it was just younger.

Major Joseph Brown arrived as the assistant adviser to the 56th Regiment in January 1971, having served a previous advisory tour in II Corps in 1968. Brown was never quite sure that the ARVN troops were "true hearted or outstanding soldiers" and had often met ARVN officers who saw their American advisers as only causing problems. His experience with the 56th Regiment was different, for it was not yet a regiment but rather an assortment of individual battalions that were at different stages of readiness, ability, and training. It was in March 1972 that the 56th Regiment was able to come together as a coherent unit for the first time. Dinh and his men then moved from their safer locations near Cam Lo to Fire Support Base C2 both to sort out the command difficulties faced by any new military formation and to gain tactical experience in forward positions along the DMZ. Brown noticed that the move to C2 caused an almost instant drop in morale, in part because it took the soldiers further away from their families. Ever resourceful, though, the families of a few of the men found their way to C2—in the middle of the war zone.[31]

The continuing drawdown of U.S. advisory forces was clearly evident in the experience of the 3rd ARVN Division. At the height of the war, there had been as many as seventy-five U.S. advisers with each ARVN regiment. These advisers served at all levels, from the regimental HQ to battalions and even companies in the field, which enabled them to obtain a full knowledge of the regiment's capabilities and foibles. By March 1972, though, the situation was so constrained that the ARVN regimental advisory staff was limited to two men, and there were so few advisers that many ARVN regiments had to do without advisory support altogether. In this difficult situation, Colonel Donald Metcalf, who served as senior adviser to 3rd ARVN Division, correctly decided to reshuffle his dwindling resources and transferred advisers from the experienced 2nd Regiment to the gathering 56th and 57th regiments.

In mid-March, Lieutenant Colonel William Camper, who had been serving with the 2nd Regiment, joined Brown and Dinh at C2. Brown had been surprised by his first contact with Pham Van Dinh. Having heard that Dinh was one of the great ARVN heroes, Brown was amused that Dinh rarely wore his uniform but always carried his .45 pistol. Regardless of Dinh's personal affectations, Brown quickly judged the 56th's commander to be one of the most able ARVN officers he had ever met and one who commanded the respect of his troops. More important, the men of the 56th performed well for their commander under fire and seemed to trust his judgment. Camper's first experience with Dinh atop C2 was rather different. Having served in an advisory capacity with 1st ARVN Division in 1965, Camper had known Pham Van Dinh as the dashing commander of the Hac Bao and had felt nothing but "admiration for a young, dynamic officer who was dedicated to the victorious survival of his men, unit and young nation." When he once again greeted Dinh some seven years later, Camper was "really surprised by his appearance." It seemed that the years of unending war had not treated Dinh well; he appeared "pudgy and unathletic" and like a man who had a great weight on his shoulders.

After unloading his gear, Camper set out to get the lay of the land in his new unit. In the Tactical Operations Center (TOC), Camper found the regimental executive officer (XO), Lieutenant Colonel Vinh Phong, to be rather uncooperative and "almost anti-U.S. in his attitude." Since the ARVN no longer had advisers at battalion level, Camper had to do his best to gather information by visiting the positions of outlying units. What he found was disturbing; the war was totally different war from what it had been in 1965. In his view, Vietnamization and ongoing protests against the war had taken their toll in a unit already stocked with "a lot of AWOLs, deserters and dissidents." On his tour of the unit with Brown, Camper reported that:

> [our] worst perceptions of the state of combat readiness were confirmed. . . . It was apparent that the units were not very well trained, motivated or ready for combat. The best information we could gather, with our limited knowledge of Vietnamese . . . was that this unit was a disaster looking for a place to occur.[32]

General Giai was fully cognizant of the weaknesses within the 3rd ARVN Division. He kept up a remarkable schedule of training and personal surveyance to try to fix the problems but was also worried that his limited troop strength while manning the farflung stationary base system inherited from the U.S. Marines left the 3rd ARVN Division an inviting, stationary target for NVA assault. Giai shared his concerns with General Lam, but the I Corps commander ignored his subordinate's requests and made certain that no complaints about the dangerous situation reached Saigon.[33]

Despite General Giai's diligent efforts, time had run out for the 3rd ARVN Division. As the North Vietnamese massed for an allout invasion, General Truong recalled, "in no way could . . . the 3rd Division be considered as fully prepared to fight a large, conventional action." It had been the sad fate of both Giai and Dinh to inherit cobbled-together units that were only partly ready and to serve, as they had in Lam Son 719, an I Corps staff that, in Truong's opinion, "lacked the experience, professionalism and initiative required of a field staff during critical times during battle."[34]

Camper had been accurate in his perceptions of Dinh; he *was* a man weighed down by the burdens of a war that was, in his view, going wrong. The American exit from the conflict, something that Dinh had never fully believed would happen, was very nearly complete, and South Vietnam stood alone. Amid political maneuvering, nobody at the highest levels seemed to care that the 3rd ARVN Division had been placed in such a vulnerable position. His soldiers could no longer feed their families and had to be kept in line through strict discipline, rather than by reliance on their own spirit and courage. Dinh had devoted his life to his nation and to the ARVN, but nothing at the center ever seemed to change. In his mind, none of the weaknesses illustrated so graphically in Lam Son 719 had been addressed; many had worsened. Earlier in his career, Pham Van Dinh had rushed into hopeless situations, with the Hac Bao, in Hue City during Tet, and at Tun Tavern, always confident of support and victory. By March 1972, all that had changed, and the ARVN hero was left in doubt and with, in his words, "some problems in my head."

The Easter Offensive

As Dinh's mood darkened, NVA forces gathered for the Nguyen Hue Offensive, named in honor of Emperor Quang Trung, a Vietnamese hero who in 1789 had dealt the Chinese a resounding defeat at the outskirts of Hanoi. Even though productive peace talks were ongoing in Paris, Hanoi saw 1972 as the perfect year to seek victory. It was a chance to lash out and humiliate the dwindling American force and to destroy their puppets through cathartic military victory rather than by negotiation.

North Vietnam committed nearly its entire combat force—fourteen divisions, twenty-six separate regiments, and supporting armor and artillery units—into the coming battles. The three-pronged offensive, with attacks aimed at An Loc in the south, Kontum in the Central Highlands, and Hue/Da Nang in the north, took the form of conventional, frontal assaults against thinly held ARVN defensive lines. While the fighting on the southern and central fronts was pivotal to the overall outcome of the offensive, the invasion across the DMZ and from Laos posed the most immediate threat to the units of the 3rd ARVN Division. Against General Giai's untested division, Hanoi's B-5 Front gathered the offensive might of three divisions, plus supporting armor, artillery, and sapper units. To the north, the 308th Division readied along the DMZ, while the 304th Division lurked across the border in Laos and the 324B Division moved into the A Shau Valley.[35]

The enemy buildup did not go unnoticed by the South Vietnamese or MACV, and by late 1971 it had become common knowledge that NVA forces would mount an attack on South Vietnam, but nobody seemed to know when or where. In December 1971, General Westmoreland, then Army Chief of Staff, visited I Corps on a whirlwind return trip to Vietnam. He told General Giai over dinner that he thought the NVA would strike in Quang Tri Province, at Kontum, and further south. Although his prediction was prescient, his opinion was as yet in the minority.[36] The threat, though, was so real that ARVN forces were placed on full alert around Tet in 1972. Despite the fears and anxieties, the historically preferred day for communist attacks came and went without major incident, but the NVA buildup continued.

Tension throughout South Vietnam mounted; everyone waited for the assault to begin. Abrams cabled Washington that the NVA was preparing its largest offensive since Tet 1968. ARVN intelligence indicated that the communist assault would "dwarf all other previous attempts in scale" and would consist of an invasion by at least ten divisions. In I Corps, available information indicated a general NVA buildup in the area, but the threat seemed greatest to the west on the oft-used invasion route from Laos to Hue City. General Lam thought that the NVA would follow a comfortable and predictable pattern of slow logistical buildup, followed by a strike from the highlands. He oriented his defensive efforts accordingly; he was simply unable to grasp the idea that the NVA would attempt a brazen assault directly across the DMZ. General Giai, though, could not afford such beliefs and fumed at the lack of time and effort on the part of I Corps in the north; Lam developed no overall plan of defense for the DMZ at all. As time slipped away, General Giai, with little support from his superiors, worked hard to prepare his officers and men for the impending attack.[37] His division had never before acted in battle as a unit and was largely forgotten by its supreme command.

While his staff developed the plan for defending the DMZ against attack, General Giai continued to rotate his units among the regimental areas of operation both to familiarize them with the varied terrain of the DMZ and to avoid "fire base syndrome" among his troops. Although the possibility of an NVA offensive loomed, on 30 March, Giai went ahead with a scheduled troop rotation, which included moving Dinh's 56th Regiment from the area of C2 west to Camp Carroll and to fire support bases Khe Gio and Fuller, while the 2nd Regiment left those bases to move to C2. Normally such a relief in place calls for incoming units to join outgoing units on the front lines to hand off command so that there is never a time when the defenses are unmanned. However, there were so few forces available to the 3rd ARVN Division that both the 56th and the 2nd Regiments would be in transit at the same time, leaving both units exposed and critical base areas undefended.[38]

At 0900 on 30 March, the 56th and 2nd regiments began their exchange of areas of operation. Dinh and his compatriots shut down their TOCs, disassembled unit radios, and placed their gear aboard jeeps and trucks; in the words of Colonel G. H. Turley, who served as the senior Marine adviser in northern Quang Tri Province, much of the 3rd ARVN Division "went nontactical for the duration of the rotation and was temporarily unable to perform as a viable fighting force."[39] At that precise moment, when the 3rd ARVN Division was most vulnerable, the NVA 308th Division, heralded by a massive artillery barrage, thundered across the DMZ and sliced the 2nd and the 56th regiments to ribbons.[40]

In the morning of 30 March 1972, three regular divisions, two tank regiments, five artillery regiments, and at least one sapper battalion attacked the 3rd ARVN Division from the north across the DMZ and from the western highlands near Khe Sanh. Thousands of shells whistled in from NVA long-range 130mm field guns, along with hundreds of 122mm rockets, causing great destruction at the ARVN fire bases in the area, including Camp Carroll, Mai Loc, Sarge, Khe Gio, and Fuller in the west and Alpha 2, Alpha 4, Charlie 1, and Charlie 2 in the north. Every major ARVN installation was pounded by fire, even including the Dong Ha and Quang Tri combat bases. All across the area, ARVN commanders and their advisers realized that, in the words of Marine Major Jim Joy, serving with the 147th Vietnamese Marine Brigade at FSB Mai Loc, "this was the real thing."[41]

Amid the punishing barrage, NVA ground forces moved forward; from the north, four spearheads of the NVA 308th Division assaulted across the DMZ and initially aimed at the destruction of the most exposed ARVN fire bases at A1, A2, A4, and Fuller. To the west, elements of the 304th Division and the 26th Regiment assaulted the 147th Vietnamese Marine Brigade positions at Nui Ba Ho, Sarge, and Holcolmb. Calls went out from the sorely pressed ARVN units for air support, but marginal weather limited what support was available.[42] Nearly everything that could have gone wrong did so, leaving the 3rd ARVN Division alone in a perfect storm of battle. General Truong later remarked:

> The unexpected assault across the DMZ caught the forward elements of the 3rd Division in movement, only partially settled into defensive positions they had not been in for some time, locally outnumbered three-to-one, and outgunned by the enemy artillery. The ARVN defenses in the DMZ area were designed to counter infiltration and local attacks. There were no positions prepared to give the depth to the battlefield that would be required to contain an attack of the size and momentum of the one that had now fallen upon them.[43]

Just after 1130 hours, Dinh, Camper, the headquarters company, and a single infantry company arrived atop Camp Carroll. Though the base boasted a formidable arsenal of twenty-two artillery pieces, including 155mm and 105mm batteries, and the only battery of mighty 175mm guns available along the DMZ, Camp Carroll was meant to provide fire support for units in the field—not to stand against NVA ground assaults. Within minutes, the first NVA artillery shells rained down on Camp Carroll; in the first hour alone, two hundred rounds, mainly from 130mm guns, blanketed the base, a total that rose to two thousand rounds by the end of the day. The accurate and persistent fire sent ARVN soldiers and their advisers scurrying for their bunkers, before either Dinh or Camper even had a chance to reconnoiter their new base or organize its defense. Camper recalled:

> [The fire] immediately destroyed all the radio antennas that were hanging out all over the bunkers. It caused tremendous morale problems. . . . We had no radio contact with the battalion north of the river, and my jeep was destroyed and my radios were destroyed in the first hour. The artillery knocked out the generators and the lines leading to the bunkers. . . . It was difficult for the regiment to operate. . . . Some of the troops made it back to Camp Carroll. I don't know what happened to the rest of them.[44]

The fighting battalions of the 56th Regiment had exited C2 in good order; the 3rd Battalion left first, bound for Khe Gio, followed by the 1st Battalion, which was tasked with guarding Route 9 while its sister units were in transit, then moving to FSB Fuller. Some elements of the 2nd Battalion remained behind, along with Colonel Phong and Major Brown, to hold C2 and await the arrival of the 2nd Regiment at that location, while other elements of the battalion moved south of Route 9. The NVA attack caught the battalions while they were on the move, causing great initial confusion. Having left first, elements of the 3rd Battalion, under the command of Major Ha Thuc Mau, succeeded in reaching Khe Gio, which immediately fell under heavy pressure from NVA infantry attacks. On C2, Phong, Brown, and the remaining units of the 2nd Battalion took heavy incoming fire, while their sister companies were stranded to the south in open and easily observed terrain amid the enemy fire. In the north, the 1st Battalion, under the command of Major Ton That Man, was in an especially vulnerable position, strung out along Route 9. It received increased attention from the NVA artillery, which halted the battalion's advance and prevented it from ever reaching FSB Fuller. As a result, Fuller remained in the hands of the stranded 1st Battalion of the 2nd Regiment.

Camp Carroll and the outlying fire support bases had enough supplies for several days of normal operations, but times were anything but normal. Even though ARVN artillerists had a difficult time returning fire amid the NVA barrage, it was obvious that their ammunition stocks would not last long during such an intense battle. Food and water were less of an issue, but the pounding by NVA guns had closed the military service road that connected Camp Carroll to Cam Lo where it joined with Route 9 and led to the ARVN stockpiles at Dong Ha. Though the NVA had not yet physically blocked the road, and military units still moved along it, supplies had already ceased to flow.[45] The volume of incoming fire and the poor weather grounded efforts at air resupply. Dinh realized that a prolonged battle would test his young unit to its very limits.

As night closed on the first day of the NVA offensive, the ARVN positions in the area continued to reel under heavy fire. During that day, eleven thousand rounds had struck the various ARVN bases and surrounding villages. Although the entire front remained active, the situation was especially bleak at the Vietnamese Marine fire bases of Nui Ba Ho and Sarge, which guarded the ARVN western flank and formed a forward defensive screen for both Camp Carroll and Mai Loc. Having closed in on Nui Ba Ho from three sides, the NVA launched a succession of human wave assaults on the desperate defenders, while NVA infantry also began to probe the defenses at Sarge. An AC-119 "Stinger" aircraft arrived and began to orbit above the fighting, but in the deteriorating weather it could not locate the defenders. American advisers at both locations broke cover and utilized infra-red strobes to guide the aircraft, which then dropped flares to illuminate the scene. Fearing an air attack, the NVA assault suddenly slacked off, but the weather worsened further and forced the Stinger to depart the scene. The NVA pressure then resumed unabated.[46]

At the 3rd ARVN Division headquarters, the situation that evening was grim, and General Giai and his U.S. adviser, Colonel Metcalf, struggled to keep up with events. As they huddled together over a tactical map, Metcalf painted a dismal picture. The units of the 3rd ARVN Division were vulnerable in their fire bases, which were never meant to face such a threat and without defensive depth would easily be surrounded and destroyed, one by one. Metcalf advised withdrawing from the bases to a more coherent line of defense behind the water barrier of the Cua Viet River.[47] Such a withdrawal, though, was fraught with difficulties, and, since the ARVN defenses were as yet standing firm, Giai decided that it was not time for such desperate measures. General Giai reported the situation to General Lam at I Corps and requested both reinforcements and strategic guidance, but, as he had in the Laotian incursion, Lam remained indecisive. He passed on the reports to Saigon, but with little urgency. Neither Lam nor the JGS had ever believed that the DMZ would be the focal point of an invasion, and they were slow to accept the reality of the situation.

That evening, Dinh attempted as best he could to sort out the situation in his own AO. Struggling to maintain only intermittent contact with his own battalions, Dinh was able to discern that NVA infantry was closing in on both Fuller and Khe Gio. Reports indicated that while 3/56 remained under steady fire, it had overcome the initial shock of battle and seemed ready to fight. 1/56 had organized itself into defensive positions on a hilltop and had fought off several enemy attacks.[48] But, with the fighting centered to his immediate north and west, it became increasingly obvious to Dinh that the NVA was focusing its efforts on tightening a noose around Camp Carroll. Dinh, though, remained confident and judged the situation to be, in his words, "bad but not too bad."

On the morning of 31 March, as inclement weather continued to hamper air support, NVA artillery fire reached a crescendo and again focused on the most vulnerable ARVN bases. In the east, battalion-size NVA forces laid siege to C1 and A2. Despite support from U.S. naval gunfire, by evening it had become apparent to the advisers on the scene that the beleaguered fire bases would not be able to hold out much longer. In the west, NVA artillerists kept up their relentless pressure on Nui Ba Ho and Sarge, while infantry readied for renewed human wave assaults. Across the front, ARVN defensive lines were stretched to the breaking point.

At the same time, NVA forces continued to pummel Dinh's 56th Regiment. North of Route 9, 1/56 made contact with an NVA battalion, which resulted in a fierce battle before the NVA force retreated. Making matters worse, 1/56 caught sight of four enemy tanks, which indicated that an armored thrust in the direction of Camp Carroll was imminent.[49] To the east, Dinh called 2/56 to Camp Carroll in an effort to buttress its defense. Caught in an open area, though, 2/56 fell under heavy enemy fire as soon as it began its move. Phong, with Brown at his side, halted the move toward Camp Carroll and opted to continue only after darkness had disrupted the NVA forward artillery observers. However, even at night, the deadly accurate fire continued to whistle in every time that 2/56 attempted to move, preventing the unit from making any headway.

The situation, though, was most serious in the northwestern sector of Dinh's AO, which faced one of the main thrusts of the NVA offensive. Artillery fire pummeled the 3/56 in and around Khe Gio and the 1/2 defenders at Fuller. Successive massed NVA infantry assaults slowly drove back the ARVN defenders and penetrated the perimeters of the fire bases. By noon on 31 March, both Khe Gio and Fuller had been overrun, with heavy ARVN losses. Though 3/56 and 1/2 remained operational and engaged in a fighting withdrawal to the south, both units were in grave danger of being surrounded and destroyed. Some men within both units fled the battle, in part out of fear for their families caught up in the chaos, while others fought on. As the NVA battered all of the units under his command, Dinh felt helpless. He could issue orders over the intermittent communications network and help direct artillery fire, but, whereas he had hoped to draw his units together in a defensive stand at Camp Carroll, Dinh now realized that he had "no control" over the rush of events.

The tactical situation for Dinh and the 56th Regiment worsened that evening, even as NVA artillery fire began to slacken. To the west, as darkness closed in and poor weather still hindered air support, NVA infantry rushed the defenses of Nui Ba Ho and broke through to the command bunkers on the forlorn hilltop. The remaining thirty to forty Vietnamese Marines and their U.S. Marine adviser, Captain Ray Smith, made their way through their own wire and booby traps in a desperate effort to evade the North Vietnamese encirclement. Further south, the Vietnamese Marine defenders of Sarge were also in a fight for their lives, and at 0340 they were forced to abandon the base. Both groups of Vietnamese Marines and their advisers began a treacherous journey through enemy-held terrain amid a tremendous downpour in an effort to link up with friendly forces at Mai Loc. Eventually, some 170 of the 300 Vietnamese Marines who had been at Nui Ba Ho were successful, while the survivors of Sarge did not reach the Mai Loc area for two full days—just in time to be swept up in the evacuation of that base.[50]

The fall of Khe Gio, Fuller, Nui Ba Ho, and Sarge in quick succession left Camp Carroll alone to guard the northwestern flank of the ARVN lines, with the support of the Vietnamese Marine base at Mai Loc to the south. Making matters worse, NVA infantry had cut the military service road from Mai Loc through Camp Carroll to Cam Lo, and a resulting Vietnamese Marine counterattack failed to reopen the road, which left both Camp Carroll and Mai Loc even more dependent upon nonexistent air resupply. The NVA then increased the volume of its artillery fire on Camp Carroll. Camper grimly noted that, for the first time, the barrage included the use of direct-fire weapons: the NVA infantrymen had closed with the defenders of the 56th Regiment atop Camp Carroll and were readying for an infantry assault on the increasingly isolated base.

As news trickled through of the fall of the outlying fire support bases, the morale of the defenders of Camp Carroll began to plummet. Dinh realized that the situation was dire and that his untested units now formed the last line of the ARVN's crumbling defensive network, a network that was never supposed to stand in the face of such a test and that stood in service of a military that seemingly had no plan to salvage the situation. Dinh firmly believed, though, that all was not lost and that a quick reinforcement of the DMZ front was the key to success. He passed his advice on to General Giai, along with the warning that under present circumstances the 56th Regiment could hold out against sustained NVA attack for only a few more days before having to give way, as had the other bases in the area. Giai responded by informing Dinh that he had already lodged requests for reinforcements and that those requests were under consideration. Dinh was skeptical. How long would the government wait to send reinforcements? If it tarried too long, all of Quang Tri Province might be lost; the 3rd ARVN Division could not hope to stand for long on its own against such odds. Giai agreed and promised to do what he could to help. Dinh was also unhappy to learn that Lieutenant Colonel Tung, commander of the 2nd Regiment, had never reached his regimental TOC at C2. While troops of the 2nd Regiment went forward, since the base had fallen under NVA artillery fire, Colonel Tung remained behind near Cam Lo. In Dinh's view, no matter the risk, a regimental commander should be at his TOC to set an example for his men. The crisis was at hand, and Dinh had to trust that the JGS and ARVN high command would react accordingly and do everything in their power to salvage the situation. He also had to hope that the tactical leadership on the ground would be up to the considerable task. Memories of

Lam Son 719 and an increased feeling of isolation as the NVA assault continued, though, served to fuel Dinh's growing doubts.

The Noose Tightens

On 1 April, as the NVA closed in on Camp Carroll from both the north and the west, disaster struck along the eastern portion of the ARVN defensive line. Furthest north along the DMZ, the isolated outposts of the 57th Regiment, from A1 to A4 (which in an earlier incarnation had been known as Con Thien), had been under withering NVA shelling for two days and now faced NVA ground assault. As the tiny ARVN bastions were buffeted by the storm of attack, U.S. advisers caught in the maelstrom called for helicopter evacuation.

At A2, which was nearly surrounded, a daring U.S. chopper pilot braved the pounding fire to rescue First Lieutenant Joel Eisenstein's small advisory group and a U.S. naval gunfire spot team. As he moved toward the helicopter, Eisenstein noticed that ARVN dead and wounded were everywhere, while other ARVN soldiers were being struck by small-arms fire. The NVA were at hand. As he got aboard the chopper, Eisenstein recalled:

> The look of desperation was all about them [the ARVN soldiers]. I will never forget the look in one Vietnamese soldier's eyes as he stared at me across the skid pad of the helicopter. We were slowly rising and he was trying to make motions to get aboard. I had to take my foot and push him back into the crowd that was gathering underneath the helicopter.[51]

The successful rescue had been necessitated by the reality of a deteriorating front line. However, to the ARVN soldiers on the ground, it was a fatal blow, for they knew that, if the Americans were leaving, the situation was lost. The ARVN soldiers felt abandoned by their advisers and by their own military. Why should the Americans be able to leave aboard a helicopter, while they had to stay and face their fate at the hands of the North Vietnamese? A short while later, the NVA overran A2.

At the 3rd ARVN Division HQ, General Giai searched for an answer to the deteriorating situation. Again Metcalf suggested that the only remedy was a general withdrawal from the fire bases that were still holding out in the north. As the historian Dale Andrade recorded:

> [The 57th Regiment] was clearly doomed. The troops had not been settled into their new positions following the rotation of 30 March, but even if they had been, it is unlikely they could have withstood the terrific pounding from North Vietnamese artillery. By the afternoon of 1 April, the northern face of the Ring of Steel [defending Quang Tri Province] was untenable.[52]

Having hoped to hold firm in his first line of defense, as he had been ordered by the JGS, General Giai now realized the loss of A2 had forced his hand and in the early evening ordered a general withdrawal to a new line of defenses on the Cua Viet River, which involved having the 57th Regiment fall back to the area just north of Dong Ha while the 2nd Regiment retreated to Cam Lo.

What was to be an orderly withdrawal, though, soon became difficult to control. Colonel Metcalf remarked that the 57th and the 2nd regiments:

> weren't prepared for it. . . . You know it takes a great deal of expertise to withdraw correctly. . . . And suddenly these people were asked to do things that . . . they just had no backup or experience in how to do. . . . I mean you are going to have some sort of filtering of the information right down to the individual himself because he doesn't understand that he is supposed to stand here and guard while this man comes back and sets up guards behind him. He doesn't grasp that at all. All he sees is everybody else leaving and what he doesn't know begins to bother him and the next thing you know he is leaving too. So then pretty soon you don't have an orderly withdrawal from firebases that you can no longer retain. . . . And it gets out of hand quickly, almost too quickly. Especially if someone screams "Tanks" or "Incoming" then the control becomes just that much less.[53]

As ARVN defenses collapsed in the east, further isolating Camp Carroll, Dinh continued to try to gain control over the deteriorating situation in his own AO. To the northwest, 3/56, which now held the most isolated position of all in the ARVN line, fought on near Khe Gio but had to pull back in the face of stiffening NVA ground assaults. In an attempt to stabilize his lines and logistics, Dinh ordered part of 1/56 to push toward Khe Gio while other elements of the unit attempted to reopen Route 9. Both efforts failed. The NVA massed for the kill and succeeded in surrounding and destroying two companies while their parent units withdrew to the south. Dinh then ordered the remnants of the units to fall back on the relative safety of Camp Carroll.

To the east, 2/56 continued its slow journey toward Camp Carroll and had been joined by armored reinforcements. Still, though, the NVA fire rained down, forcing the unit to lie low for several hours. Once forward movement had started again, Colonel Phong came to Brown with some bad news. A company guarding the flanks of their movement had been ambushed and annihilated by a considerable enemy ground force. Time was running out for 2/56, for the NVA was now closing in on Camp Carroll from all sides.

Even as Colonel Phong and Major Brown continued their perilous journey, the NVA launched its first infantry assault on Camp Carroll. On the morning of 1 April, sappers probed the western defenses of the fire base in several places, searching for a weakness. By afternoon, the communists attacked in a human wave, which, though the defenders brushed it aside with relative ease through the use of small arms, claymore mines, and direct fire artillery, was an obvious portent of things to come. Although the massed ranks of enemy soldiers formed an inviting target, overcast skies continued to limit available air support. Even so, in a selfless move, the defenders of Camp Carroll diverted their last air sortie of the day to aid the Vietnamese Marines who were still in dire straits after their withdrawal from Nui Ba Ho and Sarge.[54]

Inside the wire at Camp Carroll, Dinh became increasingly concerned. Food and ammunition began to run low, and there was no real hope of resupply. The severance of all logistic support lines also meant that there were no medevacs for the wounded or dead. As at Lam Son 719, ARVN troops had to stack their dead or bury them in shallow graves, while the wounded suffered without treatment. The presence of body bags and scores of wounded only served to remind the ARVN soldiers of the precariousness of their situation and was of great personal discomfort to Dinh, who remarked that the sad spectacle "hit my heart hard, and the hearts of our soldiers."

Still more wounded trickled in as the remnants of 1/56 and 3/56 made their way to Camp Carroll. As commander of the Hac Bao, Dinh had been involved in small-unit combat, where even a bloody day had resulted in the loss of only perhaps three men dead. During the worst day in his command career, amid the carnage of the Tet Offensive in Hue City, Dinh had lost twenty men killed. On 1 April 1972, Dinh came to the realization that he had already lost five hundred men during the Easter Offensive. Pham Van Dinh had been a consummate practitioner of the ARVN's standard wartime role in the slow and grueling routine of battle during the American war; he was comfortable and had thrived within that military reality. However, a new and horrible day had dawned as Dinh and his men faced the big-unit war. The record numbers of casualties were profoundly troubling, but the effort remained worth the cost if victory or even tactical salvation still beckoned.

Dinh received word from the survivors of the northern battles and from NVA prisoners that his tattered command now faced the weight of much of the 308th NVA Division. Aware of the imminent danger, Dinh passed the information on to General Giai, who informed Dinh that more help was on the way. General Giai was indeed under the impression that massive reinforcements would be forthcoming in time to salvage the difficult situation. Once the strength of the NVA offensive had become clear, President Thieu had remarked to Giai, "Let them come and we will finish the war right here in Quang Tri Province." The president's plan called for American air power and the commitment of the Vietnamese Marines and Airborne, Saigon's strategic reserve, to destroy the NVA in its tracks.[55] The president, though, went back on his word. The airborne, after all, was President Thieu's most loyal unit, and developing attacks in the central highlands and near Saigon meant that General Giai received reinforcements only in dribs and drabs and in numbers insufficient immediately to alter the strategic reality of NVA dominance in the region.

Facing the fight of his life, Dinh received a call from General Lam at I Corps that he hoped would bring good news of reinforcements or of a plan to save his unit from its exposed position and almost certain destruction. Instead, General Lam brusquely informed Dinh that he would receive no reinforcements and that he was to hold his position at all costs and to the last man. Lam then cut the connection and went to play his evening tennis match. In Dinh's mind, the 56th had been abandoned. It seemed like the horror of Lam Son 719 all over again: a unit stranded atop a hill was to be sacrificed to the vanity of the same politicized commander who had so botched the invasion of Laos. Nothing had changed. The older generation, the men who were ready to squander lives for political gain, remained in complete control, and Dinh, like Tran Ngoc Hue before him, would pay the price. Dinh was crestfallen; his world—the world of war that he had known for so long—was in disarray. Camper noticed an instant transformation in Dinh's demeanor and surmised later that at the root of Dinh's destruction was "the order to hold at all costs. That was our order. . . . There was no possibility of reinforcement, relief or what facing the Commander of the 56th."[56]

That evening, General Giai made the decision to shift his divisional HQ from Ai Tu south to Quang Tri, which was doubtless the correct tactical move, for Ai Tu was under constant threat from NVA 130mm artillery. It was neither a question of flight nor of bravery, but rather a question of command: under the intense enemy fire, General Giai had a difficult time remaining in contact with his battered units. However, there had been a rumor going around all day that the 3rd ARVN Division HQ was preparing to flee. With no process in place for such a move, the divisional radio connections to their units in the field simply went dead. In the words of Colonel Turley, who was present at Ai Tu and remained behind at what became 3rd Division Forward:

> Confused by the disorder around them, South Vietnamese radio operators began radioing their observations to fellow communicators located away from the division headquarters. Thus, it was only a matter of hours before all elements of the division were aware of the hasty withdrawal to Quang Tri City. On the besieged fire bases . . . rumors abounded that the division headquarters at Ai Tu had been abandoned. The rippling effect of such rumors further eroded the South Vietnamese resolve to fight.[57]

At nearly the same time, the remnants of 2/56, along with Colonel Phong and Major Brown, reached Camp Carroll. Camper was overjoyed to see Brown, for the two had lost contact and Camper had feared Brown dead. For Dinh, the moment of reunion was somber. Colonel Phong reported heavy losses during the journey and confirmed that the NVA were close behind, which meant that Camp Carroll was completely surrounded.

Pham Van Dinh's Tactical Operations Center at Camp Carroll. Photograph Courtesy of William Camper.

The events of the evening were another blow to Dinh's psyche. From atop Camp Carroll, at the far end of ARVN's faltering communications network, it seemed that the 2nd Regiment, whose commander had never even bothered to make his way to C2, and the 57th Regiment had fled. Garbled reports also indicated that General Giai, Dinh's trusted superior, had done the same. Only the 56th and the Vietnamese Marines remained in their original AOs, ordered not to surrender an inch of ground even as all others made their own way to safety. Dinh and his men were now alone.

Amid his growing crisis of conscience, Dinh made contact with his wife back in Hue, who was days away from giving birth to their third child. He felt a strong urge to go to them but did not inform her of his difficulties and instead told her to take care of the children and to go to church often. After ending the call, Dinh spent the night in his TOC. It was the dark night of his soul. In many ways, all of his experiences in Vietnam's war rushed together in a moment of supreme agony. The ARVN had once been a young force, one with problems but also full of potential. For years, from the political battles of 1966 to Tet to Hamburger Hill and Lam Son 719, Dinh had realized that there were two paths to victory: the Americans would win through brute force or South Vietnam would come of age. As he sat alone atop Camp Carroll, Dinh believed that both possibilities had come to an end. The United States had abandoned South Vietnam, and the leaders of his own nation and the ARVN had never reformed and were quite willing to sacrifice both him and his men for nothing.

Amid his shattered thoughts, Dinh found himself on the verge alternately of rage and depression. He was furious at the situation, at years of toil and blood he had invested, only to be left abandoned on a hilltop while those for whom he fought fled or played tennis. He was sad for his men, who, it seemed, would never again see their families, men he believed would soon be dead atop a forlorn hill without graves. Were either the South Vietnamese or the Americans worthy of such complete sacrifice? He yearned for a time of peace, with the killing stopped and Vietnam whole again. His thoughts finally settled on a single decision; he "had to save the lives of his people. Nobody could save our lives but me." His goal was now simple—the survival of his men.

Surrender at Camp Carroll

As morning dawned on 2 April, Easter Sunday, in the east, ARVN defenders of the 57th Regiment, the 20th Tank Squadron, and the 3rd Marine Battalion repulsed successive NVA assaults aimed at the seizure of the critical Dong Ha Bridge. As the battle raged, streams of civilians continued their trek south from the war zone, sapping the already low morale of the 57th Regiment, which, as General Truong later commented, "broke ranks around noon and withdrew to the south in disorder . . . when they saw the disorder and panic among these refugees—among whom were their own families and relatives—the panic was contagious."[58] As the ARVN defensive line neared collapse, General Giai, demonstrating great personal bravery, rushed to the battlefield and rallied his men. As the panicked soldiers ran past him, screaming "tank," he grasped one by the scruff of the neck and said, "Show me a tank . . . and we will destroy it together."[59]

The bold action of General Giai succeeded, and the ARVN troops held in place south of the Cua Viet River. Still, the situation was precarious, as the NVA gathered near the Dong Ha Bridge. In a confused series of events, the bridge was eventually blown up by 1630, which both denied the NVA a route further south and gave the 3rd ARVN Division precious time to rally its confused and battered forces.[60] The line had stabilized, but once again reports of panic and flight had reached the distant defenders of Camp Carroll, who faced their own trial by fire.

In the predawn darkness on 2 April, B-52s struck the NVA positions around Camp Carroll, which Camper hoped would slow the pace of enemy action. At first light, though, heavy artillery fire resumed, followed by a ground assault. The ARVN defenders pushed the NVA back in furious fighting, and the scene momentarily calmed as the communists paused to regroup. In the wake of what had been the heaviest assault yet, Camper and Brown checked the defensive perimeter, which had yet to be breached. Brown did his best to encourage the men and told them that if they had repulsed this attack, then they would be able to stand against anything the NVA could dish out.

Camper found the situation difficult and commented, "Troop morale was poor, casualties high, the artillery positions were still intact and usable during lulls in incoming fire. Food was getting low and small arms ammunition also." Without reinforcements, Camp Carroll, in his opinion, would be able to hold out for a few more days. Further south, the Vietnamese Marines at Mai Loc, though not as sorely pressed, found themselves in a similar predicament. With dwindling supplies and a deteriorating tactical situation, they began to consider evacuating their exposed position.[61]

Dinh contacted 3rd ARVN Division HQ and reported on events to Giai's executive officer, Lieutenant Colonel Cuong. Dinh then asked how he could be expected to continue the battle without support, supplies, or reinforcements. The XO had no real answer for Dinh, and General Giai was unavailable, dealing with the crisis at Dong Ha. The lack of any news, coupled with the fact that General Giai was devoting his time to a regiment that was fleeing from battle, only served to solidify Dinh's belief that "nobody was looking after my regiment any more. We were alone."

At 1400, a second NVA human wave assault struck the defenses of Camp Carroll from the west near the main gate. Though again repulsed, the attackers had come so close that their bodies festooned the perimeter wire of the camp. As the fighting raged, Dinh received a call from the NVA. The caller said that he was near and knew all about both Dinh and his men and of their danger. The caller then went on to make an offer; if Dinh surrendered, he and his men would be welcomed by the NVA. If they did not, they would die. The transmission then ended. Camper, who like everyone else atop Camp Carroll did not know of Dinh's short conversation with the enemy, contacted Dinh to speak of a possible helicopter resupply mission. After speaking with his U.S. adviser, Dinh then received a second transmission from someone who claimed to be the commander of communist forces in the area. He repeated the earlier offer and stipulated that it was the last such offer that Dinh would receive. Dinh responded that he would need time to meet with his regimental staff and requested a ceasefire. The NVA representative complied.

Just before 1500, the battalion commanders and regimental staff present at Camp Carroll, some thirteen men, met in the TOC. Dinh informed his gathered subordinates that the situation was bad and that they did not have the strength to hold out long against the constant enemy assaults. He then bared his soul and said, "If we continue to fight, many people will be killed. Even if we die or are wounded and win a victory, nobody will take care of us. Now we must take care of ourselves." Dinh then told the group of the NVA offer of surrender and asked for their ideas on what should they do: should they fight on, break out, or surrender? If the assembled officers wanted to continue the fight, Dinh indicated that he would accede to their wishes. Only Major Ton That Man of 1/56 spoke in favor of continuing the resistance.[62] The remaining staff sat silently; they had no answers. Dinh went on to say that at age thirty-five he had done well in the ARVN and was to be promoted to full colonel in just two months. He had a good family, as did all of the men present. It was his opinion that their families, and those of their men, would be happiest if they survived to return home one day. If nobody had any other options, Dinh counseled surrender. The vote was unanimous.[63] Dinh informed the NVA of the decision and arranged for a longer ceasefire while his staff prepared for the surrender. The NVA officer had one last request: he wanted the U.S. advisers who accompanied the 56th Regiment. Dinh replied that the advisers had long since left Camp Carroll.

Both Camper and Brown noticed that an eerie silence had descended upon the fire base since the last NVA infantry attack. Suspicious, both men sought information but were informed that Dinh and his staff were in a meeting and could not be disturbed. The two Americans returned to their own bunker to ready for what they thought might be the evacuation of Camp Carroll. A few minutes later, Dinh descended the steps of their bunker. Before Camper and Brown stood a truly broken man. On the verge of collapse and weeping, Dinh required two attempts to deliver the news: the men had chosen not to fight anymore, and he was going to surrender Camp Carroll to the NVA. Distraught, Dinh went so far as to suggest that both he and they commit suicide or that Camper and Brown attempt an escape amid the confusion of the surrender itself.[64]

The Americans refused to follow Dinh's advice, and instead Camper suggested a breakout to the south toward Mai Loc, utilizing the two light tanks and three ONTOS vehicles on hand. Dinh refused; the battle was over. Camper then told Dinh that since he would not accept their plan, there was nothing further that he could do for him. The two shook hands, and Camper informed Dinh that he would call MACV for help with his escape. If no help was available, he and Brown would move alone through the wire, rather than surrender. As Dinh turned to leave, Camper recalls:

> I was extremely angry and somewhat frightened at the prospects of being dragged off to North Vietnam. I'm ashamed of my thoughts, but I considered killing the colonel at that moment, but . . . it was not my nature to take advantage of an unsuspecting person. The colonel left.[65]

As Dinh left, the advisers got on the radio to ask for help and quickly went about the destruction of classified documents in their bunker.

With no helicopter evacuation immediately available, and assuming that the ARVN surrender was imminent, Camper and Brown made their way out of their bunker in a desperate attempt to escape to the south. On their journey, the Americans were joined by a handful of ARVN soldiers who refused to give themselves up to the enemy. Even before the members of the tiny group made it out of their own barbed wire, though, an enemy unit opened fire and put an end to their chances of escape. Camper once again got on the radio to report his situation and was informed that a C-47 helicopter, which was delivering supplies to Mai Loc, was being diverted to his position. Switching to the helicopter's frequency, Camper guided the craft, with the callsign Coachman 005, to the fire base's landing zone. Coachman 005 responded with the heartening news that its journey would be quick because, unlike during the past three days, "there was no artillery fire, no anti-aircraft fire, everything was calm." Only as the chopper neared the ground did NVA small-arms fire erupt, which was quickly suppressed by two Cobra gunships. When the helicopter touched down, Brown and a few of the Vietnamese who had taken part in the breakout attempt got on board. Camper recalls:

> Then a bunch of Vietnamese tried to get on, a lot of the Vietnamese that were surrendering tried to get on. I had a little problem; I kind of went berserk. I threw some people off. Everyone who did not have a weapon was not allowed on the plane. Joe Brown kept yelling at me, "Colonel, for God's sake get on here!"[66]

The helicopter took off, and Camper, Brown, and some thirty ARVN soldiers left, never to see Camp Carroll again.

Afraid that Dinh was using the chopper for his personal departure, the NVA announced that it was prepared to open fire on the craft with artillery and anti-aircraft guns. Dinh, though, reassured the NVA that he was still there and that the chopper was only a medevac for his most badly wounded men, and he stayed on the radio the entire time that it took for the helicopter to come and go. Dinh knew perfectly well what the helicopter was for, and, though he had not been able to provide for his advisers' safety, he did what he could to cover their departure. If he had taken the two Americans prisoner and brought them with him into captivity, he would have been treated as a hero in North Vietnam. Dinh also knew that the NVA would be vindictive if they ever discovered that advisers had actually been present at Camp Carroll and that Dinh had allowed them to escape.[67]

As his remaining men gathered atop Camp Carroll, Dinh announced the impending surrender and told the assembled men that they did not have to follow him; those who did not want to surrender were free to hide or escape and try to evade capture in the confusion. As the time for the end of the NVA ceasefire drew near, Dinh moved to the front of the group and led the way out of Camp Carroll's main gate. In the rush Dinh had not taken time to destroy the formidable array of artillery pieces atop the fire base, nor was anything done to aid those who did not wish to surrender. The United States could later use air strikes to destroy the artillery, and those who did not wish to surrender had to make that difficult decision on their own.[68] In Dinh's mind, the fate of the artillery and of those who chose not to surrender was now secondary. Amid his crisis of the soul, Dinh judges that he did the best he could with the consent of his entire staff to "accomplish his last job—to save the lives of his men."

Becoming the Enemy

That night, near Khe Gio, Dinh met with a high-ranking NVA officer, while the six hundred or so men he led into captivity received rations. Dinh informed his captor that his men were through fighting and wanted to get back to their families. The remnants of the 56th Regiment moved on foot for four days before they reached and crossed the Ben Hai River into North Vietnam. It was not the way that Dinh had expected to enter the country of his enemy: as a prisoner. Dinh was not sure what to expect, possibly torture and certainly imprisonment. In his boot, he carried a tiny pistol with two rounds, and he planned to use it to shoot his interrogator and them himself if the situation became unbearable.[69]

Once in North Vietnam, Dinh and Phong were separated from the others and taken aboard a truck for a three-day ride to Hanoi. Unlike Tran Ngoc Hue before him, Dinh was not made the subject of public ridicule; instead, he and Phong were kept under strict lock and key, guarded by five armed men. At night, the small group slept under whatever cover they could find, and during the day they rolled perpetually northward. For much of the journey, Dinh watched as a seemingly endless parade of NVA military formations headed south. The files of young men all seemed devoted to their cause; North Vietnam appeared stronger than he had ever believed. He was now certain that South Vietnam would lose its war.

After about a week of travel, Dinh and his officers arrived in Hanoi, where they were met by a delegation of high-ranking NVA officers. The men who had been their lifelong enemies complimented Dinh on his surrender and commented that his actions had saved the lives of many men, both NVA and ARVN. The treatment came as something of a surprise to Dinh, who still kept his small pistol in his boot. While the NVA officials interrogated the more junior officers, they never once asked either Dinh or Phong for information. They were prisoners of great value, a potential propaganda gold mine, and were treated accordingly.

After a few days, Dinh and his cadre of officers moved to Son Tay Prison Camp, where they were held in their own barracks separate from the remainder of the prison population and were not put to the manual-labor regimen that characterized the lives of so many ARVN prisoners. Instead, the group from Camp Carroll received reeducation in the hope that they would defect. Each day, Dinh and his officers sat through classes taught by NVA luminaries and faculty members from the University of Hanoi, receiving classic communist indoctrination. For six hours every day, the information came in waves: the communists *were* the Vietnamese people, while the southern government and its servants were puppets of American imperialism; the North and the Viet Cong were fighting for independence and liberty as they had against the French, while the south fought only for foreign greed; the Americans had duped the brave men of the ARVN to fight for a cause that was not theirs; ARVN's corrupt leadership had betrayed them. Although the classes did not lead Dinh suddenly to jettison his past, they did strike a chord with a man beaten down by years of warfare. These men, his captors, were Vietnamese, too, and were not that different from him.

After a month in captivity, Dinh faced the inevitable day of reckoning; a group of the very highest-ranking officers in the NVA arrived and offered Dinh and Phong equivalent rank in service of North Vietnam if they chose to defect. Amid a swirl of emotions, Dinh considered the offer to join with the military force that he had fought against for so long—with the Hac Bao, in Hue City, in Quang Dien District, atop Hamburger Hill. As Dinh stood face to face with what to any soldier, much less a hero, was unthinkable, the NVA representatives began to take a harder tack. The men who had surrendered at Camp Carroll were being held in captivity near Vinh and were engaged in manual labor on road-building projects. Their lives were good compared to that of other ARVN prisoners, but their lives could get hard very quickly. At that moment, it became clear; the NVA was ordering Dinh to defect and utilizing his men as a form of blackmail. Dinh believed that if he refused, "maybe I would get some problems and my people would get problems too."

Caught in the confluence formed by the meeting of his past and the paths of his future, Dinh searched for an answer. He and his men were through fighting; that was the core reason for their surrender. Dinh informed his captors that, regardless of his actions, neither he nor his men would ever fight again, and, most important, they would never take up arms against their ARVN brethren.[70] Though he believed that the communists were misguided in their approach, Dinh was first and foremost a citizen of Vietnam. He wanted to see his nation reunited; he wanted himself and his men to rejoin their families in a nation at peace. Dinh had come to the conclusion that South Vietnam would not be the engine of Vietnamese reunification, the guarantor of Vietnamese peace. In an action that he held to be true to his Vietnamese heart, Dinh took the fateful decision to betray South Vietnam and defected. Dinh, the Young Lion of Hue, became the enemy.

After the Surrender

On 2 April, General Giai had left the battlefront for a short meeting with President Thieu. Upon his return, Giai learned from his XO, Lieutenant Colonel Cuong, that Dinh had called and said goodbye. Initially, Giai did not discern the true meaning of the cryptic message and frantically sought information concerning the fate of the 56th Regiment and the western line of ARVN defenses. Only later, in a meeting with Colonel Camper, did General Giai learn the truth of events. Incredulous, Giai refused to believe that Dinh had actually surrendered until he received confirmation of the news from survivors of the 56th Regiment. Only then did General Giai come to grips with the horrible fact that the young man in whom he had invested so much trust had given up the fight.

The sudden surrender of the 56th Regiment and the loss of Camp Carroll unhinged Giai's careful planning and dislocated the western defenses of the 3rd ARVN Division just as the tactical situation in the east seemed to solidify. At Mai Loc, the 147th Vietnamese Marine Brigade now was in a precarious position, and, like the 56th Regiment, its leaders felt that they were on their own. Though his adviser, Major Jim Joy, remained skeptical, the 147th's commander decided that the loss of Camp Carroll made Mai Loc untenable and asked for and received permission to evacuate to the east. The exodus from Mai Loc took place under heavy fire, but the Vietnamese Marines kept good order and made their way to Quang Tri. The fall of Camp Carroll and the retreat from Mai Loc constricted the defensive perimeter of the 3rd ARVN Division ever further and allowed the NVA to edge closer to Dong Ha and Quang Tri.[71]

Although the situation remained precarious, the ARVN stood firm in its new line of defenses, as the NVA regrouped from its exertions and readied another attack. In an effort to make good their losses and hold firm, the ARVN finally sent reinforcements pouring into the area, including the 369th Vietnamese Marine Brigade and four ranger groups. Even as the tactical outlook brightened, General Lam, who remained clearly overmatched and did not even bother to visit his units in the field, made two critical command errors. Instead of utilizing the much-needed reinforcements to stabilize and add depth to his defensive lines, Lam ordered a counterattack against the massing enemy. Further, Lam assigned the counterattack as well as command of all of the new units to the already overburdened staff of the 3rd ARVN Division but provided neither additional support in logistics nor the signal communications essential for effective command and control. Worse yet, General Giai now faced a situation reminiscent of Lam Son 719, with units under his titular control that actually listened and responded more to their own, independent command structure.

After standing against a renewed NVA attack on 9 April, ARVN forces began their own offensive, dubbed Operation Quang Trung 729, but the tired and disorganized troops gained little ground. The ARVN attack instead degenerated into a costly battle of attrition over which General Giai enjoyed only limited control as the attached units under his command went their own respective ways. General Truong, who would later have to pick up the pieces of the debacle when he assumed command of I Corps, in May, was incensed by the command difficulties faced by General Giai, difficulties that verged upon insubordination, and later stated that the parent units of the marines and rangers:

contributed much to the confusion of command and control by elaborating on General Giai's orders or by questioning and commenting on everything concerning their units. They were not the only ones to do this, however. General Lam himself frequently issued directives by telephone or radio to individual brigade commanders, especially to the 1st Armor Brigade commander (who belonged to the same branch) and who rarely bothered to inform General Giai about these calls. General Giai often learned of these directives only after they had been implemented and these incidents seriously degraded his authority. Distrust and insubordination gradually set in and finally resulted in total disruption of command and control in the front line in northern MR-1.[72]

In the wake of an NVA attack on 27 April, disaster again struck the South Vietnamese defenders, due in large measure to chronic difficulties of command and control. The NVA assault came from all directions, and, though losses were heavy, the ARVN soldiers initially held their own. General Lam, however, became increasingly concerned about the security of Highway 1, which served as the main supply route into the area. As a result, the 1st Armored Brigade commander, without bothering to inform General Giai, ordered his 20th Tank Squadron, which had been holding a critical portion of the defensive line along the Cua Viet River, to pull back south to clear enemy elements from the critical supply route. As soon as they saw the tanks race away, the ARVN troops were gripped with panic, broke ranks, and sought safety. Before General Giai was even aware of what was happening, many of his troops had reached Quang Tri Combat Base, and the Cua Viet line of defenses had been handed to the enemy on a silver platter.[73]

In an ironic twist, after the surrender of Camp Carroll, Colonel Camper and Major Brown were reassigned to serve as advisers with the 2nd Regiment. Having had previous experience with the unit, Camper had reassured Brown that the 2nd was a quality outfit and would not collapse and leave their lives once again in peril. However, as NVA units bore down on their position near the Quang Tri bridges, Camper and Brown felt an eerie sensation as it became apparent that command and control within the regiment had failed and that several battalions in the area were in full flight. As the duo left the regimental TOC to assess the deteriorating situation, an artillery round exploded, and Brown watched in horror as Camper collapsed, struck by shrapnel in the face and neck. Brown did the best he could to patch up his buddy. Camper recalled:

> I tried to tell Joe Brown what had happened to me but I was unable
> to speak coherently; one of the fragments had damaged my vocal
> cords and blood inside my face and skull was choking me. Joe laid
> me down so I could drain. The last thing I remembered vividly was
> lying in the dirt, in some kind of potato patch, so that my mouth,
> nose and face could drain.[74]

Joseph Brown quickly arranged for the evacuation of his wounded
comrade, while he made his own way to the divisional advisory headquarters at Quang Tri.

Once again General Giai demonstrated his personal bravery by
rushing to the battlefront to restore order, but it was too late. Amid the
growing despair, the momentum of the NVA assault compelled General Giai, on 30 April, to advocate a plan that had his units withdrawing to more defensible lines south of the Thach Han River. Informed of
the plan, General Lam tacitly concurred, and the ARVN units began
their withdrawal the following morning. Even as the difficult tactical
maneuver began, though, on directions from President Thieu, Lam
countermanded his approval and instructed Giai to hold at all costs.
Shocked by this confusing development, General Giai attempted to recall his order for withdrawal, but all was chaos. Some units had already departed, while commanders of others refused to "stay there
and die" on General Lam's orders.

The withdrawal quickly degenerated as units streamed away from
the front lines in disorder. In desperation, General Giai ordered the
last coherent unit in the area, the newly refurbished 147th Marine Brigade, to mount a defense of the imposing structure of the Quang Tri
Citadel. The Marine commander, though, on his own recognizance decided that the position in Quang Tri was untenable and informed General Giai that "my troops are leaving." With his command crumbling
around him, Giai phoned General Lam, who spoke to each of the 3rd
ARVN Division's available commanders in turn and told them to obey
orders and stand firm. While on the phone, all agreed, but once the
connection was cut they told General Giai that they were still leaving.
Colonel Metcalf, the senior adviser to the 3rd ARVN Division, chroni-
cled the last minutes of the collapse of Quang Tri and wrote that the
ARVN soldiers, as Dinh before them, wondered about the wisdom of
fighting on:

Whose side are we on here, nobody will take care of us, everybody is beginning to leave. You could walk out on one of the little streets there in the Citadel and see soldiers everywhere you looked packing their Hondas, their personal gear on trucks, loading their Hondas, getting on their Hondas themselves and out the gate they were going. There was no control. It had finally got to the point where everyone was so interested in themselves and their own evacuation that they weren't really paying any attention to what tactical integrity or continuity they probably may still have had. [75]

The same command inefficiencies and military realities that had played such a role in Dinh's decision to surrender now cost General Giai his career. The entirety of Quang Tri Province had fallen to the NVA, while General Giai and his advisers narrowly escaped from the Quang Tri Citadel with their lives in a daring U.S. helicopter rescue mission. For Joseph Brown, who was getting a reputation as being bad luck, the flight from the citadel was his third and last emergency extraction as an ARVN unit crumbled around him. Upon his arrival in Da Nang, General Giai was placed under arrest and, in a last act of bravery and devotion, composed a letter in which he took all responsibility for the collapse at Quang Tri. When Colonel Metcalf saw the letter, he was shocked and responded, "General Giai that isn't true. You didn't order the evacuation." Giai stopped his friend short with the statement "I know, but I am the commander; I assume responsibility for everything."[76]

General Giai was sentenced to five years in prison for his failure at Quang Tri, another victim of an ARVN command system that was not yet ready to face the challenges presented by large-scale conventional warfare. Giai became the ARVN's scapegoat. In the ultimate irony and indignity, when South Vietnam fell, in 1975, the North Vietnamese found Giai in prison, then put him into their own "reeducation" camps for a further twelve years.

The fate of General Lam, whose incompetence had done so much to wreck both the invasion of Laos and the ARVN's defensive efforts against the Easter Offensive, was representative of the rampant politicization of the ARVN. Branded by Abrams and others as the true reason for the collapse of Quang Tri Province, Lam was removed from his command but called in several favors and got kicked upstairs in Saigon's military hierarchy, ironically receiving the post of head of the

Ministry of Defense's anticorruption campaign. Both Dinh and Hue had long realized that many within the highest levels of ARVN leadership needed to be replaced; the young patriots needed to be given the time to rise in power and to gain the opportunity to lead. Instead, Dinh and Hue were now gone, while men like Lam survived. General Cao Van Vien later commented that Lam was ill equipped to be a corps commander, and his comments reflect the viewpoints of Dinh and Hue:

> Looking back on that difficult period of time, I can now see that it was perhaps unrealistic to expect perfection from a corps commander. The kind of training and experience, the influence of politics on officers of General Lam's generation and their very background did not contribute to the cultivation of military leadership required by the circumstances.[77]

On 3 May, President Thieu ordered General Truong to take command of I Corps. Gone were the competing systems of command; gone were the bickering and uncertainty that had run rampant under General Lam's command. As he had so often done before, General Truong inspired his men to great sacrifice for their nation. While the battered 3rd ARVN Division left the line to refit and restructure, General Truong, in mid-May, directed the 1st ARVN Division and heavy reinforcements from the Vietnamese Marines and airborne forward into limited counterattacks.

Although the situation remained in flux, with both sides attempting to regain the initiative, General Truong developed a bold scheme for an advance designed to retake Quang Tri City. Though he had to work hard to convince Saigon of the merits of his audacious plan, General Truong succeeded, and, on 28, June I Corps launched Operation Lam Son 72. By 7 July, under cover of a punishing air attack, ARVN forces once again neared Quang Tri City, which the NVA determined to hold to the last man. The battle then degenerated into a test of wills between six NVA divisions and three ARVN divisions. In the maelstrom, the ARVN units performed well and pressed the NVA ever further into a hellish environment of urban warfare that dwarfed the more famous fighting in Hue City during the Tet Offensive. Finally, on 16 September, Vietnamese Marines regained the Quang Tri Citadel, which had fallen so easily only a few months before, and unfurled the

South Vietnamese flag once again atop the tortured ruins of the once beautiful structure. During the last ten days of the assaults on the Citadel, the fighting had reached a tremendous crescendo, in which 2,767 enemy troops were killed while the Vietnamese Marines lost an average of 150 men per day.[78]

Foreshadowing the Future

After initially faltering, the ARVN had held firm not only in I Corps but also in savage struggles around Kontum and An Loc. The fighting had been difficult, with South Vietnam losing 8,000 KIA and 3,500 missing, while the NVA suffered as many as 40,000 killed out of a total of 200,000 committed to battle.[79] In many ways, the struggle across South Vietnam during the Easter Offensive, one of the largest and most important battles of the entire war, represented the ARVN at its best and served to vindicate the American war. Even without American ground support, the ARVN had fought long and well, aided by the remaining U.S. advisers and lavish use of air power. The Easter Offensive left many believing that the ARVN's future was bright. In the greatest test of Vietnamization, the ARVN had stood and repulsed an all-out attack by the NVA.

General Abrams was quite frank in his estimation of ARVN performance during the Easter Offensive and remarked at the time:

> There's been some poor performances. But there *always* have been poor performances in war—in war or anything else. And I think that there always will be. . . . Some poor performances are not going to lose it. It's the *good* performances that are going to win it. . . . But—I *doubt* the fabric of this thing could have been held together without U.S. air. But the thing that had to happen before that is the Vietnamese, some numbers of them, *had* to stand and fight. If they didn't do that, *ten times* the air we've got wouldn't have stopped them. So—with *all* the screwups that have occurred, *and* with all the bad performances that have occurred—they've been there, we wouldn't be where we are this morning if some numbers of the Vietnamese hadn't decided to stand and fight. . . . And the reason, the *first* reason, is that the Vietnamese, including the 3rd Division, have decided by god

they've gone far enough and they're going to fight if they get some kind of chance.[80]

The initial performance of the ARVN during the Easter Offensive, however, had also indicated that the future remained in some considerable doubt. General Truong reflected:

South Vietnamese authorities reacted just as they had during past periods of increased activity. All deployments and reinforcements were continued in the same piecemeal, fractional manner, a brigade here, a battalion there. The initial efforts were indecisive and not enough to regain the initiative. . . . It showed that our systems for command and control and our techniques of employment of forces were not adequate to counter the conventional, combined-arms tactics being used by the NVA.[81]

The ARVN had lingering morale and leadership problems, but the potential was there; the hard-fighting willingness to sacrifice was there. The ARVN had already fought for nearly twenty years and seemed prepared to fight on for many more to come. By the end of the war, one in six South Vietnamese men were serving in the active military[82] in a war effort that cost the ARVN more than 200,000 dead. The ARVN had been constructed, shunted aside, and reconstructed to fight within an American rubric of war, which left it dependent on the United States for supplies and all-important firepower. Even with those difficulties and their constant problems of command, the ARVN had proved in the Easter Offensive that it was able to succeed within the confines of the American war, and changes in the wake of the Easter Offensive seemed to indicate that ARVN was finally serious about reform. However, the habits of nearly twenty years were difficult to break, and time had run out. The United States made good its exit from the war in early 1973, via a peace treaty that left communist forces in place even as American forces withdrew completely. American money and American firepower, which Abrams realized made the difference in the war, were gone, but the NVA and its sources of external support remained.

No matter what grand claims were made on behalf of Vietnamization, the ARVN was not yet ready to prosecute the war alone—and the outcome was inevitable. The ARVN had been created as a mirror image of the U.S. armed forces, the military of a first-world nation that could not be supported by the tattered economy of a third-world nation. Lavishly strong on paper, the ARVN fought on and struggled to change, but, ironically, in many ways it proved not to be Vietnamese enough in structure and form to withstand the American withdrawal and the eventual stripping of funding that followed.[83] Once the United States left the conflict completely, the ARVN's fate quickly became clear.

10

Journeys Home

Life in the Wake of a Lost War

WHILE DINH WENT through a personal metamorphosis in the wake of Operation Lam Son 719 and the Easter Offensive, Tran Ngoc Hue came to terms with the sad reality of life as a prisoner of war. After reaching Hanoi in the spring of 1971, Hue spent the next six months in the soul-wrenching loneliness of solitary confinement at the Hanoi Hilton.[1] After his recovery, although his captors denied him direct contact with his wife and children, they allowed Hue to make one statement on the radio, informing them that he was alive. He had barely enough food to survive and slept on the cold, hard floor of his tiny cell, but there was no torture. Hue's NVA captors seemed content to let time and solitude take their toll on his psyche.

Hue's interrogation sessions, welcome human interactions that punctuated the unending solitude, were rather odd, for, while his captors asked him many questions, they seemed more keen on giving him information. The communists gleefully demonstrated a shockingly complete knowledge of the ARVN defenses along the DMZ—especially the Dong Ha Combat Base and Camp Carroll. The communists indeed knew more information about these places than Hue did himself—and he had been stationed there. With a feeling of utter helplessness, Hue realized both that the ARVN was shot through with spies and that the NVA was preparing for a massive offensive against his comrades in I Corps. The reverse interrogation was a cunning ploy, for the NVA did not want information from Hue; they instead hoped that a demonstration of their mastery of the strategic situation would cause him to defect once he faced the inevitability of communist victory.

For the first time, Tran Ngoc Hue began to despair at the prospect that South Vietnam seemed destined to lose its war. Yet, unlike Dinh, and against the hopes of his captors, Hue channeled his despair into renewed resistance. In Dinh's case, abandonment and loss of hope had led to an acceptance of a more malleable form of nationalism in which Dinh saw his captors as Vietnamese not unlike himself and viewed the North as the vehicle through which peace could be obtained. To Hue, though, the actions of his captors only further fueled the deep dislike that he had held for the communists since witnessing Viet Minh atrocities in Ke Mon as a child. If South Vietnam was destined to fall, Hue decided that he would fight on, even if his only weapon was a steadfast resolve to deny his captors the satisfaction of breaking his spirit.

After six months in Hanoi, Hue was transferred to the POW camp at Son Tay, where on the wall of his new cell he found scrawled the names of numerous American pilots who had been held there previously. Although he remained in solitary confinement, Hue was surprised to receive blankets, double rations, and even cigarettes. The rationale behind the improved treatment was clear; the peace negotiations were going well, and the communists plainly hoped that their coming offensive would result in either a military or a negotiated victory. As the Easter Offensive ran its course, though, the NVA personnel progressively became more silent. Their mood darkened further when the first U.S. bombers streaked overhead and pummeled areas in and around Hanoi. Expecting "some kind of uprising" from the now jubilant ARVN prisoners, the NVA redistributed most of the population of Son Tay to other facilities in its vast network of POW camps. Hue found himself shuttled north to Cao Bang and Nang Son camps but eventually made his way back to Son Tay, where he soon made a surprising discovery.

Through the prison grapevine, Hue learned that, in his absence, Dinh and the group of officers who had surrendered at Camp Carroll had taken up residence at Son Tay. It was no coincidence that Dinh and his men, who lived in a communal setting, were placed in the building that adjoined the solitary-confinement cells of Hue and the other officers who had been captured in Laos. Through his wall, Hue, in his enforced solitude, could hear Dinh and his men speaking and going about their lives, even as they discussed their decision to defect. After Dinh had made his fateful choice, the NVA organized a conference between the prisoners from Laos and those from Camp Carroll, a grandstand effort intended finally to overcome the resistance of Tran Ngoc Hue.

Hue, accompanied by Colonel Nguyen Van Tho, Lieutenant Bui Van Chau, and Major Nguyen Van Thuan, sat in his prison-issue garb on one side of the conference table as Dinh and Phong entered the room, wearing much more comfortable civilian clothing. The two heroes of the ARVN, who had shared so much in common in defense of their nation for so long but who had come to such different ends, stood face to face. Dinh, who Hue remembers as perpetually happy because of his tendency to look on the bright side of life, seemed well and fit. Dinh expressed great joy at seeing that Hue, the brave young combat leader whom he "had been so very close with," was still alive. The two groups sat down, and Dinh began the conversation by asking Hue where he was now being held; he was surprised to learn that Hue had been on the other side of his own wall for nearly two weeks. The meeting did not take the ominous form of an interrogation, nor did Dinh directly urge Hue and his officers to defect. Instead, the groups exchanged pleasantries and discussed the war and family life. The NVA, though, used the meeting in a simple, straightforward manner. Dinh and his men, who were cooperating, were better fed, made small salaries, and had contact with their families; while Hue and his men faced years of unending solitary confinement.

After the meeting, Hue's captors whisked him and his fellow officers away to Hanoi for an offensive of kindness. After being so long alone and hungry in cramped cells, Hue and his compatriots found themselves in hotels, wearing civilian garb, and treated to restaurants and theater performances in the evenings. By day, the group strolled by the lakes and through the streets of Hanoi and went to visit factories that churned out war material. After witnessing the benefits of cooperation firsthand, and after being exposed to the example of Pham Van Dinh, Hue and his men were offered equivalent ranks in the NVA if they chose to defect. They could enjoy the fruits of peace and cooperation or endure years of solitary confinement. It was their choice.

The more lenient treatment, though, had failed to achieve its goal. Hue had found the spectacle of the NVA leading Dinh around like a "dog on a leash" to be quite sobering and felt only pity for his ex-comrade in arms, once a hero but now someone he judged a broken man. Hue thanked his guides and guards for their offer but politely declined to defect, claming that he "was not worthy of such an honor." Instead, he simply asked to be released so that he could return to his family and live the remainder of his life as a civilian. The NVA refused Hue's request and took the recalcitrant prisoner back to his life of loneliness in Son Tay. Tran Ngoc Hue had retained his honor, but at what price?

For their part, Dinh and Phong had accepted the NVA offer of equivalent rank on one condition: that they not be asked to "take any action or provide any information that would run counter to the interests of their old friends in the ARVN." Surprisingly, the NVA had been quick to accept their offer. In Dinh's estimation, the communists' desire to count such a "brave and famous" defector among their ranks was propaganda goldmine enough to offset any failure to gain information or extract some kind of effort from Dinh and Phong. In Dinh's words, "The NVA wanted to have me, and that was enough for them."

For the next three years, Dinh worked in a staff position and mainly wrote to chronicle his experiences in war, something that would become common among ARVN officers at war's end.[2] Dinh had enough to eat, a salary, and comfortable housing. As the war continued, Dinh even had the luxury of summer vacations at the seaside east of Hanoi, but he duly noted that even on such occasions the NVA sent along its "guides." His new comrades would never fully trust an ARVN hero turned traitor. Though life was physically pleasant, it was not a happy time for a man who had been a warrior, but he consoled himself with thoughts of impending peace. An end to the killing was his cherished goal; Vietnam would be whole again, even if it meant the fall of the nation to which he had given so much of his life.

Life for U.S. and ARVN POWs changed abruptly in January 1973 with the signing of the Paris Peace Accords and the final withdrawal of the United States from the Vietnam War. Though the peace was only short lived and signed the death warrant for South Vietnam, it also called for POWs to be repatriated to their home countries. Unaware of the signing of the Paris Peace Accords, Tran Ngoc Hue and his fellow prisoners at Nang Son camp were surprised to receive a visit from a Christian chaplain from eastern Europe. Sitting before his attentive audience, the chaplain informed the assembled prisoners that the government of North Vietnam was not atheist and that the nation enjoyed freedom of religion. As a mark of that freedom, the chaplain presented the prisoners with two copies of the Bible. The entirely new form of propaganda piqued the curiosity of the group; something special was afoot if a chaplain was singing the praises of the northern government. The anticipation in the room rose as the chaplain droned on about the joys of religious freedom in a communist state. At the end of his discourse, though, the chaplain blithely announced what all of the prisoners had not dared to hope—peace was at hand, and they were to be returned to South Vietnam.

Some of the hard-bitten warriors wept openly, while Tran Ngoc Hue maintained a mask of calm, though inwardly he was elated by the prospect of rejoining his family. The prisoners all received new clothing and additional rations before boarding trains and trucks for the journey south to Quang Tri Province, which after the Easter Offensive served as the new border between North and South Vietnam. In Hue City, Hue's wife, Cam, heard of the impending prisoner repatriation over the radio and made her way to the exchange point along the Thach Han River. She did not know when her husband would arrive among the throngs of returnees, but she planned to be there to celebrate his arrival no matter how long she had to wait.

Tran Ngoc Hue arrived in Quang Tri Province amid a crowd of ex-ARVN officers and enlisted men and made his way toward the point of exchange—South Vietnam, his home, was within sight. Suddenly, though, a NVA officer broke into the ranks and removed Hue and the other prisoners who had been captured during Lam Son 719 from the main body of men. So close to freedom, Tran Ngoc Hue learned that he was not to be released. Since he had been captured in Laos, he was "technically" a prisoner not of the NVA but instead of the Pathet Lao, and the peace treaty in Vietnam did not apply to him. Tran Ngoc Hue had stood firm and rejected the overtures of the NVA, and it was now time for him to pay the price. The exquisite mental agony of allowing him very nearly to touch freedom and his family and then snatching them away was well planned and devastating. South of the river, Cam waited for days as ARVN soldiers streamed back; she stood alone while other families shared their joyful reunions. Even after it was obvious that there would be no more prisoners crossing the bridge to freedom, she waited in a forlorn hope that her husband would somehow materialize and take her into his arms. Finally, she made her lonely way back to Hue City to continue to care for her young family, even as her husband returned to the north to endure ten more years of captivity.

Upon their return to the Hanoi area, many of the seventy remaining officer prisoners of Lam Son 719 shaved their heads and staged hunger strikes, which sparked a brutal response on the part of the NVA. Though he took part in the protest, Hue never received a

Tran Ngoc Hue's wife, Tran Thi Cam, and her three daughters in a family portrait taken while Hue was a prisoner of war. Photograph Courtesy of Tran Ngoc Hue.

beating, for he had warned his captors that he would commit suicide before allowing them to treat him in such a manner. Amid his depression, Tran Ngoc Hue, who was from a Buddhist family, turned to the Bible that he had saved since the meeting with the chaplain. Reading the Bible cover to cover several times, Tran Ngoc Hue took solace in its verses and lessons and found both the strength to continue his life and faith that he would eventually rejoin his family.

The Fall of South Vietnam

As Tran Ngoc Hue languished in continued solitary confinement and Pham Van Dinh continued his staff work in Hanoi, the war between North and South Vietnam continued—a war that both Dinh and Hue knew would end in inevitable defeat for the ARVN. Neither man, though, could have expected the speed with which the defeat came. In 1974, members of the NVA leadership asked Dinh what he thought would happen if their military launched an all-out assault into the South. Dinh responded that the ARVN was a formidable foe, especially in armor and artillery, and that the NVA gains would be fitful at best.

When the main NVA attack rolled forward, in March 1975, Dinh listened on the radio as events unfolded. Severely weakened by dramatic cutbacks in U.S. aid, the ARVN could no longer rely on the long-standing firepower edge that had so defined its role during the American phase of the Vietnam War. ARVN units were very nearly immobile due to fuel shortages, advanced armor and aircraft were mothballed because of a lack of spare parts, and artillery batteries were often limited to firing a few rounds per day. Without the full support of its ally, the ARVN was very much a fish out of water; the legacy of the American war had come home to roost. The first major communist blow fell in the central highlands, and the heavily reinforced and lavishly supplied NVA units made good initial progress against their now outmatched foe. President Thieu and his over politicized command structure then compounded the difficult situation by ordering a withdrawal from the highlands and the preparation of a defensive line that ceded the northern half of South Vietnam to the communists. Mired amid a throng of refugees on the difficult mountain roads and harassed by deadly accurate NVA fire, the ARVN staged a retreat that soon became a rout. As the ARVN front in the central highlands collapsed, the NVA attacked in the north. Surrounded and with little hope of survival, the once-proud units of I Corps collapsed in record time.

Dinh was shocked by the catastrophic nature of the ARVN defeat but was secretly inspired in mid-April by the gallant efforts of the 18th ARVN Division to stem the NVA tide at the crossroads of Xuan Loc, north of Saigon. Under the command of Brigadier General Le Minh Dao, the 18th ARVN Division held out for nearly a week against the might of four NVA divisions, reinforced by armor and artillery regiments. The hopeless struggle, which was among the bloodiest battles of the entire war, represented to Dinh what the ARVN could have been. General Dao was one of the young patriots who both Dinh and Hue had hoped would one day lead their nation to victory. It was a sobering thought for Dinh; the whole of ARVN could have been as good and strong as the 18th ARVN Division. All of South Vietnam could have fought that hard. He could have fought that hard at Camp

Carroll—but to what end? For the continued survival of leaders who were more worried about their power than about their nation? For President Thieu, who fled South Vietnam a rich man just days after the fall of Xuan Loc? The epic battle, in Dinh's mind, represented a microcosm of the ARVN experience in the Vietnam War, in which bravery and potential were both ill served and ill fostered by the bankrupt leadership of a generation gone astray. Dinh was more certain than ever after Xuan Loc that he had made the correct decision not to sacrifice the lives of his men for the like of President Thieu. It was not he who was the traitor for his actions at Camp Carroll; the leaders of South Vietnam had long before betrayed their own people.

In the solitude of his tiny cell, Tran Ngoc Hue was dependent upon his captors for information regarding the fall of his beloved nation. As the days in 1975 wore on, Hue received more and more breathless accounts of communist victory from his jailers, who were especially expansive when they delivered his meals. Hue thought that the tales of South Vietnam's collapse were just another psychological ploy, another form of mental torture. Eager that the prisoners should witness their moment of glorious victory, the NVA guards rigged a speaker system in the camp and played continuous coverage of the fighting as reported by the neutral and thus believable British Broadcasting Corporation. Allowed out of their cells to witness the jarring, ultimate defeat of the ARVN, Hue and his fellow prisoners of Lam Son 719 huddled in small groups and wept as Saigon fell and their war ended. Without a nation to call home, none of the prisoners knew what to expect next.

Once the truth of the collapse of the regime in Saigon had become clear, the prison guards could not resist taunting Hue and his fellow prisoners. On one occasion, though, Hue noticed that his captors did not expound as usual on the destruction of the ARVN; instead, they seemed puzzled and pensive. The inquisitive guards informed Hue that some of the South Vietnamese officer class, men whom the communists considered essentially American stooges, had fled in terror— a reaction that they had expected. However, several officers had chosen to commit suicide rather than surrender, a reaction that baffled the North Vietnamese.[3] Why did these men sacrifice all for a puppet nation? They asked Hue if these graduates of both Thu Duc and the VNMA had been brainwashed during their training. Hue responded that it was not the training but rather a devotion to Vietnam and a strong connection to the nation's martial past that had driven the officers to accept death over dishonor.

With the war over and peace at hand, on 2 May 1975, Pham Van Dinh made his way back to Hue City to reunite with his family after three years of separation but found his home deserted. Most of his family had fled to Saigon in advance of the approaching war. His eldest son, though, had remained behind for school, and there was a brief and happy reunion. A month passed before the remainder of Dinh's family, including his father and mother, could hazard a journey up the tortured remnants of Highway 1 to rejoin him in Hue City. When they finally arrived, though, Dinh was overjoyed; the entirety of his family had survived the conflict, the biggest victory of his life.

Pham Van Dinh, the young lion, had returned to Hue City, the city that he once had helped to save, the city where he and the men of 2/3 had jubilantly hoisted the South Vietnamese flag after the horror of Tet '68. However, the young hero was back in the uniform of an NVA lieutenant colonel. Although he remained confident that he had acted honorably, Dinh was understandably concerned about his reception in his home town. After years of difficult war, though, the people of Hue, in Dinh's words, "did not worry about my uniform, and knew that I was not their enemy." Soon Dinh began to meet some of his old soldiers from Camp Carroll on the streets. Several invited him to their homes to thank him both for saving their lives and for protecting the future of their families. Regardless of the justifications for his decisions, Dinh had been saddened and very nearly broken by his experiences of 1972; meeting the men who had served under his command and receiving their thanks was an important moment of absolution for a hero turned traitor. To Dinh, "it was the best gift of my life."

Reeducation

The Vietnamese communists inherited a country that had been ravaged by thirty years of constant warfare. The infrastructure of the nation lay in ruins, millions of refugees wandered the battered countryside, and the communists made matters worse by enacting their long-awaited societal revolution. Economically, the new system suffered both from botched attempts at agricultural collectivization and from increasing isolation from the West, leading the country into the depths of fiscal despair. With little hope for the future, some 1.5 million Vietnamese fled their homeland, often by boat, seeking sanctuary in the West. The so-called boat people of the Vietnamese Diaspora became the most compelling image of a nation and a war that the world was diligently attempting to forget.

The forced reunification of Vietnam also involved a purge of South Vietnamese society, which, while not as brutal as what took place in the killing fields in neighboring Cambodia, ripped the heart out of what had been South Vietnam and the ARVN. Though thousands of "undesirables" were executed after the conflict, the most enduring image of postwar Vietnam in the West is that of the reeducation camp.[4] Very nearly all South Vietnamese government functionaries, ARVN officers, and ARVN enlisted men were rounded up, often called to central points in villages by loudspeakers blaring their names, and taken away without notice to the camps. Though exact numbers remain in considerable doubt, several hundred thousand prisoners were housed in some 150 camps and subcamps, often located at ex-ARVN bases. For ARVN enlisted men, the stint in the camps was only of a few months' duration and involved a mix of manual labor and classes on communist ideology. However, for some officers and government officials, the ordeal of reeducation lasted more than a decade.

After the close of the conflict, the life of Tran Ngoc Hue changed only subtly. No longer technically a prisoner of war, Hue was transferred to a larger camp that quickly began to fill with ARVN officers deposited there in the wake of South Vietnam's military defeat. The camp commandant greeted the new arrivals with a stern warning and stated, "This is the Socialist Republic of Vietnam. You came to this camp to learn about our system and to work hard. If you learn these lessons well, you will be liberated. If not, you will be jailed until your fetters rot."[5] With that the prisoners moved off to their new quarters, tiny communal facilities constructed of cinder blocks with only concrete beds for comfort. For Hue, the simple act of living as a member of a group again after so many years of solitary confinement was both jarring and also wonderfully reassuring. However, a lack of certainty regarding the future ate away at the psyche of the new prisoners; nobody knew what to expect or whether the prisoners would ever see their families again.

Although Hue spent time in several reeducation camps, mainly those located near Hanoi and in the far north of the recently reunified country, he discovered that there were two main types of camps: those devoted mainly to labor and those devoted mainly to teaching. In the labor camps, inmates followed a strict schedule: 0500, wake up; 0530–0600, exercise; 0600–0630, eat breakfast; 0700, go to work; 1200, break for lunch; 1300, back to work; 1800, break for dinner; 1900, go to a classroom in which one of the camp guards read aloud the party newspaper. The prisoners would then practice patriotic songs, listen to a critique of the work they had done for the day by the camp guards, and finally receive their work assignment for the next day before retiring to bed at 2300.

Although inmates conducted all of the work that kept the reeducation camps running, from cooking to laundry, the prisoners most often found themselves also involved in backbreaking agricultural labor, such as clearing unused land by hand to plant rice or manioc. One of the most difficult tasks involved moving earth and stones by hand to form dams in streams to create ponds for aquaculture. Once the land around a camp was cleared, the work routine settled down into the daily grind of planting, tending, and harvesting rice and vegetables, closely mimicking the life of a typical Vietnamese peasant. Without access to fertilizer, the inmates had to rely on their own urine and excrement to make the land fertile, a practice that often resulted in the spread of virulent disease among a prison population already weakened by its toils. Though the camps achieved considerable success in their agricultural labors, the government confiscated most of the food that the camps produced for distribution to a population that was increasingly destitute and famine-ridden during the period of Vietnam's isolation from the West. The ARVN prisoners learned from their captors that "Our people are poor and hungry due to the war. We do not have enough rice to feed both the people and you, so you will have to eat manioc and your ration will be 1.5 kilos per day per man"—barely enough to survive.

On occasion there was a break in the monotony of seemingly endless labor, when select ARVN prisoners, usually higher-ranking officers, including Hue and Giai, were sent for short stays in camps devoted to intense political indoctrination. In their new setting, prisoners were first bombarded with lectures on the evils of American imperialism. Further lessons instructed the inmates that South Vietnam had been the stooge of American imperialism and that the nation and its ARVN servants had been enemies of the people of Vietnam. In preparation for their inevitable return to agricultural toil, prisoners next faced a battery of lessons that centered on the healing nature of physical labor. Such labor could even cleanse the hearts of ARVN criminals and transform them into solid, hardworking members of the communist state. After their studies, the inmates discussed the lessons that they had learned with their NVA instructors in a communal setting for up to two weeks. Finally, the prisoners had to write and then rewrite the results of the cumulative lessons, in tomes that sometimes ran to hundreds of pages in length. The prisoners also had to write of their experiences in the ARVN and of what a grave mistake it had been to serve the puppet regime.

Chronically underfed and overworked, the ARVN inmates of the reeducation camps suffered from all manner of disease, which resulted in thousands of unchronicled deaths, although there were few beatings and no institutionalized torture in the camps. In Hue's view, the communists did not need to rely on such obvious techniques to bedevil their defeated enemy. Instead, they relied on the subtle pains of hunger, exhaustion, and separation from family "and tried to kill us by disease." Each camp contained a tiny graveyard, and, as time slowly went by, even Tran Ngoc Hue, an optimist buoyed by his new-found religious beliefs, began to wonder when he too would lie in a lonely grave amid the hills of northern Vietnam.

As a member of the military of the reunified Vietnam, Pham Van Dinh found that his experience with reeducation camps differed considerably from that of his old comrade Hue. Dinh was assigned to work as one of the teachers at two small reeducation camps in the vicinity of Hue City, one of which was located at the former ARVN base camp at Ai Tu. The inmates of both camps were mainly officers of lower rank who were from the area of Hue City; many were men that Pham Van Dinh had known well and worked closely with in his previous life as an ARVN officer, but they were now prisoners and Dinh was their instructor. Though Dinh's subject matter centered on the people's struggle in revolutionary war and the meaning of Vietnamese independence, he focused his teaching on a simple and powerful message: no matter what they had all hoped for, no matter what their sacrifice had been, the war was over, and South Vietnam was no more.

The people of Vietnam, even those who had been such bitter enemies, had to do their best to "forget everything and work together for the future of the nation."

Despite Dinh's past, he felt that he did well in the teaching position and even served honorably. While he wished that there were no reeducation camps at all, they were a reality of Vietnamese life. Dinh's ex-ARVN brethren who populated the camps at which he worked had a simple goal; to finish their reeducation as quickly as possible and to return to their families. In his mind, Dinh helped to facilitate that goal. Additionally, Dinh did what he could to ease the lives of the inmates of his camps, and was instrumental in arranging for the prisoners to obtain passes to spend some precious time with their nearby families.

Placing Dinh in charge of the reeducation of his one-time comrades was no doubt a test on the part of his newfound communist compatriots and can be seen as both a form of subtle torture and a sad joke at the expense of the ARVN traitor. The time spent as an instructor at the reeducation camps was an especially dark one for Dinh, causing him to doubt the wisdom of his decision to defect. Wedged uncomfortably between the world of his past and the future that he had chosen, though, Dinh did the best he could to rationalize his incongruous position by doing what he could to work toward a Vietnamese reconciliation. By striving for the day when the veterans of Vietnam's civil war would live together in unity and peace, Dinh was able to place his actions in reeducation camps in the same light as he had both his surrender and defection. He was trying to save the lives of those under his care.

After a stint of only six months as a teacher in the reeducation camps, Dinh was transferred to a new position. In the new Vietnamese world, military officials had to serve alongside very nearly all civilian political appointees, and, as a result of his close connections to the area, Dinh was chosen to serve as deputy chief of the sports office of Thua Thien Province, under the direction of Nguyen Tuy, who coincidentally had been Dinh's English teacher in high school. Dinh soon came to love the job, which he quickly discovered was one of healing, a notion that was now central to his hopes for the future. In focusing on sports, Dinh learned that "people make friends and have great joy," something that he believed was sorely needed in his war-torn nation.

With one brief hiatus, Dinh served in the position of deputy sports director for nearly a decade. The tasks in his new position were varied and included the construction of a new, lit soccer stadium that seated up to twenty thousand spectators, enabling the citizens of Hue City to enjoy some of the first nighttime sporting events in the entire country. The office also conducted campaigns to promote public health, specifically discouraging the evils of excessive drinking and smoking. Finally, it was Dinh's office that oversaw all of the myriad aspects of public recreation, from the placing of ping pong tables in parks to the realities of founding physical education programs in all of the province's schools. To Dinh, being a part of the joy of sporting events and working with the children of the city after so many years of warfare was like therapy. Gone were the doubts forced upon him by his period in the reeducation camps; it was one of the happiest times of Dinh's life.

Cambodia

In 1978, in the midst of organizing the construction of the new soccer stadium for the Hue City area, Dinh received a delegation of army officers who posed an intriguing question: what in his view would be the best method to launch an invasion of Cambodia? Dinh, like most Vietnamese, was aware of the border rivalry that had simmered between the victorious Vietnamese communists and their erstwhile Khmer Rouge Cambodian allies. The Pol Pot regime, which had launched genocidal efforts to purge its own population of "unwanted elements," had also committed atrocities against members of Cambodia's Vietnamese minority and had laid waste to border areas claimed by Vietnam. The simmering tension between the two Indochinese neighbors was also part and parcel of an ongoing feud between two communist giants. China saw Cambodia as its client state and viewed Vietnam increasingly as a geopolitical pawn of the Soviet Union.

Dinh answered his military superiors honestly and advocated an air mobile assault on Phnom Penh in the event of war. Whether or not Dinh's cogent advice had any effect on the overall planning, in December 1978 the Vietnamese, using six coordinated corps-size combined-arms mechanized columns, along with a division-size amphibious assault along the coast and a massive airlift of troops to an LZ outside the Cambodian capital, quickly crushed Cambodian resistance and seized Phnom Penh in a swift, blitzkrieg-like campaign.[6] In what was the first major use of airmobile tactics by the communist forces in Vietnam, Dinh reported that there were so many helicopters plying the airways that some of his colleagues joked that the Americans must have returned to battle.

Within a few days, the victorious Vietnamese forces installed a compliant government in Phnom Penh and went about the mission of hunting down and destroying the remnants of the Khmer Rouge. Although the conflict did not involve Dinh directly, it did great damage to his hopes for a prosperous and peaceful future for Vietnam. Pol Pot's followers, backed by other smaller groupings, continued a low-level guerrilla campaign against the Vietnamese for nearly a decade. The continuing war forced Vietnam to keep substantial armed forces in Cambodia and helped to drain the national economy of much-needed resources. Finally, the Vietnamese occupation of Cambodia fatally damaged any chance that Vietnam would enjoy a quick rapprochement with the United States. Vietnam now found itself drained by a long war against irregular forces, while the repercussions of continued isolation from the West destroyed what little economic progress that had been made in the difficult years since the fall of Saigon.

The most immediate impact of the Vietnamese takeover of Cambodia, though, was an uncomfortable reminder of Vietnam's distant past. On 17 February 1979, 100,000 Chinese soldiers invaded the northern provinces of Vietnam and eventually seized the towns of Cao Bang and Lang Son. Vietnamese provincial forces, though, held their own in the difficult and mountainous terrain that they knew so well. After losing as many as twenty thousand dead, the Chinese halted their advance, having moved forward into Vietnam to a depth of only sixty kilometers, and laid waste to the Vietnamese countryside that had fallen under their control.

As Vietnam girded itself for another major war, Dinh was recalled to active service in Hue City and was asked to attend a conference of senior leaders intended to develop a tactical appreciation of the Chinese invasion, a conference headed by the NVA's legendary commander General Vo Nguyen Giap. As the conference wore on, General Giap turned to Dinh and stated that, since the onset of the Chinese invasion several ex-ARVN officers and noncommissioned officers had written and indicated their desire to join the new Vietnamese army to fight against the Chinese. Suddenly the reason behind Dinh's abrupt recall to active service became clear. General Giap asked Dinh if he believed that the ex-members of ARVN were genuine in their professed desire to join with their recent enemies to fight against Vietnam's ancient foe. Dinh assured the general that his onetime comrades would prove trustworthy and tenacious fighters and advised that Vietnam seize upon the nationalist moment to achieve a true reunification in the face of the mighty Chinese threat.

General Giap thought Dinh's reasoning sound, and before he left the meeting he promised to pursue the idea of reintegrating men of the ARVN back into the military. The questions of whether ex-members of the ARVN would have flocked to the defense of a flag that they had once fought against, of whether the communists would have emptied the reeducation camps in a nationalist call to arms, however, proved moot. Denied meaningful international support for their efforts and suffering heavy casualties, the Chinese declared that they had taught the Vietnamese a sufficient lesson and withdrew their forces after only a month. The brief glimmer of hope that Vietnam would bind its wounds in the face of a grave threat was gone; instead of serving to reunite the people as one, the threat was resolved, and the reeducation camps remained in place, the occupation of Cambodia continued, and Vietnam spiraled into economic chaos.

Life after War

The devastation wrought by the war with China, the slow drain represented by the ongoing struggle in Cambodia, continued isolation from the West, dwindling support from a Soviet Union increasingly preoccupied with its own problems, the flight of so many of its best and brightest, and the sheer economic burden on an underdeveloped nation of maintaining one of the world's largest standing armies conspired to transform the reunified Vietnam into one of the world's poorest nations by 1980. Famine periodically struck, while inflation rates reached a high of 600 percent. The all-important level of agricultural output fluctuated with the weather but remained on the whole low even as Vietnam achieved a 3 percent birthrate, one of the highest in the world.[7]

The economic despair caused a continuation of the Vietnamese Diaspora, which changed somewhat in character as many ethnic Chinese, fearing for their lives as the feud between their adopted country and their ancestral homeland simmered, fled Vietnam. Conditions in the reeducation camps reached new lows as more and more food was diverted to the needs of the wider population. A regimen of strict rationing took hold in the nation, and even the family of a high-ranking army officer like Pham Van Dinh received barely enough rice to make ends meet. The situation was so bad that Dinh believed that his nation was reaching its breaking point and that a popular uprising might result.

One night in late May 1983, more than twelve years after his capture in Laos, amid the monotonous sameness of his endless labors, Tran Ngoc Hue had a dream. He stood in a huge cathedral as a man in clerical vestments placed his hand on Hue's head and whispered that he would soon be free. Hue awoke with a start; he and his fellow prisoners continually dreamed of their release, but this dream somehow seemed more vivid and clear. He forced himself to go back to sleep and prayed for another such dream, believing that if it came again, it would come true. His prayers were answered: again he dreamed of the same cathedral, where he was visited by two priests who calmly told him not to worry, for he would soon be released. A bang came at the door; it was 0500 and time to begin the workday. Hue ran to one of his fellow prisoners and told him the good news; he was going to be freed.

One week later, as the inmates gathered to make their way out into the rice fields, the moment came. Every morning an army officer addressed the group, gave out the day's news, and made work assignments. On some treasured days the officer also carried a list. When the men saw that the officer carried the list, anticipation coursed through the crowd; it was a list of those to be released that day. To the prisoners, the release lists seemed capricious in nature. There were no steps that a prisoner could undertake to ensure his release, no test of loyalty that he could pass. The contents of the list, then, were always a mystery and led to suspense that only added to the subtle torture faced by the ARVN prisoners. For the lucky few, jubilation followed the reading of the list, but for those who did not hear their names it was always a crushing blow. After more than a decade of disappointment, as his dream had foretold, Tran Ngoc Hue finally heard his name intoned. Unlike the others on the list, Hue did not leap or break down in joyful tears; he simply gathered his few belongings and left.

Receiving a train ticket and a small amount of money meant only to be enough to feed him on his journey, Tran Ngoc Hue made his way to the south. While in reeducation, Hue had been able both to send and receive mail from his wife, Cam, who had warned him not to return to Hue City. It was her belief that he was too well known there and that he might be harmed or returned to prison. Heeding Cam's advice, Hue made his way to Saigon, where an underground ARVN community existed.

Learning of her husband's release only after his arrival in Saigon, Cam hurried to his side for a reunion filled not only with joy but also with bittersweet tears for what the family had lost. The children barely recognized their father; the youngest had been only two months old when Hue departed for Laos in 1971, and now she was more than twelve. Cam had labored long and hard to care for the family in the years of her husband's absence, one of the millions of unsung female heroes of the Vietnam War. She had first continued her work as a nurse, but, after the fall of South Vietnam, she, as the wife of a "puppet military officer," had been forced to abandon her job. Living at the home of her in-laws, Cam toiled at whatever odd job she could find to make ends meet. As a result of the constant work and the nearly unimaginable stress of being a single parent in times of both war and tremendous economic despair, Cam was in failing health, but still she labored on.

The Vietnam to which Tran Ngoc Hue returned in 1983 was nearly unrecognizable. The ARVN that he had served and the nation that he had so loved were no more, expunged from the national memory so thoroughly that even the massive Saigon ARVN cemetery, which housed the graves of several thousand soldiers, was soon to be destroyed. Moreover, though freed, Hue remained under a close government watch that amounted to house arrest, which made it impossible to find any type of employment. Frustrated by continued poverty and his inability to care for his family, Hue did what he could, but the survival of the family still depended in large measure on Cam, who found work as a home nurse.

While Tran Ngoc Hue and his family endured a life of repression, hard work, and destitution, the economically beleaguered Vietnamese government announced in 1985 a new policy of *doi moi,* or renovation, which allowed for the gradual introduction of some aspects of a free-market economy. These changes, which were initially slow and halting, had little immediate impact on or meaning for Tran Ngoc Hue, for employment even in a free-market Vietnam was reserved only for those with "clean" records. However, *doi moi* proved a major influence on the life of Pham Van Dinh. While Hue lived in poverty as a result of his unbending allegiance to his lost nation, Dinh, while by no means rich, lived in the same home in Hue City that his family had occupied during the war and made his way to and from his government job on a Honda moped. After the worst of the economic turmoil had passed, Dinh and his family lived in relative comfort as part of the ruling system.

As part of the *doi moi* program, the Vietnamese government created special military units in each province that were tasked with the economic betterment of the area. In 1985, Dinh moved from his position as deputy chief of the sports office in Thua Thien Province to command of the economic unit for the province, which initially controlled agricultural production of more than fifty hectares of land. The unit not only oversaw farming activity on the land under its direct control but also built roads, founded schools, and managed timberland. The economic units also played a role in the gradual demobilization of the massive Vietnamese military, which had been such a drain on the national economy. Dumping hundreds of thousands of ex-soldiers into an already overburdened job market would have been a cataclysmic error. Instead, the economic units eased soldiers back into the economy. The soldiers first opened new land and new jobs in schools and then were civilianized into those new positions.

As *doi moi* ran its slow but successful course, Pham Van Dinh began a second life as a small businessman. Many in Hue City were wary of the reforms and feared risking their savings in a difficult business environment, but Dinh decided to gamble on Vietnam's economic future. In 1989, Dinh took his first steps into the nascent world of Vietnamese capitalism and bought an IFA cargo truck built in East Germany, the first privately owned truck in Hue City. With his twenty-six-year-old son serving as his driver and sole employee, Dinh used the truck to launch a small transport company that hauled goods to and from places as distant as Saigon and Hanoi. Although Dinh eventually procured another truck, within three years he divested himself of the business; *doi moi* had opened the door of change far enough that many people in Hue and throughout Vietnam had bought trucks, and the competition in the haulage industry had become too great. Though he had not succeeded, Pham Van Dinh still hoped to find a business venture that would be large enough to involve his entire family and to enable him to retire from the military.

Vietnamese and American Dreams

Dave Wiseman had never given up the search for Tran Ngoc Hue after Lam Son 719. After returning from Vietnam in 1972, Wiseman had been assigned to the Norfolk, Virginia, Naval Station, where he tried to search through any available records for news regarding the fate of his dear friend. Four years later, Wiseman was assigned to Marine headquarters, where he inquired again, but still he found nothing. After retiring from the service, in 1980, Wiseman relocated to the Washington, DC, area where he continued his search. The only things that he ever heard, though, were rumors that Hue had been killed in Laos or that he had died in prison. However, without positive proof of Hue's demise, Wiseman refused to give up hope.

When thousands of Vietnamese refugees, including officers who had been released from prison camps, began to arrive in the nearby suburbs of northern Virginia, Wiseman, equipped with a picture of Hue, launched a one-man search party throughout the Vietnamese expatriate community. After showing Hue's picture to hundreds of expatriates without any results, in July 1990 Wiseman attended a dinner for the Families of Vietnamese Political Prisoners Association. As the picture was passed around yet another table of expatriates, Ngo Duc Am, a former prisoner in Vietnam and a cousin of Hue's wife, Cam, positively identified Hue and informed the jubilant Wiseman that Hue and his family were alive and well in Saigon.[8]

A few weeks later, Tran Ngoc Hue was astonished to receive a letter from his old adviser and was honored to learn that Wiseman had never forgotten their friendship and had searched for him for so long. Amazingly, the authorities had failed to open the letter, and Hue also discovered $100 in cash, a princely sum for someone who was so destitute. The kindness was overwhelming, and Hue sat down in tears before he could finish the letter, in which Wiseman offered Hue and his family what help he could, ranging from money to medicine to aid in reaching the United States. With a burden lifted from his shoulders, a weight of nearly twenty years since he had been captured, Tran Ngoc Hue strode without fear to the Hotel Caravelle. He did not give any thought to the watchful eyes of the police; he thought, "Let them see me!" At the hotel, he sent off a fax to Wiseman, a very public act in a suspicious and closed country. The fax thanked his dear friend for his help but kindly rejected the offers of money. What Hue and his family wanted was out of Vietnam, "at any price."

Dave Wiseman took Hue's appeal to heart and immediately began to work through the auspices of the recently inaugurated Humanitarian Operation, an agreement implemented in a rapprochement between Washington and Hanoi designed in part to allow prisoners of the reeducation camps who had been incarcerated for more than three years and their families to emigrate legally to the United States. For his part, Hue had to endure the bureaucratic nightmare of attempting to acquire passports and exit visas from a government that resented his very existence. He also had to borrow money for the transportation costs for him and his family from the U.S. State Department, with the promise that he would repay the loan in five years. The process was agonizingly slow and required nearly all of Hue's time as Cam's health continued to deteriorate. Every month for more than a year, $100 in cash arrived like clockwork from Dave Wiseman, which allowed Hue and Cam to keep going.

On 7 November 1991, Tran Ngoc Hue, his wife, Cam, and their three daughters boarded an aircraft in what had once been Saigon and departed their homeland for a new life. After considerable delay in Bangkok and Paris, the Trans touched down at National Airport, in Washington, DC. There they met and fell into the arms of their gracious friends and benefactors, the Wisemans. What faced the Trans, though, was daunting—a new beginning, penniless and homeless in a new and strange country. Wiseman, with help from fellow Marines, though, had thought of everything; the Trans had a fully equipped apartment in Falls Church, Virginia, complete with TV, cable, and schoolbooks for the children, waiting for their arrival.

The Trans worked hard to adjust to life in their new home. The children enrolled in English classes, while Hue and Cam immersed themselves in the Vietnamese émigré community. In January 1992, the Trans were asked to attend a meeting with General Carl Mundy, the Commandant of the U.S. Marine Corps. In an emotional meeting, General Mundy presented Tran Ngoc Hue with the U.S. Bronze Star and Silver Star, both of which he had earned in fighting during 1968 but had long since lost. Though the faces around him were not Vietnamese and he still longed for the land of his ancestors, Tran Ngoc Hue was truly happy for the first time in more than twenty years. He had finally come home.

In 1990, Pham Van Dinh saw something amazing in Hue City. Americans, mainly veterans but also a scattering of intrepid businessmen and tourists, were beginning to trickle back to Vietnam. As the Vietnamese economy rebounded and relations with the West continued to warm, the number of tourists, especially from Australia and France, continued a slow rise and gave Dinh an idea. As Hue received his decorations from the hand of General Mundy, Dinh sat in the lobby of a bank and took out a loan to build a small hotel in Hue City. Still in the military, Dinh left the management of the business to his eldest son, and, of the hotel's remaining staff of ten, five were from Dinh's immediate family. It seemed like the Vietnamese version of the American dream, a business opportunity that allowed Dinh's family to work and prosper as one.

After nearly four years of operating the Sunflower Hotel, having made enough money to at least make a dent in their considerable mortgage on the property, Dinh found that the continued warming of relations between the United States and Vietnam played an ever-increasing role in his life. With his fluency in English, Dinh had become in demand as a specialized tour guide for Americans who wanted to investigate the famed Vietnam War sites that dotted what had once been I Corps, from distant Hamburger Hill to the nearby Hue Citadel. In 1996, through an American veteran named Courtney Frobenius, the proprietor of Vietnam-Indochina Tours, Dinh received a surprising request. General John Cushman, once the commander of the 2nd Brigade of the 101st Airborne, which had fought alongside Dinh's 2/3 ARVN in Quang Dien District in the wake of the Tet Offensive, was going to travel to Hue City and wanted to see the areas where his unit had been active. Cushman stayed in the Sunflower Hotel, and Dinh served as his guide throughout the journey. Later Dinh also served as a guide for two additional groups of 101st Airborne veterans and also attended the ceremony in honor of Pete Peterson's arrival as the first U.S. Ambassador to Vietnam since the end of the conflict. It was a truly happy time for Dinh. Both his family and their business were doing well, and his new nation was mending relations with the land of his one-time allies. Dinh had found his place in a land that he called home.

Full Circle

Tran Ngoc Hue threw himself into the hustle and bustle of American life and worked as many as three jobs at a time to repay his debts and to rebuild the fortunes of his family. Wiseman was amazed at the zeal demonstrated by his friend and stated:

> He paid back the State Department $4000 for his airline tickets within a year and even gave me back the security deposit on the apartment. You think of trying that. I helped get him a job at the Marine PX, but the Commandant of the Marine Corps knew him well enough by then that I think my influence was small.[9]

After his stint at the Marine PX, Hue secured a position working at the Navy Federal Credit Union. Though Cam still suffered from health issues that dated back to the rigors of life alone while caring for a young family in time of war, she also worked fulltime to help make a better life in their adopted land. In September 1994, the Trans moved to a new home of their own in Falls Church, and in 1995 they sponsored the nine members of another former South Vietnamese POW family in their own efforts to reach the United States.

On 29 February 1997, as Dinh watched Vietnam and the United States reconcile, Tran Ngoc Hue and his entire family took the oath that made them citizens of the United States of America. Since that time, all three of Hue's daughters have successfully graduated from the University of Maryland: two have married and now have families of their own. In 2002, Tran Ngoc Hue assented to be interviewed for this project, and, as we sat down to work, it quickly became apparent to me that Hue is a man at peace. Though he had been through the turmoil born of years of war, had very nearly died, and had endured years of imprisonment and hardship; Tran Ngoc Hue believes himself to be one of the luckiest men in the world and thanks God every day for having answered his prayers. In one of the most poignant moments of our long conversations, Hue leaned in and said, "I once did not think that I would survive to see my wife and children again. But I did. I lived to see them all, and even my grandchildren. I have lived to see them successful in life. What a blessing. Every day I live the American dream."

The previous spring I had undertaken a month-long series of interviews with Pham Van Dinh. Our discussions began well enough and concentrated on his early life and first years of service in the ARVN. Dinh seemed to be utterly at peace and was happy to give his honest recollections of service to a nation that he had once so obviously loved. Only when we reached the difficult subject of his surrender and defection did Dinh begin to show any emotion. It was almost as if in the interviews he had been able to relive his life as a renowned ARVN officer; the path of his future was as yet untrod, and hope remained. Discussion of his surrender, though, brought reality and all of its attendant pain rushing back. As the subject of the interview touched on the moment of his surrender, Dinh became more and more introspective and began to ask questions of me, sobering and troubling questions. Why did America not push its advantage after Tet '68 and win ultimate victory? Why had America chosen, instead, to exit the conflict and leave the ARVN abandoned and alone against its formidable foe? At one point, as we spoke of his unit being surrounded on Camp Carroll, Dinh leaned in toward me and, with tears in his eyes, asked a question that had obviously gnawed at the very core of his being for thirty years: "America is still in South Korea. Why are you not still in South Vietnam? What did we do wrong?"

As our interviews neared their conclusion, I asked Pham Van Dinh why he had chosen to put himself through the pain of the interviews at all. He responded that there were many reasons that he should not tell his story. In the wake of the upheaval that surrounded his canceled public address, he now realized that many in the United States greatly disliked him. No matter how much historical sleuthing I did to corroborate his story, those people would not only continue to vilify him but also brand us both liars. He also admitted the fundamental irony represented by his presence in the United States. The present Vietnamese government, to which he had defected and which he still served, would not allow him to tell his story in Vietnam. However, in Dinh's mind, the reasons both to speak and to be totally candid about his past outweighed the obvious risks. As he aged, Dinh was well aware that the interviews represented his only chance to tell the truth of some of the most important events of the war, no matter what the cost. He closed the interviews by stating that he "wanted people to know the story of our country and the story of the war" and hoped that his story "would help young people and old people to understand and learn from both my victories and my mistakes."

The Vietnam War had finally come full circle. Tran Ngoc Hue, who had fought so valiantly for so long and who had paid such a high price for his bravery, has found peace and a new home in the United States. Pham Van Dinh, who had also fought valiantly for so long but in the end had fallen short of the traditional definition of a hero, can find true peace in neither a transformed Vietnam nor the United States. When Dinh returned home, he went about gathering additional information to supplement our interviews. After a few communications, though, there was nothing but silence. A few months later, I learned that Dinh had suffered a major stroke and that his life was in peril. Although he endured a long and painful recovery process, Pham Van Dinh remained very weak and unable to speak, making the reasoning behind his willingness to tell the truth about the events of his life all the more prophetic.

The story of Pham Van Dinh and Tran Ngoc Hue is, in the end, like a Greek tragedy. Both men struggled diligently for years and came tantalizingly close to victory before the fates dealt them defeat through no fault of their own—separate yet related personal defeats caused by the terrible confluence of events that was the flawed U.S./South Vietnamese war in Vietnam. Dinh and Hue, two young heroes with so much in common, made vastly different decisions in the face of adversity. Although Dinh and Hue have led very different lives since those eventful days, it is a reflection of the Vietnam War's complexity that both men firmly believe that in the closing moments of their war and ever since, they have each followed quintessentially Vietnamese paths of honor.

Conclusion

THE LIVES OF Pham Van Dinh and Tran Ngoc Hue were both dominated and defined by the Vietnam War. Choosing similar paths, Dinh
and Hue embraced a noncommunist nationalism fueled largely by a
fundamental Vietnamese value: family. Driven by the tenants of *on*
and *hieu*, as well as by an almost paternalistic devotion to their fledgling nation, the two comrades fought hard and prospered within the
context of a war dominated by American, not South Vietnamese, military and political needs. Although Dinh and Hue realized, as did so
many other U.S. and South Vietnamese combat officers, that both the
war and the South Vietnamese systems were flawed, they fought on,
exhibiting a level of stoicism and resilience that are among the hall-
marks of Vietnamese martial history. Pham Van Dinh and Tran Ngoc
Hue were Vietnamese warriors, in the best tradition of their ancestors.

The life stories of Pham Van Dinh and Tran Ngoc Hue also reflect
an ARVN that was a complex institution, that, although all too often
either ignored or portrayed as a hapless victim of history in the West,
played an integral role in the Vietnam War. Hue's sterling career, ranging from his efforts to recapture Hue City in 1968 to his final moments
in command during Lam Son 719, represented the best of the ARVN:
dedication, honor, and duty. While Dinh also fought well, from the
founding of the Hac Bao to Tun Tavern, the conclusion of his career
seems to represent only the archetypal traits ascribed to the ARVN:
cowardice and duplicity. The actions of Dinh and Hue seem simple on
the surface, but a fuller understanding of the context of their actions as
their careers in the ARVN came to an end reveals profound lessons
about the ARVN and its war.

Within a broader context, although the tenacity displayed by
Hue's 2/2 during Lam Son 719 highlights the best characteristics of
the ARVN, the destruction of the battalion also represents both the
American construct of the war and the ARVN at their worst. Due in
part to issues of American politics, the operation took place two years

too late, and the ARVN, having long functioned as an adjunct of an American war, proved to be both tactically and politically lacking. Without advisers, much less the support of U.S. combat forces, the ARVN demonstrated that it was not ready to shoulder the burden of war alone, yet the withdrawal of U.S. forces only accelerated. Problems ranging from tactical tinkering by President Thieu to outright insubordination by powerful and politically motivated generals also demonstrated that the pace of South Vietnamese military and political reform had been far too slow.

Dinh's end, too, was far from simple, and fits into a broader understanding of the Vietnam War. The historian Robert Brigham has argued that the South Vietnamese leadership did not provide the national identity required to support a long and grueling war. He contends:

> Over time the ARVN created a subnational culture that focused the war's meaning on family survival. Servicemen arrived at a shared understanding that the war was no longer about "the national question" but about something more elemental. Drawing on cultural and historical traditions, the ARVN redefined the meaning of the war. What held it together in the face of enormous difficulties was a growing belief among soldiers that military service was actually a way to increase the odds that their individual families would survive intact. . . . Still, most soldiers accepted (and continue to accept) an unfavorable reputation as a small price to pay for accomplishing their main objective: saving their families.[1]

Over time, Dinh's men, the long-suffering soldiers of the ARVN, became even more important to him than his blood family. In that context, Dinh's decision both to save his family of soldiers and to ensure the futures of their own families can be seen as a very Vietnamese act.

The events that led to Dinh's defeat atop Camp Carroll were also part of the legacy of a bifurcated war. An attempt to compensate for the departure of American forces from the DMZ and a politicized ARVN high command combined in the creation of the deeply flawed 3rd ARVN Division. The decision to assign the new formation to defend one of the most dangerous areas of South Vietnam, command gaffes at I Corps, and supply and communications problems all conspired to leave Dinh and his command in a nearly hopeless situation. Unlike Hue when confronted with faced similar circumstances, though, Dinh chose to surrender and defect. Although in some ways his actions are understandable, Dinh ultimately abandoned the cause of his ARVN compatriots. In the years that followed, many others within the ARVN came to the same conclusion that Dinh reached in 1972: their war was lost. Some broke and ran; others fought on to the bitter end, but few followed Dinh's path—a path of a broken soul that to most ARVN veterans mocks the sacrifice of those who fell for the cause of their nation.

The fates that befell Dinh and Hue, in large part consequences of the dysfunctional nature of the military that they served, are symptomatic of the flawed nature of the Vietnam War as a whole. One of America's chief mistakes was conducting the war through traditional, Western means. Assuming a leading role in the conflict in 1955, the United States in general and MAAG in particular failed to view the coming war as an insurgency and instead worked to craft the wreckage of the VNA into an ARVN of standard infantry divisions based on the American model. Efforts to implement effective counterinsurgency and to win the "hearts and minds" of the South Vietnamese population were halting and often emanated only from officers of lower rank. The American military system was slow to adapt and was headed at its most critical juncture by a COMUSMACV who was "bored" by pacification. As a result, promising counterinsurgency schemes and developments, such as Pham Van Dinh's experience in Quang Dien District, went largely unnoticed until the advent of Abrams's command, when it was too late. Reliant on traditional modes of war and American firepower, the ARVN was neither tied to the social and economic realities of Vietnam nor prepared for the war that it actually faced.

Attritional military victories both veiled and exacerbated the fundamental problems that defined the allied war effort. Supremely confident of their ability, incoming U.S. forces essentially pushed the ARVN to one side in an attempt to destroy the communist threat singlehandedly. The policy proved to be shortsighted. Due in part to limits placed on the use of military force for geopolitical reasons, a corresponding escalation of the conflict by the North Vietnamese, and the stalwart nature of the Viet Cong insurgency, the Americans could not hope to win by traditional methods of warfare alone. The best hope for success instead lay in a symbiosis of U.S. and ARVN efforts and the creation of a South Vietnam that was capable of ensuring its own survival.

Yet, as the American war in Vietnam progressed, the relationship between the United States and South Vietnam remained fatally flawed as the Americans and the ARVN fought two different wars in the same country. Innovation within the dual system again came from officers in the field, who held more junior ranks and who served at the nexus of the U.S./ARVN symbiosis. Both American and Australian advisers, along with their Vietnamese counterparts, toiled in near-anonymity to ensure an effective synthesis of U.S./ARVN effort and ability. The efforts of the advisory system, however, always remained secondary to a more traditional American reliance on brute force. Other efforts at achieving a true unity of effort in Vietnam, best evidenced by the successes achieved by Colonel John Cushman's 2nd Brigade of the 101st Airborne in conjunction with the 1st ARVN Division in Quang Dien District, were never truly systematized and came too late to alter the strategic reality of a bifurcated war.

Endemic problems within the structure of the South Vietnamese state and military further weakened the allied war effort. The leadership of both the South Vietnamese state and the ARVN were holdovers from the French colonial regime and were all too often interested first in obtaining and then in retaining personal power. With political loyalty serving as the ultimate arbiter of worth within the upper echelons of the ARVN command structure, there was little impetus for far-reaching military and societal reform. Tutored as they were in the American belief in the efficacy of traditional military victory, too few South Vietnamese leaders saw a compelling rationale for undertaking a painful transformation of their dysfunctional political and military systems.

Both the Americans and their South Vietnamese clients were confident of victory, and as a result neither ally devoted enough time or effort to the creation of a South Vietnam fully capable of defending itself. In many ways, the United States prosecuted its own war in Vietnam, while the leadership of South Vietnam was too quick to allow American battlefield successes to obscure long-term weaknesses within in its own society and military. The American reliance on traditional methods of warfare, when combined with the failure of the South Vietnamese leadership to institute systemic reforms, combined to create an ARVN that was dependent on U.S. logistic support and firepower. Relegated to a position of secondary importance, the ARVN actually functioned quite well within the rubric of the war, winning substantial victories alongside its American allies, from the recapture of the Citadel in Hue City to battles in the A Shau Valley. But, when American troops began to withdraw from the conflict, the flaws of the American way of war in Vietnam and the failure of South Vietnam's political and military elite to undertake needed reform became tragically clear.

Despite the best efforts of an innovative core of young U.S. and ARVN officers and a belated effort on the part of MACV, the results of the powerful confluence of American military traditionalism and South Vietnamese systemic intractability were evident in both Lam Son 719 and the Easter Offensive. Although in both cases ARVN personnel fought bravely, the command failures of the ARVN, when combined with the withdrawal of U.S. combat forces, foreshadowed the defeat of South Vietnam. At the highest level, Lam Son 719 and the Easter Offensive demonstrated that, despite its firepower and size, the ARVN was neither tactically nor strategically ready to face the NVA without substantial U.S. aid. On the lowest level, amid the fighting on two hilltops as their units were being destroyed, Pham Van Dinh and Tran Ngoc Hue faced in very personal ways the ramifications of the failures of both the United States and South Vietnam at war.

While it is right to remember the Vietnam War as representative of the myriad failings of military and political imagination in both America and South Vietnam, an understanding of the lives of Dinh and Hue reveals a further truth about the conflict. For all of the strategic failures on the part of the United States, and for all of the systemic failures on the part of South Vietnam, the alliance between U.S. and ARVN forces in the conflict achieved considerable success. Although the upper echelon of the ARVN remained deeply flawed, the lower levels of the ARVN, epitomized by Dinh and Hue, fought with valor for years. And, while the strategic structure of the war rested on misguided assumptions, the U.S./ARVN alliance usually bested the vaunted VC and NVA in battle and came tantalizingly close to military victory in the year after the Tet Offensive.

The Vietnam War sends a grave warning regarding the projection of military force into the complex internal conflicts of other nations. Although firepower and attrition nearly succeeded in obtaining a military victory in the traditional sense in Vietnam, it remains doubtful whether faltering American will or a dysfunctional South Vietnamese state would have been able to transform strategic victory into long-term systemic success. In addition to tactical dominance, the Vietnam War required a true symbiosis and unity of effort on the part of U.S. and ARVN forces and a corresponding devotion to duty and willingness to accept change on the part of the South Vietnamese government. The raw material for success was on hand: stalwart warriors and leaders within both the ARVN and the U.S. military, firepower supremacy, and talented advisers. A more cooperative military and political structure better capable of first discerning and then learning from its failings might have made the final chapters of the lives of Pham Van Dinh and Tran Ngoc Hue very different. In the end, though, the great martial deeds and the tragic ends of the military careers of Dinh and Hue stand as testimony to both the great strengths and the equally great weaknesses of the combined U.S./ARVN war in defense of South Vietnam.

Notes

Notes to the Preface

1. In Vietnamese names, the family name comes first, while the given name appears last. Though it is in many ways improper, in most cases when only a single name is used, this book will utilize the first name of the person in question. In other words, Tran Ngoc Hue will be referred to as Hue, and Pham Van Dinh will be referred to as Dinh. This name usage is done to simplify matters for a Western readership, and the author makes apologies to any Vietnamese readers who might take offense at the practice.

Notes to the Introduction

1. For a revealing account regarding the nature of the Vietnamese expatriate community in the United States see Andrew Lam, *Perfume Dreams: Reflections on the Vietnamese Diaspora* (Berkeley, CA: Heyday Books, 2005).

2. Dale Andrade, *America's Last Vietnam Battle: Halting Hanoi's 1972 Easter Offensive* (Lawrence: University Press of Kansas, 1995); Colonel G. H. Turley, *The Easter Offensive, Vietnam, 1972* (Annapolis, MD: Naval Institute Press, 1985).

3. Andrew Wiest, ed., *Rolling Thunder in a Gentle Land: The Vietnam War Revisited* (Oxford: Osprey, 2006), 26.

4. The historiographical balance has begun to tip, as a growing number of scholars focus their attention on the ARVN. The important books and studies in the field now include Robert Brigham, *ARVN: Life and Death in the South Vietnamese Army* (Lawrence: University Press of Kansas, 2006); Phillip E. Catton, *Diem's Final Failure: Prelude to America's War in Vietnam* (Lawrence: University Press of Kansas, 2002); and Thomas R. Cantwell, "The Army of South Vietnam: A Military and Political History, 1955–1975" (unpublished Ph.D. dissertation, University of New South Wales, 1989). Mark Moyar's massive *Triumph Forsaken, The Vietnam War, 1954–1965* (Cambridge: Cambridge University Press, 2006), also pays a great deal of attention to South Vietnam and the ARVN. James Willbanks also pays special attention to the ARVN in his pivotal works *The Battle of An Loc* (Bloomington: Indiana University Press, 2005) and *Abandoning Vietnam: How America Left and South Vietnam Lost Its War*

(Lawrence: University Press of Kansas, 2004). There also exists a move among ARVN veterans of the war to chronicle their own experiences. Relatively few of these accounts have made the crossover to major English-language presses. As interest in the field expands, more graduate students are turning to the ARVN as a focus of their research, including Jason Stewart at the University of Southern Mississippi, who is working on a Ph.D. dissertation concerning the command of ARVN general Vu Van Giai.

5. For a full account of America's role in the ARVN's defeat see Willbanks, *Abandoning Vietnam.*

Notes to Chapter 1

1. Stanley Karnow, *Vietnam: A History* (New York: Viking, 1983), 138.

2. The vast majority of information concerning the lives and recollections of Pham Van Dinh and Tran Ngoc Hue is drawn from a series of tapes made of the author's interviews with the two men. The tapes are now housed at the Center for Oral History and Cultural Heritage at the University of Southern Mississippi. In an effort to avoid repetitiveness in the notes, the author will only rarely give specific references to taped material when necessary. Notes in each chapter, though, will isolate the tapes that contain the information contained in that chapter. Information contained in this chapter can be found on Pham Van Dinh interview tapes 1–2, and Tran Ngoc Hue interview tape 1.

3. Brigham, *ARVN,* 51.

4. For widely differing views on the nature of the Buddhist movement in Vietnam see Moyar, *Triumph Forsaken,* and Robert J. Topmiller, *The Lotus Unleashed: The Buddhist Peace Movement in South Vietnam, 1964–1966* (Lexington: University Press of Kentucky, 2002).

5. By Dinh's reckoning, only some 15 percent of the Vietnamese population was able to afford the type education that he received.

6. Cantwell, "The Army of South Vietnam," 2.

7. Ibid.; Ronald H. Spector, *United States Army in Vietnam. Advice and Support: The Early Years, 1941–1960* (Washington, DC: Center of Military History, 1983), 165.

8. Anthony James Joes, *The War for South Viet Nam, 1954–1975,* rev. ed. (Westport, CT: Praeger, 2001), 85.

9. Brig. Gen. James Lawton Collins, *Vietnam Studies. The Development and Training of the South Vietnamese Army, 1950–1972* (Washington, DC: Center of Military History, 1975), 12–13.

10. Andrew Krepinevich, *The Army and Vietnam* (Baltimore: Johns Hopkins University Press, 1986), 21.

11. Spector, *Advice,* 225.

12. Ibid., 256.

13. Cantwell, "The Army of South Vietnam," 16. Also see Tran Van Don, *Our Endless War: Inside Vietnam* (San Raphael, CA : Presidio Press, 1978), 171.

14. Don, *Our Endless War*, 149; Brigham, *ARVN*, 5.

15. Brigham, *ARVN*, 5–7, 11.

16. Catton, *Diem's Final Failure*, 87.

17. John A. Nagl, *Learning to Eat Soup with a Knife: Counterinsurgency Lessons from Malaya and Vietnam* (Chicago: University of Chicago Press, 2005), 120.

18. Lt. Gen. Ngo Quang Truong, *Indochina Monographs. Territorial Forces* (Washington, DC: Center of Military History, 1980), 25.

19. Lt. Gen. Ngo Quang Truong, *Indochina Monographs. RVNAF and U.S. Operational Cooperation and Coordination* (Washington, DC: Center of Military History, 1980), 173.

20. Cantwell, "The Army of South Vietnam," 23.

21. Arnold Isaacs, *Without Honor: Defeat in Vietnam and Cambodia* (Baltimore: The Johns Hopkins University Press, 1983), 102.

22. Cantwell, "The Army of South Vietnam," 33, 38, 40.

23. Ronald Spector, *After Tet: The Bloodiest Year in Vietnam* (New York: Free Press, 1993), 101.

24. Joes, *War for South Viet Nam*, 87.

25. Research for this book involved interviews and contact with numerous U.S. and Australian advisers to ARVN units. Though in the interviews I certainly learned of instances of ARVN inefficiency, all of the advisers in question expressed respect for their ARVN counterparts and the units under their command.

26. Jeffrey J. Clarke, *The U.S. Army in Vietnam. Advice and Support: The Final Years, 1965–1973* (Washington, DC: Center of Military History, 1988), 12–14.

27. Moyar, *Triumph Forsaken*, 169.

28. Military History Institute of Vietnam, *Victory in Vietnam: The Official History of the People's Army of Vietnam, 1954–1975*, translated by Merle Pribbenow (Lawrence: University Press of Kansas, 2002), 111–112.

29. Moyar, *Triumph Forsaken*, 208.

30. Ibid., 196.

31. Lt. Gen. Dong Van Khuyen, *Indochina Monographs. The RVNAF* (Washington, DC: Center of Military History, 1980), 11; Joes, *War for South Viet Nam*, 91; Collins, *Development and Training*, 29.

Notes to Chapter 2

1. Information contained in this chapter can be found on Pham Van Dinh interview tapes 2–9 and on Tran Ngoc Hue interview tapes 1–2.

2. Cantwell, "The Army of South Vietnam," 218, 223; Clarke, *Advice and Support*, 29.

3. The British remained interested observers throughout the Vietnam War, and papers in the British National Archives in Kew represent an underutilized source for understanding Vietnam. Though the collections are scattered from the files of the Foreign Office to the files of the War Office, papers exist on myriad topics ranging from ambassadorial critiques of American tactics, to the workings of the British Jungle Warfare school in Malaya (which trained scores of South Vietnamese officers), to the comings and goings of Sir Robert Thompson, lauded for his actions in Malaya and constant adviser to the Americans in Vietnam. The papers concerning the Jungle Warfare School are located in DO 169/109.

4. Collins, *Development and Training*, 32.

5. Ibid., 34.

6. Bui Tin, "Fight for the Long Haul: The War as Seen by a Soldier in the People's Army of Vietnam," in Wiest, ed., *Rolling Thunder*, 60.

7. Brigham, *ARVN*, 41.

8. In 1967, the VNMA permanently converted to a four-year program.

9. Cantwell, "The Army of South Vietnam," 210, 218; Clarke, *Advice and Support*, 29.

10. Collins, *Development and Training*, 16–17, 28, 30. The training, abilities, and usage of the Regional and Popular Forces would remain a critical question regarding the overall military abilities of South Vietnam.

11. For an important revisionist account of Diem's downfall see Moyar, *Triumph Forsaken*, chs. 11–12.

12. Ibid., 283.

13. H. R. McMaster, *Dereliction of Duty: Lyndon Johnson, Robert McNamara, the Joints Chiefs of Staff and the Lies That Led to Vietnam* (New York: Harper, 1997), 198–199.

14. Cantwell, "The Army of South Vietnam," 124, 129.

15. Moyar, *Triumph Forsaken*, 284.

16. Khuyen, *The RVNAF*, 13.

17. Clarke, *Advice and Support*, 503, states, "Between 1964 and 1972 consumer prices in South Vietnam rose 900 percent and the price of rice 1400 percent, while incomes rose only about 300 percent for officers and, at most, 500 percent for enlisted men. During the same period the official dollar-piaster [the local currency] exchange rate increased from VN$35 to VN$420, was continuing to rise, and was undercut by a black-market rate that was considerably higher. As a result, a full colonel in the South Vietnamese Army saw his monthly salary shrink from about US$400 to US$85; an army captain, from US$287 to US$61; and a private, from US$77 to US$30."

18. Khuyen, *The RVNAF*, 346.

19. Cantwell, "The Army of South Vietnam," 190.

20. Brigham, *ARVN*, 51–52.

21. The dynamics of how the Viet Cong came to dominate some communities in South Vietnam have been studied at great length. Though based on research on other areas of South Vietnam, the conclusions of these studies have wider validity and serve to inform the conclusions reached by the present author. Perhaps the most important studies in this area are David W. P. Elliott, *The Vietnamese War: Revolution and Social Change in the Mekong Delta, 1930–1975* (New York: M. E. Sharpe, 2003); Jeffrey Race, *War Comes to Long An: Revolutionary Conflict in a Vietnamese Province* (Berkeley: University of California Press, 1972); and Eric Bergerud, *The Dynamics of Defeat: The Vietnam War in Hau Nghia Province* (Boulder, CO: Westview Press, 1990).

22. Brigham, *ARVN*, 15.

23. Truong, *RVNAF and U.S. Operational Cooperation*, 169.

24. Cantwell, "The Army of South Vietnam," 254.

25. Nagl, *Learning to Eat Soup with a Knife*, 127.

26. Ibid., 116.

27. Cantwell, "The Army of South Vietnam," 141.

28. Karnow, *Vietnam: A History*, 437.

29. McMaster, *Dereliction of Duty*, 204–205.

30. Cantwell, "The Army of South Vietnam," 247.

31. Krepinevich, *The Army and Vietnam*, 196.

32. Truong, *Territorial Forces*, 75–76; Truong, *RVNAF and U.S. Operational Cooperation*, 165; George MacGarrigle, *United States Army in Vietnam. Combat Operations. Taking the Offensive: October 1966 to October 1967* (Washington, DC: Center of Military History, 1998), 7.

33. Truong, *RVNAF and U.S. Operational Cooperation*, 164.

34. Ibid., 172.

35. Terry Gill interview.

36. Cantwell, "The Army of South Vietnam," 281–282.

37. Gill interview; Geoffrey Annett interview.

38. Collins, *Development and Training*, 35.

39. Gill interview; Annett interview.

40. Though the People's Army of Viet Nam (PAVN) is the correct descriptor for North Vietnamese regular forces, this study utilizes the more commonly used North Vietnamese Army (NVA).

41. The tactic of "hanging on to the belts" of opponents called for VC and NVA forces to allow U.S. or ARVN forces to advance to close range before opening fire. Such tactics sought to minimize U.S. or ARVN use of supporting air or artillery firepower.

42. Sorley, "Conduct of the War in Vietnam," in Wiest, ed., *Rolling Thunder*, 178–179.

43. Gill interview.

44. R.L.B. Cormack, "The Buddhists, 1963–1968," a report on the Buddhist crisis filed by the British embassy in Saigon, 1 August 1968. Foreign Office Documents, FCO 15/770, British National Archives.

45. For a full discussion of the Buddhist movement of 1966 see Topmiller, *The Lotus Unleashed*. For an alternate view of the nature of the Buddhist movement see Moyar, *Triumph Forsaken*.

46. Cantwell, "The Army of South Vietnam," 143–144.

47. Clarke, *Advice and Support*, 130.

48. Topmiller, *Lotus Unleashed*, 37.

49. Frances FitzGerald, *Fire in the Lake: The Vietnamese and the Americans in Vietnam* (New York: Vintage Books, 1973), 375.

50. Topmiller, *Lotus Unleashed*, 38–39; FitzGerald, *Fire in the Lake*, 374.

51. Clarke, *Advice and Support*, 131–132.

52. Ibid., 136.

53. The information for this account comes from Pham Van Dinh interview tape 8 and is augmented by information from Topmiller, *Lotus Unleashed*, 80.

54. Clarke, *Advice and Support*, 138–139; Cantwell, "The Army of South Vietnam," 147.

55. Dinh's account of his actions at Lang Co Bridge is corroborated by his Australian adviser Terry Gill's account of the story.

56. FitzGerald, *Fire in the Lake*, 387.

57. Cantwell, "The Army of South Vietnam," 148.

58. George Smith, *The Siege at Hue* (Boulder, CO: Lynne Rienner, 1999), 13.

59. Cantwell, "The Army of South Vietnam," 311.

Notes to Chapter 3

1. There exists a vibrant historical controversy regarding Westmoreland's handling of the Vietnam War that centers on whether he simply misjudged the nature of the war or whether his failure was rooted in his being hamstrung by his own government. Nearly every history of the Vietnam War contains some judgment on Westmoreland's command abilities. Central to the present debate, though, is Lewis Sorley's *A Better War: The Unexamined Victories and Final Tragedy of America's Last Years in Vietnam* (New York: Harcourt Brace, 1999), which contends that the strategy of General Creighton Abrams was superior to that of Westmoreland. Also see Samuel Zaffiri, *Westmoreland* (New York: Morrow, 1994); and William Westmoreland, *A Soldier Reports* (New York: Doubleday, 1976).

2. MacGarrigle, *Combat Operations*, 3.

3. Edward Murphy, *Semper Fi Vietnam: From Da Nang to the DMZ, Marine Corps Campaigns, 1965–1975* (Novato, CA: Presidio, 1997), 37–38.

4. Krepinevich, *The Army and Vietnam,* 190.

5. For more information on the innovative nature of CAPs see Michael Peterson, *The Combined Action Platoons: The U.S. Marines' Other War in Vietnam* (New York: Praeger, 1989).

6. James Coan, *Con Thien: The Hill of Angels* (Tuscaloosa: University of Alabama Press, 2004), 24.

7. Information contained in this chapter can be found on Pham Van Dinh interview tapes 10a, 10b, and 11 and on Tran Ngoc Hue interview tape 2.

8. Bob Jones interview tape 1. Jones initially served as Senior Adviser to the 1st Battalion, 3rd Regiment of the 1st ARVN Division and later as Senior Adviser to the Hac Bao.

9. After their first introduction in the text, ARVN units will be referred to by their accepted numerical abbreviation. Thus, 2nd Battalion, 3rd Regiment will be referred to as 2/3 ARVN.

10. Mark Moyar, "Villager Attitudes During the Final Decade of the Vietnam War," Texas Tech University Vietnam Center Web site. Available at http://www.vietnam.ttu.edu/vietnamcenter/events/1996_Symposium/96papers/moyar.htm. Quoted in Gerard DeGroot, *A Noble Cause? America and the Vietnam War* (New York: Pearson, 2000).

11. Nguyen Cao Ky, *Twenty Years and Twenty Days* (New York: Stein and Day, 1976), 80.

12. Sorley, "Conduct of the War in Vietnam," 178.

13. It can be argued that Westmoreland's failure to see the interconnected nature of attrition and pacification was the critical mistake of the entire war.

14. Richard Hunt, *Pacification: The American Struggle for Vietnam's Hearts and Minds* (Boulder, CO: Westview Press, 1995), 34, 89–90.

15. Lewis Sorley argues convincingly in *A Better War* that pacification had in many ways succeeded as part of Abrams's "One War" strategy by 1972.

16. Brig. Gen. Tran Dinh Tho. *Indochina Monographs. Pacification* (Washington, DC: Center of Military History, 1980), 16.

17. Gen. Cao Van Vien, Lt. Gen. Ngo Quang Truong,; Lt. Gen. Dong Van Khuyen, Maj. Gen. Nguyen Duy Hinh, Brig. Gen. Tran Dinh Tho, Col. Hoang Ngoc Lung, and Lt. Col. Chu Xuan Vien, *Indochina Monographs. The U.S. Adviser* (Washington, DC: Center of Military History, 1980), 152.

18. Ibid.

19. Tho, *Pacification,* 39.

20. Truong, *Territorial Forces,* 89.

21. Nagl, *Learning to Eat Soup with a Knife,* 120–121.

22. Tran Van Don, *Our Endless War,* 153.

23. Collins, *Development and Training,* 41.

24. Truong, *Territorial Forces*, 54.

25. Collins, *Development and Training*, 42; Cantwell, "The Army of South Vietnam," 180.

26. Truong, *Territorial Forces*, 51–53, 85, 102–104.

27. Ibid., 97–98.

28. Ibid., 97.

29. After the onset of CORDS and through the later guidance of Abrams, many of the worst problems with the Regional and Popular Forces were eradicated. Also, in major part because of the destruction of the Viet Cong during the Tet Offensive, pacification reached new heights after 1969. However, the war also changed, becoming much more a traditional conflict. In the end, even the revitalized RF/PF were unable to stand effectively against such threats. For a fuller history of the pacification campaign see Hunt, *Pacification*. Regarding the later history of the RF/PF, little has yet been written, and it seems a fruitful and important area for new research.

30. Jones interview tape 1.

31. Nagl, *Learning to Eat Soup with a Knife*, 159.

32. Ibid., 160.

33. Krepinevich, *The Army and Vietnam*, 182; Nagl, *Learning to Eat Soup with a Knife*, 160.

34. Clarke, *Advice and Support*, 175.

35. Ibid., 233–234.

36. Hunt, *Pacification*, 75.

37. Ibid.

38. Ministry of Defense, Vietnamese Institute for Military History, "The 1968 Tet Offensive and Uprising in the Tri-Thien-Hue Theater" (*Huong Tien Cong va Noi Day Tet Mau Than o Tri-Thien-Hue*). Translated by Robert Destatte and Merle Pribbenow for The United States Army Center of Military History Histories Division, 6,12.

39. Jim Coolican interview tape 1.

40. Information on VC atrocities is taken from Hue interview tape 2 and Bob Jones interview tape 1.

41. Vien et al., *Adviser*, 187.

42. Clarke, *Advice and Support*, 60.

43. Clarke, *Advice and Support*, 59–60; Vien et al., *Adviser*, 7; Courtney Frobenius interview; Jim Joy interview; Benjamin Harrison interview.

44. Clarke, *Advice and Support*, 58–59.

45. Ibid., 62.

46. Krepinevich, *The Army and Vietnam*, 23.

47. Vien et al., *Adviser*, 31–32.

48. Clarke, *Advice and Support*, 62. Like many advisory practices, though,

the rotation system changed and lengthened during the period of drawdown of U.S. forces after 1969.

49. Vien et al., *Adviser*, 90–91.

50. George O. Adkisson interview.

51. Coolican interview tapes 1–2.

52. Ian McNeill, *The Team: Australian Army Advisers in Vietnam, 1962–1972* (New York: Hippocrene, 1984), 72, 91.

53. Gill interview; Russell Smith interview; Annett interview.

54. McNeill, *The Team*, 124.

55. Annett interview; McNeill, *The Team*, 97–100.

56. Gill interview.

57. The quotations are taken from Coolican interview tape 1. However, every adviser interviewed for this project, from corps level down to company level, echoed Coolican's sentiments. Remarkably, even William Camper, who had his life put in danger when his counterpart, Pham Van Dinh, surrendered at Camp Carroll, retains his belief in the ARVN and its ability.

58. Vien et al., *Adviser*, 58.

59. Ministry of Defense, "The 1968 Tet Offensive," 19.

60. Jack Shulimson, Lt. Col. Leonard Blasiol, Charles Smith, and Capt. David Dawson, *U.S Marines in Vietnam: The Defining Year, 1968* (Washington, DC: U.S. Marine Corps History and Museums Division, 1997), 101–103.

61. Ibid., 104.

62. Hue interview; Coolican interview, tape 1.

63. Shulimson, *The Defining Year*, 104–105.

64. Coolican interview tape 1.

Notes to Chapter 4

1. See Ministry of Defense, "The 1968 Tet Offensive."

2. James H. Willbanks, "The Battle for Hue, 1968," in William Robertson and Lawrence Yates, eds. *Block by Block: The Challenges of Urban Operations* (Fort Leavenworth, KS: U.S. Army Command and General Staff College Press, 2003), 123. Also see James H. Willbanks, *The Tet Offensive; A Concise History* (New York: Columbia University Press, 2006).

3. Ministry of Defense, "The 1968 Tet Offensive," i. The italics are in the original.

4. Eric Hammel, *Fire in the Streets: The Battle for Hue, Tet 1968* (Chicago: Contemporary Books, 1991), 8.

5. Murphy, *Semper Fi Vietnam*, 189.

6. William (Joe) Bolt interview.

7. Information contained in this chapter can be found on Pham Van Dinh interview tapes 11–13 and Tran Ngoc Hue interview tapes 3–4.

8. Coolican interview tape 2; Adkisson interview.

9. Department of the Army, 45th Military History Detachment, "The Battle of Hue, 19 March 1968," 4–5.

10. Ministry of Defense, "The 1968 Tet Offensive," 29.

11. Smith, *The Siege at Hue*, 171. Information regarding Hue's role in the battle comes primarily from the Hue interview tapes but is augmented by detail from Smith, *The Siege at Hue*, and Hammel, *Fire in the Streets*. Footnotes are used only when the interview information is augmented by information from these sources.

12. Smith, *Siege*, 23–24.

13. Coolican interview tape 2.

14. Ibid.

15. 1st U.S. Marine Division, "Combat After Action Report, TET Offensive, Hue," National Archives, College Park, 51.

16. Ministry of Defense, "The 1968 Tet Offensive," 50.

17. Adkisson interview; Coolican interview tape 2; Hammel, *Fire in the Streets*, 40; Smith, *Siege at Hue*, 35–38.

18. Smith, *Siege at Hue*, 39.

19. 1st U.S. Marine Division, "Combat After Action Report," 52; Smith, *Siege at Hue*, 43–54.

20. 1st U.S. Marine Division, "Combat After Action Report," 52.

21. Ibid., 71.

22. Bolt interview.

23. McNeill, *The Team*, 141–142.

24. Bolt interview.

25. Department of the Army, "The Battle of Hue," 7.

26. Headquarters I Corps Advisory Group, Advisory Team 1, "After Action Report of the Enemy's TET Offensive," National Archives, College Park, 8, 11.

27. Ibid., 16.

28. Department of the Army, "The Battle of Hue," 6.

29. Smith, *The Siege at Hue*, 122.

30. Hammel, *Fire in the Streets*, 254.

31. The South Vietnamese had been very reluctant to utilize indirect firepower to aid in the assault amid the historic buildings of the Citadel. As a result, the first heavy bombing raid did not take place until 7 February, and the return of poor weather and the desire to spare Vietnamese history from destruction limited the use of indirect firepower for the remainder of the battle.

32. Bolt interview.

33. Coolican interview tape 2.

34. Hammel, *Fire in the Streets*, 297.

35. William Keith Nolan, *Battle for Hue: Tet, 1968* (Novato, CA: Presidio, 1983), 158.

36. Department of the Army, "The Battle of Hue," 8.

37. Smith, *The Siege at Hue*, 155.

38. Ibid.

39. In the fighting against the final NVA offensive in Hue City, the Hac Bao accounted for 150 enemy dead. I Corps Advisory Group, "After Action Report," 11.

40. Smith, *The Siege at Hue*, 166. The attention lavished on American exploits, and the paucity of coverage of the Vietnamese aspects of their own war, clouded the ability of the American people and indeed the American military fully to understand the conflict in Vietnam. The problem has been perpetuated by a similar tendency in the historical coverage of the war.

41. Hammel, *Fire in the Streets*, 303.

42. Dinh interview tape 12; I Corps Advisory Group, "After Action Report," 12.

43. Coolican interview tape 2; Nolan, *Battle for Hue*, 171.

44. Smith, *The Siege at Hue*, 167.

45. Nolan, *Battle for Hue*, 87.

46. Ibid., 185.

47. Department of the Army, "The Battle of Hue," 14.

48. Smith, *The Siege at Hue*, 169.

49. Bolt interview.

50. Adkisson interview.

51. I Corps Advisory Group, "After Action Report," 3.

Notes to Chapter 5

1. McNeill, *The Team*, 152.

2. Shulimson et al., *U.S Marines in Vietnam*, 241. Though U.S. and ARVN estimates of enemy dead and wounded are sometimes rightly questioned, it remains obvious that the NVA and VC suffered a tremendous setback in the Tet Offensive.

3. Ibid., 225.

4. Spector, *After Tet*, 118; Hunt, *Pacification*, 173. By midyear, forces in I Corps were as follows: 3rd Marine Division and the 1st Brigade of the 5th Mechanized Division were responsible for Quang Tri Province. Further south, the 101st Airborne Division and the 1st Cavalry Division operated in an arc around Hue City in Thua Thein Province. In Quang Nam, Quang Tin, and Quang Ngai provinces, the 1st Marine Division and the Americal Division held sway. Additionally, Gen. Hoang Xuan Lam of I Corps controlled thirty-

four thousand ARVN regulars, with the seventeen maneuver battalions of the 1st ARVN Division operating in Quang Tri and Thua Thien, while the twelve battalions of the 2nd ARVN Division operated in Quang Tin and Quang Ngai provinces. Further augmenting the total, 49,800 troops of the RF/PF worked throughout the region. Source: Charles R. Smith, *U.S. Marines in Vietnam: High Mobility and Standdown, 1969* (Washington, DC: U.S. Marine Corps History and Museums Division, 1988), 3.

5. Clarke, *Advice and Support*, 293. In 1968, South Vietnamese forces reached a total of 798,682 men, with the following breakdown: ARVN 324,637; Vietnamese Navy, 19,661; Vietnamese Air Force, 16,161; Vietnamese Marines, 9,000; RF, 152,549; PF, 151,945; National Police, 79,729; Civilian Irregular Defense Groups, 45,000. Source: Cantwell, "The Army of South Vietnam," 240.

6. Clarke, *Advice and Support*, 293, 296, 298, 399–301.

7. Shulimson, *The Defining Year*, 250.

8. The information for this chapter comes from Pham Van Dinh interview tapes 13–15 and Tran Ngoc Hue interview tapes 4–5.

9. Lt. Gen. John H. Cushman, "A Personal Memoir, An Account of the 2nd Brigade 101st Airborne Division, Sept. 1967–June 1968," Author's Collection, 61. The memoir contains fragments of several operational orders, as well as articles and comments on operations of the 2nd Brigade. Footnotes for such material denote the origin of the document in question but also indicate that the information from the document in question is taken from Cushman's memoir.

10. Truong, *Territorial Forces*, 119.

11. Annex A (Intelligence) to Frag Order 8 to OPORD 5–68 (Operation Jeb Stuart), in Cushman, "A Personal Memoir," 56.

12. Cushman, "A Personal Memoir," 64; Bolt interview.

13. Bolt interview; Cushman, "A Personal Memoir," 94.

14. Cushman, "A Personal Memoir," 55.

15. Brig. Gen. John Cushman, "How We Did It in Thua Thien," *Army*, May 1970, in Cushman, "A Personal Memoir," 80.

16. Truong, *Territorial Forces*, 119–120.

17. Ibid.

18. Spec. 4 Robert Johnson, "Liberation of Quang Dien," *Rendezvous with Destiny*, in Cushman, "A Personal Memoir," 165.

19. Cushman, "How We Did It," in Cushman, "A Personal Memoir," 81–82.

20. Cushman, "A Personal Memoir," 113–117.

21. Sources for the fighting at Phouc Yen include Cushman, "A Personal Memoir," 122–127; Cushman, "How We Did It," in Cushman, "A Personal Memoir," 83–84; Hue interview; Coolican interview.

22. Cushman, "A Personal Memoir," 159.

23. Cushman, "How We Did It," in Cushman, "A Personal Memoir," 85.

24. Truong, *Territorial Forces*, 122.

25. Ibid., 123.

26. The arrival of new units in 1968 necessitated a change in the American command system in I Corps. In February, MACV created the Provisional Corps, consisting of the 1st Air Cavalry Division, the 101st Airborne Division, and the 3rd Marine Division, which took operational control of Quang Tri and Thua Thien provinces. The Provisional Corps remained subordinate to the III MAF.

27. Shulimson, *The Defining Year*, 252–253; Spector, *After Tet*, 138; Lt. Gen. Willard Pearson, *Vietnam Studies. The War in the Northern Provinces, 1966–1968* (Washington, DC: Department of the Army, 1975), 89.

28. Pearson, *War in the Northern Provinces*, 91.

29. Advisory Team 3, "Combat After Action Report Lam Son 216," 31 May 1968, National Archives, College Park; Shulimson, *The Defining Year*, 253.

30. Spector, *After Tet*, 140.

31. Advisory Team 3, "Combat Operations After Action Report, Lam Son 225," 27 September 1968 (Washington, DC: National Archives, 1968).

32. Bolt interview.

33. Advisory Team 3, "Combat Operations After Action Report, Lam Son 225."

34. Bolt interview.

35. Shulimson, *The Defining Year*, 412; Bolt interview.

36. Travis Kirkland interview.

37. Advisory Team 3, "Combat Operations After Action Report, Operation LAM SON 265," National Archives, College Park.

38. Smith interview.

39. Wally Sheppard interview.

40. Smith interview.

41. Tom Jaco interview.

42. Jaco interview.

43. Kirkland interview.

44. The Military History Institute of Vietnam, *Victory in Vietnam*, 229, 238.

45. Spector, *After Tet*, 282.

46. Hunt, *Pacification*, 172–173.

47. Tho, *Pacification*, 17.

48. Collins, *Development and Training*, 85.

49. Lewis Sorley, ed., *Vietnam Chronicles: The Abrams Tapes, 1968–1972* (Lubbock: Texas Tech University Press, 2004), 113.

50. William Colby, *Lost Victory* (Chicago: Contemporary Books, 1989), 213.

51. Sorley, *Abrams Tapes*, 117. Emphasis in the original.

52. Willbanks, *Abandoning Vietnam*, 12–15.

53. Clarke, *Advice and* Support, 391–393.

54. Truong, *RVNAF and U.S. Operational Cooperation*, 179.

55. Ibid., 181.

56. Clarke, *Advice and Support*, 393.

Notes to Chapter 6

1. Sorley, *A Better War*, 88, 104.

2. Information contained in this chapter can be found on Pham Van Dinh interview tapes 15–16 and Tran Ngoc Hue interview tape 5.

3. The detailed information regarding Operation Apache Snow and the resulting struggle at Hamburger Hill comes from the following sources: 22d Military History Detachment, Narrative, Operation "Apache Snow," 101st Airborne Division U.S. Army Military History Institute, Carlisle Barracks, Carlisle, Pennsylvania; 3rd Brigade, 101st Airborne Division, Summary of Action and Results, Battle of Dong Ap Bia, 24 May 1969, U.S. Army Military History Institute; Lt. Gen. Richard Stilwell, XXIV Corps After Action Report, Operation Apache Snow, 27 August 1969, U.S. Army Military History Institute; Lt. Col. Weldon F. Honeycutt, 3rd Battalion 187th Airborne Infantry, Combat After Action Report, Operation APACHE SNOW, 20 June 1969, U.S. Army Military History Institute. To avoid repetition, footnotes will accompany only information specific to one source or direct quotes.

4. Samuel Zaffiri, *Hamburger Hill: The Brutal Battle for Dong Ap Bia, May 11–20, 1969* (Novato, CA: Presidio, 1988), 83.

5. Honeycutt, 3rd Battalion 187th, Combat After Action Report.

6. Ibid.

7. 22d Military History Detachment, Operation "Apache Snow," p. 10.

8. Zaffiri, *Hamburger Hill*, 166.

9. Honeycutt, 3rd Battalion 187th, Combat After Action Report.

10. Zaffiri, *Hamburger Hill*, 228–229.

11. 3rd Brigade, 101st Airborne Division, Summary of Action and Results, Battle of Dong Ap Bia. Appendix I. AP Account of Hill 937 Battle by Jay Scarbutt.

12. Harvey Zimmerle interview.

13. Zaffiri, *Hamburger Hill*, 231–232.

14. Honeycutt, 3rd Battalion 187th, Combat After Action Report.

15. Zaffiri, *Hamburger Hill*, 269.

16. The information on the 2/3 ARVN's role in the battle for Dong Ap Bia comes from several sources in addition to the extensive oral interview with Pham Van Dinh. Again, footnotes will be kept to a minimum except in cases of direct quotes or very specific information. The sources include: interview with

Maj. Harvey Zimmerle, who served as senior adviser with 2/3 ARVN; interview with Lt. Col. Cecil Fair, who served as senior adviser with the 3rd ARVN Regiment; interview with Warrant Officer Max Kelly, who was an AATTV adviser with 2/3 ARVN; interview with Lt. Mai Xuan Tiem, who was a platoon commander of 2/3 ARVN.

17. Kelly interview.

18. Ibid.

19. In an action on 1 June, after 2/3 had been tasked with an RIF mission in the A Shau Valley, both Carr and Campbell were killed in action. The loss of the two young men hurt Zimmerle deeply, as did the fact that these brave American soldiers never received their historical due for their actions at Hamburger Hill.

20. Dinh interview; Mai Xuan Tiem interview.

21. Zimmerle interview.

22. Col. Wilson C. Harper, Headquarters United States Military Assistance Command, Vietnam, Memorandum for the Record, ARVN Participation in Attack on Hill 987, 22 May 1969, U.S. Army Military History Institute.

23. The timing of the incident fits in well with Honeycutt's after-action report, which makes reference to 2/3's receiving friendly mortar fire at and after 0942.

24. Cecil Fair interview.

25. Ibid.

26. Kelly interview.

27. Lt. Col. Weldon Honeycutt interview.

28. General Truong did, however, play a leading role in the compilation of the Indochina Monographs, an important series of appreciations of the conflict written by ARVN officers after their emigration to the United States.

29. Gen. Ngo Quang Truong interview.

30. Harper, Memorandum for the Record.

31. Sorley, *Abrams Tapes, 1968–1972*, 194.

32. Nagl, *Learning to Eat Soup with a Knife*, 173.

Notes to Chapter 7

1. McNeill, *The Team*, 156–157.

2. Smith, *High Mobility and Standdown*, 52.

3. Clarke, *Advice and Support*, 310, 313.

4. Ibid., 316–320.

5. Spector, *After Tet*, 100.

6. Smith, *High Mobility and Standdown*, 294. Though the exact percentages of villages considered secure are always in doubt, it is certain that by 1969 pacification in I Corps had reached its highest level to date.

7. Hunt, *Pacification*, 195.

8. John M. Shaw, *The Cambodian Campaign: The 1970 Offensive and America's Vietnam War* (Lawrence: University Press of Kansas, 2005), 21–22. Also see Dale Andrade, *Ashes to Ashes: The Phoenix Program and the Vietnam War* (New York: Lexington Books, 1990); William Colby, *Lost Victory* (Chicago: Contemporary Books, 1989); and Mark Moyar, *Phoenix and the Birds of Prey: The CIA's Secret Campaign to Destroy the Viet Cong* (Annapolis, MD: Naval Institute Press, 1997).

9. The Military History Institute of Vietnam, *Victory in Vietnam*, 246.

10. Sorley, *Abrams Tapes*, 363, 126.

11. Clarke, *Advice and Support*, 335.

12. Ibid., 336.

13. Shaw, *Cambodian Campaign*, 49.

14. Smith, *High Mobility and Standdown*, 131.

15. Vu Van Giai interview.

16. Ibid.

17. The information for this chapter comes from Pham Van Dinh interview tapes 17–21 and Tran Ngoc Hue interview tapes 5–6.

18. Giai interview.

19. 2nd Regiment Advisory Team, Advisory Team 3, After Action Reports, December 1969–February 1971. National Archives, College Park.

20. 2nd Regiment Advisory Team, Advisory Team 3, After Action Report, 14 July 1970. National Archives, College Park.

21. Gordon Greta interview.

22. E. L. Devereaux, "A VVA Veteran Profile—Harry Hue Tran: 'Every Day I Live the American Dream,'" April 30, 1996. Author's Collection, 7.

23. 2nd Regiment Advisory Team, Advisory Team 3, After Action Report, 21 October 1970. National Archives, College Park.

24. "Reunited 20 Years Later," *Washington Post*, November 21, 1991, D 14.

25. Devereaux, "A VVA Veteran Profile," 7.

26. McNeill, *The Team*, 162–163.

27. Capt. W. R. Deane, Monthly Report, 3/54 ARVN, June 1970, 4. Australian War Memorial.

28. Bill Deane interview.

29. McNeill, *The Team*, 170.

30. Truong's words spoken to Lt. Col. J. A. Clark, then Commanding Officer AATTV, quoted in McNeill, *The Team*, 171.

31. Graham A. Cosmas and Lt. Col. Terrence P. Murray, *U.S. Marines in Vietnam: Vietnamization and Redeployment, 1970–1971* (Washington, DC: U.S. Marine Corps History and Museums Division, 1986), 84.

32. Jaco interview. In keeping with Dinh's reputation, Jaco (who later rose to the rank of lieutenant general) heard and believed that Dinh had met

his end by charging with his pistol drawn toward an enemy tank—fighting to the last. When the author informed Jaco of Dinh's surrender, he was at first shocked but then expressed a confidence that the Dinh he knew was a true combat officer and must have made the correct decision under trying circumstances.

33. Headquarters 54th Regiment Advisory Team, 1st Infantry Division (ARVN), Combat After Action Report, 25 October 1970. National Archives, College Park.

34. Headquarters 54th Regiment Advisory Team, 1st Infantry Division (ARVN), Combat After Action Reports, May 1970–July 1971. National Archives, College Park.

35. Jaco interview.

36. Harrison interview.

37. Jaco interview.

38. Keith Nolan, *Death Valley: The Summer Offensive, I Corps, August 1969* (Novato, CA: Presidio, 1987), 10–11.

39. Deane interview.

40. Jaco interview.

41. Greta interview.

42. Willbanks, *Abandoning Vietnam*, 28; Clarke, *Advice and Support*, 344–345.

43. Giai interview; Harrison interview; Jaco interview.

Notes to Chapter 8

1. Shaw, *The Cambodian Campaign*, 34, 51, 54.

2. Maj. Gen. Nguyen Duy Hinh, *Indochina Monographs. Lam Son 719* (Washington, DC: Center of Military History, 1979), 7; Shaw, *Cambodian Campaign*, 161.

3. Clarke, *Advice and Support*, 421.

4. Ibid., 232–233.

5. Hinh, *Lam Son 719*, 53.

6. Ibid., 33–35, 42, 54–55; Cantwell, "The Army of South Vietnam," 337.

7. Truong, *RVNAF and U.S. Operational Cooperation*, 179.

8. There is an emerging debate over whether or not MACV expected stiff enemy resistance in Laos. Lewis Sorley has provided evidence that Abrams forecast that the NVA had a significant fighting force in the area and could "be expected to defend his base areas and logistics against any allied operation" (Sorley, *A Better War*, 235). However, Col. Arthur Pence in his After Action Report for Lam Son 719 contended that "It was apparent at this time that United States intelligence felt that the operation would be lightly opposed" (Hinh, *Lam Son 719*, 57). Whether or not it constituted part of the planning, Lam Son

719 certainly better fit a "best-case scenario" than one that predicted strong enemy resistance.

9. Hinh, *Lam Son 719*, 157; Cantwell, "The Army of South Vietnam," 338.

10. Project CHECO, *Lam Son 719, 30 January–24 March 1971: The South Vietnamese Incursion into Laos* (Directorate of Operations Analysis, CHECO/ CORONA HARVEST Division, 1971), 3–4; Hinh, *Lam Son 719*, 37–40.

11. Brig. Gen. Sidney B. Berry, Final Report. 101st Airborne Division Airmobile Operations in Support of Operation Lam Son 719, 8 February–6 April 1971. May 1, 1971, I, 7–8.

12. Information contained in this chapter can be found on Pham Van Dinh interview tapes 21–23 and Tran Ngoc Hue interview tapes 6–7.

13. Hinh, *Lam Son 719*, 82; Project CHECO, *Lam Son 719*, xv.

14. Military History Institute of Vietnam, *Victory in Vietnam*, 274.

15. McNeill, *The Team*, 174–175.

16. Project CHECO, *Lam Son 719*, 35–36, 40.

17. The detailed information on the progress of the assault is taken in the main from Hinh, *Lam Son 719*; Project CHECO, *Lam Son 719*; Brig. Gen. Sidney B. Berry, 101st Airborne Division Airmobile Operations in Support of Operation Lam Son 719, 20 March 1971; and Brig. Gen. Sidney B. Berry, Final Report. 101st Airborne Division Airmobile Operations in Support of Operation Lam Son 719, May 1, 1971. Information on the progress of the 1st ARVN Division is taken from Advisory Team 3, Combat After Action Report, Lam Son 719, National Archives, College Park. Footnotes will be kept to a minimum except in cases of direct quotations and in cases where there exists a discrepancy in the documentation.

18. Project CHECO, *Lam Son 719*, 43.

19. Ibid., 47.

20. Sorley, *A Better War*, 247.

21. Ibid., 248.

22. Keith Nolan, *Into Laos: The Story of Dewy Canyon II/Lam Son 719; Vietnam 1971* (Novato, CA: Presidio, 1986), 105, 145.

23. Ibid., 147.

24. Harrison interview.

25. Project CHECO, *Lam Son 719*, 11.

26. Sorley, *A Better War*, 257.

27. Hinh, *Lam Son 719*, 159.

28. Jaco interview.

29. Hinh, *Lam Son 719*, 158.

30. Sorley, *A Better War*, 256–257; Project CHECO, *Lam Son 719*.

31. Hinh, *Lam Son 719*, 161.

32. Harrison interview.

33. Advisory Team 3, Combat After Action Report, Lam Son 719, 13–14.

By the end of February, 1st ARVN Division had amassed an impressive string of victories and had accounted for 1,088 enemy dead at a cost of only 58 friendly KIA.

34. Giai interview.

35. Sorley, *A Better War*, 254.

36. Hinh, *Lam Son 719*, 103.

37. Giai interview.

38. Sorley, *A Better War*, 255.

39. Casualty figures and combat force totals for both sides in Operation Lam Son 719 remain in considerable doubt. The estimate of three thousand NVA dead and an overall figure of twelve thousand NVA casualties by 11 March as well as total force estimates can be found in Project CHECO, *Lam Son 719*, 67.

40. Rich Johnson interview; Nolan, *Into Laos*, 279.

41. Johnson interview.

42. Advisory Team 3, Combat After Action Report, Lam Son 719, 21–24.

43. Devereaux, "A VVA Profile," 9.

44. Project CHECO, *Lam Son 719*, 75–77; Nolan, *Into Laos*, 318.

45. Dinh interview; Hinh, *Lam Son 719*, 168.

46. Hinh, *Lam Son 719*, 140–141.

47. Headquarters 54th Regiment Advisory Team, 1st Infantry Division (ARVN), Combat After Action Report, 20 April 1971, National Archives, College Park.

Notes to Chapter 9

1. Willbanks, *Abandoning Vietnam*, 115.

2. Ibid., 122.

3. Maj. Gen. Nguyen Duy Hinh, *Indochina Monographs. Vietnamization and the Cease-fire* (Washington, DC: Center of Military History, 1980), 88–89.

4. McNeill, *The Team*, 178.

5. Hinh, *Vietnamization*, 22, 25–26.

6. Turley, *The Easter Offensive, Vietnam, 1972*, 24–25.

7. Lt. Gen. Ngo Quang Truong, *Indochina Monographs. The Easter Offensive of 1972* (Washington, DC: Center of Military History, 1979), 16.

8. Clarke, *Advice and Support*, 450.

9. McNeill, *The Team*, 178.

10. Hinh, *Vietnamization*, 36–44.

11. Collins, *Development and Training*, 108–109.

12. Hinh, *Vietnamization*, 90.

13. Ibid., 464–469.

14. Willbanks, *Abandoning Vietnam*, 116–117.

15. Lt. Col. William Camper, Interview Transcript, Turley Papers, 14.

16. Information contained in this chapter can be found on Pham Van Dinh interview tapes 23–31.

17. Cantwell, "The Army of South Vietnam," 356.

18. Headquarters 54th Regiment Advisory Team, 1st Infantry Division (ARVN), Combat After Action Report, Lam Son 487 and 720, 10 July 1971, National Archives, College Park.

19. Giai interview.

20. Truong, *Easter Offensive*, 18.

21. Col. Donald J. Metcalf Interview Concerning the Fall of Quang Tri, Turley Papers, 23–24.

22. Ibid., 24.

23. McNeill, *The Team*, 185.

24. Giai, taped interview.

25. Giai interview.

26. Headquarters U.S. Army Advisory Group, 3rd Infantry Division (ARVN), Narrative Summary of ARVN Effectiveness, 9 January 1972, National Archives, College Park, 3, 6.

27. Giai taped interview.

28. Headquarters U.S. Army Advisory Group, 3rd Infantry Division (ARVN), Narrative Summary of ARVN Effectiveness, 6.

29. Truong, *Easter Offensive*, 166.

30. Headquarters U.S. Army Advisory Group, 3rd Infantry Division (ARVN), Narrative Summary of ARVN Effectiveness, 4.

31. Joseph Brown interview.

32. William Camper interview, 4–6.

33. Andrade, *America's Last Vietnam Battle*, 35.

34. Truong, *Easter Offensive*, 20–21.

35. Andrade, *America's Last Vietnam Battle*, 29; Truong, *Easter Offensive*, 13.

36. Giai interview.

37. Ibid.; Truong, *Easter Offensive*, 12, 23–24; Cantwell, "The Army of South Vietnam," 355; Project CHECO, *The 1972 Invasion of Military Region I: Fall of Quang Tri and Defense of Hue*. Directorate of Operations Analysis. CHECO/CORONA HARVEST Division, 1973, 8.

38. Truong, *Easter Offensive*, 23–24; Camper interview, 6–7.

39. Turley, *The Easter Offensive*, 35.

40. Controversy has dogged the timing of the troop rotation. Was it sheer luck that caused the NVA to attack at the perfect time, or was there a more sinister explanation? To Turley, the coincidence of the NVA attack was just too overwhelming and led to a hypothesis that "The precise timing of the multitude of events about to unfold could not have happened just by chance" (Turley, *The Easter Offensive*, 36.) While the vaunted NVA intelligence network, as it

had in the case of Lam Son 719, might well have gained some prior knowledge of ARVN movements in the DMZ, the cases against General Giai and Pham Van Dinh, perhaps the most obvious candidates for treason, are weak and do not fit the course of future events. In Dinh's case, the troop rotation left him and the 56th Regiment in danger of destruction, caught in the midst of the deadly NVA surge. General Giai spent more than a decade in North Vietnamese prisons and "reeducation" camps. A traitor in ARVN's midst either would have been conveniently absent during the assault, rather than in its midst, or would have avoided prison at the hands of his communist captors. The rotation had in fact been planned for some time and was designed to allow the 2nd Regiment, which had been in place at Camp Carroll for months, a chance to recuperate from its exertions. At worst, then, the rotation was a needless gamble in a precarious time—a gamble that left Dinh and his 56th Regiment caught in the open facing the brunt of the largest NVA offensive to date in the war.

41. Joy interview.

42. Project CHECO, *The 1972 Invasion*, 15, 18; Turley, *Easter Offensive*, 53. The detailed information regarding the course of the Easter Offensive in I Corps comes from the following sources: Advisory Team 155, Advisor After Action Reports (3rd ARVN Division), March-May 1972 (Easter Offensive), National Archives; Truong, *Easter Offensive*; Turley, *Easter Offensive*; Project CHECO, *The 1972 Invasion*; Camper interview; Brown interview; Camper, Interview Transcript, Turley Papers; Giai interview; Giai taped interview; Andrade, *America's Last Vietnam Battle*; Advisory Team 155, Surrender at Camp Carroll, 13 April 1972, Turley Papers; Col. Donald J. Metcalf Interview Concerning the Fall of Quang Tri, Turley Papers; Col. Donald J. Metcalf, "Why Did the Defense of Quang Tri Province, SVN, Collapse?," Turley Papers; Lt. Col. William Camper, Memorandum on Surrender at Camp Carroll, 13 April 1972, Turley Papers; Maj. Jim Joy, USMC, Mai Loc After Action Report, Jim Joy Personal Collection; Joy interview; Capt. Nguyen Dinh Nhu interview; Lt. Mai Xuan Tiem interview; Lt. Col. Vinh Phong interview; Maj. Ton That Man interview. To avoid repetition, footnotes will accompany only information specific to one source or direct quotes.

43. Truong, *Easter Offensive*, 25.

44. Camper, Interview Transcript, Turley Papers, 4–5.

45. Joy interview.

46. Turley, *Easter Offensive*, 66–68; Joy, Mai Loc After Action Report, 3–4.

47. Giai interview.

48. Ton That Man interview.

49. Advisory Team 155, Advisor After Action Reports (3rd ARVN Division), March–May 1972 (Easter Offensive), 1.

50. Joy, Mai Loc After Action Report, 6–9.

51. Turley, *Easter Offensive*, 96.

52. Andrade, *America's Last Vietnam Battle*, 58.

53. Col. Donald J. Metcalf Interview Concerning the Fall of Quang Tri, Turley Papers, 2–3.

54. Camper interview, 8.

55. Giai interview.

56. Camper, Interview Transcript, Turley Papers, 14.

57. Turley, *Easter Offensive*, 113.

58. Truong, *Easter Offensive*, 29.

59. Andrade, *America's Last Vietnam Battle*, 59.

60. Though the events concerning the destruction of the bridge remain in doubt, for a fuller study of the event see John Miller, *The Bridge at Dong Ha* (Annapolis, MD: Naval Institute Press, 1998).

61. Camper interview, 8–9; Joy, Mai Loc After Action Report, 11.

62. Man interview.

63. Dinh's account of the secretive meeting is substantiated by interview information from Lt. Col. Vinh Phong, Maj. Ton That Man, and Capt. Nguyen Dinh Nhu. All were at the meeting and agree that the main point of the meeting was saving the lives of the men and that the agreement to surrender was unanimous, with Major Man abstaining.

64. After so many years, Dinh, Camper, and Brown have recollections of the meeting that differ in detail. Camper and Brown both indicate that Dinh said that he had shot two of his own men earlier in an attempt to make them continue the fight. Dinh adamantly denies the remark. The details of the meeting recorded here are formed through a compilation of all three accounts; a compilation that attempts to rely on the printed record of events dictated shortly after the fall of Camp Carroll.

65. Camper interview, 10.

66. Camper, Interview Transcript, Turley Papers, 10.

67. Lt. Col. Vinh Phong was also surprised to see the helicopter land at Camp Carroll, and assumed it was for Dinh. However, when Dinh remained on the radio and did not depart, Phong was even more surprised but came to suspect the purpose of Dinh's actions.

68. Though Dale Andrade includes a paragraph in his book that contends that an artillery battery manned by Vietnamese Marines refused to surrender at Camp Carroll and resisted to the last man, the only account of the action comes from a lone message received from an adviser at Mai Loc before the surrender. Dinh and the other Vietnamese witnesses at Camp Carroll remember no such resistance.

69. A complicating factor in understanding Dinh's actions is the fact that shortly after his surrender, an NVA radio broadcast was made in which Dinh

announced his surrender and urged other ARVN units to do the same. While it is doubtless true that such a radio broadcast did indeed take place (a full transcript of the broadcast can be found in Camper, Interview Transcript, Turley Papers), Dinh and Phong deny that they ever took part in such a broadcast and contend that it was a North Vietnamese propaganda ploy.

70. Though the personal rationale for his defection can of course only come from Dinh himself, his version of events and his description of his overriding concern for his men and their families are echoed by the accounts of Col. Vinh Phong, Capt. Nguyen Dinh Nhu, and Lt. Mai Xuan Tiem.

71. Joy, Mai Loc After Action Report, 15–17; Joy interview.

72. Truong, *Easter Offensive*, 38.

73. Andrade, *America's Last Vietnam Battle*, 111; Truong, *Easter Offensive*, 39; Giai interview.

74. Turley, *Easter Offensive*, 263; Brown interview; Camper interview.

75. Metcalf interview, 10.

76. Ibid., 15.

77. Gen. Cao Van Vien, *Indochina Monographs. Leadership* (Washington, DC: Center of Military History, 1980), 139; Andrade, *America's Last Vietnam Battle*, 143.

78. Truong, *Easter Offensive*, 65–71.

79. Sorley, *A Better War*, 339.

80. Sorley, *Abrams Tapes*, 825–826. Emphasis in the original.

81. Truong, *Easter Offensive*, 169.

82. Brigham, *ARVN*, 1.

83. Isaacs, *Without Honor*, 129.

Notes to Chapter 10

1. Information contained in this chapter can be found on Pham Van Dinh interview tapes 31–38 and Tran Ngoc Hue interview tapes 7–9.

2. General Lam Quang Thi contends that in 1973 Dinh returned to Quang Tri Province in an effort to talk ARVN troops there into surrendering amid battle; General Lam Quang Thi, *The Twenty-Five-Year Century* (Denton: University of North Texas Press, 2001), 293. Dinh, though, contends that he spent the entire time between his surrender in 1972 and the end of the war in 1975 in Hanoi.

3. Upon the news of surrender, five South Vietnamese generals famously committed suicide rather than surrender to the North Vietnamese. An unspecified number of less senior officers also committed suicide. Lieutenant General Lam Quang Thi, "A View from the Other Side of the Story: Reflections of a South Vietnamese Soldier," in Wiest, *Rolling Thunder*, 133.

4. Wiest, *The Vietnam War, 1956–1975,* 85.

5. Giai interview. Though they were often housed in separate camps, General Vu Van Giai, Tran Ngoc Hue, and the other ARVN prisoners in reeducation camps in the main experienced similar treatment. The information on camp routine and conditions comes jointly from the interviews with Giai and Hue, but footnotes will again be kept to a minimum.

6. See Merle L. Pribbenow, "A Tale of Five Generals: Vietnam's Invasion of Cambodia," *The Journal of Military History* 70, no. 2 (April 2006): 459–486.

7. Wiest, *The Vietnam War,* 88. For further information on postwar Vietnam see Hy V. Luong, *Postwar Vietnam: Dynamics of a Transforming Society* (Singapore: Institute of Southeast Asian Studies, 2003), and Robert Templer, *Shadows and Wind: A View of Modern Vietnam* (New York: Penguin, 1998).

8. "Veteran Friends, Reunited," *Washington Post,* November 21, 1991 D14.

9. Devereaux, "A VVA Veteran Profile—Harry Hue Tran," 11.

Notes to the Conclusion

1. Brigham, *ARVN,* 110.

Bibliography

Interviews

Extensive oral interviews with Pham Van Dinh and Tran Ngoc (Harry) Hue form the bedrock source for this work. The tapes resulting from the series of interviews (some fifty-five hours of interviews in all) are now open to use by researchers. These and the additional taped interviews conducted by the author are housed in the Center for Oral History and Cultural Heritage at the University of Southern Mississippi. Written interviews are also open for research purposes and, along with copies of other relevant primary source material, are housed in the McCain Library and Archives at the University of Southern Mississippi.

Tape Interviews

The subjects of these interviews usually served in many positions during their tenure in Vietnam. Only the positions most relevant to the present study are listed in parentheses, along with their rank at the time.

Capt. Jim Coolican (Senior Adviser to 2/3 ARVN April–November 1967, Senior Adviser to the Hac Bao November 1967–March 1968); Col. Cecil Fair (Senior Adviser to the 3rd Regiment, 1969); Maj. Gen. Vu Van Giai (Commander 1st ARVN Division Forward, 1970–1971, Commander 3rd ARVN Division 1972), interview courtesy of Jason Stewart; Col. Ben Harrison (Senior Adviser 1st ARVN Division 1971, Senior Adviser Airborne Division 1971); Maj. Tom Jaco (Senior Adviser, 54th Regiment, 1970–1971, Deputy Adviser, I Corps 1971); Capt. Travis Kirkland (Senior Adviser to the Hac Bao, 1968–1969); Capt. Richard Johnson (Operations Officer 173rd Aviation Company 1971), interview courtesy of Jim Williams; Capt. Bob Jones (Senior Adviser to the Hac Bao, May–November 1967); Warrant Officer Max Kelly (Australian Army Training Team, Adviser 2/3 ARVN 1968–1969); and John Klose (S-3 223rd Aviation Battalion 1971), interview courtesy of Jim Williams.

Written Interviews

Col. George O. Adkisson, (Senior Adviser 1st ARVN Division); Warrant Officer Geoffrey Annett (Australian Army Training Team, Adviser, Hac Bao 1966;

2nd Battalion, 1st Regiment 1967); Warrant Officer Doug Bell (Australian Army Training Team, Adviser 1st Battalion, 54th Regiment 1970); Capt. William J. Bolt (Senior Adviser 2/3 ARVN 1967–1968, Senior Adviser Hac Bao 1968); Lt. Col. William Camper (Senior Adviser 56th Regiment 1972); Col. John H. Cushman (Commander 2nd Brigade, 101st Airborne Division); Capt. W. R. Deane (Australian Army Training Team, Adviser 3rd Battalion, 54th Regiment 1970); Warrant Officer Keith Forden (Australian Army Training Team, Adviser Hac Bao 1969–1970); Capt. Courtney Frobenius (Senior Adviser 43rd Vietnamese Ranger Battalion 1970–1971); Maj. Gen. Vu Van Giai (Commander 1st ARVN Division Forward 1970–1971, Commander 3rd ARVN Division 1972); Warrant Officer Terry Gill (Australian Army Training Team, Adviser Hac Bao 1966); Capt. Gordon Greta (Assistant Adviser, 2nd Battalion, 2nd Regiment 1970–1971); Maj. Jim Joy USMC (Senior Adviser Brigade 147 Vietnamese Marine Corps); Maj. Ton That Man (Commander 1st Battalion, 56th Regiment); Warrant Officer Bruce McIlwraith (Australian Army Training Team, Adviser RF/PF forces in southern I Corps 1967); Capt. Nguyen Dinh Nhu (56th Regiment); Lt. Col. Vinh Phong (Executive Officer, 56th Regiment); Capt. Walter Sheppard (Australian Army Training Team, Senior Adviser 1st Battalion, 51st Regiment 1969–1970); Capt. Russell Smith (Australian Army Training Team, Senior Adviser 1st Battalion, 5th Regiment 1969; 2nd Battalion, 1st Regiment 1970); Capt. Charles Thurmond (adviser to the Reconnaissance Company of the 1st ARVN Division 1968); Lt. Mai Xuan Tiem (Platoon Commander 2/3 ARVN, Operations Officer 56th Regiment); Lt. General Ngo Quang Truong (Commander 1st ARVN Division 1966–1970, Commander I Corps 1972), Harvey L. Zimmerle, USMC (Senior Adviser 2/3 ARVN 1968–1969).

Unpublished Primary Sources

1st U.S. Marine Division, Combat After Action Report, TET Offensive, Hue. National Archives and Record Center, College Park, MD.

2nd Regiment (ARVN) Advisory Team, Advisory Team 3, Combat After Action Reports, July 1970–March 1971. National Archives, Washington, DC.

3rd Brigade, 101st Airborne Division, Summary of Action and Results, Battle of Dong Ap Bia, 24 May 1969. U.S. Army Military History Institute, Carlisle Barracks, Carlisle, PA.

22d Military History Detachment, Narrative, Operation "Apache Snow," 101st Airborne Division. U.S. Army Military History Institute, Carlisle Barracks, Carlisle, PA.

Advisory Team 3, Combat After Action Report, Lam Son 719. National Archives and Record Center, College Park, MD.

Advisory Team 155, Adviser After Action Reports (3rd ARVN Division),

March–May 1972 (Easter Offensive). National Archives and Record Center, College Park, MD.

Advisory Team 155, Surrender at Camp Carroll, 13 April 1972. Turley Papers, Marine Corps University Research Archives, Quantico, VA.

Col. G. O. Adkisson, Headquarters I Corps Advisory Group Advisory Team 1, After Action Report of the Enemy's TET Offensive, 9 April 1968. National Archives and Record Center, College Park, MD.

Brig. Gen. Sidney B. Berry, 101st Airborne Division Airmobile Operations in Support of Operation Lam Son 719, 20 March 1971. Author's Collection. Courtesy of Jim Williams.

Brig. Gen. Sidney B. Berry, Final Report. 101st Airborne Division Airmobile Operations in Support of Operation Lam Son 719, 8 February–6 April 1971, May 1, 1971. Author's Collection. Courtesy of Jim Williams.

Lt. Col. William Camper, Interview Transcript. Turley Papers, Marine Corps University Research Archives, Quantico, VA.

Lt. Col. William Camper, Memorandum on Surrender at Camp Carroll, 13 April 1972. Turley Papers, Marine Corps University Research Archives, Quantico, VA.

Lt. Gen. John H. Cushman, "A Personal Memoir, an Account of the 2nd Brigade 101st Airborne Division, Sept. 1967–June 1968." Author's Collection.

Capt. W. R. Deane, Monthly Report, 3/54 ARVN. Australian War Memorial: Official Record, AWM 293; Records of the Australian Army Training Team Vietnam (AATTV), Item 14, AATTV Reports, June 1970.

Department of the Army, 45th Military History Detachment, "The Battle of Hue, 19 March 1968." Courtesy of Jim Coolican.

Foreign Office Papers. British National Archives, Kew, United Kingdom.

Wilson C. Harper, Memorandum for the Record, ARVN Participation in Attack on Hill 937, 22 May 1969. U.S. Army Military History Institute.

Headquarters 3rd ARVN Regiment Advisory Team 3, Combat After Action Reports, May 1968–November 1969. National Archives and Record Center, College Park, MD.

Headquarters 54th Regiment Advisory Team, 1st Infantry Division (ARVN), Combat After Action Reports, May 1970–July 1971. National Archives and Record Center, College Park, MD.

Headquarters I Corps Advisory Group, Advisory Team 1, After Action Report of the Enemy's TET Offensive. National Archives and Record Center, College Park, MD.

Headquarters U.S. Army Advisory Group, 1st Infantry Division (ARVN), Final Combat Operation After Action Feeder Report, Lam Son 719, 25 April 1971. National Archives and Record Center, College Park, MD.

Headquarters U.S. Army Advisory Group, 3rd Infantry Division (ARVN),

Narrative Summary of ARVN Effectiveness, 9 January 1972. National Archives and Record Center, College Park, MD.

Lt. Col. Weldon F. Honeycutt, 3rd Battalion 187th Airborne Infantry, Combat After Action Report, Operation APACHE SNOW, 20 June 1969. U.S. Army Military History Institute, Carlisle Barracks, Carlisle, PA.

Maj. Jim Joy, USMC, Mai Loc After Action Report. Jim Joy Personal Collection.

Travis Kirkland Diary and Papers. Courtesy of Travis Kirkland.

Col. Donald J. Metcalf Interview Concerning the Fall of Quang Tri. Turley Papers, Marine Corps University Research Archives, Quantico, VA.

Col. Donald J. Metcalf, "Why Did the Defense of Quang Tri Province, SVN, Collapse?" Turley Papers, Marine Corps University Research Archives, Quantico, VA.

Ministry of Defense, Vietnamese Institute for Military History, "The 1968 Tet Offensive and Uprising in the Tri-Thien-Hue Theater" [*Huong Tien Cong va Noi Day Tet Mau Than o Tri-Thien-Hue*], trans. Robert Destatte and Merle Pribbenow for the U.S. Army Center of Military History, Histories Division. Author's Collection.

Lt. Gen. Richard Stilwell, XXIV Corps After Action Report, Operation Apache Snow, 27 August 1969. U.S. Army Military History Institute, Carlisle Barracks, Carlisle, PA.

Published Primary Sources

Tran Van Don. *Our Endless War: Inside Vietnam* (San Raphael, CA: Presidio Press, 1978).

Nguyen Cao Ky. *Twenty Years and Twenty Days* (New York: Stein and Day, 1976).

Sharp, Admiral U.S.G. *Strategy for Defeat: Vietnam in Retrospect* (Novato, CA: Presidio, 1978).

Sorley, Lewis, ed. *Vietnam Chronicles: The Abrams Tapes, 1968–1972* (Lubbock: Texas Tech University Press, 2004).

Thi, Lam Quang. *The Twenty-Five-Year Century* (Denton: North Texas Press, 2001).

Walt, Lewis. *Strange War, Strange Strategy: A General's Report on Vietnam* (New York: Funk & Wagnalls, 1970).

Westmoreland, William. *A Soldier Reports* (New York: Doubleday, 1976).

Unpublished Secondary Sources

Cantwell, Thomas R. "The Army of South Vietnam: A Military and Political History" (Sydney: University of New South Wales, 1989).

Devereaux, E. L. "A VVA Profile—Harry Hue Tran: 'Every Day I Live the American Dream.'" April 30, 1996. Author's Collection.

Johnson, Lt. Col. Richard. "Lam Son 719: Perils of Strategy." Strategy Research Project, U.S. Army War College, Carlisle Barracks, Carlisle, PA.

Williamson, Maj. Curtis. "The U.S. Marine Corps Combined Action Program (CAP): A Proposed Alternative Strategy for the Vietnam War" (Quantico, VA: U.S. Marine Corps Command and Staff College, 2002).

Published Government Documents

Clarke Jeffrey J. *United States Army in Vietnam. Advice and Support: The Final Years* (Washington, DC: Center of Military History, 1988).

Collins, Brig. Gen. James Lawton. *Vietnam Studies. The Development and Training of the South Vietnamese Army, 1950–1972* (Washington, DC: Center of Military History, 1975).

Cosmas, Graham A., and Lt. Col. Terrence P. Murray. *U.S. Marines in Vietnam: Vietnamization and Redeployment, 1970–1971* (Washington, DC: U.S. Marine Corps History and Museums Division, 1986).

Hinh, Maj. Gen. Nguyen Duy. *Indochina Monographs. Lam Son 719* (Washington, DC: Center of Military History, 1979).

Hinh, Maj. Gen. Nguyen Duy. *Indochina Monographs. Vietnamization and the Cease-fire* (Washington, DC: Center of Military History, 1980).

Khuyen, Lt. Gen. Dong Van. *Indochina Monographs. The RVNAF* (Washington, DC: Center of Military History, 1980).

Lung, Col. Hoang Ngoc. *Indochina Monographs. Strategy and Tactics* (Washington, DC: Center of Military History, 1980).

Lung, Col. Hoang Ngoc. *Indochina Monographs. The General Offensives of 1968–69* (Washington, DC: Center of Military History, 1981).

MacGarrigle, George. *United States Army in Vietnam. Combat Operations. Taking the Offensive: October 1966 to October 1967* (Washington, DC: Center of Military History, 1998).

Melson, Charles D. *U.S. Marines in Vietnam: The War That Would Not End, 1971–1973* (Washington, DC: U.S. Marine Corps History and Museums Division, 1977).

Pearson, Lt. Gen. Willard. *Vietnam Studies. The War in the Northern Provinces, 1966–1968* (Washington, DC: Department of the Army, 1975).

Project CHECO. *Lam Son 719, 30 January–24 March 1971: The South Vietnamese Incursion into Laos.* Headquarters, Pacific Air Forces Directorate of Operations Analysis. CHECO/CORONA HARVEST Division. 1971.

Project CHECO. *The 1972 Invasion of Military Region I: Fall of Quang Tri and Defense of Hue.* Headquarters, Pacific Air Forces Directorate of Operations Analysis. CHECO/CORONA HARVEST Division. 1973.

Shulimson, Jack, Lt. Col. Leonard Blasiol, Charles Smith, and Capt. David

Dawson. *U.S Marines in Vietnam: The Defining Year, 1968* (Washington, DC: U.S. Marine Corps History and Museums Division, 1997).

Smith, Charles R. *U.S. Marines in Vietnam: High Mobility and Standdown, 1969* (Washington, DC: U.S. Marine Corps History and Museums Division, 1988).

Spector, Ronald H. *United States Army in Vietnam. Advice and Support: The Early Years, 1941–1960* (Washington, DC: Center of Military History, 1983).

Starry, Gen. Donn. *Vietnam Studies. Mounted Combat in Vietnam* (Washington, DC: Department of the Army, 1989).

Telfer, Maj. Gary, Lt. Col. Lane Rogers, and Keith Fleming. *U.S. Marines in Vietnam: Fighting the North Vietnamese, 1967* (Washington, DC: U.S. Marine Corps History and Museums Division, 1984).

Tho, Brig. Gen. Tran Dinh. *Indochina Monographs. Pacification* (Washington, DC: Center of Military History, 1980).

Truong, Lt. Gen. Ngo Quang. *Indochina Monographs. The Easter Offensive of 1972* (Washington, DC: Center of Military History, 1979).

Truong, Lt. Gen. Ngo Quang. *Indochina Monographs. RVNAF and U.S. Operational Cooperation and Coordination* (Washington, DC: Center of Military History, 1980).

Truong, Lt. Gen. Ngo Quang. *Indochina Monographs. Territorial Forces* (Washington, DC: Center of Military History, 1980).

Vien, Gen. Cao Van. *Indochina Monographs. Leadership* (Washington, DC: Center of Military History, 1980).

Vien, Gen. Cao Van; Lt. Gen. Ngo Quang Truong; Lt. Gen. Dong Van Khuyen; Maj. Gen. Nguyen Duy Hinh; Brig. Gen. Tran Dinh Tho; Col. Hoang Ngoc Lung; and Lt. Col. Chu Xuan Vien. *Indochina Monographs. The U.S. Adviser* (Washington, DC: Center of Military History, 1980).

Books

Andrade, Dale. *America's Last Vietnam Battle: Halting Hanoi's 1972 Easter Offensive* (Lawrence: University Press of Kansas, 1995).

Andrade, Dale. *Ashes to Ashes: The Phoenix Program and the Vietnam War* (New York: Lexington Books, 1990).

Bergerud, Eric. *The Dynamics of Defeat: The Vietnam War in Hau Nghia Province* (Boulder, CO: Westview Press, 1990).

Blaufarb, Douglas. *The Counterinsurgency Era: U.S. Doctrine and Performance 1950 to the Present* (New York: Free Press, 1977).

Braestrup, Peter, ed. *Vietnam as History: Ten Years after the Paris Peace Accords* (Washington, DC: University Press of America, 1984).

Brigham, Robert. *ARVN: Life and Death in the South Vietnamese Army* (Lawrence: University Press of Kansas, 2006).

Buttinger, Joseph. *Vietnam: A Dragon Embattled* (New York: Praeger, 1967).

Caputo, Phillip. *A Rumor of War* (London: Pimlico, 1999).

Catton, Phillip E. *Diem's Final Failure: Prelude to America's War in* Vietnam (Lawrence: University Press of Kansas, 2002).

Coan, James. *Con Thien: The Hill of Angels* (Tuscaloosa: University of Alabama Press, 2004).

Colby, William. *Lost Victory* (Chicago: Contemporary Books, 1989).

Davies, Bruce, and Gary McKay. *The Men Who Persevered* (Crows Nest, Australia: Allen & Unwin, 2005).

DeGroot, Gerard. *A Noble Cause? America and the Vietnam War* (New York: Pearson, 2000).

Duiker, William. *The Rise of Nationalism in Vietnam, 1900–1941* (Ithaca: Cornell University Press, 1976).

Duiker, William. *Sacred War: Nationalism and Revolution in a Divided Vietnam* (Boston: McGraw-Hill, 1995).

Elliott, David W. P. *The Vietnamese War: Revolution and Social Change in the Mekong Delta, 1930–1975* (New York: M. E. Sharpe, 2003).

FitzGerald, Frances. *Fire in the Lake: The Vietnamese and the Americans in Vietnam* (New York: Vintage Books, 1973).

Frankum, Ronald. *Like Rolling Thunder: The Air War in Vietnam, 1964–1975* (New York: Rowman & Littlefield, 2005).

Gibson, James. *The Perfect War: Technowar in Vietnam* (Boston: Atlantic Monthly Press, 1986).

Hammel, Eric. *Fire in the Streets: The Battle for Hue, Tet 1968* (Chicago: Contemporary Books, 1991).

Harrison, Maj. General Benjamin. *Hell on a Hill Top: America's Last Major Battle in Vietnam* (New York: I Universe, 2004).

Head, William, and Lawrence Grinter, eds. *Looking Back on the Vietnam War* (Westport, CT: Praeger, 1993).

Hunt, Richard. *Pacification: The American Struggle for Vietnam's Hearts and Minds* (Boulder, CO: Westview Press, 1995).

Isaacs, Arnold. *Without Honor: Defeat in Vietnam and Cambodia* (Baltimore: Johns Hopkins University Press, 1983).

Jamieson, Neil L. *Understanding Vietnam* (Berkeley: University of California Press, 1993).

Joes, Anthony James. *The War for South Vietnam, 1954–1975,* rev. ed. (Westport, CT: Praeger, 2001).

Karnow, Stanley. *Vietnam: A History* (New York: Viking, 1983).

Kinnard, Douglas. *The Certain Trumpet: Maxwell Taylor and the American Experience in Vietnam* (London: Brassey's, 1991).

Kolko, Gabriel. *Anatomy of a War: Vietnam, the United States, and the Modern Historical Experience* (New York: Pantheon, 1985).

Krepinevich, Andrew. *The Army and Vietnam* (Baltimore: Johns Hopkins University Press, 1986).

Lam, Andrew. *Perfume Dreams: Reflections on the Vietnamese Diaspora* (Berkeley, CA: Heyday Books, 2005).

Lehrack, Otto. *No Shining Armor: The Marines at War in Vietnam* (Lawrence: University Press of Kansas, 1992).

Luong, Hy V. *Postwar Vietnam: Dynamics of a Transforming Society* (Singapore: Institute of Southeast Asian Studies, 2003).

McMahon, Robert, ed. *Major Problems in the History of the Vietnam War* (Lexington, MA: D. C. Heath, 1995).

McMaster, H. R. *Dereliction of Duty: Johnson, McNamara, the Joint Chiefs of Staff, and the Lies That Led to Vietnam* (New York: Harper, 1998).

McNeill, Ian. *The Team: Australian Army Advisers in Vietnam, 1962–1972* (New York: Hippocrene, 1984).

Metzner, Edward P. *Reeducation in Postwar Vietnam: Personal Postscripts to Peace* (College Station: Texas A&M University Press, 2001).

Military History Institute of Vietnam. *Victory in Vietnam: The Official History of the People's Army of Vietnam, 1954–1975,* trans. Merle Pribbenow (Lawrence: University Press of Kansas, 2002).

Miller, John. *The Bridge at Dong Ha* (Annapolis, MD: Naval Institute Press, 1998).

Moss, George. *Vietnam: An American Ordeal,* 4th ed. (New York: Prentice Hall, 2002).

Moyar, Mark. *Phoenix and the Birds of Prey: The CIA's Secret Campaign to Destroy the Viet Cong* (Annapolis, MD: Naval Institute Press, 1997).

Moyar, Mark. *Triumph Forsaken: The Vietnam War, 1954–1965* (Cambridge: Cambridge University Press, 2006).

Murphy, Edward. *Semper Fi Vietnam: From Da Nang to the DMZ, Marine Corps Campaigns, 1965–1975* (Novato, CA: Presidio, 1997).

Nagl, John A. *Learning to Eat Soup with a Knife: Counterinsurgency Lessons from Malaya and Vietnam* (Chicago: University of Chicago Press, 2005).

Nguyen, Tin. *General Hieu, ARVN: A Hidden Military Gem* (San Jose: Writers Club, 2000).

Nolan, William Keith. *The Battle for Hue: Tet, 1968* (Novato, CA: Presidio, 1983).

Nolan, William Keith. *Into Laos: The Story of Dewy Canyon II/Lam Son 719; Vietnam 1971* (Novato, CA: Presidio, 1986).

Nolan, William Keith. *Death Valley: The Summer Offensive, I Corps, August 1969* (Novato, CA: Presidio, 1987).

Peterson, Michael. *The Combined Action Platoons: The U.S. Marines' Other War in Vietnam* (New York: Praeger, 1989).

Pike, Douglas. *PAVN: People's Army of Vietnam* (Novato, CA: Presidio, 1986).

Race, Jeffrey. *War Comes to Long An: Revolutionary Conflict in a Vietnamese Province* (Berkeley: University of California Press, 1972).

Record, Jeffrey. *The Wrong War: Why We Lost in Vietnam* (Annapolis, MD: Naval Institute Press, 1998).

Robertson, William, and Lawrence Yates, eds. *Block by Block: The Challenges of Urban Operations* (Fort Leavenworth, KS: U.S. Army Command and General Staff College Press, 2003).

Shaw, John. *The Cambodian Campaign: The 1970 Offensive and America's Vietnam War* (Lawrence: University of Kansas Press, 2005).

Sheehan, Neil. *A Bright Shining Lie: John Paul Vann and America in Vietnam* (New York: Random House, 1988).

Smith, George W. *The Siege at Hue* (Boulder, CO: Lynne Reinner, 1999).

Sorley, Lewis. *A Better War: The Unexamined Victories and Final Tragedy of America's Last Years in Vietnam* (New York: Harcourt, Brace, 1999).

Spector, Ronald. *After Tet: The Bloodiest Year in Vietnam* (New York: Free Press, 1993).

Templer, Robert. *Shadows and Wind: A View of Modern Vietnam* (New York: Penguin, 1998).

Topmiller, Robert J. *The Lotus Unleashed: The Buddhist Peace Movement in South Vietnam, 1964–1966* (Lexington: University Press of Kentucky, 2002).

Turley, Col. G. H. *The Easter Offensive, Vietnam, 1972* (Annapolis, MD: Naval Institute Press, 1985).

Vandiver, Frank. *Shadows of Vietnam* (College Station: Texas A&M University Press, 1997).

Wiest, Andrew. *The Vietnam War, 1956–1975* (Oxford: Osprey, 2002).

Wiest, Andrew, ed. *Rolling Thunder in a Gentle Land: The Vietnam War Revisited* (Oxford: Osprey, 2006).

Willbanks, James H. *Abandoning Vietnam: How America Left and South Vietnam Lost Its War* (Lawrence: University Press of Kansas, 2004).

Willbanks, James H. *The Battle of An Loc* (Bloomington: Indiana University Press, 2005).

Willbanks, James H. *The Tet Offensive; A Concise History* (New York: Columbia University Press, 2006).

Zaffiri, Samuel. *Hamburger Hill: The Brutal Battle for Dong Ap Bia, May 11–20, 1969* (Novato, CA: Presidio, 1988).

Zaffiri, Samuel. *Westmoreland* (New York: Morrow, 1994).

Articles

Cushman, Brig. Gen. John. "How We Did It in Thua Thien." *Army* (May 1970). In Lt. Gen. John H. Cushman, "A Personal Memoir." Author's Collection.

Fulbrook, Capt. Jim. "LamSon 719." *U.S. Army Aviation Digest* (June 1986). Author's Collection.

Johnson, Spec. 4 Robert. "Liberation of Quang Dien." *Rendezvous with Destiny.* In Lt. Gen. John H. Cushman, "A Personal Memoir." Author's Collection.

Moyar, Mark. "Villager Attitudes during the Final Decade of the Vietnam War." Texas Tech University Vietnam Center Web site. http://www.vietnam.ttu.edu/vietnamcenter/events/1996_Symposium/96papers/moyar.htm.

Pribbenow, Merle L. "A Tale of Five Generals: Vietnam's Invasion of Cambodia." *Journal of Military History* 70, no. 2 (April 2006): 459–486.

Sloniker, Mike. "The Easter Offensive of 1972 to the War's End in January 1973." Unpublished article for the Vietnam Helicopter Pilots Association. Author's Collection.

Sloniker, Mike. "The First Regional Assistance Command." Unpublished article for the Vietnam Helicopter Pilots Association. Author's Collection.

Sloniker, Mike. "Lam Son 719." Unpublished article for the Vietnam Helicopter Pilots Association. Author's Collection.

Sorley, Lewis. "Courage and Blood: South Vietnam's Repulse of the 1972 Easter Invasion." *Parameters* (Summer 1999): 38–56.

"The Black Panther (Hac Bao) Company," in *Chien Si Cong Ha* [*The Republican Combatant*], 15 August 1969.

Newspaper Articles

"Reunited 20 Years Later." *Washington Post,* November 21, 1991, D14.

Index

Abrams, General Creighton, 71, 125, 195, 300, 312n29; command abilities of, 310n1; and Easter Offensive, 243, 270–271; and Hamburger Hill, 174; and One War strategy, 153–155, 311n15; and planning of Lam Son 719, 199; plans for 1969, 157; and prosecution of Lam Son 719, 205–206, 217–218; replaces Westmoreland, 153; and results of U.S./ARVN I Corps offensive of 1968–1969, 152–153; and U.S. withdrawal from Vietnam, 180–182, 194, and weaknesses of RF/PF, 179

Abrams Tapes, The, 174

Adkisson, Colonel George, 99, 104–105, 109; and Pham Van Dinh, 122

Advisers, 3, 8, 24, 26, 32, 38, 51, 56, 82–91, 143–151, 184–186, 213, 238–241, 251, 301; Advisory Team 1, 122–123; Advisory Team 155, 238; and ARVN fighting methods, 46, 81–82, 146–147; base camps, 144–146; battalion staff, 85; cannot accompany ARVN into Laos, 203, 216; and control of firepower, 85, 90–91, 203, 212; language difficulties, 86–87; nature of advisory effort, 84–85, 143; opinion of ARVN, 90, 185, 190–194, 307n25, 313n57; rations, 145; tour of duty, 87, 132n48; training, 86, 143; withdrawal of, 230–231, 240. *See also* Australian Army Training Team Vietnam (AATTV)

Agroville Program, 23, 70

Andrade, Dale, 6, 252, 326n68

Apache Snow operation, 158–175. *See also* Hamburger Hill

Ap Bac, Battle of, 28, 35

Army of the Republic of Vietnam (ARVN), 2–5; airmobility, 51–52; armament of, 41–42, 55; and Buddhist crisis, 59–62; and Cambodian Incursion, 197–198; CIA report on abilities of, 180; complexity of, 298; and counterinsurgency, 22–23, 27, 32, 47; creation of, 22–24; desertion, 23, 232, 238; detachment of battalions to districts, 77–78; draft, 23; and fall of South Vietnam, 278–280; family and, 40–41, 192, 232, 299; fighting methods, 41–43, 46–47, 149–150, 199–201; graft, 24, 39–40, 73–74, 80, 180; highlands battles of 1970, 186–190; historiography, 5, 25, 96–97, 298, 305n4; immobility, 236; initial military performance, 27–29; leadership qualities, 32, 56, 190, 209, 233, 271, 279–281, 301; loss of initiative to the NVA, 54; military situation in I Corps during U.S. withdrawal, 183–195; modernization plans for, 126–127, 231–232; morale, 49, 188, 191–193, 226, 233–234, 271; officer class, 18–19, 25–26, 44–45, 233; and overthrow of Ngo Dinh Diem, 36–38; pay, 39–40, 180, 232, 308n17; politicization of, 21, 24–26, 36–37, 47–48, 71, 78, 127, 178–180, 210–211, 218, 227, 236, 268–269, 279, 299, 301; relationship to U.S. forces, 8, 48, 67, 76–77, 87, 129–133, 136–137, 155–156, 190–194, 199–201, 210–211, 231, 251, 271–272, 300–303; reliance on firepower, 23–24, 49, 85, 90–91, 147, 194, 199, 203, 211–212, 231, 271, 301; response to U.S. withdrawal, 181–182, 186, 230–233, 235; reverses in 1964–1965, 48; roots of, 19–22; situation after Lam Son 719, 229–230, 233–234; strength of, 6, 27, 34–35, 126, 231–232, 316n5; training of, 32; unready to shoulder the burden of the war after Lam Son 719, 227, 299, 302. *See also* Advisers; Hamburger Hill; Lam Son 719;

ARVN (*continued*)
Pacification; Reeducation; Regional and Popular Forces (RF/PF); Tet Offensive; U.S./ARVN I Corps offensive of 1968–1969

Army of the Republic of Vietnam, units of: I Corps, 46, 48, 57–61, 66–67, 124–128, 139, 141, 147, 149, 151, 154–156, 180–182, 190, 194, 200–201, 210–211, 218, 225–226, 230–231, 234–237, 242–243, 248, 265–266, 299; III Corps, 75, 181, 186, 197; IV Corps, 213, 232; 1st Division, 4, 13, 32, 50, 52, 54, 57–64, 67, 88, 98–104, 106–107, 109–115, 118–122, 124–125, 131, 138–140, 147, 149, 151, 154, 171, 182, 191, 194, 201, 203–205, 207, 213–215, 226, 233–237, 241, 269; 2nd Division, 41, 67, 88, 236–237; 3rd Division, 226, 235–242, 244–245, 262, 265–269, 299; 18th Division, 279; 21st Division, 130; 25th Division, 236; Airborne Division, 200–201, 203, 208, 211, 213, 269; Marine Division, 210–211, 213–214, 223–224, 238, 247–249, 269; 1st Armored Brigade, 201, 203, 208; 147th Marine Brigade, 245, 247–249, 264–265, 267; 1st Ranger Group, 203; 1st Regiment/1st Division, 214–215; 2nd Regiment/1st Division, 214, 236, 244; 54th Regiment/1st Division, 145, 187–193, 202, 234–235; 2nd Regiment/3rd Division, 239–240, 246, 250, 252, 256, 266, 324n40; 56th Regiment/3rd Division, 236–238, 240–241, 244–262, 324n40; 57th Regiment/3rd Division, 236–238, 251–252, 256–257; 1st Airborne Task Force, 109; 1st Battalion/1st Regiment/1st Division, 43–45, 54, 218; 2nd Battalion/1st Regiment/1st Division, 218; 3rd Battalion/1st Regiment/1st Division, 215, 218; 4th Battalion/1st Regiment/1st Division, 158, 204, 215, 218–220; 2nd Battalion/2nd Regiment/1st Division, 157, 183–185, 193, 202, 214, 216, 220–223, 234, 298; 3rd Battalion/2nd Regiment/1st Division, 221; 4th Battalion/2nd Regiment/1st Division, 110–111, 215, 220–221, 223, 236; 5th Battalion/2nd Regiment/1st Division, 157, 215, 220, 236; 1st Battalion/

3rd Regiment/1st Division, 110–111, 114, 157, 204; 2nd Battalion/3rd Regiment/1st Division, 77–81, 106–109, 111–115, 118–119, 122–123, 133, 136, 138–142, 148–149, 157, 164–174, 204, 212, 281, 294; 3rd Battalion/3rd Regiment/1st Division, 32, 38, 41–42, 109, 220; 4th Battalion/3rd Regiment/1st Division, 109, 204, 220; 1st Battalion/54th Regiment/1st Division, 234; 2nd Battalion/54th Regiment/1st Division, 187–190, 234; 4th Battalion/54th Regiment/1st Division, 234; 2nd Battalion/6th Regiment/2nd Division, 236; 1st Battalion/2nd Regiment/3rd Division, 246, 249; 4th Battalion/2nd Regiment/3rd Division, 240; 1st Battalion/56th Regiment/3rd Division, 236, 239–240, 246, 248, 253; 2nd Battalion/56th Regiment/3rd Division, 246, 248–249, 253; 3rd Battalion/56th Regiment/3rd Division, 246, 248–249, 252; 1st Battalion/57th Regiment/3rd Division, 236, 239; 1st Airborne Battalion, 203; 2nd Airborne Battalion, 204, 214–215; 3rd Airborne Battalion, 204, 209; 7th Airborne Battalion, 111; 8th Airborne Battalion, 203; 9th Airborne Battalion, 111, 204; 21st Airborne Battalion, 209; 11th Armored Squadron, 203; 17th Armored Squadron, 203, 208; 20th Armored Squadron, 257, 266; 7th Cavalry, 102, 111, 114, 116; 101st Combat Engineer Battalion, 204; 3rd Marine Battalion, 257; 21st Ranger Battalion, 204; 39th Ranger Battalion, 206–207; Hac Bao Company, 4, 50–55, 60–64, 68–69, 82–83, 87–88, 98–103, 110, 115–116, 118–119, 122–123, 133–136, 141–142, 149, 221, 253, 263, 298; Reconnaissance Company, 99–100, 119–120

A Shau Valley, 43, 45, 52, 130, 137–139, 142, 180, 186–187, 201, 234–235, 243, 302. *See also*, Apache Snow operation; Hamburger Hill

Attleboro, Operation, 65–66

Australian Army Training Team Vietnam (AATTV), 88–90, 124; relationship with American advisers, 90; size of, 88; supply, 89; training, 88

Bao Dai, 14, 19; relationship to Pham Van Dinh, 13
Batterall, Colonel Ray, 210
Binh Trams, 202, 222
Bishop, Colonel Bertram, 130, 132
Bolt, Captain Joe, 130, 140, 143, 152; and Pham Van Dinh, 122; and Tet Offensive, 106–109, 113; and Tran Ngoc Hue, 141–142, 150–151; transfer to Hac Bao, 141
Brandt, Captain Keith, 218–219
Brigham, Robert, 12, 299
British Broadcasting Corporation, 280
British National Archives, 308n3
Brown, Major Joseph, 240, 246, 248, 255, 266–268; and Pham Van Dinh, 241; and surrender at Camp Carroll, 260–261, 326n64
Buddhism, 278, 306n4; and 1966 uprising, 57–62, 310n45; and Ngo Dinh Diem, 35–36; place in Vietnamese society, 14
Bui Van Chau, Lieutenant, 274

Cambodia, 282; Vietnamese invasion of, 286–287
Cambodian Incursion, 197–198; ARVN performance in, 197–198; NVA losses in, 197–198; results of, 198
Cam Lo, 247, 252
Campbell, Private Billy, 169, 319n19
Campbell, Captain D. H., 124
Camp Carroll, 2, 183–184, 245–253, 255–261, 263, 273–274, 279–281, 296, 299, 324n40
Camper, Lieutenant Colonel William, 151, 250, 264, 266–267; arrival at Camp Carroll, 245; and ARVN morale after Lam Son 719, 233–234; and Pham Van Dinh, 240–241; and situation at Camp Carroll, 246, 258; and surrender at Camp Carroll, 255, 269–261, 326n64; weakness of 3rd Division, 241
Cantwell, Thomas, 44, 47
Cao Bang Prison Camp, 274
Cao Van Thu, 43
Cao Van Vien, General, 68, 86–87; opinion of Hoang Xuan Lam, 269; and planning of Lam Son 719, 199; and prosecution of Lam Son 719, 205
Carr, Sergeant Bertram, 169, 319n19
Catholics: and Ngo Dinh Diem, 35; opposition to communism, 12, 18; and schools, 15
Chaisson, Brigadier General John, 125
Chase, Captain Jack, 116–117
Chiem Uc, Lieutenant, 43
China, invasion of Vietnam, 286–288
Civil Guard, 35, 73
Civil Operations and Revolutionary Development Support (CORDS), 71, 74, 312n29
Clifford, Clark, 126–127
Colby, William, 153
Collins, General James, 74
Combined Campaign Plan for 1969, 155
Cong Ton Nu Thi Nhan, 12
Conmy, Colonel Joseph, 161, 171, 173
Con Thien, 66
Coolican, Captain James, 84, 87, 134; appointed to the Hac Bao, 82; and Pham Van Dinh, 81–82; and Tet Offensive, 99, 104, 110, 115; and Tran Ngoc Hue, 88, 92
Cooper-Church Amendment, 198, 203
Cronkite, Walter, 96
Cushman, Colonel John, 129–130, 294, 301; belief in U.S./ARVN cooperation, 130–132, 136; and cordon tactics, 132–136; reliance on constant pressure on NVA, 132. See also U.S./ARVN I Corps offensive of 1968–1969
Cushman, Lieutenant General Robert, 125, 181

Da Krong Valley, 187, 234–235
Da Nang, 51, 67, 140; and Buddhist crisis, 57–60, 62
Davidson, General Phillip, 71
Davis, Major General Raymond, 177
Deane, Captain Bill, 187–189, 193
Defense Language Institute, 86
Delaware, Operation, 138–139
Demilitarized Zone, 32, 52, 65–66, 148, 177, 182–185, 187, 201–202, 237–239, 243–245, 273, 299
Democratic National Convention, 96
Dewy Canyon II, Operation, 201, 203
Dien Bien Phu, 13, 21
Dong Ap Bia. See Hamburger Hill
Dong Ha, 182, 185, 226, 245, 247, 273; bridge at, 257–258, 326n60

Dong Van Khuyen, Lieutenant General, 39–40
Dong Xoai, 48
Du Quoc Dong, Lieutenant General, 208

Easter Offensive, 5, 8, 91, 273–274, 277, 302; I Corps command problems, 242, 248, 265–268; I Corps misjudges NVA axis of advance, 244; 3rd Division headquarters shift to Quang Tri, 255–256; adviser's opinion of 3rd Division, 238–241; air support, 245, 247, 253, 258; ARVN Lam Son 72 counteroffensive, 269–270; ARVN losses in, 270; ARVN preparation for, 243–244; ARVN Quang Trung 729 counteroffensive, 265; ARVN troop rotation before, 244–245, 324n40; collapse of Cua Viet line of defenses, 266; creation of 3rd ARVN Division, 235–239; Day 1 of, 245–248; Day 2 of, 248–250; Day 3 of, 251–257; Day 4 of, 257–262; defense of Fuller and Khe Gio, 248–249; effects of fall of Camp Carroll, 264–265; infantry assaults on Camp Carroll, 253, 258; lack of ARVN reinforcements, 254; Marine defense of Mai Loc, 247, 249, 258, 264–265; Marine defense of Nui Ba Ho and Sarge, 247, 249; morale at Camp Carroll, 250, 253, 258; Ngo Quang Truong's assessment of 3rd Division, 236, 239, 242; NVA artillery support, 245–248; NVA buildup for, 243; NVA losses in, 270; NVA planning, 243; NVA strength, 245; quality of troops in 3rd Division, 237; retreat to Cua Viet River, 251–253; supplies at Camp Carroll, 247, 250, 253, 258; surrender at Camp Carroll, 259–262, 326n63, 326n64, 326n68; as a victory or a defeat, 270–271; weather and, 245, 247–248, 253; withdrawal to Thach Han River, 267–268. *See also* Abrams, General Creighton; Brown, Major Joseph; Camper, Lieutenant Colonel William; Hoang Xuan Lam, General; Metcalf, Colonel Donald; Pham Van Dinh, Colonel; Ton That Man, Major; Vu Van Giai, Brigadier General
Eisenstein, First Lieutenant Joel, 251

Fair, Lieutenant Colonel Cecil, 171–172
Families of Vietnamese Political Prisoners Association, 292
Family: and the ARVN, 40–41, 56, 192, 232, 299; importance in Vietnamese life, 12, 23, 227; and RF/PF, 74
France: foundation of Vietnamese National Military Academy, 33; soldiers and Ke Mon, 17; and Vietnamese education, 15; and Vietnamese National Army, 19–21
Frobenius, Courtney, 294

Geneva Accords, 12, 15, 21
Gia Hoi District, 108
Gia Long, 97
Gibson, Lieutenant Jimmy, 169
Gill, Warrant Officer Terry, 56
Go Noi Island, 139
Goodpaster, General Andrew, 154–155
Gravel, Lieutenant Colonel Mark, 105–106
Great Society Program, 48, 126
Gregory, Colonel Arthur, 46
Greta, Captain Gordon, 185, 193–194, 216, 222–223

Hai Van Pass, 60, 91
Hamburger Hill, 182, 214, 263, 294; 2/3 ARVN ordered off summit, 171–172; ARVN participation in, 164–174; 2/3 ARVN seizure of summit, 168–170; controversy concerning seizure of, 172–175; effect of, 158, 166, 175–176; final assault on, 167–171; first assaults on Hamburger Hill, 159–162; first move into the A Shau Valley, 159–160; friendly fire, 162, 170–171, 319n23; NVA defenses, 160, 162–163; NVA forces at, 159–160; NVA losses at, 167; public opinion and, 164; renewed assaults on, 162–166; U.S. losses, 161–162, 164, 168; U.S. reinforcements for, 161. *See also* Apache Snow operation; Honeycutt, Lieutenant Colonel Weldon
Hamlet Evaluation System (HES), 179
Hammel, Eric, 117
Hanoi, 14, 222, 243, 262, 273–274, 293
Harkins, Lieutenant General Paul, 28
Harper, Colonel Wilson, 174

Harrison, Colonel Benjamin, 191, 194, 212
Ha Thuc Mau, Major, 246
Heinl, Colonel Robert, 229
Henry, Sergeant Paul, 169
Hiestand, Colonel Harry, 172
Hill 937. *See* Hamburger Hill
Hoa Lo Prison, 222, 273–274
Hoang Xuan Lam, General, 186; appointment as I Corps commander, 61; command difficulties of, 210–211; command failures during Easter Offensive, 265–269; decision to withdraw from Laos in Lam Son 719, 216–217; and fall of Fire Support Base 31 in Lam Son 719, 208; indecision during Easter Offensive, 248; informs Pham Van Dinh to hold to last man during Easter Offensive, 254; and planning of Lam Son 719, 200; plan to retake the initiative in Lam Son 719, 213–214; as politicized commander, 209; promotion after Easter Offensive, 268–269; and stall of Lam Son 719 at A Loui, 205, 207; unprepared for Easter Offensive, 242; and withdrawal from Laos in Lam Son 719, 218, 220. *See also* Cao Van Vien, General
Ho Chi Minh, 11, 15, 18, 20, 58
Ho Chi Minh Trail, 137, 222; NVA dependency on Laotian branches of, 198. *See also* Lam Son 719
Honeycutt, Lieutenant Colonel Weldon, 159–167; 170, 173; confidence at Hamburger Hill, 159, 163; and controversy over seizure of Hamburger Hill, 173; convinces Zais to allow 3/187 to participate in final assault on Hamburger Hill, 165; realizes NVA troop strength at Hamburger Hill, 160–161
Houng Tra District, 134
Hue City, 1, 4, 11–12, 16, 39, 51, 52–53, 64, 79, 82–83, 129, 137, 140, 150, 186, 221, 234, 242, 263, 277, 281, 284, 286, 290–291, 294, 298, 302; and Buddhist crisis, 57–58, 60–62; as focus of Tet Offensive, 97–98, 124. *See also* Tet Offensive
Humanitarian Operation, 293
Huynh Van Cao, General, 60–61

Improvement and Modernization Program, 231–232

Indochina Monographs, 319n28

Jaco, Major Tom, 145–146, 190–194, 210, 320n32
Joes, Anthony James, 25
Johnson, General Harold, 76
Johnson, Lyndon, 38, 48, 71, 76; ends graduated escalation, 126
Johnson, Captain Rich, 216, 219–220
Johnson, Specialist Robert, 131–132
Jones, Captain Bob, 82–84
Jones, Major General William, 182
Joy, Major Jim, 245, 264
Jungle Warfare Centre, 89
Jungle Warfare School, 32, 50, 308n3

Kelly, Warrant Officer Max, 168, 171–173
Ke Mon Village, 16–17, 221, 274
Kennedy, John F., 35
Khe Sanh, 2, 66, 125, 128, 139, 201, 210, 216, 223, 226, 234–235, 245
Khmer Rouge, 287
Kirkland, Travis, 147
Kissinger, Henry, 154, 177
Komer, Robert, 71
Kontum, 243
Korean War, 22–24, 168
Krepinevich, Andrew, 86

LaHue, Brigadier General Foster, 105
Laird, Melvin, 154–155, 175, 177
Lam Quang Thi, General, 327n2
Lam Son 216, 138
Lam Son 225, 140–141
Lam Son 265, 142
Lam Son 487, 234
Lam Son 719, 91, 195, 233, 242, 273, 277, 280, 298, 302; 1st ARVN Division earns special praise in, 213, 322n33; air support for, 203–204, 208, 211, 220–221; allied belief that NVA would not resist, 198, 200, 202–203, 321n8; ARVN command difficulties during, 210–211, 218; ARVN decision to withdraw, 217; ARVN drive stalls at A Loui, 205; ARVN losses, 207, 209, 223–224; ARVN over reliance on U.S. fire support, 211; ARVN retakes the initiative, 212–215; ARVN strategy, 200–201; ARVN troop strength, 204–205; ARVN withdrawal

Lam Son 719 (*continued*)
  phase, 217–224; destruction of 2/2,
  220–223; effect on South Vietnamese
  morale, 225–226; evacuation of Ranger
  South, 208; fall of Fire Support Base 31,
  208–209, 212; fall of Fire Support Base
  Lo Lo, 218; fall of Ranger North, 207;
  as illustrative of ARVN's strengths, 224;
  as illustrative of ARVN's weaknesses,
  224–225; initial NVA counterattacks,
  206–209; initial phase of operation,
  203–206; loss of G3 and G4, 204–205,
  210; media coverage, 225; NVA losses,
  207, 209, 218, 322n33, 323n39; NVA
  preparations for, 202; NVA reinforcements, 205; planning of, 199–201; politicized ARVN decision making during,
  205, 207–209, 213–214, 216, 218; pre-
  invasion phase, 203; secrecy and, 200,
  202; strike on Tchepone, 216–217;
  Tchepone as a symbolic target, 214; as
  test of U.S./ARVN war structure, 199–
  200; terrain and, 201; timing of, 198–
  199; U.S. losses in, 224; U.S. pressure
  for, 199; U.S. helicopter pilots and, 211,
  216, 218–220; as a victory or a defeat,
  225, 229; weather and, 204, 206
Lam Son 720, 234
Land to the Tiller Program, 192, 229
Lang Co Village, 60–62
Laos, 52, 83, 91, 125, 139, 143, 180, 198,
  227, 234, 274, 277; base areas in, 67, 152,
  157, 177; infiltration from, 137–138;
  possible invasion of, 158. *See also* Lam
  Son 719
Le Minh Dao, Brigadier General, 279
LeRoy, Cathy, 109
Lodge, Henry Cabot, 35
Lon Nol, General, 197

Marxism, 20
McCain, Admiral John, 199
McCann, Captain Pat, 189
McNamara, Robert, 35, 77; and ARVN
  politicization, 36
McNeil, Ian, 89, 231
Media coverage: and Ap Bac, 28; and
  Hamburger Hill, 164–165; and Lam Son
  719, 225; and Tet Offensive, 96, 109,
  116–117, 126, 315n40

Metcalf, Colonel Donald, 236–237, 240;
  on ARVN retreat to the Cua Viet River
  during Easter Offensive, 252; advises
  Vu Van Giai to retreat behind Cua Viet
  River on first day of Easter Offensive,
  247; and court martial of Vu Van Giai,
  268; and withdrawal to Thach Han
  River, 267–268
Military Assistance and Advisory Group,
  Vietnam (MAAG), 76; and creation of
  the ARVN, 22–23, 84, 300; reliance on
  conventional operations, 22–23
Military Assistance Command, Vietnam
  (MACV), 44, 62, 125, 174, 181, 185, 230,
  233, 302; foundation of, 28. *See also*
  Abrams, General Creighton; Tet
  Offensive; Westmoreland, General
  William
Morrison, Jack, 144
Mundy, General Carl, 293–294

Nang Son Prison Camp, 274, 276
National Security Study Memorandum 1,
  154
Navy Federal Credit Union, 295
Ngo Dinh Diem, 12–13, 14–15, 57, 59; and
  counterinsurgency, 22–23; fails to
  spread government to the countryside,
  27; overthrow of, 35–36, 308n11; and
  politicization of the ARVN, 24–25;
  regime of, 26
Ngo Duc Am, 292
Ngo Quang Truong, General, 4, 67, 73, 81,
  138, 141, 147, 152, 227, 257, 319n28; and
  3rd ARVN Division, 236, 239, 242, 245;
  and advisers, 24; appointment to I
  Corps, 269; appointment to IV Corps,
  214; appointment to 1st ARVN Division, 63; and Buddhist crisis, 62; command style, 69–70; and commitment of
  American ground forces, 49–50; and
  counterinsurgency, 23–24; and desertion, 232; and failure of I Corps command during Easter Offensive, 265–
  266; and Hamburger Hill, 164, 173;
  highlands battles of 1970, 186–190; and
  Pham Van Dinh, 68–69, 188; and
  RF/PF, 73, 131; and Tet Offensive, 97–
  104, 106–107, 109–115, 118, 121, 123;
  and Tran Ngoc Hue, 69–70; and

U.S./ARVN cooperation, 131, 137, 156; and U.S. withdrawal, 230

Ngo Van Chung, Colonel, 102

Nguyen Cao Ky, Air Vice Marshal: and Buddhist crisis, 57–60, 62; and politicization of ARVN, 47–48, 78, 178; rise to power, 47

Nguyen Chanh Thi, General, 58–59

Nguyen Duy Hinh, General, 200–201, 210–211, 217, 224

Nguyen Huu Chuoc, Captain, 221

Nguyen Khanh, General, 47, 57

Nguyen Tai Thuc, Lieutenant, 61

Nguyen Tang, 40

Nguyen Thi Nghia, 14

Nguyen Tri Phuong, 14

Nguyen Van Chau, 33

Nguyen Van Chuan, General, 50, 52, 58–60, 63, 69

Nguyen Van Dai, Colonel, 70

Nguyen Van Duong, Colonel, 55

Nguyen Van Thieu, General, 57, 62; and Easter Offensive, 254, 267; and fall of South Vietnam, 279–280; and planning of Lam Son 719, 199; and politicization of ARVN, 47–48, 78, 178; and prosecution of Lam Son 719, 205, 207–210, 213–214, 216; rise to power, 47

Nguyen Van Tho, Colonel, 274

Nguyen Van Thuan, Major, 274

Nixon, Richard, 154; and Vietnamization, 175, 177, 181, 229

Nolan, Keith, 121, 192, 208–209

North Vietnamese Army, 1, 6, 22, 66–67; armament of, 55; and Cambodian Incursion, 197–198; commitment of regular forces, 53–54, 66; dependency on Laotian branches of the Ho Chi Minh Trail, 198; and fall of South Vietnam, 278–280; and highlands battles of 1970, 186–190; and pacification, 179; reaction to ARVN success in 1962–1963, 28; situation after Lam Son 719, 229; situation after the overthrow of Ngo Dinh Diem, 37; situation after U.S./ARVN I Corps offensive of 1968–1969, 177, 181, 184; tactics, 54, 128, 181, 184, 309n41; Thon Hoi Yen battle, 54–55. *See also* Easter Offensive; Hamburger Hill; Lam Son 719; Pham Van Dinh, Colonel; Reeducation; Tet Offensive; U.S./ARVN I Corps offensive of 1968–1969

North Vietnamese Army, units of: B-5 Front, 243; 2nd Division, 205; 304th Division, 205, 243; 308th Division, 139, 205, 207, 243–245, 254; 320th Division, 205; 324B Division, 205, 243; 4th Regiment, 100; 6th Regiment, 100; 83rd Regiment, 54–55; 90th Regiment, 128; 803rd Regiment, 140; 8th Battalion, 66th Regiment, 187; 12th Battalion, 4th Regiment, 130; 12th Sapper Battalion, 103; 318th Battalion, 190–191; 800th Battalion, 100–101, 103; 802nd Battalion, 100–101, 103

O'Daniel, Lieutenant General John, 22

O'Reilly, Fire Support Base, 189–190

Pacification, 67, 70–81, 179, 300; Accelerated Pacification Program, 152; ARVN shifted to, 49; politicization of, 179; success of, 229, 311n15, 312n29, 319n6

Paris Peace Accords, 276

Pathet Lao, 202, 277

Pellerin School, 15–16

Pence, Colonel Arthur, 212, 321n8

Perfume River, 97, 103–104, 106–109, 111

Peterson, Ambassador Pete, 294

Pham Van Chieu, General, 59

Pham Van Dinh, Colonel, 4, 6–7, 47, 48, 90, 145–146, 156, 324n40; at 1st Division Forward, 182; as 2/3 commander, 72–73, 79–81, 98–99, 106–109, 111–115, 118, 120–123, 129–130, 138–142, 158, 164–176; as 54th Regiment XO, 188–189, 190–193; as 56th Regiment commander, 237–238, 244–262; and advisers, 148–151, 190–192, 240–241; and ARVN fighting methods, 42–43; and ARVN politicization, 178; and ARVN training, 32; author's first meetings with, 1–2; and Buddhist crisis, 60–62, 68; as a businessman in postwar Vietnam, 291–292; captivity, 262–263; childhood, 11–13, 15–16, 29; and Chinese invasion of Vietnam, 287–288; in command of economic unit for Thua Thien Province, 291; defection, xviii, 6, 264, 276, 300, 327n70, 327n2; as deputy sports

Pham Van Dinh (*continued*)
    director of Thua Thien Province, 285–
    286, 289; as district chief, 72, 76, 78–81;
    doubts South Vietnam can survive, 235,
    242; and Easter Offensive, 244–262;
    effect on of losses during Easter Offen-
    sive, 254; and fall of South Vietnam,
    278–281; and family, 107, 111, 120, 281;
    feeling of helplessness during Easter
    Offensive, 249, 254–256, 258; first bat-
    tles, 41–43; founds a school for 54th
    Regiment, 192; as Hac Bao commander,
    50–56, 60–63, 68–69; and Hamburger
    Hill, 158, 164–176; interviews, xviii, 3,
    9, 296–297, 306n2; and Lam Son 719,
    202, 226–227; leadership, 26, 56, 298;
    military training, 16, 31–33; and over-
    throw of Ngo Dinh Diem, 38; and paci-
    fication, 49, 72–73, 79–81; radio broad-
    cast after surrender, 326n69; and reedu-
    cation, 284–285; relationship to his
    men, 55–56; as representative of officer
    class, 19, 37; reputation, 190–191; return
    to Hue City, 281; and RF/PF, 79–80;
    surrender, 2, 5, 259–262, 299–300,
    326n64; and Tet Offensive, 98–99, 106–
    109, 111–115, 118, 120–123; and Thon
    Hoi Yen battle, 54–55; and Tran Ngoc
    Hue, 53, 115, 183, 274–275; and Tun
    Tavern, 188–189; and U.S./ARVN I
    Corps offensive of 1968–1969, 129–130,
    138–142; and U.S. withdrawal, 177, 195,
    233, 235; and Vietnamese invasion of
    Cambodia, 286. *See also* Brown, Major
    Joseph; Camper, Lieutenant Colonel
    William; Easter
    Offensive; Hamburger Hill
Pham Van Hoa, Colonel, 171
Pham Van Phu, Major General, 214, 234
Pham Van Vinh, 12–13
Pham Xuan Nhuan, General, 58–60, 62
Phan Gia Lam, Lieutenant, 116
Phnom Penh, 286
Phu Bai, 53, 62, 83, 105, 157, 192, 239;
    training center at, 32, 35, 38
Phu Loc, 91–92, 99, 112
PK 17, 39, 138, 140, 149
Pol Pot, 287
Procup, Colonel Wayne, 132
Program for the Pacification and Long-
    Term Development of South Vietnam
    (PROVN), 76–77, 153

Quang Dien District, 69, 76, 78–81, 98,
    129–137, 141, 263, 294, 300–301
Quang Nam Province, 41, 67, 78, 138,
    177
Quang Ngai Province, 67, 177
Quang Tri Combat Base, 245, 266–270
Quang Tri Province, 128, 177, 234, 243,
    250, 268–269, 277
Quang Trung, 242
Quang Trung 729, Operation, 265

Reeducation, 263, 282–285, 287–288,
    328n5
Regional and Popular Forces (RF/PF), 35,
    49, 67, 72–80, 92, 134, 231–232, 237;
    Abrams's opinion of, 179; armament,
    75, 80; effectiveness of, 312n29; training,
    74, 79–80, 308n10; and U.S./ARVN I
    Corps offensive of 1968–1969, 129, 131–
    132, 136–137
Ripcord, Fire Support Base, 189
Rolling Thunder, 48
Rosson, Lieutenant General William, 138

Scharbutt, Jay, 164
Schwarzkopf, General Norman, 63
Self-Defense Corps, 35, 73
Sheppard, Captain Wally, 144–145
Smith, George, 111
Smith, Captain Ray, 249
Smith, Captain Russell, 144–145
Song Be, 48
Song Bo River, 128, 134
Son Tay Prison Camp, 263, 274–275
Sorley, Lewis, 311n15, 321n8
South Vietnam: agriculture, 23; ARVN
    and government of, 24–25, 36–37; class
    and, 13; control of countryside, 71, 152;
    economic weakness, 232; education,
    306n5; failure to reform, 27, 45, 71–72,
    156, 177–180, 232, 301; fall of, 278–281,
    327n3; Land to the Tiller Program, 192;
    leadership, 26, 47–48, 80; nationalism,
    6, 18, 20–21, 26, 298; and rejection of
    PROVN, 77–78; religion and 12–15, 27,
    35; resiliency of population, 95–96; war
    dead, 6. *See also* Army of the Republic

of Vietnam (ARVN); Buddhism; Catholics; Easter Offensive; Family; Lam Son 719; Ngo Dinh Diem; Pacification; Regional and Popular Forces (RF/PF); Tet Offensive; U.S./ARVN I Corps offensive of 1968–1969; Viet Cong
South Vietnamese Air Force, 60
South Vietnamese Ranger School, 32, 43
Spector, Ronald, 25, 139
Strategic Hamlet Program, 23, 70
Street Without Joy, 52
Struggle Movement, 58–62
Sunflower Hotel, 294

Ta Bat Fire Base, 43, 45, 138
Tam Ky, 41, 78
Taylor, Maxwell, 49; and ARVN politicization, 36; and commitment of American ground forces, 48
Tchepone, 198, 200–202, 205, 207, 214–217, 224
Tet Offensive, 4, 6, 95–125, 140, 175, 242, 281, 296; aftermath shifts initiative to U.S./ARVN, 125, 127, 312n29; aimed at ARVN, 96–99, 105–106; as American defeat, 96, 124; ARVN casualties, 111, 114, 121, 125; ARVN counterattack, 109–111, 114–116, 118–119; ARVN lack of firepower in, 108–110, 113; atrocities and, 124; battle for MACV compound, 98; as communist defeat, 95–96, 124, 125; defenses of Hue City, 99–100; failure of NVA to retain initiative, 103–104; holiday, 99; indirect firepower and, 314n31; initial fighting, 100–109; marginalization of ARVN contribution, 116–117, 120–121, 315n40; NVA defenses, 113–114; NVA/VC losses, 110, 114, 123, 125, 315n2; post Tet U.S./ARVN offensive plan, 125–126; preparation for, 79, 91–92, 97–98; rationale for, 95; struggle for MACV compound, 104–105; U.S. casualties, 114, 121; U.S. Marine counterattack in the citadel, 112–115; U.S. Marine role in battle, 121; refugees, 125
Thich Tam Chau, 57
Thich Tri Quang, 57–58
Thompson, Major Robert, 112, 115, 117, 119–120; on Pham Van Dinh, 122

Thompson, Sir Robert, 308n3
Thon Hoi Yen, 54
Thon Than Trung Village, 133
Thua Thien Province, 128, 130, 136, 177, 186, 234, 285, 291
Thu Duc Reserve Officers School, 16, 31–32, 33, 63, 280
Toan Thang 41. See Cambodian Incursion
Toan Thang 43. See Cambodian Incursion
Toan That Dinh, General, 60
Ton Huyen Trang, Captain, 184
Ton That Man, Major, 246, 326n63; speaks against surrendering at Camp Carroll, 259
Tran Huu Chuong, 14, 16
Tran Huu Dieu, 14
Tran Ngoc Hue, Lieutenant Colonel, 4, 6–7, 47, 48, 90, 156, 173, 193; as 2/2 commander, 157, 183–185, 202, 214–216, 220–221; and advisers, 82–83, 87–88, 148–151, 185–186; as aide to General Nguyen Van Chuan, 50, 53–54, 58–63; and ARVN fighting methods, 46–47; and ARVN politicization, 178; and Buddhist crisis, 58; capture, 221–222; childhood, 11, 13–14, 16–18, 29; and defense of the DMZ, 183–185; emigration, xvii–xviii, 292–294; and fall of South Vietnam, 278–280; family, 100–101, 110, 290; first battles, 43–46; as Hac Bao commander, 82–83, 87–88, 91–92, 99–104, 110, 115–116, 118–123, 128–129, 133–136, 141–142, 157; and Hamburger Hill, 175–176; interviews, 3, 9, 295–296, 306n2; and Lam Son 719, 202, 214–216, 220–221; leadership, 26, 69, 298; life in the United States, 295; life under house arrest, 290–292; malaria, 157; marriage, 68; military training, 33–34, 43; and pacification, 49; and Pham Van Dinh, 53, 115, 183, 274–275; Phouc Yen battle, 134–136; Phu Loc battle, 91–92; prison, 5, 221–222, 273–278, 280, 282–284, 289; and prisoner exchange, 276–277; release from prison, 289; and religion, 222, 276, 278, 295; as representative of officer class, 19, 37; and Tet Offensive, 99–104, 110, 115–116, 118–123; Thon Lang battle, 128–129, and U.S./ARVN I Corps offensive of 1968–1969, 133–136,

Tran Ngoc Hue (*continued*)
141–142; and U.S. withdrawal, 177,
194–195. *See also* Lam Son 719
Townsend, Major General Elias, 153
Tran Thi Cam, 68–69, 186, 216, 277–278,
290, 292–293
Tran Van Don, General, 22
Truehart, William, 27–28
Truong Thieu Sinh Quan, 17
Truong-Tien Bridge, 107–108
Tun Tavern, 187–190, 193, 242, 298; ARVN
losses in, 189; ARVN morale in, 188
Turley, Colonel G. H., 6, 244, 324n40; and
shift of 3rd Division headquarters to
Quang Tri during Easter Offensive, 255

Uc Dai Loi House, 89
Unified Buddhist Church, 57
United States: commitment of ground
forces to Vietnam, 31, 48; and counterinsurgency, 47; and creation of the
ARVN, 22–23; drop in military morale,
192–193; fighting methods, 46; first battles with the NVA, 56; Officer Candidate School, 31; and overthrow of Ngo
Dinh Diem, 25–26; and peace negotiations, 126; and planning of Lam Son
719, 199; political expediency of withdrawal, 127, 154–155, 177, 194, 230;
relationship to postwar Vietnam, 287,
293–294; relationship to South Vietnam,
8, 26, 48–49, 82, 155–156, 199–201, 300–
303; and Vietnamese nationalism, 21;
withdrawal from Vietnam, 127, 180–
183, 194, 198–199, 230–231, 271, 276.
See also Abrams, General Creighton;
Army of the Republic of Vietnam
(ARVN); Cambodian Incursion; Hamburger Hill; Lam Son 719; Pacification;
Tet Offensive; U.S./ARVN I Corps offensive of 1968–1969; Westmoreland,
General William
United States military, units of: Provisional Corps, 317n26; III Marine Amphibious Force (MAF), 66–67, 125, 128,
181; 1st Cavalry Division, 138, 140; 1st
Marine Division, 66, 105; 3rd Marine
Division, 66, 139, 154, 182, 239; 101st
Airborne Division, 138, 140, 142, 182,
189–190; Americal Division, 66; 3rd

Brigade, 1st Cavalry Division, 115, 181;
1st Brigade, 5th Mechanized Division,
182, 203, 239; 2nd Brigade, 101st Airborne Division, 129–136, 151, 154, 294,
301; 196th Infantry Brigade, 230; 1st
Battalion, 1st Marines, 105; 1st Battalion
5th Marines, 91–92, 112–117; 1st Battalion, 7th Cavalry, 138; 3rd Battalion,
187th Infantry, 158–168, 170–174; 1st
Battalion, 501st Infantry, 132–134; 2nd
Battalion, 501st Infantry, 133–134, 158,
167; 1st Battalion, 502nd Infantry, 129–
130, 135–136; 1st Battalion, 506th Infantry, 158, 161–163, 165–167; 2nd Battalion, 506th Infantry, 165–167; 2nd Battalion, 5th Marines, 105; Combined Action
Platoons (CAP), 66, 91–92, 311n5
University of Maryland, 3
University of Southern Mississippi, 1;
Center for Oral History and Cultural
Heritage, 10, 306n2; McCain Library
and Archive, 10
U.S. Army Special Warfare School, 86
U.S./ARVN I Corps offensive of 1968–
1969, 128, 175; Abrams's opinion of,
152–153; assaults in the lowlands, 128–
137; cooperative nature of, 130–132;
and cordon tactics, 132–136; drive into
the highlands, 137–142; force levels
during, 315n4; NVA historians and,
151–152; NVA/VC attacks during, 139–
140; NVA/VC casualties in, 130, 136,
139, 141; Phouc Yen battle, 134–136;
results of, 152–153, 177–179, 181,
319n6. *See also* Apache Snow operation;
Hamburger Hill
U.S.-South Vietnamese Combined Campaign Plan, 77

Vann, Colonel John Paul, 28
Viet Cong, 1, 6, 35, 39, 41, 46, 51, 54–55,
66–67, 69, 70, 72, 74, 76–77, 91–92, 125,
179, 312n29; and Ap Bac, 28; in the A
Shau Valley, 43, 45; atrocities, 82; and
Buddhist crisis, 61; and control of South
Vietnamese people, 42–43, 309n21;
foundation of, 27; and nationalism, 33;
in Quang Dien District, 79–81; strength,
37, 53, 177; tactics after U.S./ARVN I
Corps offensive of 1968–1969, 181.

See also Tet Offensive; U.S./ARVN I Corps offensive of 1968–1969

Viet Minh, 13, 15, 16, 19, 21; attack at Ke Mon, 16–17; founding, 11; nationalist roots, 19

Vietnam: postwar economic turmoil, 288–289; postwar *doi moi* policy, 290–291

Vietnamese Diaspora, xvii, 4, 282, 288–289

Vietnamese expatriate community, 3, 292, 305n1

Vietnamese indigenous units, 19–20

Vietnamese Joint General Staff, 22, 40, 64, 199–200

Vietnamese National Army, 13–14, 22; creation of, 20; politicization of, 21; problems in, 21

Vietnamese National Military Academy, 3, 17, 33–34, 35, 280

Vietnamization, 155, 158, 175, 180–181, 197, 229, 271. *See also* United States, withdrawal from Vietnam

Vinh Phong, Lieutenant Colonel, 241, 246, 248, 255, 262, 275, 326n67; defection, 263–264

Vo Nguyen Giap, General, 287–288

Vu Van Giai, Brigadier General, 324n40; appointed to command 3rd Division, 237–238; in command of 1st Division Forward, 183, 188; court martial of, 268; decision not to retreat behind Cua Viet River on first day of Easter Offensive, 247–248; and Dong Ha Bridge, 257–258; learns of surrender of Camp Carroll, 264; and Pham Van Dinh, 183; and plan for a lighting raid on Tchepone during Lam Son 719; 214; preparation for Easter Offensive, 243; promises reinforcements for the 56th Regiment during the Easter Offensive, 250, 254; and reeducation, 283; and retreat to the Cua Viet River during Easter Offensive, 252; shift of 3rd Division headquarters to Quang Tri during Easter Offensive, 255–256; and South Vietnamese morale after Lam Son 719, 226; training of 3rd Division, 241–242; and U.S. withdrawal from Vietnam, 182

Walt, Lieutenant General Lewis, 66

Westmoreland, General William, 36, 48, 70, 72, 84, 125, 153, 155; on advisory effort, 85; command abilities of, 310n1; and Easter Offensive, 243; and pacification, 71, 77, 300, 311n13; rejection of PROVN, 77; and relationship to ARVN, 49; strategy of, 65, 71, 77; and Tet Offensive, 96

Weyand, Sergeant Richard, 151

Williams, Lieutenant General Samuel, 22–23

Wiseman, Lieutenant Colonel David, 151, 185–186, 216, 222–223; emigration of Tran Ngoc Hue, xvii–xviii, 292–293, 295

World War II, 11, 20, 168

Xepon River, 201, 205, 215

Xuan Loc, Battle, 279–280

Zais, Major General Melvin, 164–165

Zimmerle, Captain Harvey, 148, 191; and Hamburger Hill, 168–173, 319n19

About the Author

ANDREW WIEST is Professor of History at the University of Southern Mississippi, where he also serves as co-director of the Center for the Study of War and Society. He has taught as a visiting professor at both the U.S. Air Force Air War College and the Royal Military Academy, Sandhurst. He is the author of several books, including *Haig: The Evolution of a Commander* and *Passchendaele and the Royal Navy*. He is editor of *Rolling Thunder in a Gentle Land: The Vietnam War Revisited* and co-editor of *War in the Age of Technology: Myriad Faces of Modern Armed Combat*.

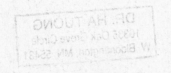